History of the Justices of the Peace

History of the
Justices of the Peace

by

Sir Thomas Skyrme

KCVO, CB, CBE, TD, JP, DL, MA

Of the Inner Temple, Barrister-at-Law

Volume II
England 1689-1989

Published by Barry Rose and the Justice of the Peace
Chichester
England

©1991 Sir Thomas Skyrme KCVO, CB, CBE, TD, JP, DL, MA

ISBN No.
1 872328 50 4

British Library Cataloguing in Publication Data
Skyrme, *Sir* Thomas
History of the Justices of the Peace
Vol. 2
I. Title
344.20716

ISBN 1-872328-50-4

Typeset by Countrywise Press, Chichester
Printed and bound by BPCC Wheatons

CONTENTS

TABLE OF STATUTES CITED IN VOLUME II

ERRATA

Please note:

Page 280, footnote 14, the reference should be to p.331 *post*.

Page 308, footnote 44, the reference should be to p.268 *ante*.

Page 417, footnote 2, the reference should be to p.300 *ante*.

Page 423, footnote 10, the reference should be to p.161 *ante*.

CASES

CHAPTER I

THE AGE OF INDEPENDENCE, POWER AND "DECLINE" 1689 - 1820

PART I - THE RULERS

The justices reach the zenith of their power and influence - Undisputed rulers of the countryside - Assessment of their work and qualities; Obvious defects but some traditional criticism unjustified; Individual justices among leaders of reform - Advent of party political influence; Appointments dominated by politics during first half of eighteenth century - The personnel of the commissions - Rise in importance of clerical justices

If we were asked to name a period in English history during which the county possessed the largest measure of self-government, when its local administrators were most effectively free from superior control, either by the National Executive, Parliament, or the Law Courts, we should suggest the years between 1689 and 1835, or, more precisely, the century that elapsed between the accession of the House of Hanover and the close of the Napoleonic wars.[1]

DURING THE CENTURY AND A HALF which followed the "Glorious Revolution" of 1689 the Justices of the Peace enjoyed far greater freedom from external control than at any other time in their history. A period began in which they ceased to be accountable to any other authority in respect of their administrative functions and their judicial decisions were subject to less scrutiny by the higher courts than was the case before or since. They were able to conduct local affairs as they thought fit. They could introduce new ideas at their whim and, if they failed to perform their duties, there was little fear of punishment. The Sovereign, the Council and even Parliament left the justices largely to their own devices. Indeed, as will be shown later, Quarter Sessions even assumed a paramount role in legislation both at local

---

1. Webb, *ELG, The Parish and the County,* p. 309. The Webbs also commented that "at no period did the landed gentry enjoy so large a measure of local autonomy and irresponsible power as between the accession of the House of Hanover and the close of the Napoleonic wars. It was the 'local self-Government' of each county by a Commission of the Peace made up of voluntarily serving territorial magnates and landed gentry, that seemed to Rudolph von Gneist, the greatest foreign student of English Local Government, the most unique, distinctive and admirable feature of the British constitution." *ELG,* vol. 4, *Statutory Authorities for Special Purposes,* p. 389.

and national level. The influence which the justices were able to exert in all quarters was enhanced by the fact that they now operated as a body - albeit one that was often divided between political parties - instead of as eminent individuals, which had been a characteristic of earlier periods. The justices' unfettered authority, together with further additions to their powers and functions and an extension of their influence on national affairs, all contributed to mark the eighteenth century as the period in which they reached their zenith, and throughout the century they jealously insisted upon the retention of this unique position.

This same period, however, has sometimes been described as one of decline in which the justices exhibited increasing arrogance and selfishness towards the community with whom they steadily declined in favour. Historians have tended to be highly critical of the justices during this era, but their research has been restricted until recently by a paucity of written material, and they have been obliged to base their judgments upon a limited number of public records illuminated by anecdotal evidence contained in the works of contemporary writers, many of them authors of fiction. These writers, notably Fielding and Smollett, were condemnatory of the justices, their novels depicting both urban and rural justices as being what Edmund Burke described in Parliament as "elderly, greedy, corrupt, who had attained office by improper means." Fielding's Squire Western in *Tom Jones* was ready to exceed his power without compunction, and was only deterred from sending his sister's maid to prison for having been rude to her mistress because his clerk reminded him that "he had already had two informations exhibited against him in the King's Bench, and had no curiosity to try a third."[2] Fielding also portrayed JPs in a disparaging manner in some of his other works which provided outstanding examples of sadism and corruption. Examples were Justice Squeezum in *Rape upon Rape,* Jonathan Thrasher in *Amelia* and Justice Frolic in *Joseph Andrews* who took obvious pleasure in sentencing anyone to imprisonment and to a "little correction, too, a little stripping and whipping." The fact that Fielding himself became chief magistrate at Bow Street would have made his readers assume that his descriptions must be accurate.

Tobias Smollett, although his characterization did not equal that of Fielding, depicted the magisterial tyrant forcefully in the character of Justice Gobble, in *The Adventures of Sir Launcelot Greaves,* who had made his fortune as a London tradesman, secured the support of a nobleman "who had a post at court," married a rich widow and bought a property in the country where he settled and, by means of a bribe to the nobleman, secured his appointment to the Commission of the

2.   *Tom Jones,* bk. vii, ch. ix.

Peace. His service on the bench was marked by pomposity and self-indulgence with malice towards any who crossed his path and cruelty to the defenceless creatures who were brought before him. He habitually sat in his own parlour, accompanied by his wife who constantly urged him to impose the harshest punishments.

The *Gentleman's Magazine*, which was the source of much comment on current affairs during the century, contains letters condemning the presence on the commissions of unsatisfactory justices. In 1788 there were two such letters written by the same correspondent, one of which began by commenting that if the Lords Lieutenant were not more careful in their selection of those "who apply to have their names inserted in the commission, in a few years it will be found difficult to prevail upon men of fortune and abilities to act." He then went on to give a graphic description, quoted by the Webbs, of two justices of whom he had had experience.

"In the first place the neighbouring justice is a well-meaning man, with some share of parochial knowledge. But alas! all his good qualities are rendered useless by passions ungovernably furious, a fantastic whimsical wife, and a penchant for strictly enforcing the game laws. ... Without any justice in the neighbourhood of property or importance sufficient to withstand his outrages, he is degenerated into that worst of all despots, a judicial tyrant. ... In the other parish the principal justice is a good-natured fox-hunter, who spends his days on horseback and his evenings in eating and drinking. He regularly attends the justices' meeting, and when business begins pouring in, he opens as follows, first taking out his watch. "Well, gentlemen, you are better acquainted with Burn and Blackstone than I am; you will recollect that dinner is to be ready at four." He then retires to an adjoining room, which he devotes to a more pleasing amusement with the landlord's daughter; his humble brethren are too well bred to break in on his pleasures. Thus, though naturally a good kind of man, he gives up his neighbours to pettifoggers and half-gentlemen, who torture the laws to base purposes of petty quarrels, low prejudices, and mercenary cabal."[3]

Later novelists continued to paint the same picture, Dickens being an eminent example in his portrayal of Mr Fang in *Oliver Twist.* The character of Fang was generally recognized as being based upon a real magistrate, Allan Laing of the Hatton Garden police office who was notorious for his harshness and insolence. Although the public could be excluded from the police offices, this did not apply to the Press, and Dickens succeeded with the help of a reporter friend in being present

3.   *Gentleman's Magazine,* April 1788, p. 315.

in Laing's court. Dickens's oblique attack on Laing in *Oliver Twist,* combined with a campaign mounted by the journal *Figaro in London,* resulted in Laing's dismissal by the Home Secretary. Fang, like Squeezum, was an urban magistrate in Middlesex and, as will be seen in ch. IV, these areas did contain justices who were little better than the characters portrayed in the novels. Those in the rural areas, on the other hand, were not so deserving of censure. Even Fielding and Smollett introduced justices whose characters were acceptable, such as Squire Allworthy, Justice Worthy and Sir Launcelot Greaves, all of whom may have been fairly representative of many of the real-life justices in that they seem to have had a reasonable idea of their duties and powers.

Until recently there has been little evidence available to rebut the adverse image created by the novelists and other writers of the eighteenth and nineteenth centuries. The characters depicted were generally assumed to be typical of the eighteenth century justice, whereas the records which are now available suggest that they were a-typical; yet even today the Dickensian view prevails. Accessible records of the magistrates' proceedings and of their private correspondence during this period were comparatively sparce until the mid-twentieth century, and those which could be easily consulted tended to support the generally accepted view. The Webbs, when compiling their monumental history of local government embracing the Poor Law, licensing, highways and prisons, were deprived of a significant amount of the material which is available to the historian today, and their judgment of the JPs must have been adversely affected. They recognized that the Squire Westerns were exceptional; "from the evidence before us, we infer that these evilly disposed Rulers of the County were, even in Middlesex, a minority of the whole, whilst in the other Counties they were certainly merely exceptional."[4] They went on, however, to paint the following picture of the majority of magistrates.

"The bulk of the local squirarchy who were in the Commission of the Peace were "average sensual men," too well off to care to make a trade of justice, too pugnaciously independent to serve the caprices of powerful neighbours, too anxious to live in peace and enjoy their sporting privileges unimpaired to wish to act in ways that would seem arbitrary or oppressive to their tenants and labourers. Their motives for undertaking the unremunerated and troublesome office of justice of the peace were, for the most part, quite ordinary; their fathers had done so before them; it was convenient to themselves and to their fellow-parishioners to have a justice near by; they

---

4.   *ELG, The Parish and the County,* p. 347.

instinctively disliked the intervention of any other person in the village that they dominated or over the estate that they owned. Their worst characteristics were indolence and ignorance."

This somewhat negative assessment of the Justices of the Peace was probably accurate so far as it went, but there was another side of the coin.

Today it is possible to examine a new wealth of written material which has become accessible during the past few decades. Much of this can be found in the archives which have now been collected in the county record offices and it consists not only of official documents and records of proceedings, but also numerous diaries and a vast amount of private correspondence. This new evidence does not immediately reverse the impression that the justices had many shortcomings when judged by modern standards. They did not hesitate to behave in a thoroughly unseemly manner if they were faced with a threat to their dignity. The gentry and members of the nobility would react like spoilt children when anyone had the audacity to besmirch their reputation. There were many instances in the nineteenth as well as the eighteenth century. In the 1830s a Gloucestershire JP, Colonel William Berkeley who later became Lord Segrave, violently assaulted the editor of the county newspaper because he had published an article criticizing his behaviour. A few years later Berkeley's brother, who was also on the Gloucestershire commission, assaulted and injured the editor of a London magazine which had denigrated him and his family. Both brothers continued to sit as magistrates after committing these acts of violence. Such cases were not uncommon, but on the other hand the evidence now available reveals a good deal to the justices' credit.

It must be accepted that, to the observer of today, many of the eighteenth century justices appear arrogant and ambitious and also vindictive and tyrannical, ready to abuse the authority of their office when it suited them to do so and having little regard to the sufferings of their fellow creatures. These were not, however, the exclusive characteristics of the magistrates. They applied to all the upper classes, and also to those of lower degree when they had an opportunity to exhibit them. Generally, the justices behaved no worse than most of their fellow countrymen and there were numerous instances when their conduct was clearly above the average. There is no evidence that they were more lax in the performance of their duties than were members of the Government or of Parliament or the holders of other public offices at that time. It was an age of arrogance, loose morals and acute class distinctions, and one might have expected that those who were able to assume the mantle of local deities would have behaved in a more self-centred and inconsiderate manner than did most of the justices during this period. In fact, there is ample evidence that they exhibited certain qualities which were in advance of the generality of their society. In particular, they had a clear sense of responsibility. Most were impressively conscientious in the performance of their duties and, contrary to general belief, they showed real concern for the welfare of the local population. It is true that they often appeared to be intolerant and selfish, but once their position was clearly established they took a genuine pride in maintaining the standards of their local communities. Most justices were concerned for the well-being of the people in their area, and an aspect of this was seen in the many instances where, both in and out of court, they acted in a diplomatic or conciliatory manner and attempted to resolve differences which had arisen between individuals or groups. Blackstone considered that one of the justices' most important functions was "healing petty disputes and preventing vexatious prosecutions." It became customary for all local problems to be laid before the nearest justice. On these occasions they were able to achieve more successful results than a regular court of law or Government officer because they could handle the problem in an informal atmosphere and with a close understanding of the problems arising in their neighbourhood.

Furthermore, some individual justices were foremost among those who initiated the beneficial reforms which were ultimately adopted. Whereas there were numbers of compassionate individuals throughout the whole population, there were also justices who shared their sentiments and took positive steps to implement them. Some of these were conspicuous in their achievements, such as the prison reformer, Sir George O. Paul of Gloucestershire, or the Reverend H. Zouch of Yorkshire who, among a number of activities, wrote a pamphlet on the social problem of the day entitled *A Few Words on Behalf of the Poor.* The Rev. Henry Bryant, a Norfolk justice, reminded his colleagues that "it is indifferent to the pauper to what parish he belongs; but it cannot be indifferent to him that he belongs to no parish." There were many others who supported these progressive policies. Time after time in the diaries of individual justices and in the prolific correspondence of the squirearchy, one finds comments which demonstrate humane concern about the plight of individuals and a real interest in improving existing conditions so as to ameliorate the lot of those who were not to blame for the position in which they found themselves. There was also a compassionate approach to major issues, even to the treatment of offenders.

Contrary to widespread belief, it is clear from court records that the justices did not normally inflict maximum penalties and that it was quite common for them to impose fairly lenient sentences. It is true that they were apt to be harsh when their own interests were involved, though not invariably so, while on other occasions they were far more considerate than is generally supposed. Recent research in different parts of the country supports the view that although the maximum permitted sentences for convicted criminals were harsh by modern standards and although one can occasionally find instances of the maximum penalty being imposed for apparently trivial offences, in the main justice was fairly administered according to the standards of the time. As we shall see, this was the case even in the enforcement of the game laws where the justices' conduct has always been regarded as ruthlessly selfish and cruel.

Although the justices' Government was oligarchical, their attitude towards the community for which they were responsible has been rightly described as paternalistic; but this went considerably further than being merely condescending or patronizing as the term may imply. The eighteenth century saw the development of humanitarianism, which was advanced not by the Government but by individuals and associations. Some of the individuals who played a leading role in this movement were the JPs and they were often supported by the body of their fellow magistrates.

One may well condemn the eighteenth century justices for being selfish and vindictive and for showing philanthropic proclivities only when they had achieved their ambitions and when it suited them to rule their domains as benevolent despots. This judgment should, however, be tempered by the recognition that a significant number of the justices were imbued with genuine humanity and would have exhibited this even if they had not achieved office; while the others, who fell into the general category, made up for their shortcomings by governing the country in as efficient and scrupulous a manner as the extraordinarily deficient system would allow. Blackstone, who was no great supporter of the justices, admitted when he wrote in the middle of the century that "the country is greatly obliged" to them for undertaking this onerous work. Having regard to the defects of the system, the Government of the country by unpaid, untrained, part-time officers was a remarkable achievement. On the whole it worked successfully and this could only have been accomplished by men who were intelligent and competent and who possessed a considerable sense of responsibility.

These redeeming features may be pleaded in mitigation of the sentence which most recent observers have been inclined to impose upon the eighteenth century justices, but it must be recognized that their reputation among their contemporaries deteriorated markedly during this period, giving impetus to the reforming movements which reached their goal in the legislation of the following century.

In this chapter we will look at the general picture of the Justices of the Peace in the eighteenth century and examine the principal developments which brought them to the apogee of their power and influence. This will be followed in chs. II and III by a description of changes which took place in the routine work of the justices and an account of those functions and activities which tended to stain their image in the eyes of the public and which contributed to the replacement of the justices in their administrative role by other institutions under the reforms of the nineteenth century.

The eighteenth century Commissions of the Peace

It is well known that when James II fled the country he threw the Great Seal into the Thames, hoping thereby to disrupt the Government of anyone who presumed to succeed him. There was, however, no problem because a new seal of the realm is always made whenever there is a change of sovereign. Immediately after James's departure a group of peers assumed the powers of Government on an interim basis and issued a Declaration which included authority for all Protestant justices to remain in office for the time being. It is questionable whether anyone had legal authority to act as a justice in these circumstances, but in fact the Protestant members of the commissions continued to operate on a reduced scale in most areas. In a few instances, Quarter Sessions were held, but only to dispose briefly of matters of urgency.

At this time there were 58 county commissions in England and Wales. In addition to these there were certain liberties and towns which had their own commissions, but these varied in number from time to time during the century and a half after the Revolution.[5]

In 1689 there was a slight variation from the normal practice in that Lord Chancellor Jeffreys was succeeded, not by a new Keeper of the Great Seal but by three commissioners who performed the same functions. In the same month a committee of the Privy Council was appointed to prepare lists of potential justices for submission to the commissioners. The committee seems to have consulted various local magnates, including Lords Lieutenant, though it is not clear precisely how they proceeded. They then forwarded their lists to the commissioners who, under instructions from the King, proceeded to make the appointments without questioning any of the recommendations, though there was some delay in preparing the new commissions and a number of counties did not receive one for several months.

5.　　The following had separate commissions at some time during this period: The Isle of Ely, the Soke of Peterborough; the Liberties of Cawood, Otley, Ripon, St Albans, St Peter at York, Southwell and the Tower of London; the Cinque Ports; the cities of Oxford and Westminster; the boroughs of Bedford, Buckingham, Cambridge, Haverfordwest, Macclesfield, Malden, Poole, Saffron Walden, St Albans (separate from the Liberty), Sudbury, Taunton, and New Woodstock.

Importance had always been attached to the inclusion in each commission of a number of persons with knowledge of the law and, as we have seen, this was a reason for the establishment of the *Quorum*, but by the seventeenth century it had lost its significance because by then most justices were included in it even when they had no legal qualification.[6] Moreover, there was less need for lawyer justices than there had been in the past because the Clerk of the Peace, who was always present at Quarter Sessions, was legally qualified and was in a position to advise his justices on points of law, and also most chairmen of Quarter Sessions had studied law. The Webbs and other historians were wrong, however, when they said that by 1689 the *Quorum* clause "had become a mere form, as the practice was to name in each commission all the justices as of the *Quorum*."[7] There were others, such as Maitland and Blackstone who were under the impression that it had become customary to omit just one justice from the *Quorum* as a matter of form,[8] but here again there was a misapprehension. In fact, as is shown in Appendix II, the number of justices who were not in the *Quorum* remained fairly large for some time after the Revolution, and even in 1702 there were many counties where the exclusions were substantial; in Norfolk as many as thirty were not in the *Quorum*. In only four English counties (Durham, Oxfordshire, Rutland and Westmorland) and one Welsh (Radnorshire) was there only one justice omitted from the *Quorum*. From the beginning of the eighteenth century, however, the proportion of non-*Quorum* justices did drop. Lord Cowper, who held the Great Seal from 1705 to 1710 and from 1714 to 1718, rarely omitted a justice from the *Quorum*, and Lord Harcourt (1710 to 1714) never did so. None the less, as will be seen in the list set out in Appendix II, a few such omissions remained for some years thereafter. The *Quorum* was finally abolished by an Act of 1753.[9]

In the eighteenth century the commissions continued to be issued to certain liberties and boroughs as well as to counties. At the beginning of the century new commissions were generally issued every fifteen months, but this was extended to three years and by the 1730s the interval became much longer. The need to issue commissions at short intervals ceased when the Lord Chancellor adopted a new method of appointment by signing "fiats" containing the names of new justices

6. Dr Burn also gave as a reason "learning being now greatly advanced and improved since the first institution of this office, this distinction is not of much use." *Justice of the Peace*, 19th ed 1800 III, p. 16.
7. *ELG., The Parish and the County*, p. 303.
8. F.W. Maitland, *Justice and Police* London (1885) p. 81 and note 2; William Blackstone *Commentaries on the Laws of England*, i. 340.
9. 26 Geo. II, c. 27. This provided that even if an Act specified that a document had to be signed by a justice of the *Quorum* it was legally valid though none of the justices were of the *Quorum*.

and directing that they be added to the commission. This was done without requiring a new commission to be issued. A similar system came to be used for the removal of names, but this could also be achieved by means of a writ of *supersedeas*. Lambard[10] said that *supersedeas* was the only way in which a justice could be removed short of issuing another commission, but it was little used until the end of the 1730s.[11] The practice was revived by Lord Chancellor Macclesfield and even more so by his successor, Lord Hardwicke. It would seem that a justice against whom a complaint had been made would be given an opportunity to answer the charge.[12] After the Lord Chancellor had personally considered the case the writ would be issued directing the justice to cease acting as such, and this had the effect of virtually removing him from the commission. From that time *supersedeas* was used regularly to deal with justices whose conduct demanded immediate suspension from duty.[13] Those whose behaviour, though reprehensible, was less serious were removed in a more leisurely manner under a fiat.

This new procedure for both appointment and removal of justices resulted in long periods elapsing between the issue of new commissions. Thus, in Gloucestershire, the commission was not renewed for over 40 years (between 1769 and 1809) and names were added or removed by means of the Lord Chancellor's directions conveyed in his fiats. It was necessary, however, to introduce a change in the format of the commission itself. Previously the names of the justices were set out in the body of the commission and were followed by instructions. Under the new arrangements names were added at the foot of the old commission.

Official documents, including Commissions of the Peace, were permanently anglicized by an Act of 1733, and thenceforth all commissions were worded in English instead of Latin. From 1736 all pleadings in court had to be in English instead of in French or Latin. In 1752 the Gregorian was substituted for the Julian calendar and the legal year began on January 1 instead of March 25. An Act of 1760

---

10.   *Eirenarcha*, pp. 74-75.
11.   Lionel Glassey found only one issue of a *supersedeas* between 1675 and 1720 - that of John Rotherham who was put out of the Middlesex and Westminster commissions by Lord Macclesfield in July 1719 because he had sent the Russian Minister an insulting letter and had committed one of his servants to prison. *(Politics and the Appointment of Justices of the Peace, 1675-1720* OUP, (1979) p. 19-20). There were, however, instances of the whole body of justices on a commission being suspended by *supersedeas* issued through the Crown Office instead of the Court of Chancery which had been the normal practice. For example, a writ of *supersedeas* was issued to all the St Albans justices in 1685 and to those in Macclesfield in 1711. PRO, Index 4215, p. 120; Index 4216, p. 230.
12.   Norma Landau, *The Justices of the Peace, 1679-1760*, p. 129. For examples of such cases see *ibid.*, pp. 130-131.
13.   Norma Landau found that under Hardwicke 14 justices were suspended in 20 years and a further 22 during the remainder of the century. *Op. cit.*, p. 129.

provided that no Commission of the Peace should in future be determined on the death of the sovereign.

All commissions were passed under the Great Seal by the Clerk of the Crown in Chancery on the instructions of the Lord Chancellor, except in the County Palatine of Lancaster where the seal was that of the Duchy and was operated on the instructions of the Chancellor of the Duchy. When a new commission was issued it was sent by the Crown Office to the area to which it applied, a record being kept in the Crown Office docket book. The Clerk of the Crown held office for life and was sometimes at loggerheads with the Lord Chancellor and his staff, which caused serious delays and errors in the issue of commissions.

The Lord Chancellor also had three secretaries who were quite distinct from the Clerk of the Crown: the Principal Secretary, the Secretary of Commissions, who was responsible for Justices of the Peace, and the Secretary of Presentations who dealt with ecclesiastical patronage. These three were personal appointments by the Lord Chancellor and when he left office they too usually relinquished their posts, destroying at the same time any papers and files which might have disclosed embarrassing secrets to their successors. By the twentieth century the Principal Secretary had become the Permanent Secretary, who also invariably held the entirely distinct office of Clerk of the Crown in Chancery. The Secretaries of Commissions and Presentations remained, but whereas the latter's duties were much the same as in the eighteenth century, that of the Secretary of Commissions had changed fundamentally. In the eighteenth century he was responsible not only for Commissions of the Peace but also of oyer and terminer, gaol delivery, sewers, and charitable uses. By 1960 he was no longer concerned with the last four of these but had assumed responsibility for stipendiary magistrates, General Commissioners of Income Tax and a number of other matters unconnected with Justices of the Peace. It is not known precisely when the first Secretary of Commissions was appointed, but Francis Bacon had such a Secretary in 1618, and it had become a regular appointment by 1689. As already mentioned, the office of Secretary of Commissions, being a personal appointment by the Lord Chancellor, as it still is, terminated when the Lord Chancellor himself vacated office. The only exception to this during the eighteenth century was the poet, John Hughes, who became Secretary of Commissions in October 1717, during Lord Cowper's second tour of office, and continued to serve under Lord Macclesfield. By the twentieth century the Secretary of Commissions, though still appointed personally by the Lord Chancellor, was usually retained in office by successive Chancellors until he retired or was transferred to some other appointment.

Party Politics

The most outstanding feature of the Commissions of the Peace at the
end of the seventeenth and during the first half of the eighteenth
century was the impact made by party politics. Political parties were in
evidence before 1688 in the rivalry of the Court and Country parties
and this had some influence on public appointments.[14] Justices were
sometimes removed from the commissions because they were thought
to be opposed to the Government, though it was more usual for men
to be appointed to the commissions because they were supporters of
the Court party rather than for their opponents to be removed. It was
not until after the advent of the Whigs and Tories that party warfare
had a serious effect on the Justices of the Peace. The Whigs appeared
in 1679 in the aftermath of the Popish Plot and the exclusion crisis
when an attempt was made to exclude the future James II from the
throne. The Tory party emerged immediately afterwards, but were the
successors of the earlier Anglican and squirearchical party which, as
we have seen, was created in 1661 and was composed of Cavaliers who
were aggrieved because they did not recover the lands they had been
forced to sell. Both parties appreciated the importance of the
Commission of the Peace as a political weapon and they sought to
manipulate it to their advantage. From the beginning of the eighteenth
century one sees attempts by both parties to increase their
membership of the commissions and to curtail that of their opponents.
For a few years following the Revolution, however, there was little sign
of this. Both Whigs and Tories (if not too extreme in their views) were
appointed justices and neither party dominated the commission.
Likewise, the Government itself was composed of moderates from
both parties. A change came in 1693 when the Commissioners of the
Great Seal, who had proved to be largely ineffective, were replaced by
a new Lord Keeper, John Somers.[15]

The appointment of Somers marks the beginning of party
domination of the Commissions of the Peace which occurred at the
same time as the introduction of party Government at national level.
Somers was a Whig and his appointment coincided with the formation
of a predominantly Whig ministry. As soon as he assumed office
inquiry was made as to the political connections of existing justices,
and for this purpose Assize Judges were instructed to report those who
refused to act because they were dissatisfied. Following these inquiries
a number of justices were removed in 1693, and still more in 1694,
though dismissals fell far short of the numbers who lost office in the
purges of Charles II and James II. In 1696 the removals increased after

14. A notable example occurred in 1676 when Lord Townshend was replaced by the Earl of
    Yarmouth as Lord Lieutenant of Norfolk because the latter supported the Court party.
15. Somers was appointed Lord Chancellor and made a baron in 1697.

the attempted assassination of William III when, in a wave of popular support for the King, an Act was passed requiring all office holders including justices to take a special oath of allegiance.

Under Somers substantial dismissals were made in some counties, though many were unaffected. There were some Tory justices from well established families who were indispensable in running local affairs and whose conduct was such that there were no obvious grounds for removing them apart from their political allegiance. Most were allowed to remain. Moreover, in the rural areas the Whigs had considerably fewer supporters of sufficient calibre to serve on the commissions than did the Tories who were the party of the country gentry.

Nevertheless, Somers did manipulate the commissions in favour of the Whigs, and for this he was strongly criticized by his opponents. In 1699 the Commons appointed a committee to examine the commissions as they then were and also to note those who had been appointed or dismissed during the previous seven years. They concluded that, in appointing numbers of Whig supporters, Somers had lowered the standard of those on the commissions. The committee reported in March 1700 and this was followed by a petition from the Commons to the King that "Gentlemen of Quality and Good Estates" should be appointed to the commissions and that "Men of Small Estates should be omitted." The King replied: "I am of the Opinion that Men of the best Quality and Estates are more proper to be entrusted in the Commission of the Peace and Lieutenancy, and Directions shall be given accordingly."

The Tories gained the ascendency in the Commons in 1700 and the members of the Whig junta were removed from office. Somers himself was removed in April and a month later Nathan Wright, a Tory, was appointed in his place. His appointment was followed by a further investigation by a Commons committee. At that time the Lord Chancellor did not have unfettered authority over the appointment of justices. It was considered quite normal for the King to require the Privy Council to advise when a major reconstitution of the commissions was contemplated, and there was nothing strange in one or other of the Houses of Parliament conducting its own inquiry.

The Commons committee of 1700 recommended that all justices removed from office since 1696 should be restored, provided that they had taken the prescribed oaths. This was broadly accepted, and about two-thirds of those previously removed were reinstated. Also the Lords Lieutenant, *Custodes* and Assize Judges were asked to submit new names for appointment. Among the new appointees were all Members of Parliament, many of them Tories, who were not already justices. The revision of 1700 resulted in a great number of new appointments and few omissions, so the commissions became considerably larger. The majority of those omitted were men of small estate, who were removed in conformity with a definite policy of increasing the standard of the individual magistrates, but many of the new justices came from families who would not have been represented on the commission a generation earlier. They had recently progressed up the social ladder and had secured political backing for their personal advancement. The removal of the less prosperous justices did not please the Whigs, who voiced their indignation in both Houses of Parliament, but Wright declined to alter the position to any appreciable extent except in Cheshire, although shortly before his removal from office in 1704 he went rather further in restoring Whig justices who had been dismissed since 1700. Throughout his term of office Wright does not seem to have been guided by strong partisan motives. He wanted to appoint those who would make sound justices and to remove only those who were ineffective, but he allowed himself to be guided by influential colleagues and local magnates. In particular, the period following William III's death in March 1702 saw an eclipse of the Whigs and the ascendency of the Tories, and in addition to changes in the membership of the commissions several Whig Lords Lieutenant and *Custodes* were replaced by Tories.[16] The benches remained predominantly Tory until Cowper was appointed, after an interval, to succeed Wright in October 1705.

The appointment of Cowper was the outcome of an alliance of Marlborough and Godolphin with moderate Whigs rather than with moderate Tories. Cowper was Chancellor when England and Scotland were united in 1707 and he was the first Lord Chancellor of Great Britain. He was to serve on the Woolsack for two separate terms, totalling nine years in all. Although a Whig, he made far fewer adjustments to the commissions than his Tory predecessor. Norma Landau estimates that between 1705 and early 1707 he dismissed only 79 justices in counties where Wright had removed 587.[17] Political manipulation of the commissions continued, however, for nearly half a century. The fact that, for the time being, there were not more drastic changes on party lines was because the Governments were still coalitions and included both Whig and Tory Ministers. Cowper, as a Whig, took steps to readjust the commissions so as to balance the Tory ascendency created by Wright, but he did not resort to any drastic action and does not seem to have deliberately manipulated the commissions in favour of his own party to any appreciable extent. Like his predecessor, however, he had to rely upon local recommendations

16.   Four Whig Lieutenants and six Whig *Custodes* were replaced by Tories, but in April 1705, shortly after Wright had left the Woolsack, five Tory Lieutenants were replaced by Whigs.
17.   *Op. cit.,* p. 83. See also Herts RO, Panshanger MSS D/EP F152. List of those put in and out of commission by "my Lord Keeper."

for most of the candidates with the result that some commissions saw remarkably little change. Cowper does seem to have recognized the problem created by the numerous justices who failed to perform their duties and he attempted to include a larger number of active magistrates.

The importance of the commissions in the political field was enhanced by the realization that they could strengthen a party's chances of success in Parliamentary elections. In addition to rewarding supporters and punishing opponents by granting or denying appointment, it came to be recognized that the JPs themselves could exercise considerable influence over the voters. The courts were used to disseminate political propaganda and the electorate were more ready to accept statements made by JPs than by other members of the community who were not on the commission. If electors showed an unwillingness to do so the justices could make life very difficult for them in numerous ways. Improper threats were sometimes made, including the taking away of the licence of a publican. Daniel Defoe records an incident when a clergyman was imprisoned as a vagabond solely because the justices disapproved of his political views. In 1714 Cowper received a letter from a Warwickshire magnate saying:

"I take this occasion to observe to you that in case there is not some Regulations here in the Commission of the Peace as well as in other Places, the Tory Interest will always inevitably prevail, for the Bench of justices have such an Influence over the Freeholders in this county that they insult those poor wretches to such a degree that out of fear they seem to lose all sense of liberty ..."[18]

The justices' exercise of their powers was also of political significance in that it could affect the financial burden of the tax-payers in their area. Lord Chancellors also had in mind the possibility of securing the goodwill of some of their party's less staunch opponents who might be induced to transfer their allegiance if they were placed on a commission. Likewise it was thought sensible to avoid alienating moderate opponents to the extent of removing them from the bench. They tended to remain quiet while they were left in office. It is difficult to measure the success of this policy but it certainly had the effect of increasing the number of local gentry on the commissions. The same tactics were adopted to a greater or lesser extent under each of the Lord Chancellors during the first part of the century and the vicissitudes are recorded in detail in Lionel Glassey's *Politics and Appointment of Justices of the Peace, 1675-1720.*[19]

18. Letter from George Lucy. Herts RO, Cowper, Panshanger MSS. D/EP F154.
19. OUP (1979).

Cowper's first term of office came to an end in 1710 when he was replaced by the Tory, Harcourt,[20] who was more thorough in manipulating the commissions. In the following years a large number of new appointments were made - significantly more than under Cowper - the majority being Tories but there were also a few Whigs. Harcourt also removed more than twice as many justices as his predecessor, but left far more Tories than Whigs on the commissions. By 1714 only a small proportion of Whig justices remained, but Harcourt was under increasing pressure from the Tory leader, Bolingbroke, to eliminate even these. They were probably saved from extinction by the death of Queen Anne in July 1714 which was followed by a rout of the Tories and the establishment of a predominantly Whig ministry. This was the beginning of a long period of Whig hegemony during which the Tories, who were discredited by their exhibition of Jacobite sympathy in the 1715 uprising, were able to exert little influence on national affairs.

Under the Regency Act the Commissions of the Peace did not terminate until six months after the death of the Queen, by which time George I had assumed the crown. Two months after the Queen's death Cowper returned to the Woolsack, and so ended the four-year period of Harcourt's Chancellorship during which the Tories had dominated the commissions. Under Harcourt the swing to the Tories had been greater than that to the Whigs under Cowper, but the position varied considerably in different areas, probably depending upon the advice received from the localities. Whereas some county commissions had been swung dramatically in favour of the Tories, others had seen little change. There is also evidence that Harcourt appointed some prominent Jacobites who were prepared to support the succession to the throne of the Pretender on the Queen's death.[21]

Harcourt's term of office also marked a development in the independence of the Lord Chancellor's control over magisterial patronage. Throughout his term there were virtually no interventions by the Privy Council nor by Parliament nor the Secretaries of State requiring the appointment or removal of certain justices, as had occurred previously as a matter of course.

After the accession of George I the party political tide again turned and there was reorganization of the commissions in favour of the Whigs, accompanied by the replacement of Tory Lords Lieutenant and *Custodes* with Whigs in more than half the counties. Cowper, however, resisted the demands of his more zealous colleagues and did not leave as many Tories out of the commissions as they wished. He seems to have been concerned more with balancing the benches and rectifying

20.   Harcourt became Lord Keeper in October 1710 and Lord Chancellor in April 1713.
21.   See Glassey, *op. cit.*, pp. 232-3.

the discrepancies of his predecessor than with creating substantial Whig majorities. In this he may have been motivated by a desire to avoid driving the Tory gentry, who constituted a formidable force in many counties as well as in Parliament, into active opposition to the Government. He realized that too drastic a purge of the commissions could be counterproductive in that it might lead to powerful bodies of discontented men concluding that the only chance of re-establishing their authority lay in a united attack on those in office. Cowper was criticized by the Whigs for not transforming the commissions more drastically in their favour, but he explained his policy in a memorandum to the King in 1715. He drew attention to the change which had taken place as a result of party conflict in the removal of justices from the commissions at the beginning of the century. He observed that:

"But so late as in my own memory of business, very few if any were displaced without cause assigned & proved, because it was justly thought to be an injurious disgrace on any Gent[leman] in this country to be turned out ... unless for some known or evident reason ...

But as the two parties grew more & more set & violent against one another, this commendable tenderness, I may say justice, began by degrees to be laid aside. Gentlemen well qualify'd were put out of that Commission without formal hearings or even so much as proof ex parte of any misbehaviour in their Duty. When I had the Honour of the Great Seale the first time, I cannot accuse myself of that last mention'd practice & yet by perserverance in putting in those who were best inclin'd to the Protestant Succession & leaving out, as fast as I could discover them, those who were of too inferior a Condition & taking all just advantages of proof against those who discovered a disaffection to the true interest of their country, I can truly say, the Commissions of the Peace were at my surrendering the Seale in a very good state with a sufficient balance in favour of the honest interest."[22]

Cowper pointed out that it would have been unjust and would have done more harm than good to remove justices merely on "private whispers," but on the other hand he was prepared to dismiss those who showed their disaffection by neglecting to act. The memorandum also explained that on the King's accession Cowper had done his best, within the limited time available, to

"turn out according to the best accounts I could get, great numbers of persons disaffected & otherwise not well qualifyd, & put in all I

---

22.   Herts RO, Cowper, Panshanger MSS. D/EP F152. Memorandum for George I.

could have well recommended as to Estate & affection to your Government: and as to those who wer of Estate and quality Sufficient in their Country, but were represented by Your Majesty's friends as of suspected inclinations; I thought it for Your Majesty's interest not to displace them on bare general suspicion; unless they who solicited their Removal would give in writing some particular instance or objection to their conduct ... This I required not that [it] would have been any defence to me in case the contrary party had proved strong enough to call my Conduct in Question; but that at least I might by having recourse to my papers, be able to allege a reason for my proceedings to any that should come to expostulate with me ..."[23]

In April 1718 Cowper resigned because of ill-health and was succeeded by Thomas Parker (later Earl of Macclesfield) who was also a Whig. He adopted a moderate policy on the composition of the commissions, but continued to remove the more active Tories, especially those suspected of supporting the Jacobites. In the result, the Tories, though not entirely eliminated, were left in a small minority in most areas and local Government was dominated by the Whigs. Macclesfield was reluctant, however, to disgrace anyone without good reason by dismissing them from a commission, and in some counties where the Tory justices had been allowed to remain in office they were in a majority. The seriousness attached to dismissal from the commissions had already been stressed in the oft quoted comment by Dr William Lloyd in a letter to Cowper in 1709: "It must be allowed that the honour of being in, is not so great as the disgrace of being turn'd out of the commission."[24] On the other hand, new Tory justices were seldom appointed and by the time that Macclesfield (impeached for financial irregularities) ceased to be Lord Chancellor in 1725, and was succeeded in 1726 by Peter King, the Whigs were in the majority on almost all commissions.

King's appointment was marked by a slackening of party political bias in magisterial appointments. George I himself was averse to partisan manipulation of the commissions and he instructed King to include all gentlemen of rank and quality in each commission unless they were in direct opposition to the Government. King followed these instructions and reinstated a few of those who had been removed by his predecessors because of their political persuasions. Charles Talbot, who succeeded King as Lord Chancellor in 1733, followed much the same policy but seems to have been careful to restrict the number of Tories who were appointed, although they were not automatically

23.　　*Ibid.*, Quoted by Glassey, *op. cit.*, pp. 251-2.
24.　　Herts RO, Cowper, Panshanger MSS D/EP F55.

excluded. Consequently, when Talbot retired four years later most commissions had a clear Whig majority.

Talbot was succeeded in 1737 by the Earl of Hardwicke, who was to remain in office for 26 years and who took a close interest in the commissions over which he exercised firm control. Hardwicke adopted the principle that no justice should be removed from the commission because of his political views but only on grounds of misconduct, and there is no evidence that he ever directed a removal for political reasons. Consequently, to be dismissed became an even greater disgrace than before and most justices remained in office for life. Their position was therefore more akin to that of the professional Judges who also held office for life. The Act of Settlement of 1701 finally established security of office for the higher judiciary who thereafter held office during good behaviour subject to a power of removal by the Sovereign on an address presented by both Houses of Parliament. These provisions did not apply to the Justices of the Peace who continued to hold their appointments at the pleasure of the Sovereign, but from the end of the 1730s their appointments were seldom terminated except on the grounds of misconduct or inability.

Hardwicke's policy reflected the changing attitude of many of the Whig ministers. A long period of Whig hegemony gave rise to the formation of dissatisfied groups among the Whigs themselves, some of whom were prepared to consider alliances with Tory factions. Henry Pelham, who became head of the Whig Government in 1743, later entered into an alliance with an opposition group which included both Whigs and Tories. The Government were then forced to agree in principle to the admission of Tories to the commissions in reasonable numbers. The agreement virtually confirmed what the King had had in mind 20 years earlier. In future, proper regard was to be had to the appointment to all commissions of "gentlemen of Figure and Fortune well affected to His Majesty's Government, without distinction of parties." From now onwards numbers of Tories were regularly included in the commissions, although Hardwicke still tried to maintain a Whig preponderance where this could reasonably be achieved. It would be true to say, however, that from 1745 onwards appointments to the commissions no longer depended to any appreciable extent upon party affiliation, and still less did removal, though political debate continued to be a prominent feature of Quarter Sessions and Petty Sessions.

The importance of Quarter Sessions in the political field increased greatly in the eighteenth century. It was no doubt for this reason that Robert Walpole, who was a JP for Norfolk, continued to serve on the commission throughout his life, even during the twenty-one years when he was in all but name Prime Minister, and he always attended Quarter Sessions whenever he was able to do so. Justices' diaries contain frequent entries recording their attendance at meetings prior to sessions with colleagues belonging to their own party. On these occasions they would decide upon their candidates for Parliament and for various local offices. The meeting at which the appointment of the latter was finally made by the assembled justices for the county was often a contentious affair. The Rev. F.E. Witts of Gloucestershire records the election of the governor of the gaol in Gloucester on the September 13, 1836:

"We arrived as the Magistrates were congregating for the election of a Governor of the Gaol. We assembled in the Crown Court, Bathurst[25] presiding. One hundred and six justices were assembled. The Lord Lieutenant Lord Segrave, the Duke of Beaufort, Lord E. Somerset, Lord Bathurst, Lord Redesdale were present, and most of the leading gentry both Conservative and Whigs, but there was a large preponderance of the latter actuated by a double motive. To bring in a partisan and show the strength of the party on the one hand and on the other to favour a man to whom on the score of poverty the appointment was of the utmost importance and who was connected with some old and influential families."[26]

By the accession of George I the election of the chairman of Quarter Sessions had become an important political contest because the influence he could exert was considerable. Even in counties where one party had an overwhelming majority among the justices there were strong political undercurrents. In a diary entry of October 16, 1833, the Rev. F. Witts describes the election of Mr Bathurst (who presided at the election of the governor of the gaol mentioned above).

"It had been rumoured that the Whig party would have proposed some magistrates of their own politics; but as they would have had little chance in a court the majority of whose members hold Tory opinions it was prudent of them not to make the trial. Mr Bathurst was brought up at the Bar, is a sound lawyer, a very steady, upright grave man."

The chairman's charge to the Grand Jury was used to disseminate political propaganda and often dealt with a range of political issues of national as well as local significance. Similar pronouncements had been made through the Grand Jury at Assizes since the latter part of the seventeenth century when these juries began to include a

25.   This was C. Bragge Bathurst junior, the son of the Right Hon. C. Bragge Bathurst, mentioned below at p. 27, who had also been Chairman of Quarter Sessions. The Lord Bathurst referred to later in the present extract was Henry, 4th Earl Bathurst.
26.   *The Diary of a Cotswold Parson*. The Rev. F.E. Witts, 1783-1854. Ed. David Verey (1977) Alan Sutton.

substantial number of justices. Political debate continued to be a prominent feature of Quarter Sessions well into the nineteenth century.

Importance of the Lords Lieutenant and Custodes Rotulorum in the appointment process

We have seen how, during the first half of the eighteenth century, the composition of the commissions was influenced by party politics, but this varied considerably from one county to another, largely because the Lord Chancellor, although invested with overriding authority to adjust the commissions at his discretion, was obliged to act upon local advice. In the early part of the century, recommendations were sought and received from a number of local interests and not exclusively from the Lord Lieutenant or the *Custos Rotulorum*. Sometimes the Lord Chancellor used another magnate to examine the Lord Lieutenant's list and to report secretly on the candidates. An example of this is to be found in Gloucestershire while Hardwicke was Lord Chancellor. The Earl of Berkeley, Lord Lieutenant and *Custos*, although a Whig, wished to include some Tories in the commission so as to lower the heat of the opposition, while making sure that there was a Whig majority. When Berkeley asked for a new commission to be issued in 1739 Hardwicke instructed Sir John Dutton, a former Whig Member of Parliament for the county, to consider Berkeley's list in secret. Dutton reported that several nominees were unacceptable and they were dropped.[27] It was also the practice to consult the Assize Judges, and sometimes these volunteered information without waiting to be asked. For example, in 1700 Lord Chief Baron Ward disclosed that the Cornwall justices were inadequate because only twenty of them were performing their duties.[28]

In the latter part of the century it was almost invariably the Lord Lieutenant, who was also usually *Custos Rotulorum,* upon whom appointments and removals depended. As Lord Melbourne observed in the early nineteenth century, Justices of the Peace "are selected according to the peculiar notions and circumstances of each Lord Lieutenant." Lord Brougham, who was Lord Chancellor under William IV, said that "some Lord Lieutenants appoint men for their political opinions, some for their activity as partisans in local contests." This, however, requires qualification because responsibility for the commission and for those appointed to it rested strictly with the *Custos Rotulorum* and not with the Lord Lieutenant. By the end of the

27. BL, Add. MSS 35601, ff. 128, 145-6.
28. PRO, Privy Council Miscellaneous Papers, P.C., 1/1/50: April 18, 1700.

eighteenth century both offices were usually held by the same person, whereas this had not been so in the earlier part, and there were instances of two persons with opposing political views serving as Lieutenant and *Custos* in the same county. Thus in Northamptonshire, the Whig Earl of Monmouth was Lord Lieutenant while the Tory Viscount Hatton was *Custos.* The difference between the offices of Lieutenant and *Custos* for magisterial purposes does not seem to have been fully appreciated even by Lord Chancellors and other Ministers. One finds that much correspondence relating to justices was addressed to the Lord Lieutenant on the assumption that responsibility for their appointment rested solely with his office. On the other hand it was common during the first part of the eighteenth century for both the Lieutenant and the *Custos* to be consulted on proposed appointments, and the Privy Council Committee of 1700 asked that lists of all justices who had been removed since 1696 be sent to both Lieutenants and *Custodes,* and also to Assize Judges, for comments, and they were also invited to suggest candidates for inclusion in the new commissions. The distinction between the two offices became of less importance as they came to be held by the same individual, and henceforth references to Lord Lieutenant will be intended to include *Custos,* but the two offices remain distinct even to the present day. The Lord Lieutenant is appointed by the Sovereign on the advice of the Prime Minister, whereas the *Custos Rotulorum* or Keeper of the Rolls is appointed by the Lord Chancellor.[29]

The Lord Lieutenant had become the dominant figure in the county in consequence of his original military role, but this aspect of his work declined, especially after the Napoleonic Wars. The decline was accelerated when the militia became moribund and, although the Lieutenancy played a part in the yeomanry which largely replaced the militia, the need to have local forces ready to disperse riots diminished with the establishment of county police forces. The Lord Lieutenant had long had some responsibility for the county justices, and as the office came to be held jointly with that of *Custos* the holder was clearly identified as head of the magistrates in the county.

Lords Lieutenant were always persons of eminence, and sometimes they were also leading national figures active in the central arena with little time to devote to their Lieutenancy duties. For instance, Marlborough was Lord Lieutenant of Oxfordshire and Godolphin of Cornwall. Cowper became Lord Lieutenant of Hertfordshire in 1710. The Whig ministry which began in 1715 contained three Lords Lieutenant; the Duke of Devonshire (Derbyshire), Townshend (Norfolk) and Doddington (Somerset). All three retained their

29.   Administration of Justice Act, 1973, s. 1(2).

Lieutenancies when dismissed from the Government in 1717. Even when they were not Ministers many Lieutenants were inclined to spend an appreciable amount of their time in London. Some magnates still held more than one Lieutenancy at the same time. The Duke of Northumberland was Lord Lieutenant of Middlesex, Nottinghamshire and Sussex, and the Duke of Bolton of Dorset, Hampshire and Carmarthen, but Bolton was removed from all three in 1733. By the latter part of the century Lords Lieutenant usually held office for life.

By the end of the eighteenth century appointments to the commissions were almost always made in accordance with the recommendations of the Lord Lieutenant. The Lord Chancellor might add names on his own initiative but seldom did so. As early as 1749, Lord Broke, Lord Lieutenant and *Custos* of Warwickshire, reacted angrily to Hardwicke's proposal to add two justices to the list he had submitted. One of them was nevertheless appointed.[30] As regards removal, we have seen that this became rare except in cases of misconduct. Lord Eldon, a Tory who became Lord Chancellor in 1801, went further and made a rule "that however unfit a magistrate might be for his office, either from private misconduct or party feeling," he would never remove him from the commission until he had been convicted of some offence by the verdict of a court of record, adding that as the magistrates gave their service gratis they ought to be protected.[31]

The eighteenth century Justices of the Peace

It was in the eighteenth century that the term "magistrates" came to be applied to Justices of the Peace. This was an ancient title describing persons who exercised judicial and executive powers and its adoption may have been a recognition of the breadth of the justices' responsibilities. Those to whom it was applied also represented a broader based section of the community than that of the traditional JPs. We have seen that after the Restoration men of comparatively low status appeared in the commissions to a greater degree than previously. For the most part these were men who had given outstanding support to the Government and were rewarded in this way. The tendency increased after the 1689 Revolution with the growth of party politics, and this was the subject of the complaints in both Houses of Parliament which have already been mentioned. Criticism for the most part emanated from the old established county gentry who resented the need to associate with the new generation of men who had gained their position through commerce. This attitude

30. BL, Add. MSS 35603, f. 170, July 15, 1749.
31. Reported in speech by Brougham. Hansard, February 7, 1828, vol. XVIII, N.S. p. 161.

continued well into the nineteenth century, and in 1833 it gave rise to the only recorded occasion when Justices of the Peace have gone on strike. The justices of the county of Merioneth refused to perform their duties for a time because they would not serve with a newly appointed justice who, though a wealthy landowner, had once kept a retail grocery. They also objected to his being a Wesleyan Methodist, but it was his social background rather than his religious views which caused them to demonstrate their feelings in such an extreme manner. The commissioner who reported on this case supported the justices' action, explaining that it amounted to "genuine patriotism."

We have seen that in Cromwell's day it was recognized that the country could not be governed effectively by men of low degree who did not have the respect of the masses, and during the régime of the Major Generals it was agreed that the justices needed to be drawn from the leading gentry. In the eighteenth century the established county families strove, with only limited success, to maintain this principle and to prevent the appointment of men of lower social degree lest this should reflect upon the status of the existing justices. The property qualification requiring ownership of land of the yearly value of £20 which had been imposed by the Act of 1439 still applied, and there were demands, particularly from the Tory gentry, that this should be raised substantially so as to ensure that only wealthy landowners should become justices. Several attempts to amend the 1439 Act were abortive and, even when they succeeded, the result was to raise the qualification to a level far too low to ensure the elimination of the less prosperous.

An Act of 1732[32] decreed that, from March 25, 1733, no person should be capable of becoming a JP or of acting as such for any county "who shall not have an estate of freehold or copyhold ... of the clear yearly value of one hundred pounds over and above what will satisfy and discharge all incumbrances that may affect the same." No attorney, solicitor or proctor might be a JP in any county so long as he continued to be engaged in such practice. Anyone acting as a justice when not qualified under the Act was to forfeit £100, half of which was to go to the King and half to the informer bringing proceedings in the courts at Westminster. This Act did not extend to a city or town being a county of itself, nor to any other city, town, cinque port or liberty having Justices of the Peace "charter, commission or otherwise."[33]

The preamble to the 1732 Act stated that "constituting persons of

32.   5 Geo. II, c. 18.
33.   The following were also excluded from the Act; Peers and their eldest sons, knights of the shire elected to Parliament, justices of the board of green cloth (who dealt with matters within the verge of the Palaces), principal officers of the Navy, "the two Under Secretaries in each of the offices of Principal Secretary of State" and heads of colleges and halls in the Universities of Oxford and Cambridge.

mean estates to be Justices of the Peace may be highly prejudicial to the publick welfare." A further Act of 1745[34] began by observing:

"Whereas by many Acts of Parliament of late years made, the powers and authority of justices of the peace is greatly increased, whereby it is become of the utmost consequence to the commonwealth, to provide against persons of mean estate acting as such; and whereas the laws now in force are not sufficient for that purpose."

The Act went on to re-enact and extend the provisions of the 1732 statute. It was to apply to every "county, riding or division" and no one might act as a justice until he had taken the prescribed oath at general or Quarter Sessions "for which he does or shall intend to act." The oath was to begin with the words:

"I, AB, do swear, That I truly and bona fide have such an estate, in law or equity, to and for my own use and benefit, consisting of (specifying the nature of such estate, whether messuage, land, rent, tythe, office, benefice, or what else) as doth qualify me to act as a Justice of the Peace for the county, riding or division of ... according to the true interest and meaning of an Act of Parliament, made in the eighteenth year of the reign of His Majesty King George the Second, intituled, an Act to amend and render more effective an Act passed in the fifth year of his present Majesty's reign ..."

A record of the oath was to be kept by the Clerk of the Peace among the sessions records. Anyone acting as a justice when not qualified or without taking the oath was subject to a fine of £100, one moiety to go to the poor of the parish in which the offender usually resided and the other moiety went to the informer who sued and who was also given his full costs. If, however, the plaintiff discontinued the case, or was non suited, or if judgment was given against him, the person against whom he brought the proceedings was to receive treble costs. The case had to be brought within six months after the commission of the act.

There was further legislation on the subject during the last half of the century, but this made no significant difference. An Act of 1760[35] was mainly concerned with clarifying the position of those who were on the commissions at the time of the death of George II, and who were retained in office provided that they took the oaths before the Clerk of

34. 18 Geo. II, c. 20. This Act added Privy Councillors to those who were excluded from the statutory qualifications.
35. 1 Geo. III, c. 13. It was no longer necessary to sue out new writs on the death of a Sovereign, but the Act provided that on the issue of a new commission justices were to sign a roll on which the oaths had been engrossed.

the Peace. Under the Justices' Qualification Act 1774 a justice was required to possess an estate of freehold, copyhold or customary in fee of the yearly value of £100, and this was extended a year later by an Act which required only the occupation of property rated at £100. The value thus remained at £100, which by that time was not a great deal of money, and many middle class people would have had no difficulty in qualifying for appointment. Those who had recently made fortunes in trade were richer than some of the landed gentry, who resented their presence on the commission even more for this very reason. They could therefore have had little effect except to focus attention upon the status which the justices were expected to maintain. Apart from the period of the Interregnum, emphasis had always been placed upon the need to entrust the important powers of a Justice of the Peace only to men of property, and the fact that in the eighteenth century Parliament saw fit to confirm the property qualification and to raise it in value, even by a comparatively small amount, was an indication of the importance which still attached to maintaining the propertied class as the core of the magistracy.

In spite of the resistance from the squirearchy, the number of newcomers to the bench continued to increase as the Industrial Revolution, which began in the late eighteenth century, brought large fortunes to men of humble origin who then moved into country estates. It was as well that many of them were placed on the commissions for they were often the most assiduous in the discharge of their duties, and sometimes they were the only magistrates resident in the neighbourhood of towns. In fact, one of the serious defects in the magistracy of the eighteenth century was the scarcity of justices in many areas; in some places there was a total absence.[36] This was particularly marked in those parts of the country where the population had increased dramatically with the introduction of new industries, but did not include anyone who was regarded as suitable for appointment to the commission. With the exception of Middlesex and parts of Surrey no attempt was made to meet the new situation by the appointment of men in the lower social scale. The result was that the corruption which pervaded the benches in the metropolitan area was avoided elsewhere but at the expense of having to travel 20 miles or more in some places to find even one justice. Had it not been for the appointment of many clerics to the commissions the position would have been considerably worse.

A particularly unsatisfactory consequence of the absence of any justice in an area was that the local officers were unrestrained and sometimes became petty tyrants. As we shall see later there was also

---

36.   The Act 18 Geo. III, c. 49 allowed justices to act for adjoining counties because "the Administration of Justice is frequently obstructed for want of Resident justices."

the need to bring justices from long distances to deal with outbreaks of disorder and rioting, which were a common feature of eighteenth century England, and there was often long delay in securing the presence of a justice to read the Riot Act.

There were many complaints about justices who failed to act. Sometimes this came from the Assize Judges, as in the case of Chief Baron Ward mentioned above. In the early part of the century, about half of those appointed failed to take out a *dedimus,* and between Hardwicke's appointment in 1737 and 1760 only about one in every four new justices did so. This does not mean that they disdained the office. The appointment was as much sought after as ever, its rewards being the standing which it gave to the justice among his fellows and the satisfaction of domination over the inhabitants of his neighbourhood. Many of those appointed, however, sought to enjoy the distinction without accepting the burden, and it had become easier to remain on the commission without performing a share of the work. This situation began to change about the middle of the century when more emphasis was placed upon the work which the justices were required to perform, especially the maintenance of public order. As the century progressed more assiduous attention was paid by the justices to the law and to the rules of procedure. This may have been due in part to the large number of legally qualified clerical justices who, as we shall see, were among the most active magistrates towards the end of the century, and many of them were the authors of textbooks.

Notwithstanding the widening of the base on which the magistracy was founded it remained a select, oligarchical élite. Many were the sons and grandsons of justices.[37] They were the rulers of the land and membership of the commission was something to which every one of consequence aspired. As already indicated they were predominant in Parliament; most members of the House of Lords and the majority of the Commons were on a commission. A large proportion were among the principal landowners of the county, and it is a matter of considerable significance that most of these must have been the landlords of all the parish officers within their respective parishes. In the early part of the century the majority of the nobles who were justices neglected their duties, but by the end they were taking a more active interest and some became chairmen of Quarter Sessions. The same was true of Ministers in the Commons. Bragge Bathurst, father of the Gloucestershire justice mentioned earlier, was chairman of Quarter Sessions and an extremely active magistrate while serving as a

37. Details of justices on the Kent commission who were preceded by paternal ancestors and of those who were succeeded by their sons are given by Norma Laundau, *op. cit.,* Appx. B, pp. 376, 377.

Minister in three successive Governments. Bathurst was one of the many justices who were followed on the bench by their sons. In view of the political importance of Quarter Sessions one might have expected that the Parliamentarians of both Houses would have invariably concentrated their attention upon this aspect of the justices' work, but this was not so. Some devoted their time to the performance of duties within their own neighbourhood and only rarely came to Quarter Sessions. A striking example of this was Sir William Bromley who managed to perform a formidable amount of out-of-sessions work even after he became Speaker of the House of Commons and later Secretary of State.[38]

Eighteenth century justices have been portrayed as lackadaisical insofar as their magisterial commitments were concerned, but there were many, in addition to Sir William Bromley, to whom this certainly did not apply. Their numerous diaries testify to the keen and active interest they took in their work. It is also generally assumed that the justices, in common with the rest of the squirearchy, were largely preoccupied in drinking, gaming and hunting. It is true that large numbers spent a great deal of their time in the hunting field, interspersed with convivial gatherings at which much wine was consumed. The diaries record substantial meals which were a regular feature of magisterial meetings, especially Quarter Sessions. The rate of intoxication must have been high, and sometimes those who attempted to ride home afterwards failed to arrive. The Rev. F.E. Witts records the fate of Mr Winchomb Hicks, an "esteemed magistrate" who came to grief in this way after the sheriffs' dinner in Gloucestershire on March 31, 1824, when he fell off his horse and was found almost dead. It is obvious, however, that these happenings were not peculiar to the Justices of the Peace nor to the gentry who lived in the eighteenth century. Although the heavy drinking sportsman was probably typical of many of the justices during this period, fortunately for the country this did not inhibit them from devoting a substantial amount of time effectively to public service. Country-house archives and the store chests of parish churches have produced quantities of documents which show that many justices spent a prodigious amount of time and energy in discharging their numerous duties in a conscientious and public-spirited manner. In an age when it was customary for the upper classes to devote much of their days and nights to the pursuit of pleasure, it is remarkable how much time was given by some of the justices to work which, though it must have been

38.   Warwickshire County Records, eds. H.C. Johnson & N.J. Williams, 1964, IX, pp. xxxviii-xl. Sir William Bromley was first elected for Gloucestershire but became Member for Oxford University in 1700. His detailed notes of cases have survived and provide an informative picture of the single justice and his work, most of which was conducted in his own house.

of interest to them, was obviously not always enjoyable and could amount to drudgery. In 1803 the Rev. Robert Forby, a Norfolk justice, wrote to a friend bemoaning the weight of his public duties.

"Till you have experienced the heavy drudgery of an acting Justice, Deputy Lieutenant and Commissioner of the Land Tax ... on whom the burden of a large district lies, you will not readily conceive the fatigue they cause to the mind ... I return at five o'clock to a solitary dinner, which I abhor, with my head full of parish rates, surveyor's accounts, vagrants, runaway husbands, assaults, petty larcenies, militia lists and substitutes, tax duplicates and distress warrants, some or all of these jumbled together in a horrid confusion."

Those who performed these duties were intelligent and well educated. Most, like their predecessors, had studied at a university or at an Inn of Court, but whereas at the beginning of the eighteenth century the majority had been to an Inn, by the end the position was reversed and substantially more had attended a university. The higher proportion of university graduates was due partly to the large number of clerical justices who were appointed in the late part of the century, all of whom had attended a university. Apart from the clerics, however, more of the gentry were now attending universities, while study at an Inn of Court was becoming confined to those who wished to follow a legal career. Among the gentry the university would probably have been followed by the Grand Tour, during which they widened their intellectual scope and from which they returned with collections of books to embellish the inexpanding libraries which were an essential part of a gentleman's establishment. It is clear from the diaries which the owners compiled and the letters they wrote to their friends that their book collections were not merely decorative but were the source of constant interest and subject for debate.

Clerical justices

A remarkable feature of the last half of the eighteenth century was the large number of clergy who were justices and who took a prominent part in magisterial affairs. As we have seen, bishops had been included in most commissions since the early sixteenth century and a few of the junior clergy from the seventeenth, but until the mid-eighteenth century it was unusual for more than one or two of them to be justices in any county. The small number appointed was probably due to the involvement of the justices in the prosecution of recusants and non-conformists and in the enforcement of other ecclesiastical regulations, and it was not thought right to place these functions in the hands of members of the established church. In 1689, however, the so called Toleration Act[39] put an end to the persecution of those who did not conform to the established church, and by 1750 there was no continuation of the acute sectarian controversies of earlier generations. The number of clerical justices increased dramatically, except in a few counties where the Lord Lieutenant was opposed to such appointments and would not nominate any clerics. One of the reasons for choosing so large a number of justices in this category was that the clergy were generally more knowledgeable in the law than most other justices and were better adapted to the handling of matters which came before them. Moreover, almost all proved to be highly dedicated to the work, throwing themselves enthusiastically into the task, and always ready and available to deal with any problems which might arise. Some people, particularly certain bishops, questioned the propriety of involving ministers of religion in magisterial work, but it was nearing the middle of the nineteenth century before these comments had any effect on the number of appointments. As late as 1832, a Parliamentary Paper (No. 39) gave the total number of justices as 5,371 of whom 1,354 were clergymen.

Clergymen at that time were not without personal financial resources. The value of livings had risen substantially and recruitment to the clergy was drawn from a higher class than previously. The majority were members of landowning families, many being the younger sons of gentry and nobles whose elder brothers inherited the family estate, and there were instances of both brothers being included in the same commission. On other occasions they were presented to livings outside the county of their origin but were able to mix freely in the upper levels of society in their new area, and because of their background there was not a lot to distinguish between them in their social life. The country parson who, having preached his sermon on Sunday, divided the rest of the week between pastoral duties, riding to hounds, shooting game, sitting on the bench and joining his friends at convivial functions was a familiar figure of the late eighteenth and early nineteenth century. Cobbett, writing in 1826, observed that incumbents were better "known as Justices of the Peace than as clergymen."[40]

A number of prominent clerical justices are mentioned by the Webbs.[41] There was the Reverend Paley of the diocese of Durham who was asked by the Bishop in his capacity as *Custos* "to act in the Commission of the Peace for which ... he was well qualified by his talents

39.   1 William & Mary, c. 18.
40.   *Rural Rides*, vol. II, (1885) p. 168.
41.   *ELG, The Parish and the County*, pp. 350-360.

for close investigation, and by his knowledge of the criminal law ...". Paley's "penetration" and "sagacity" seem to have been greatly appreciated at Quarter Sessions, but the Webbs add that, when acting as an examining magistrate in his own parlour, his behaviour was criticized as "being hasty and irascible." The Webbs give credit to the many clerical justices who were foremost in protecting the poor and raising the standard of living among the people. The Rev. George Botts, a Suffolk justice, drew attention to the disgraceful state of the house of correction at Botesdale and was successful in obtaining improvements and in inducing his fellow justices to provide materials on which the prisoners might work and to pay an increased salary to the keeper on condition that he abandoned the taking of fees. Similarly, the Rev. John Tindel, an Essex justice, succeeded in having the county gaol at Chelmsford cleansed and improved. Among other justices who spent many years of their lives improving the prisons were the Rev. Samuel Glasse of Middlesex and the Rev. Henry Zouch of the West Riding.

From 1750 onwards it was not uncommon for clerical justices to be in a majority at Quarter Sessions and a number of them became chairmen. The Rev. Henry Zouch was one of these. He was a former schoolmaster, and his appointment in 1735 caused offence to the other justices who thought him to be unfit for the office. They pressed for the appointment of a Mr Wentworth, a wealthy landowner.[42] Hardwicke, the Lord Chancellor, after consulting the Whig Lord Lieutenant, the Earl of Malton who was also *Custos,* appointed Wentworth with the Earl's approval but did not remove Zouch. Zouch had probably been put forward in the first place because he was the Lord Lieutenant's political agent and had worked hard in the Whig cause. In spite of the initial opposition to his appointment, Zouch became chairman of Quarter Sessions and was responsible for the complete reorganization of the gaol at Wakefield.

Zouch came in for some severe criticism from the Webbs in respect of his involvement, with William Wilberforce, in the national movement for the "Reformation of the Manners of the Lower Orders." The Webbs quote a passage from his writings:

"It is found by long experience that when the common people are drawn together upon any public occasion, a variety of mischiefs are certain to ensue; allured by unlawful pastimes or even by vulgar amusements only, they wantonly waste their time and money to their own great loss and that of their employers. Nay, a whole neighbourhood becomes unhinged for many days, quarrels are too

42.   PRO, c 234/445, BL, Add. Mss., 35600, f. 89.

often promoted, and the young and inexperienced are initiated into every species of immorality."

The Webbs pointed out that although this policy, which was adopted by many other justices, both lay and clerical as well as Zouch, was to be commended in that it sought to reduce the number of alehouses, cockfights and other undesirable pastimes and also stemmed subsidized vagrancy, neither Zouch nor his fellow magistrates ever thought of providing alternative forms of recreation nor any education. "There is, to our mind, something unpleasant in the combination of luxurious living, which the wealthy Evangelicals of the end of the eighteenth century themselves indulged in, and the wholesale prescription for the lower orders of an abstinence from all sensual indulgence."

It is true that many clerical justices, like most other people at their social level, tended to be prejudiced against the lower classes, and this continued in the nineteenth century. In 1826 the Rev. F.E. Witts recorded in his diary on January 13, the trial of some weavers who "acting under the delusion so prevalent in all manufacturing districts" had engaged in disturbances with a view to obtaining higher wages. Witts, after commenting that several of them were "of very decent appearance", went on to comment that "they must be punished with severity since the indulgence shown to the Stroud rioters has failed in its effect." They were given "two years incarceration" in a house of correction. There were, however, numbers of clerical justices who strove to understand the problems of the working classes and endeavoured to lighten their load. Some of these, like the Rev. Zouch, were also chairmen of Quarter Sessions.

An example was the Rev. John Foley, who was chairman of Gloucestershire Sessions from 1796 to 1803. He was the author of *Charges delivered to the Grand Jury 1798-1804,* which contained the following advice on how to treat the lower classes. "Visit the Cottages of the Poor and by gentle modes of persuasion inculcate the necessity of sobriety, diligence, neatness and cleanliness, together with an economical management of the little earnings they obtain ... and in this way will be established a firm and compact union between the different classes of society." Yet another clerical chairman who also published his charges to the Grand Jury at about the same time as Foley was the Rev. Samuel Partridge of Lincolnshire (Parts of Holland).[43]

Probably the most famous of all clerical chairmen was the Rev. Richard Burn, Vicar of Orton and Chancellor of the diocese of Carlisle, who was chairman of Westmorland Quarter Sessions and, as we have seen, published *The Justice of the Peace and Parish Officer* in

---

43. *Seven Charges given to Grand Juries at the General Quarter Sessions of the Peace etc.* 1809.

1755. This became the standard work for justices and overseers and it ran into 30 editions, the last being published in 1869.

Among the many clerical justices of note was the Rev. Edmund Poulter, a Justice of the Peace for Hampshire who, in 1795, drafted a comprehensive report on the labouring poor which was adopted by Quarter Sessions.[44] The Webbs have pointed out that several clerical justices with reforming zeal were responsible for making the successful experiments in Poor Law administration on which the new law was subsequently based. In addition to Poulter they mention Whately of Cookham, Lowe of Bingham and Becher of Southwell,[45] but there were numbers of others. Among the clerics who left full accounts of the every day activities of eighteenth century justices was the Rev. Robert Forby of Norfolk, whose description of their exhausting burden has been cited above. Being lawyers, some of the clerical justices produced works which concentrated on the strictly legal aspects of their duties, such as the Rev. Samuel Clapham who in 1818 published *A Collection of the Several Points of Sessions Law alphabetically arranged.*

Another interesting example of a clerical justice was the Rev. W.R. Hay, who had been chaplain to the Salford house of correction and was a Lancashire justice at the time when the Industrial Revolution and its accompanying increase in population were creating a surge in crime. This threatened to overwhelm the courts of the county justices for the Salford Hundred which covered much of south east Lancashire including Manchester. The justices deputed to Hay the task of seeking Parliamentary authority for the appointment of a salaried magistrate to relieve the pressure of work. Hay had been called to the Bar and when, in 1805, he had secured the passage of the necessary Act[46] it was he who was appointed to be what was the first stipendiary magistrate for the area, a post which he held until 1823.[47] As far as is known, he did not draw the salary allowed by the Act, but he was given the living of Rochdale with a stipend of £2,500 which he held during most of his term of office.

There were many other clerical justices in addition to those already mentioned who made significant contributions to the work of the magistracy, and it would be superfluous to refer to them all. One can gain some impression, however, of the extent of their involvement by looking at just one fairly typical county, Gloucestershire. We have seen that the chairman of Gloucestershire Quarter Sessions from 1796 to 1803 was the Rev. John Foley. Another cleric to hold this office was

44. *Inquiry into the State of the Poor* by the Rev. Edmund Poulter. Hants RO, QS Minutes, July 14, 1795.
45. *ELG, The Parish and the County,* p. 356.
46. 45 Geo. III, c. 59.
47. As will be seen in ch. IV, stipendiaries had already been appointed in Middlesex.

the Rev. George Cooke who was chairman for no less than twenty years from 1813 to 1833. Only three other justices held the chairmanship for longer than this during the 260 years from 1710 when a record was first kept - the longest being twenty-five years.[48] Apart from those who became chairmen of Quarter Sessions, there were at least 55 clerical justices appointed to the Gloucestershire commission during the hundred years from 1715, and around the end of the century some 15 served at one time out of a total of little more than 100 justices (though the figures varied considerably). The impact of the clerical justices was much greater than their percentage of the total number would suggest, as they were far more frequent attenders at Quarter Sessions and other meetings than most of their colleagues, and often they were in a majority on these occasions. As in the rest of the country they were enthusiastic writers of diaries and textbooks. The diary of the Rev. F.E. Witts has already been mentioned. The Rev. Charles Coxwell wrote a narrative of his life which gives a graphic picture of his duties.[49] So too did the diary of the Rev. Francis Wells of Prestbury who was a justice for forty-one years from 1715. Esther Moir draws attention to a somewhat different type of clerical justice, the Rev. H.G. Dobyns Yate, who moved in high circles, both in Gloucestershire and elsewhere, and was often absent from the county, but he did not neglect his local duties which are recorded in his diary.[50]

There is hardly a parish throughout Gloucestershire where examples cannot be found. In the Cotswold village of Blockley[51] where these lines are being written, there were only two vicars between 1761 and 1831 and both were Justices of the Peace. Both took a very active part in magisterial affairs, particularly in those aspects which could benefit the people of the parish. This applied especially to the administration of the Poor Law, and the two vicars spent an considerable amount of their time in dealing with cases of settlement and of poor relief. The first of the two, Charles Jasper Selwyn, who held the benefice from 1761 to 1794, founded the Blockley Benefit Society for the relief of those in need. Selwyn was also one of those justices who did all the clerical work for himself and his colleagues instead of employing a clerk. This entitled him to various fees, but he never took them for himself and invariably arranged for them to be devoted to some charitable purpose, usually his Sunday school fund. Both Selwyn and his successor, William Boughton, were also concerned in another project which seems inappropriate for those holding judicial office but

---

48.　Thomas Hayward was chairman from 1743 to 1768, and had occasionally held the chair previously from 1738. Sir Frencis Adams Hyett was chairman from 1904 to 1929.
49.　*A Narrative of the life of the Rev. Charles Coxwell MA written by himself.*
50.　Gloucestershire RO PE 85. E. Moir, *British Institutions. The Justices of the Peace* (1969) p. 86. *Local Government in Gloucestershire 1775-1800*, pp. 56-7.
51.　Blockley parish at this time was an enclave of Worcestershire and did not become part of surrounding Gloucestershire until the twentieth century.

which was regarded as perfectly proper at the time when magistrates were still police as well as Judges. They were both treasurers of a society called the "Blockley Association for the Prosecution of Felons", whose members subscribed to a fund from which rewards were paid to informers. The rewards ranged from £10 in cases of highway robbery or arson to 10 shillings for the theft of turnips, potatoes and fruit. In practice the offenders who were prosecuted in this manner were seldom dangerous criminals and were usually women stealing turnips or men stealing corn for their starving families. The Association also resolved that if any alehouse keeper in Blockley should "entertain any disorderly Person or shall suffer any tippling on the Sabbath day, and more especially during the time of Divine Service, which practice we conceive to be the fundamental cause of the very many offences committed," it was their determined resolution to report him to the justice in order that his house should no longer be licensed.

The keen interest shown by the clerical justices in social problems was to be expected, but it would not have been surprising if they had been more reluctant to deal with police duties and the trial of criminal cases. In fact, they seem to have been equally enthusiastic in undertaking every branch of the justices' work. They were certainly no more lenient in their treatment of offenders than their lay colleagues. It was the common view that those who broke the law should be severely punished, and this included those who demonstrated against low wages and bad working conditions. Miss D. McClatchey, in a study of the Oxfordshire clergy between 1777 and 1869, concluded that up to the 1830s more criminal convictions were the outcome of decisions by clerical justices than by lay.[52] They were not hesitant in imposing strict penalties and in expressing their disapproval of criminals in forceful terms. There were three clergy among the 12 justices who ordered the troops to attack the crowd in Manchester in 1819 on the occasion which came to be known as the "Massacre of Peterloo," to which we refer later.

At the beginning of the nineteenth century the clerical justices were not without their critics and by 1815 they were under fire from the Radicals both in and out of Parliament. As the Webbs comment:

"In the eyes of Parliamentary Radicals of this period, the superior knowledge of law for which the clerical justices were distinguished, their greater philanthropy and, we think we may add, their higher standard of integrity, were outweighed by the objection to their political Toryism and their inclination towards increasing collective regulation."[53]

---

52.   Oxfordshire Clergy 1777-1869, Oxford UP (1960), ch. XII, passim.
53.   *ELG, The Parish and the County,* p. 358.

From then onwards there was a growing feeling that service on the bench was incompatible with a clergyman's duty to his flock, and the number of appointments dropped. In spite of this many continued to serve for a time and as we have seen, as late as 1832, a quarter of all Justices of the Peace in England and Wales were members of the clergy, but by the latter part of the nineteenth century it was generally accepted that no beneficed clergyman or minister of any denomination in charge of a church should be appointed a JP unless no other suitable person could be found in the locality.

Other justices

The clergy were not the only members of the Commission of the Peace who made their mark in the social field. There were many others, both at national and local level. An example of the latter was Charles Selwyn of Surrey who was the leader of reform in Richmond in the 1720s, while Sir George O. Paul of Gloucestershire was, as we shall see later, largely responsible for fundamental improvements to the prison system throughout the country. When we turn to the maintenance of highways we find that one of the greatest highway engineers, John Loudon MacAdam, was a justice in Bristol and a commissioner of turnpike trusts. There were also large numbers of "rank and file" justices whose names have been forgotten but who made a significant contribution to the operation of the system, as is now clear from the numerous documents which are available for scrutiny. At the other end of the scale we see the nobility taking a more active interest in magisterial work in general from the latter part of the century. They were more frequent than they had been previously in their attendance at sessions and other meetings and some became chairmen of Quarter Sessions. Some developed a sense of responsibility for conditions in their local areas and took a lead in effecting social reforms. For instance, the Duke of Richmond, when Lord Lieutenant of Sussex, was largely responsible for having new, modernized prisons built at Horsham and Petworth.

By the beginning of the nineteenth century the County Commissions of the Peace were dominated by men in the highest classes of society and, even in Middlesex, the commissions were generally free of the mean and corrupt justices who had gained appointment in the past. There were still many who had made their fortunes in trade and their numbers continued to increase, but for the most part they were now well established as wealthy landowners and were largely accepted into the social set which constituted the rulers of the countryside. Indeed, many of the old established families had augmented their incomes, and in some cases saved themselves from insolvency, by investing in trade and commerce. Almost all the justices were men of considerable wealth and were very conscious of their importance and independence and of the fact that they formed an exclusive oligarchy. Because of their wealth, they had no need to resort to corrupt practices like those of the trading justices in Middlesex and, being arrogant and jealous of their reputation, they could not contemplate behaving in a manner which might bring them into disrepute. Most were intelligent and well educated and imbued with a considerable sense of responsibility and a genuine desire to exercise their extensive powers in the interest of the community, although well aware that it was also in their own interest to do so.

These were the men who, as Justices of the Peace, enjoyed far greater authority and influence than at any other time, either earlier or later, in the country's history. They were the effective rulers of the land. They governed the countryside directly through Quarter Sessions and Petty Sessions and they influenced the Government of the country through Parliament and political channels. They were the antithesis of the doctrine of separation of powers which had recently been revived by Montesquieu, as they still exercised the threefold functions of judges, administrators and police and, totally contrary to the concept of magisterial office, they had also invaded the legislative sphere, as explained in the next chapter.

Of the eighteenth century F.W. Maitland wrote: "A history of the eighteenth century which does not place the Justices of the Peace in the very foreground of the picture will be known for which it is - a caricature."[54] Most historians have not accepted Maitland's theme. They have focused upon the central Government, while largely ignoring the total domination of local affairs by the justices and have overlooked the extent to which they influenced national issues. The justices' functions when they were at the height of their power and their ultimate decline in the public's estimation will be described in the following two chapters.

---

54. *The Shallows and Silences of Real Life. Collected Papers,* ed. H.A.L. Fisher, 1911, 1, p. 468.

CHAPTER II

THE AGE OF INDEPENDENCE, POWER AND "DECLINE" 1689 - 1820

PART II - THE COURTS AND THE MACHINERY OF GOVERNMENT

Machinery for the performance of justices' duties - Quarter Sessions and their officers - Arrogation of legislative power - The single justice; Two or more justices - Petty Sessions - Other local courts - Assizes

BETWEEN THE REVOLUTION of 1689 and the Reform Act of 1832 the justices reached their meridian. As we saw in the last chapter, their work was more extensive and their authority of greater importance to the country as a whole than at any other time before or since. This was particularly the case in respect of their administrative and executive functions, but even in the discharge of criminal judicial business, although there was a drop in the number of serious cases with which they dealt, the volume of minor crimes coming before them in and out of Quarter Sessions was considerable and their decisions were subject to less supervision than in any other period. The vast amount of administrative work was partly the outcome of a spate of legislation, much of it inspired by the justices themselves.

Dr Burn, commenting in 1785 on the amount of legislation which had been passed since his Textbook for justices was first published in 1755, wrote that

"The statutes or Acts of Parliament which have been made during the said time, connected more or less with the office of Justice of the Peace, are in number above 300; ...

By means of which statutes, so many new matters are in every session of Parliament brought under the jurisdiction of those justices, and so many alterations are made in subjects of which they before had cognizance, that every new edition, in order to keep pace with the law, is in effect a new book."[1]

In fact, an appreciable amount of the additional authority exercised by the justices came not from legislation but from innovations introduced by the justices themselves and not sanctioned by Parliament. Such was the strength of the justices at this time that they

1.　"Advertisement" to the Fifteenth Ed., 1785.

were able to act on their own initiative to a great extent without their conduct being called in question.

There was a huge increase in what may be described as public services, and in every case supervision rested with the justices. The gaols, which were previously the concern only of the high sheriff, and the houses of correction which were originally farmed out to keepers, were brought directly under the Justices of the Peace who spent considerable amounts of public money on their improvement and upkeep. Vagrancy, which had previously been dealt with merely by harsh measures of suppression, now involved much time, energy and money in resettlement and other action in relation to paupers. The work and the cost of maintaining and repairing roads and bridges increased enormously with the growth of traffic, brought about by expanding industry, a larger population and the inclination to travel. In the first part of the nineteenth century a wholly new institution appeared in the form of county lunatic asylums for which the justices became responsible.

In addition to these matters of local Government, the judicial work of the justices also increased, partly because of the larger number of presentments arising from their administrative responsibilities, but still more as a result of a sharp rise in the number of criminal cases which came before both Quarter Sessions and Petty Sessions and even before single justices. These cases arose largely as a result of the growth of population, especially in the industrial areas, but the number of minor crimes and misdemeanours coming before justices' courts was also increased by the gradual decay of the remaining manorial courts in the seventeenth century.

All this involved the justices in greater financial responsibility, entailing the handling of far larger sums of money and the keeping of more complex accounts. The Webbs estimate that the total expenditure of all Quarter Sessions in England and Wales rose from less than £100,000 a year to more than £1m between 1689 and 1835, and that during the same period the amounts spent by parishes on highways and poor relief, which was under the direction of the justices, increased from about £500,000 to between £7m and £8m.[2]

Machinery for the performance of justices' duties

At the beginning of the eighteenth century the machinery through which the justices discharged their expanding duties remained basically the same as it had been for the previous three centuries. The old judicial process still operated even in respect of purely administrative business. Much time was spent at Quarter Sessions in hearing

2.   *ELG, The Parish and the County,* p. 181.

presentments against those who failed to perform their public duties and in trying and imposing punishment upon the offenders, but although the justices' sessions continued to be generally regarded as constituting courts of law, a greater distinction began to be drawn between purely judicial work and that which was concerned with local administration. Another significant change which occurred during the eighteenth century was that many administrative functions came to be performed by new, paid officials, appointed by and responsible to the justices. This applied particularly to the Poor Law, rating, highways and bridges and to gaols. The cost of public works was borne by rates levied by the justices on individual members of the population. Instead of penalties being imposed on parishes and other areas for failure to perform some public duty, the necessary work was carried out under the direction of the justices, who allocated the necessary funds from the rates. These reforms were, however, defective in that the officials upon whom the justices had to rely were sometimes persons to whom the work had to be contracted and whose sole object was to conduct it to their own financial advantage.

In attempting to perform their administrative functions the justices came more and more to act in accordance with policies and rules of procedure which they themselves, in the absence of directions from above, were obliged to formulate.

Another notable change in the eighteenth century was the transfer of work from Quarter Sessions to the justices out of sessions. Previously, the greater part of the justices' work had been handled in Quarter Sessions, but a large amount of business was now transferred to one or more justices operating in their local parts of the county. In consequence of this Quarter Sessions were less involved in trials of first instance but acquired a substantial appellate jurisdiction. They were now obliged to hear a vast number of appeals against decisions by single justices or by Petty Sessions.

Quarter Sessions

Quarter Sessions, as the focal point of all local affairs, were supposed to be an occasion for much pomp and ceremony at which everyone of significance in the county was present. Sometimes they were indeed marked by considerable pageantry and were attended by the majority of magistrates, headed by the Lord Lieutenant and *Custos,* and by all the county and parish officers - high constables, the high sheriff, coroners, petty constables, bailiffs of hundred and liberties, gaolers, keepers of houses of correction and numerous citizens who were to form the juries. In practice, attendance varied considerably, depending upon the place in which the sessions were held, the season of the year and especially upon the importance of the matters to be discussed. There were occasions when only three or four justices and a small number of officials were present. Larger numbers assembled for the opening of the sessions but would depart at an early stage, leaving the work to be completed by a few dedicated colleagues. Edmund Bohun, writing in 1693, mentions justices "who come and take the King's wages and before half the business is done betake them to the tavern; leaving two or three to finish and conclude the business."[3] The Webbs draw attention to the bill of the Clerk of the Peace for Dorset in 1752 which contains numerous items for messengers sent on horseback to justice after justice to get even two to hold a court,[4] and Dr Burn, writing in 1776, recalls many Quarter Sessions which were attended by only two or three justices and adjourned sessions where none appeared at all. It seems probable, however, that these quotations give a false impression of the normal size of Quarter Sessions benches in the eighteenth century. Burn was referring to sessions in Yorkshire where attendances were exceptionally small and there can be little doubt that the Webbs were wrong when they wrote that "right down to the last quarter of the 18th century it was evidently unusual for the Bench at Quarter Sessions to consist of more than three or four Magistrates ..." An analysis of attendances made by Esther Moir[5] leads to the conclusion that the Webbs "grossly underestimated the numbers." Her figures are largely based on Gloucestershire where attendances at the single centre in Gloucester tended to be greater than at sessions in other counties where they were held in more than one place, but the average attendance at Gloucestershire Quarter Sessions was 13 between 1775 and 1780; this dropped to eight from 1780 to 1785 but reached an average of 20.5 at every session between 1785 and 1790. Research throughout the rest of the country supports her conclusions, and her own study of the Estreat of Fines for 1785 shows that Middlesex, which headed the list, averaged as many as 50 JPs per session, followed by Essex and Surrey each with 25. Even in counties having constant adjournments there were usually six, though Holland, which was a part of Lincolnshire having its own sessions, had only three.[6]

It is difficult to gauge the numbers who attended Quarter Sessions

3.   *The Justice of the Peace, His Calling and Qualifications,* p. 166.
4.   ELG, *ibid.,* p. 422, n. 3.
5.   *Local Government in Gloucestershire, 1775-1800* (1969) pp. 44-45. Published by the *Bristol and Gloucestershire Archaelogical Society, Records Section,* vol. VIII.
6.   *Ibid.,* p. 77, n. 30.

at any one time because, as we have seen, the Clerks of the Peace did not record all those who were present, and because no record was kept to show whether a justice who attended on the first day remained throughout the sessions. It is clear that attendances were low in the middle of the eighteenth century, but by the beginning of the nineteenth they had improved in numbers and in quality. The work was no longer left to a few dedicated magistrates who were prepared to give the time, but most of whom were not at the top of the social scale. Instead, it was usual, at least by the end of the eighteenth century, for a significant proportion of the most prominent gentry in the county to be present, including the Lord Lieutenant and other members of the aristocracy, who for some time had been conspicuous by their absence but who were now taking a more active interest in the work. The total number of participants was also substantial. It was still the case, however, that numbers increased spectacularly when a matter of particular interest was to be decided. Mention has been made earlier of the statement by the Rev. Witts that 106 justices were present for the election of the governor of Gloucester gaol in 1836. This was almost the total number of justices on the Gloucestershire commission at the time, apart from Privy Counsellors and those who had not qualified or were unavoidably absent. The rise in numbers present at sessions towards the end of the century was due at least in part to the recognition of Quarter Sessions as an instrument for securing reforms and improvements in the existing system. Matters of particular current interest were the reform of the gaols, the Poor Law, the treatment of offenders, licensing policy and the ever increasing local rates.

Throughout the century attendances were larger where the sessions were held regularly in the same town which was in a central position than they were when, as often happened, they met successively in several different centres. On these occasions it was usual for only those justices who lived within a reasonable distance to be present. There were indeed some counties where Quarter Sessions were transferred by adjournment to a number of different places for the express purpose of giving equal facilities for attendance to all justices wherever they might reside. Wiltshire being a case in point. It should be added, however, that there were also occasions when adjourned sessions were held in all quarters of a county for some other specific purpose, such as to make it easier for persons who were required to take prescribed oaths before the sessions. There were also occasions when a temporary crisis made it necessary for Quarter Sessions, which normally met in one place, to be held elsewhere; as in Gloucestershire where, between 1685 and 1688, they met in Cirencester, Painswick and Wotton-under-Edge instead of in Gloucester because of a smallpox epidemic in the city.[7] There were a few counties which, during the course of the eighteenth century, divided their Quarter Sessions into two distinct courts, each with its own chairman and Clerk of the Peace, and each empanelling its own juries and levying its own rates, even though there was still only one Commission of the Peace and one Lord Lieutenant and *Custos* for the whole county. In these circumstances, which applied in Kent, Suffolk and Sussex, each county justice attended only the Quarter Sessions for the area in which he resided.[8]

The state of the roads, although improving during the century, remained a deterrent, and in winter some became virtually impassable. There were few justices who braved the elements for the Epiphany sessions, and many officers were also absentees. Most of those who attended in the earlier part of the century still rode to sessions on horseback, but as road transport improved an increasing number arrived in wheeled vehicles. The Rev. Witts recorded that Lord Edward Somerset travelled in "a phaeton with flying Steeds, old Baker and Myself in a humble gig."[9]

The justices were still entitled to receive four shillings for each day on which they attended Quarter Sessions under the Acts of 1388 and 1390. The necessary sum had to be claimed by the high sheriff in his cravings. How it was then dispersed varied from time to time and from county to county. There were still some areas where up to eight justices who attended were paid the daily sum; in others, as we have seen, the money was placed in a joint fund to defray the cost of sessions dinners.[10]

In those places where Quarter Sessions were normally held in some public hall it was usual for the justices to assemble on the first day in an inn, whence they processed formally to the courthouse. Thus, the Gloucestershire justices gathered at the King's Head at 10 am, and then proceeded in stately procession to the Booth Hall for the formal opening of the sessions. After the opening, the Gloucestershire magistrates returned to a private room in the King's Head where they

---

7. Sometimes the dates of sessions were changed to avoid some competing attraction. For example, Norfolk Quarter Sessions in July, 1652 ordered: "If St Faith's Fair falls on the day of the sessions or the next day, two justices are to attend and adjourn sessions for a week, since most men have business at the fair." *Norfolk QS Order Book*, 399.
8. There was no apparent authority for this arrangement, but in each case the position was subsequently legalized by Private Acts of Parliament and, in the case of Suffolk and Sussex, the counties themselves were divided, each having acquired a separate Commission of the Peace and Lord Lieutenant.
9. *Diary of a Cotswold Parson*, p. 130.
10. The cost of meals was sometimes defrayed by the High Sheriff himself out of his own pocket, and sometimes the sessions ordered the Treasurer to pay the bill. Thus, in 1702, the Essex sessions ordered that "the Treasurer of the East Division do pay to John Clements of Chelmsford, inn-holder the sum of £2.5.6 for justices' dinner at the adjournment of the Quarter Sessions." QS Minutes;, April 14, 1702, quoted by the Webbs, *ELG, ibid.*, p. 438.

dealt with administrative business and from which the public were excluded. This included highway maintenance, poor relief, rating and the appointment of constables and of jurors. They then adjourned again to the Booth Hall, usually on the following day, where they sat in public as a court of justice, to hear indictments and appeals and to deliver gaols. The practice of holding the judicial proceedings in public, but of excluding all except the justices and officials from the administrative meetings, was general throughout the country until the early nineteenth century, and in many counties the secrecy which surrounded county fincances and other local government matters persisted after the reforms of the 1830s.

Whereas at the beginning of the century most Quarter Sessions were held entirely in inns, by the end some counties had custom-built courthouses, but the justices still resorted to an inn for refreshment. "The custom of dining together and passing the evening in each other's company tend much to maintain that friendly harmony and mutual good intelligence which distinguishes the Gloucester Sessions." So wrote the Rev. Witts, but the same sentiments were echoed throughout the country. This does not mean that harmony invariably prevailed, especially when political issues were involved. Sometimes conflict also arose from personal disputes, as when harsh words were exchanged between Colonel Berkeley and Thomas Lloyd Baker at Gloucestershire Quarter Sessions in 1832 over the shooting of foxes,[11] but these did not develop into physical assaults as they had done frequently in the past.

The time taken to complete county sessions varied considerably, but they usually lasted from three to six days.

Chairman of Quarter Sessions

The chairman of Quarter Sessions presided over the court while it was in session and controlled the proceedings. He also supervised the business between sessions and gave instructions to the Clerk of the Peace. It was usually the chairman who delivered the charge to the grand jury at the opening of sessions.

We have seen that up to the end of the seventeenth century no county had a regular chairman of Quarter Sessions. Usually the *Custos* presided if present, but in his absence any justice might take the chair *ad hoc.* In most counties the inconvenience which this caused was remedied in the early part of the eighteenth century by the election of a chairman from among the justices present at each session. For a long time, however, there was no provision for the appointment of a chairman on a long-term basis, and some Quarter Sessions passed

11.   Gloucestershire RO, D. 471/Cl.

resolutions designed to ensure that no one could hold the office permanently. Middlesex Quarter Sessions, for instance, in 1723 resolved that no justice should be chairman for more than one year.[12] The office was important, however, not only at the sessions themselves but during the intervening period when a chairman was needed to supervise work which had to be done on their behalf. In some counties the advantage of having a regular chairman was accepted soon after the beginning of the century. Gloucestershire introduced such an arrangement in 1710 when John Viny was elected chairman and held office for nine years. Most counties had adopted the same practice by the 1790s, but a few retained the old arrangements until well into the nineteenth century.

The last chapter described some of those who held the office of chairman during this period. In the early part of the eighteenth century the chairman was usually one of the leading men in the county, but later he became less eminent. The drop in social level was probably due to the considerable amount of work involved in the office, combined with the fact that the most prominent men in the social sphere no longer felt it essential to attend all the meetings of the sessions. They appeared when there was something of special importance to discuss, but on other occasions were content to leave the business to someone else. The chairman was therefore chosen because he had the ability, the time and the willingness to devote his energy to what were becoming increasingly onerous duties. Quarter Sessions also endeavoured to choose someone with a knowledge of the law, which included the many clerics who were appointed in the latter part of the century.

The scene began to change again at the end of the eighteenth century and by the nineteenth the chairmanship of Quarter Sessions was recognized as an opportunity to dominate county affairs, and accordingly it was usually held by a person of considerable status and influence, sometimes by a member of the nobility. Owing to the weight of work, however, separate appointments were sometimes made of chairmen to preside at judicial and at administrative sittings, a lawyer being chosen for the former. For instance, in 1842, the Gloucestershire justices elected Ebenezer Ludlow, a serjeant at law, as chairman of the "Appellate and Judicial Court," and Bransby Purnell as chairman of "Financial and all General County Business."

In those counties where it was customary for Quarter Sessions to be held regularly in two or more towns it was not uncommon for different individuals to serve as chairman in each of them. Norfolk adopted a peculiar system in 1801 by electing four different justices to serve

12.   *Middlesex QS Minutes,* February 27, 1723.

consecutively as chairman at each of the four annual Quarter Sessions held in Norwich.[13]

Officers attending Quarter Sessions

Clerk of the Peace

At the beginning of the eighteenth century the only permanent officer of Quarter Sessions was still the Clerk of the Peace (except where there was also a deputy clerk) who was appointed by the *Custos*. He advised on points of law, kept records of proceedings, collected returns from constables and clerks to justices of divisions,[14] had custody of the archives and was responsible for the administration of the court and for protecting the county against charges at Quarter Sessions. Among the many records he had to keep were those of enclosure awards, applications to set up a printing press, meeting places of freemasons and non-conformists, game keepers' licences, and even licences granted to those who wished to use hair powder. Under the first Census Act, which was passed in 1801, he had to collate the returns from the constables, and later he also had to collate the lists of voters for Parliamentary elections. He also promoted Bills before Parliament when these were required. The clerks were lawyers, some having begun their careers in legal practice as attorneys or in some other local government office such as under sheriff or later as treasurer. The justices had little control over their clerk and he usually held office for life. If he misdemeaned himself in the execution of his office he might be removed on a complaint in writing to Quarter Sessions.[15] In the nineteenth century he also became liable to be removed for misconduct other than in the execution of his office.[16] Sometimes, however the clerk decided to resign in order to take up some other pursuit; a few subsequently becoming Justices of the Peace and Members of Parliament. Prior to appointment as Clerk of the Peace some had held office as high sheriff.

The clerk was still entitled to two shillings for each day he attended Quarter Sessions under the Statute of Cambridge of 1388; the fees being payable from the fines and amercements imposed by Quarter Sessions, for which the sheriff had to account to the Exchequer. This continued until repealed by an Act of 1855.[17] In addition to these payments the clerk was also entitled to demand fees from individuals

---

13. *Norfolk QS Minutes,* July 16, 1801.
14. This sometimes involved keeping registers. For instance, in 1753 an Act required registers to be kept of all alehouse licences; 26 Geo. II, c. 31.
15. 1 William and Mary, c. 2.
16. 27 & 28 Vict., c. 65, s. 2.
17. 18 & 19 Vict., c. 126.

for various functions he performed, and he received donations from the sessions themselves for exceptional service such as presenting a measure to Parliament on their behalf. Lambard also refers to certain statutory fees to which Clerks of the Peace were entitled for enrolling bargains and sales, registering badgers (persons who bought corn and other commodities to carry elsewhere to sell) and taking recognizances of persons who took rogues into their services for a year. The clerk was liable to a fine if he took more than the statutory sum, but most fees were fixed only by custom. These varied considerably from county to county and might amount to substantial sums. In 1774 the Clerk of the Peace of Cardiganshire was paid £20 a year for conveying Quarter Sessions records from one town to another, and in 1719 the Clerk of the Peace of Essex was claiming £6.13s.4d every time he sent orders to the High Constables. The clerks made clear profits from these transactions, but from time to time they were also reimbursed for the amount which they had actually expended on behalf of Quarter Sessions. A common example of this was the renting of accommodation for various purposes. Thus in 1733, Gloucestershire sessions resolved that a sum be paid towards the costs of their clerk in setting up an office for the storage of documents.[18]

Disputes sometimes arose between Clerks of the Peace and Clerks to Justices as to the fees due for work done out of sessions. In 1709, the Clerk of the Peace of Carmarthenshire sued various JPs for fees due at special sessions,[19] and in 1723 Buckinghamshire justices took action to stop Clerks to Justices depriving the county Clerk of the Peace of his fees by failing to send certificates to Quarter Sessions of licences granted to alehouse keepers and victuallers.[20]

In the eighteenth century the fees of a Clerk of the Peace were substantial, leaving him in receipt of income well exceeding his normal expenses, and there were occasions when the office was virtually bought and sold.[21]

An Act of 1817[22] empowered Quarter Sessions to settle a table of fees for their Clerk of the Peace, subject to confirmation by the Judge of Assize, but there were already proposals to pay the clerks annual salaries in lieu of fees. In 1819, the West Riding justices agreed to pay their clerk £400 a year in place of his fees. This was dropped in 1828

18. "Whereas the Clerk of the Peace for this County hath lately at his own expense taken by lease a house near the Boothall in Gloucester for the greater conveniency and more regularly placeing and keeping in the rolls and records of the Peace belonging to this county. In consideration whereof, it is ordered by this Court that the Treasurer of the County Stock do pay to the Clerk of the Peace the sum of 10 pounds towards his fitting up his said office."
19. PRO Chancery proceedings before 1714, Bridges, 235/22.
20. Buckinhamshire. Calendar of QS Records, V, 164.
21. See: *ELG, ibid.,* p. 503, n. 4.
22. 57 Geo. III, c. 91.

because the legality of the arrangement was questioned, but from 1835 many counties substituted salaries for payment by fees. This followed a recommendation by a House of Commons committee on county rates in 1834[23] that it should be within the discretion of each Quarter Sessions to continue payment by fees or to pay a salary in lieu, though leaving the clerk in receipt of fees from individuals. Parliament did not give effect to this resolution until 1851, but a Parliamentary inquiry for the years 1841-45[24] showed that many counties were then paying salaries ranging from about £180 (Anglesey) to about £4,500 (Lancashire) although deputies and other staff were paid out of these sums. In 1851 an Act (14 & 15 Vict. c. 55) authorized the payment of salaries to Clerks of the Peace instead of fees; the amount was to be recommended by Quarter Sessions and approved by the Home Secretary. Approval was given to the payment of salaries in many counties during the next few years, though the amount seems to have been somewhat lower than was the case before the Home Secretary's agreement was required. According to the House of Commons records[25] fourt-fifths of the Clerk of the Peace were in receipt of fixed salaries of between £80 and £1,600 by 1861.

High sheriffs
Although the Clerks of the Peace were the only officers of Quarter Sessions at the beginning of the eighteenth century, there were other officials upon whom the justices relied. Unlike the Clerks of the Peace, these officers were obliged to serve without remuneration in accordance with the old principle of compulsory, unpaid public service. The most eminent of these officers was the high sheriff, who was appointed by the Crown and obliged to serve unpaid for one year. At the beginning of the eighteenth century his duties included responsibility for gaols and custody of prisoners, the collection of fines and forfeitures which he paid over to the Exchequer, arranging for the election of Members to Parliament, keeping the roll of the freeholders, issuing summonses, summoning jurors for both Assizes and Quarter Sessions and the execution of the decisions of both these courts. He was also concerned in the organization of Quarter Sessions and in the payment of the daily wages to those justices who were entitled to them. Most sheriffs never went near a prison and, as we shall see, during the century they lost most of their authority in respect of the prisons.

Although the office of sheriff was still regarded as one of considerable honour and was usually held by a person drawn from the same class as most of the Justices of the Peace, it no longer carried the

23.   House of Commons: *Reports from Committees,* 1834, vol. XIV, p. 146.
24.   House of Commons: *Accounts and Papers,* 1845, vol. XXXVI, p. 265.
25.   House of Commons: *Accounts and Papers,* 1861, vol. 51, pp. 459-474.

high respect which it had done in the past. Being onerous and involving considerable expense, it was unpopular and was avoided whenever possible. Most of the work usually devolved upon an under sheriff who was a salaried official, but there was no way of avoiding the considerable financial burden which included entertaining the Assize Judges and providing dinners for the justices.

Apart from the under sheriffs, high sheriffs were assisted by bailiffs whom they appointed. As previously there were high bailiffs for the hundreds and below them other bailiffs who executed writs and served summonses.

High constables and petty constables

As the office of high sheriff decayed the work of high, head or chief constable of hundreds and liberties tended to increase in importance. We have seen that they were originally officers of the old manorial courts, but by 1689 most were appointed by Quarter Sessions, at first for a year, but later for much longer and in many counties for life. The justices' authority to appoint high constables and petty constables rested, however, on the fact that the old courts which had previously made these appointments had ceased to do so. Consequently, in the case of *R. v. Wakeford* in 1714[26] it was held that, although the justices had power to appoint a constable if, in a particular instance, a manorial court had always made the appointment and could continue to do so, then an appointment made by the justices must be quashed. High constables were still drawn from the lower middle class and were obliged to serve without remuneration, although they were entitled to certain allowances. The allowances were far exceeded by the outgoings and the office which, like that of high sheriff, was both onerous and expensive was avoided as far as possible as it had been in the past. In the latter part of the century counties began to pay their high constables small fees for certain purposes.

The work of the high constables, and that of the petty constables who served under them, involved executing most of the orders of the justices and as the justices' work increased during the eighteenth century so too did that of the constables, but at the same time their status dropped. The sessions which the high constables had held on their own slowly disappeared and such work as they did was absorbed by the justices at Petty Sessions. On the other hand, the high constable came to be saddled with numerous duties connected with local government, such as making presentments on the state of roads and bridges and sometimes even inspecting bridges themselves and carrying out repairs. Again, they had to enforce the law on weights and

26.　Sessions Cases, 98.

measures and to inspect and, where necessary, suppress public houses. Still more important, and ever more onerous, was the apportionment and collection of rates and taxes. Rates were usually collected by the petty constables, though sometimes by churchwardens and overseers, and passed to the high constables. A tax like the window tax involved the petty constables in visiting each building and recording the number of windows. More will be said about tax collection when referring to county finance in the next chapter.

The principal function of the high constables and of petty constables continued to be that of police, and they were held responsible by Quarter Sessions for dealing with cases of disorder, for handling vagrants and for apprehending breakers of the law in general. They were also responsible for keeping watch and ward. The result was singularly ineffective owing to the unsuitability of the untrained, unpaid and largely illiterate constables who generally avoided the performance of their duties whenever possible but were not averse to embezzling funds.

As we have seen, the petty constable was originally appointed by the manorial court, but by the eighteenth century the appointment was usually made by two local JPs. The petty constable levied rates on his parish, executed the warrants and orders of the justices and made presentments of offences committed in his parish. After the Revolution, Quarter Sessions still spent some time reviewing the presentments of petty constables, although these were often a formality and merely repeated that all was well in the parish. The following presentments made by constables at Essex Quarter Sessions[27] are typical of those made throughout the country at the end of the seventeenth century.

Parish of Quendon
There are none that sell ale or beer without licence.
Hues and Crys are pursued without delay.
There are no young men or maids out of service.
All the poor are well provided for.
Thomas Ripshire and the wife of Edward Camp absent from church for three days.

Parish of Rickling
No eavesdroppers nightwalkers or profaners of the Sabbath.
No young men or maids out of service.
No poor children fit to be apprentices.
No inmates.

27.　*ERO Q/SR,* vol. 24, January 8, 1686.

Alehousekeepers do observe good order.
Poor well provided for.
Stocks & Whipping posts in good repair.
Hues and Crys duly pursued.
John Squire for absenting himself from church.

During the course of the eighteenth century presentments by petty constables virtually ceased, though some were still made by the high constables on their behalf, almost always in the form "nothing presentable" or similar words. Presentments also continued to be made to Quarter Sessions by individual justices.

County treasurer

Although the various officials who have just been described acted on behalf of the justices none of them were strictly officers of Quarter Sessions apart from the Clerk of the Peace. Among the clerk's duties was the keeping of county accounts which did not occupy a great deal of time before the Revolution. From 1689 onwards, however, county finances began to create a formidable amount of work and, by the beginning of the eighteenth century, counties appointed special officers who came to be known as county treasurers. Before that time separate treasurers had sometimes been appointed for different funds; such as those collected for houses of correction, gaols, vagrants, bridges or for charitable uses, and sometimes different treasurers served in different parts of the same county. There had been occasions when Quarter Sessions in certain counties placed the rates under the responsibility of JPs nominated for the purpose, and elsewhere individuals who were not justices were sometimes appointed treasurers for particular funds. In the eighteenth century the county treasurers took over the management of all these funds. The early treasurers received no remuneration, but a few were paid special grants by Quarter Sessions for outstanding service in accomplishing specific tasks.

The terms of service of county treasurers was standardized by an Act of 1739[28] which laid down general regulations for rating, required the treasurers to submit proper accounts and confirmed that they should hold office at the pleasure of Quarter Sessions at an annual allowance of not more than £20. The remarkable increase in the financial work of Quarter Sessions at the end of the eighteenth century led to the payment of a regular but modest stipend to most, though not all, county treasurers.[29] Many of the treasurers continued to be chosen

28.   12 Geo. II, c. 29.
29.   In Gloucestershire, at the turn of the century, the treasurer was paid a salary of 12 guineas a year with an additional five guineas for making out the abstract of accounts. This was increased to 20 guineas in 1809.

from among the Justices of the Peace themselves until well into the nineteenth century when persons with financial qualifications were usually appointed, but before that the treasurer sometimes employed a deputy who presented the accounts.

As the name implies, the treasurer's functions were primarily financial, but in some instances Quarter Sessions gave them additional duties, including even the superintending of repairs to county gaols.[30]

Surveyors

Surveyors of highways, originally appointed under the Statute 2 & 3 Phillip and Mary, c. 8, of 1555, continued to operate until the nineteenth century. From 1691 they were nominated, as described later, at special highway sessions by the justices who also supervised their activities. They received no payment beyond their expenses until the Highways Act 1835[31] authorized parish vestries to pay remuneration to their surveyors, but under an Act of 1773[32] the justices, at the request of two-thirds of the parishioners assembled in the vestry, could appoint a specially skilled salaried surveyor. Little use was made of this provision until the turn of the century.

In some counties a salaried surveyor of bridges or "bridge master" was appointed as early as the seventeenth century, but the usual practice was for Quarter Sessions to nominate surveyors from time to time to inspect a particular bridge and, where necessary, to supervise the repair.[33] In either case a fixed rate of remuneration was declared at the time of appointment.[34]

Overseers of the poor

Overseers of the poor were responsible for implementing the Poor Law, which will be described in the following chapter. The churchwardens of every parish were overseers *ex officio* and in addition to them between two and four "substantial householders" were to be nominated as overseers every year, within one month after Easter, by two or more justices (one to be of the *Quorum*) "dwelling in or near the parish or division."[35] The persons nominated by the JPs were usually elected in the first instance at a meeting of the parish and a list

---

30. *ELG, ibid.,* pp. 508-509.
31. 5 & 6 William IV, c. 50.
32. 14 Geo. III, c. 78, s. 5.
33. In 1828 Gloucestershire Quarter Sessions appointed the famous engineer, Thomas Telford, to inspect the Severn Bridge at Over and, on May 5, 1828, he wrote to the Clerk of the Peace saying that he found the bridge "fully equal to anything of the kind in Europe." *Gloucestershire QS Archives 1660-1889,* p. 18. Telford was later appointed surveyor of public works for the county of Shropshire.
34. For instance, in 1761, Gloucestershire QS appointed Thomas James as surveyor of "that part of Chepstow Bridge as lyes within the county" at an annual stipend of £10. *Gloucestershire QS Minutes* Trinity Sessions, 1761.
35. 39 Eliz., c. 3, as amended by 43 Eliz., c. 2.

of names was then submitted to the justices. Anyone appointed was obliged to serve, but if it were thought that an overseer nominated by the justices was unsuitable there was an appeal to Quarter Sessions.[36] The appointment itself had to be made by the local justices and not by Quarter Sessions. Women might not be appointed overseers, but it is not clear whether a JP might serve in this capacity.[37] Failure by the justices to nominate overseers made them liable to a fine of £5 to be used for poor relief.

The overseers were required to raise "weekly or otherwise" sums of money for the relief of the poor, lame and impotent of the parish, and also materials "to set the poor on work." They supervised the distribution of relief and they provided work for the poor. This included setting to work anyone who had no means of support and no "ordinary and daily trade" and also children whose parents were thought to be unable to maintain them. The overseers also kept an eye on outsiders coming into a parish where, if unable to support themselves, they might become a burden on the community. The overseers might complain to two JPs (one of the "*Quorum)* within 40 days of a person coming to settle in a tenement of yearly value of under £10, and ask that they be removed to the place where they were last legally settled.[38] The overseers supplied the certificates which were required by persons leaving the parish to find work elsewhere (as described later). Overseers were required to meet at least once a month in the parish church, on a Sunday afternoon after service, unless excused by two justices on grounds of sickness or other just excuse. Those failing to attend or defaulting in some other way were to forfeit 20 shillings to the poor. If they did not pay this sum the amount could be levied by a warrant of two justices and, if this was ineffective, the justices might commit the overseer "to the common gaol, there to remain without bail or mainprize till the said forfeiture shall be paid."[39] Appeal from the action of the justices lay to Quarter Sessions.

Minor officers
As work increased, some Quarter Sessions appointed various minor officers who performed a variety of duties. By the end of the century most Quarter Sessions had a "cryer" who was appointed primarily to act as court usher, but was given numerous jobs including that of messenger. The Webbs mention employees of Quarter Sessions in certain counties,[40] such as "Marshals" (Devon and Dorset) and

36.　　43 Eliz., c. 2, s. 6.
37.　　Burn, *The Justices of the Peace and Parish Officer*, pp. 342-343.
38.　　13 & 14 Charles II, c. 12.
39.　　43 Eliz., c. 2.
40.　　*ELG, ibid.*, pp. 523-4.

"Common Informers" (Essex). The latter were required *inter alia* to inspect weights and measures. Quarter Sessions in other counties also came to appoint inspectors for a number of purposes, such as reporting on the price of corn and on the quality of building materials.

The new bureaucracy

The appointment of subordinate officers as described in the preceding paragraphs was a significant move towards the establishment of a local government structure. Previously, apart from the parish officers and indirectly the sheriffs, the only officials through whom the justices could operate were, as we have seen, the Clerks of the Peace. In the eighteenth century there was a fundamental change. One or more assistants were appoitned in the clerk's office while new officers like the treasurers and surveyors were added at county level and an infrastructure was created by the Clerks to the Justices out of sessions reporting to Quarter Sessions through the Clerks of the Peace. A subservient bureaucracy answerable solely to the justices was born.

Contractors

A feature of local administration in the early eighteenth century was the employment of private contractors to perform many of the jobs which had to be done. This was the usual manner in which roads and bridges were kept in repair, prisons and workhouses were administered and vagrants and convicts were transported. The work was farmed out to those who were prepared to do it in return for the prospect of making a profit out of it. This could have dire consequences, especially for the poor and the prisoners who were likely to be underfed and ill-housed.

Coroners

Among those who usually attended Quarter Sessions, at least on the first day, were the coroners. This was a more popular office than that of sheriff or constable, and when vacancies occurred there were sometimes several candidates seeking election. The coroner was elected by the freeholders for life and he held inquests into deaths in suspicious circumstances and into treasure trove. He committed persons for trial at Assizes on charges of murder or manslaughter and he presented bills on inquests to Quarter Sessions. He was paid fees and allowances.

Business at Quarter Sessions

The subjects dealt with at Quarter Sessions can be seen recorded in the order books or minute books of the period. At the beginning of the eighteenth century much time was spent dealing with political and religious matters, the latter included the licensing of Dissenters' places of worship, but by the middle of that century these had almost disappeared and, apart from criminal work, the sessions were engaged in dealing with a wide range of administrative subjects. These included, as already shown, the appointment of officers and the payment of their salaries, levying rates and settling disputed rate assessments, maintaining roads, bridges, gaols, houses of correction and other county buildings and the repair of churches, discharges from apprenticeships, discharges of insolvent debtors, poor relief and settling disputes between parishes, removal of vagrants, licences for alehouses and the suppression of disorderly or superfluous alehouses, licences to erect cottages for paupers without the statutory four acres of land, licences for private asylums[41] and theatrical performances.[42] The order books contain reports of committees on turnpike roads, on prisons and on the transport of convicts, and they note the authorization of payments of accounts of coroners and of bounties to the growers of hemp and flax, and there are numerous claims for refund of excise duty on salt lost in shipwrecks and on malt destroyed in fires. Considerable time was spent on matters concerning the raising and training of the militia, the examination of militia accounts and on payments to dependents during the Napoleonic Wars. The order books also record various regulations for such matters as rates of wages and tolls, vagrancy, and the suppression of revels, wrestling matches, disorderly alehouses and "Egyptians." The sessions compiled various lists, such as those of disabled soldiers, of persons who took the oaths of allegiance and supremacy in 1715, of persons who were papists or reputed papists, and of those to whom Tyburn tickets had been issued. The sessions also appointed inspectors for certain trades and industries. These included inspectors of "cloths, racks and tenters,"[43] of corn returns[44] and for preventing the spread of "distemper among the hornedcattle."[45] They also appointed searchers of bricks and tiles,[46] and of anything else that seemed to require attention.[47] Some of the administrative work of the justices in Quarter Sessions will be described at greater length in the next chapter.

The rest of the time spent by the justices at Quarter Sessions was occupied in the trial of criminal cases and the hearing of appeals. As

---

41.   14 Geo. III, c. 49.
42.   28 Geo. III, c. 30.
43.   13 Geo. I, c. 23.
44.   31 Geo. III, c. 30.
45.   19 Geo. II, c. 5.
46.   12 Geo. I, c. 35.
47.   At Norfolk sessions in July, 1650, "Ralph Barrett complained of men selling oysters out of season. Two justices of limit to appoint two men to taste whether oysters in season or not. Anyone selling oysters out of season to be bound over by a justice to next sessions." *Norfolk "QS Order Book,* 71.

mentioned earlier, a notable feature of proceedings during the eighteenth century was the shift of jurisdiction from Quarter Sessions to Petty Sessions, and to a less extent to single justices. This loss of work was replaced, however, by the hearing of appeals which accounted for an appreciable amount of Quarter Sessions time. The majority of appeals were against decisions of justices out of sessions, and they related not only to criminal cases but to administrative matters such as settlement, bastardy, assessment to rates and the ratification of accounts of parish officers. These functions will be described in greater detail in the following chapter.

Dress in court

A difference between the professional Judges and the Justices of the Peace which dates from this time is to be seen in the dress worn in court. Whigs and robes have been worn by the Judges continuously since this period whereas the justices have worn contemporary civilian dress, save in a few instances. It was not uncommon at this time for some of them to wear distinctive insignia, particularly in the boroughs where the mayor and aldermen often wore civic robes and chains of office. The only surviving example of this in 1989 was in the City of London where the Lord Mayor and Aldermen still robed for Petty Sessions, and so too did the other City justices (who, as explained earlier, have been appointed only since 1968) though they wore a slightly different blue and black robe from that of the Aldermen. As regards Quarter Sessions, the full-time chairmen of county sessions (who were first appointed in the mid-twentieth century) and the recorders of boroughs wore whigs and gowns, which the lay chairmen did not. A few of the latter, however, were distinguishable in other ways, the last instance being that of the chairman of Dorset sessions who, until the 1960s, wore a top hat when presiding.

The grand jury:

The grand jury occupied a key position at both Assizes and Quarter Sessions and the powers which they exercised, sometimes with dubious authority, were extensive. They numbered between 12 and 20 jurors, and a presentment was not valid unless it was supported by at least 12.

At Assizes the grand jury usually included Justices of the Peace. In 1658 the Yorkshire Assize Judges, with a view to strengthening the grand jury, ordered that six Justices of the Peace should be summoned to attend each Assize for service on the jury.[48] Justices were not present, however, on a large scale before 1680, but from then onwards the proportion increased rapidly and soon the grand juries in most counties were dominated by the justices. At Quarter Sessions the

48.   West Yorkshire, Asz. 42/1 (Summer 1658).

justices, being Judges of the court, could not also serve on the juries, although there were a few instances where one or two did so. In any event, grand juries, both at Assizes and Quarter Sessions, were composed of the most substantial citizens of the county. They served without remuneration and failure to attend was punished with a substantial fine. As previously, it was the grand jury's function in the eighteenth century to consider bills of indictment and to decide whether there was sufficient *prima facie* evidence to justify a trial, in which case, as previously, they returned a true bill, or if not they endorsed the Bill *"Ignoramus"* and the case proceeded no further. The grand jury were not concerned only with criminal charges in the usually recognized sense, but were responsible for presentments which involved the county or the parish in carrying out their public duties, and sometimes effective measures could not be taken unless the jury made a presentment, as in the case of repair of bridges.[49] Sometimes the grand jury went so far as to proclaim that certain action had to be taken, such as the repair of a prison building, and the work would subsequently be carried out in conformity with their directions.

It has been claimed that public expenditure depended upon the grand jury because the justices could not make any order for payment on the county or parish without presentment unless expressly authorized by statute.[50] There is no clear authority for this statement but it seems to reflect the practice of Quarter Sessions down to the nineteenth century. An Act of 1739[51] provided that no county funds should be spent on bridges, gaols or houses of correction, except after presentment by a grand jury, and this was extended to shire halls in 1768.[52] The enactment of 1739, insofar as it related to bridges, was criticized by Dr Burn on the ground that it made it impossible to deal with urgent repairs required in cases of emergency. While recognizing that it might be reasonable to restrain the high constables, surveyors and even the justices from "bringing a charge upon the county in such matters at their will and pleasure, and perhaps only for the private convenience of individual," Burn suggested that in cases of emergency and where the sum involved was not more than 40 shillings, the justices should have authority to meet immediately and to order the rebuilding.[53]

We have seen that the grand jury, at both Assizes and Quarter Sessions, did not confine its attention to presentments, but also

49. As mentioned above, the Statute of 1531 (22 Hen. VIII, c. 5) expressly required the presentment of a grand jury before Quarter Sessions could take the necessary steps for the repair of a bridge.
50. See J.C. Cox, *Three Centuries of Derbyshire Annals,* 1890, vol. i, p. 117, quoted by the Webbs, *ELG, The Parish and the County,* p. 449 and n. 1.
51. 12 Geo. II, c. 29.
52. 9 Geo. III, c. 20.
53. *The History of the Poor Law,* 1764, p. 246.

regarded itself as the voice of the local community and made lengthy statements on the state of the county and of the country as a whole. These might be directed to the Government or to Parliament, and they ranged from attesting allegiance to a new Sovereign to commenting on foreign affairs, and it was thought that they influenced Parliamentary voters at elections. The jury's address was usually in conformity with the views of the majority of the justices in the county, and in the case of Quarter Sessions the jury often received written instructions from the justices. Generally, grand juries exhibited a notable sense of responsibility, but there were exceptions, particularly at Quarter Sessions, in cases where the jury took the opportunity to procure the unjust indictment of personal enemies or political opponents.

By the nineteenth century the grand jury had ceased to play a leading role in local Government and its work was largely confined to criminal judicial business.

In addition to the grand jury, who were concerned with the county as a whole, there were also hundred juries at Quarter Sessions, drawn from the hundreds, liberties and boroughs which came within the jurisdiction of county Quarter Sessions. These were responsible for presentments arising from nuisances and delinquencies within the hundreds and other areas, but they had largely fallen into disuse by the early eighteenth century, and instead the presentments in these cases were made by the high constables of hundreds and the petty constables of parishes and townships.

Committees

Frequently Quarter Sessions ended before all the work was completed, but in these cases adjourned sessions were held to dispose of it. The practice also developed of assigning specific questions of importance to committees. Some were established on a permanent basis, the most common of these being one to deal with finances and accounts. Others were set up to handle temporary requirements, such as the building of a new prison or shire hall. The size of the committee varied from two or three named justices to "all acting Magistrates inclined to attend."

Arrogation of legislative authority

Probably the most remarkable development during the eighteenth century was the assumption by Quarter Sessions of the function of Parliament. The involvement of the justices in legislation took two forms; they influenced and even dictated the measures passed by Parliament, and they also created new local laws entirely at their own discretion.

Attempts by Quarter Sessions to intervene in national affairs at the beginning of the century had not been successful. In 1701 Kent

Quarter Sessions, which were predominantly Whig, petitioned the Commons that the King be supported in the war by grants of supply. This was regarded as a breach of privilege and five justices who were principally responsible for the petition were omitted from the commission when it was renewed shortly afterwards.[54] Later, however, matters of national as well as local importance were debated at length at Quarter Sessions. At these mettings the Members of Parliament who represented the county in the Commons as well as justices who were members of the House of Lords were present and subsequently conveyed the views of the sessions forcefully to Parliament. In the course of time it came to be recognized that any proposed measure which ran contrary to the views expressed in county sessions had little chance of passing the national legislature. It was also recognized that such Acts as were passed by Parliament depended for their effective implementation upon the good will of the justices. The practice therefore grew up of circulating proposed Bills to Quarter Sessions for their comments before they were submitted to Parliament, and Parliament itself was not prepared to discuss such Bills until this had been done and until the justices had signified their general approval. This applied more forcefully in respect of matters affecting local interests and, in the words of the Webbs, "so far as the internal local administration of the rural districts was concerned the House of Commons felt itself to be but the legislative clearing house of the several courts at Quarter Sessions."[55] As might be expected, the result of this phenomenon was that all Acts relating to local services enhanced the powers of the justices and ensured that all other local authorities, including the new statutory bodies, were subordinated to them. Quarter Sessions did not, however, confine themselves to local matters. Question of national importance which were only indirectly of concern to local authorities, such as foreign affairs, were also debated at the sessions whose views, if shared by those in other counties, could have a decisive impact on Parliament and the Government.

The intervention of Quarter Sessions in the legislative sphere was effected not only by influencing the national legislature in Parliament, directly or indirectly, but also by usurping the legislative process itself and arrogating law-making powers to which they had no legal title. With virtually unlimited scope in the conduct of local government it was a simple matter for Quarter Sessions, without approval from Westminster, to make regulations which were as effectice as any statute, and it was not uncommon for them to do so. There were instances of this before the eighteenth century, as for example in the creation of new offences and the definition of penalties which were to

54.   CJ, XIII, 518, 538-9, 550; PRO, C213/9, p. 25.
55.   *ELG, ibid.,* p. 544.

be imposed on those who committed them. Previously there had been a check on such activity by the scrutiny of the higher courts and the Privy Council, although some were allowed to pass without protest. By the eighteenth century, however, although these proclivities could still be checked by the courts, the occasions on which this was done were comparatively rare and there was no longer any direct intervention by the Council or the Secretaries of State.

In assuming direct legislative power the justices were probably unaware in most instances that they were acting unconstitutionally. Being charged with responsibility for maintaining law and order they took it for granted that they could do whatever they deemed necessary to achieve this object, and when regulating the behaviour of members of the public or issuing directions to parish officers it probably never occurred to them that they were exceeding their powers. It is sometimes difficult to draw the line between those functions which they exercised legally and those which were illegal. The Commission of the Peace and some statutes gave them wide discretionary powers which they were apparently intended to discharge in any manner they thought fit. Certain statutes expressly directed them to lay down rules. Moreover, their decrees were not subject to confirmation by any other authority as were the bye-laws made by later local government bodies. There were, however, many occasions when the justices, or their clerks whose duty it was to advise them, should have recognized beyond doubt that they were acting illegally. There were few appeals against their decisions, partly because of the cost of such proceedings, but it is a comment on the omnipotent position they occupied in the eye of both Government and people that their conduct was only rarely challenged.

One area in which law-making by Quarter Sessions occurred frequently was in liquor licensing. Numerous orders were made which applied to these licences and under some of them inns and alehouses had to be closed on Sundays, although there was no statutory power at that time to impose such a restriction. In asserting their responsibility for keeping the peace and for controlling vagrancy the justices exceeded their authority by placing restraints on itinerant traders. Among the Quarter Sessions who took this course were those of Kent who, in 1785, issued a regulation that "no hawker, pedlar, petty chapman, or other trading persons or persons going from town to town, or to other men's houses," should sell any goods within the county "under pain of forfeiting for every such offence the sum of 10 pounds."[56] Again, the justices' many experiments in poor relief led to various local enactments by Quarter Sessions. The most famous of

56.   Kent QS Minutes, October 4, 1785.

these became known as the Speenhamland system which is described later. Yet another area in which the justices' orders were legislative in character was that of rating.[57]

Where many Quarter Sessions clearly exceeded their authority was in the suppression of fairs. This was evidently done with a view to removing the occasion for breaches of the peace or for other illegal conduct such as the playing of unlawful games, but the justices had no mandate to close fairs even for these good reasons. The minutes of Gloucestershire Quarter Sessions contain a number of such instances when they made both general and specific orders for the prohibition of fairs, wakes, revels "and other disorderly meetings," the implication being that those attending were bound to make trouble.[58] These included gatherings at which wrestling, "cudgel playing" and other sporting events took place. To enforce their laws the justices in the area were required to bind over "those who shall presume to assemble together" to appear at the next Quarter Sessions "to answer their contempt." Although there were objections to this highhanded action the only effective opposition seems to have come from certain Lords of the Manor who stood to lose revenue if the fair was not held. On some of these occasions the fair proceeded under the auspices of the lord of the Manor and the justices did not intervene beyond ordering the constable to arrest those who committed breaches of the peace or committed other offences which were clearly breaches of the law.[59]

The justices therefore not only administered the common law and the law made by Parliament but to a significant extent they also enforced laws which they had invented and promulgated themselves without authority, guidance or supervision. They succeeded in placing themselves in the unique position of being both law makers and law enforcers.

The single justice

As already mentioned, the eighteenth century was marked by a substantial transfer of work from Quarter Sessions to justices out of sessions including single justices acting on their own. We have seen that the powers of a single justice were already wide in the time of Lambard and they covered criminal and civil jurisdiction, keeping the peace and a number of administrative subjects. Many of the statutes

57. The Webbs give many other instances. *ELG, ibid.,* pp. 533-550.
58. Gloucestershire Quarter Sessions Minutes, Epiphany and Easter 1710; Epiphany 1718, Easter 1731.
59. The Webbs describe the attempt of Surrey Quarter Sessions to suppress the Camberwell Fair in 1806 which was thwarted by the Lord of the Manor. *ELG, ibid.,* p. 537.

which conferred this authority on the single justice did not specify the procedure to be followed and left him largely to his own devices. Much of this work was conducted by the justice in the parlour of his private house which came to be known as the "justice room." He could also, if he wished, dispose of some cases on the spot. For instance, if he overheard a person swearing a profane oath, or found someone in the highway who appeared to him to be drunk, he could impose an immediate fine or order a period in the stocks or in prison. He was supposed to report every such conviction to the next Quarter Sessions, but rarely did so and most justices kept no record.

The business conducted by the single justice was substantial, and there were many who preferred to spend an appreciable amount of time on this work rather than attending Quarter Sessions. Contemporary diaries show that some justices were engaged for at least some part of three or four days a week in Petty Sessions and in acting alone. The single justice took security to keep the peace and to be of good behaviour,[60] and he made orders for imprisonment pending trial. He could impose fines for theft, for disorderly behaviour and for indulging in sports or conducting business on Sundays. He could likewise impose fines for breaches of the game laws and for possessing guns, greyhounds, snares or nets for hunting or fishing where the accused did not possess the necessary qualification. He also imposed sentences on those who destroyed hedges, on bakers who sold bread below the legal weight and on hawkers who did not have a licence. He could order distraint of goods for non-payment of fines and imprisonment of those who did not have enough money or goods to pay the fines. He imposed prison and other sentences on those whom he convicted of affray, of aiding smugglers and of theft of horses or of stealing from gardens and orchards. He sent those who refused to work to the house of correction. Whipping was a sentence frequently imposed on offenders, especially vagrants. The stocks were also a favourite option of the single justice for a variety of offenders including those who refused to work at harvest time. He could order searches to be made of suspected persons and he could arrest them when found.

The single justice was involved in many administrative matters, some of which will be described later. In his own house he would deal with innumerable problems brought to him by the inhabitants of the area in which he lived, such as non-payment of wages, labour disputes and paupers claiming that they had not received relief from the

60.　A justice could require a person to enter into a recognizance to keep the peace after he had received a complaint, but the justice did not have to wait for a complaint before binding over to be of good behaviour so long as he believed that the person was likely to commit an offence. If the person refused to be bound over the justice could commit him to prison.

overseer. He frequently apprenticed a young person to a trade, first examining the reports of the overseers and the credentials of the potential employer before making an order. The single justice administered numerous oaths which were required from individuals under various statutes. For example, an oath had to be taken before a justice by every person who was to be employed in the postal service that they would not open or delay any letter or packet which came into their hands, nor suffer anyone else to do so.[61] Outside his home he would be involved in supervising gaols and houses of correction and in inspecting alehouses, highways and bridges. This might lead to his presenting some person or body for failing to fulfil their public duty and subsequently, especially in the case of a highway, he might find himself placed in charge of the repairs and the disbursement of funds on the cost.

The most irksome of the single justice's duties arose from his continuing responsibility as a police officer for keeping the peace. There was considerable escalation of industrial unrest throughout the eighteenth century and it was the justice's duty to take steps to suppress it, as we shall see in the next chapter.

For the most part, the powers exercised by the single justice did not affect those in the upper levels of society, but they were of overwhelming importance to the majority of persons living in the area in which the justice resided, particularly the poor, the petty criminal, the officers of the parish and the justice's own tenants and employees. He could not, however, act without the co-operation of his colleagues in respect of matters of wider concern to the community, and this included the granting or withholding of a licence to an alehouse keeper even in the justice's own village. This restriction on the justice's authority proved irksome to some of the more arrogant, who attempted to flout the law and act on their own. They were rarely successful and even leading aristocrats found that the law was paramount. Norma Landau cites the example in 1742 of Lord Willoughby de Broke of Warwickshire who granted alehouse licences on his own initiative and without obtaining the signature of another justice. He was successful in this enterprise until he imprisoned a cleric without good cause. The cleric's brother, who was a justice for the county, secured support from his colleagues for a petition that Lord

---

61. 9 Anne, c. 10. A single justice could sentence a post-boy to hard labour in a house of correction for between 14 days and one month, on the evidence of one witness, for loitering on the road or failing to perform his duties in certain other ways; 5 Geo. III, c. 20, s. 20. Another provision relating to the postal system was that where it involved pecuniary penalties of £50 or more these were to be pursued in the courts at Westminster, but if they were less they could be recovered before one justice residing near to the place where the offence was committed. The justice could convict the offender and distrain his goods; 5 Geo. IV, c. 51.

Willoughby de Broke be removed from the commission, and his name was duly struck out.

Two or more justices

The numerous powers already exercised by two or more justices also continued throughout the period and tended to be more extensive than those of a single justice. They licensed and suppressed alehouses, ratified assessment to highway and poor rates, appointed overseers and surveyors, bound poor apprentices, made regulations in time of plague, licensed sick persons to go to Bath and Buxton for cure and they spent some time dealing with rogues, vagabonds, bastard children and the game laws. Wage supervision, previously undertaken at Quarter Sessions, was now the task of the divisional justices. Parish accounts, which were of growing importance, required the approval of two justices.

A further trend from the end of the seventeenth century was that in many parts of the country duties previously exercised by Quarter Sessions were delegated to small groups of justices in the area in which the matter arose. Repair of highways and buildings, resolving differences between parishes, considering appeals against rate assessment, and determining local problems were treated in this way, the justices being empowered by Quarter Sessions to settle the matter at their discretion. Sometimes a committee of justices was appointed by Quarter Sessions on a permanent basis to supervise a specific project such as the management of a gaol.

Petty Sessions

One of the most important developments in the seventeenth and eighteenth centuries was the growth of Petty Sessions. This was particularly so in the eighteenth century when there was a tendency to require matters previously dealt with by a single justice to be brought to the regular meetings of the division. One reason for this was probably the increase in party politics during the first half of the century. Members of the majority party wished to curtail the powers of the minority, and this could be done effectively only when decisions had to be taken at meetings at which their majority prevailed. At the same time, there was a continuous transfer, as already mentioned, of various classes of work from Quarter Sessions to meetings of justices out of sessions. The result of this dual transfer of work was that a large proportion of the justices' duties came to be performed at formal meetings in each division where initial decisions were taken by the justices, leaving Quarter Sessions to act as a court of appeal, apart from a few matters which had to be taken at Quarter Sessions under statutes such as bridge maintenance or licensing Dissenters' places of worship. The divisional sessions, which had become well established by the time of the Revolution in 1688, came to be referred to as Petty Sessions, though as yet there was no legal definition of the sessions nor of their function, apart from certain special meetings such as Brewster sessions after 1729.

Information on the precise work performed at Petty Sessions is meagre until divisional clerks began to keep minute books. This is because, apart from routine returns to Quarter Sessions on such matters as the grant of liquor licences, the justices were not required to submit records of their meetings to any higher court. Indeed, as they were not statutory bodies they were not obliged to keep any notes of their proceedings at all, though all justices were urged by the textbook writers to keep full notes of everything they did. Most of the powers conferred upon two or more justices did not necessarily have to be exercised at Petty Sessions but, in accordance with the trend already noted, many of these had to be enforced at Petty Sessions under directions from the justices themselves. Thus, although poor rates could be authorized by any two justices living in or near the division, these came in the course of time to be dealt with always at Petty Sessions.

The areas covered by divisions were not defined at county level and it was left to the local justices to fix the boundaries as they thought best. Likewise, they arranged the time and place of meetings. The allocation of justices to divisions was a matter for agreement among the justices, each of whom was qualified in law to sit in any part of the commission area. This is still the case today, but now each justice is appointed on the understanding that he or she will sit only in a specified division. The regular meetings of Petty Sessions were normally held in an inn, whereas the informal meetings of earlier times, usually of two justices, had taken place either in an inn or in the house of one of them.

By the end of the seventeenth century Petty Sessions were dealing with most minor crimes and local quarrels. In such cases, warrants directed that defendants should appear at Petty Sessions where they were tried summarily instead of at Quarter Sessions where they might otherwise have been obliged to appear on a recognizance for which they would have had to pay a fee.

Chairman of Petty Sessions

It was obviously convenient for one of the justices present to preside at Petty Sessions. At first the practice was to choose a chairman *ad hoc* at each sessions or for the chair to be taken in rotation. By the 1750s many benches were electing permanent chairmen, and this became the general practice by the end of the century.

Clerks to Petty Sessions

For a long time some justices had employed clerks on a personal basis to assist them in their work out of sessions. By the eighteenth century it was becoming fairly common for clerks to attend divisional or Petty Sessions as well as when a single justice sat in his own home. Experience showed that legal advice was useful on these occasions. As mentioned earlier, Squire Western found this when his clerk, who "had a qualification which no Clerk to a Justice of the Peace ought ever to be without, namely some understanding in the law of this realm," advised him that he had no power to send his sister's maid to Bridewell. It was also the clerk's duty to keep records of proceedings, to draft documents such as warrants and the orders which had to be signed by the justices, to prepare presentments to Quarter Sessions and occasionally to draft a case for submission to a barrister. During the eighteenth century it became customary for Petty Sessions to obtain a supply of books, such as copies of the statutes and magistrates' textbooks, at public expense, and it was the clerk's duty to obtain these and submit the bill to Quarter Sessions. In the course of time it became usual for Quarter Sessions to communicate with the justices acting out of sessions through the Clerk of the Peace and the clerk to Petty Sessions.

The clerks to Petty Sessions were allowed to take fees for various services they performed, in particular for each warrant and other document which they issued, though initially there was no clear legal authority for them to do so. In those cases where there was no clerk, the justices usually collected the fees and in some cases pocketed them themselves. On the other hand there were those, like the Rev. Charles Jasper Selwyn of Blockley, mentioned above, who used them for some charitable purpose. It was argued that unless fees were charged the burden of work falling upon Petty Sessions would become intolerable; on the other hand the proliferation of fees amounted in some cases to oppression.

There were many cases where charges were manifestly excessive; even a vagrant sentenced to be whipped had to pay a fee, and so too did a pauper before he could qualify for relief. Sometimes the grand jury at Quarter Sessions made presentments of excessive fees charged by clerks. In 1698 the grand jury at Essex Quarter Sessions presented several clerks "for demanding and taking extortive fees, viz. 5s for one pair of apprentices indentured for binding our parish children," and "for taking 2s.6d for confirmation of the Poor Rate." This led to some Quarter Sessions drawing up lists of fees which the clerks were allowed to charge. Gloucestershire sessions seem to have been the first to do this when, in 1718, they drew up a comprehensive table of the fees which clerks were to be allowed to take, and it was ordered that the

table should be recorded in the books of every parish.62 In 1753
Parliament intervened and enacted that Quarter Sessions in every
county should draw up a schedule of fees to be taken by Clerks to
Justices. This was to be binding upon all concerned. The table was to
be deposited with the Clerk of the Peace, but before it became
effective it had to be ratified by the Judges of Assize. It could also be
varied from time to time with the Judges' approval. Clerks who took
fees other than those as set out in the table were liable to a fine of £20.

The clerks to Petty Sessions usually held other local offices, in
particular they acted as clerks to the commissioners of land tax and of
window tax and sometimes they were treasurers of the gaols and
houses of correction and of the militia fund.

The development of the office of Clerk to the Justices at Petty
Sessions was of crucial importance to the future of the Justices of the
Peace. With the increasing complexity of the work performed by the
justices, particularly the expansion of their powers of summary
jurisdiction from the end of the eighteenth century, it is unlikely that
the lay justice system would have survived had it not embodied the
essential element of a legally qualified officer with the duty of advising
the court on the multifarious matters with which it was concerned, and
in particular on the law and legal procedure. The clerk became an
integral and indispensable part of the lay magistracy.

Other local courts

We have seen that although the importance of the old manorial courts
had been diminishing for some time they and the municipal courts
remained in operation throughout the eighteenth century. Manorial
courts still settled actions between tenants and dealt with common
nuisances. Small debts could be recovered in the hundred courts and in
the shire courts held by the sheriffs.

There were certain statutory bodies responsible for administrative
matters which were distinct from the JP's courts but whose members
were largely composed of justices, thereby increasing the latter's
burden still further. The principal bodies of this kind, which have
already been mentioned, were the commissioners of land tax, window
tax and of sewers. Almost every justice was appointed a commissioner
of land tax, and for this reason meetings of the commissioners usually
coincided with those of the justices. The justices' clerk served both
bodies. Under 43 Geo. II, c. 48 a JP could act as a land tax
commissioner even if he were not listed as a commissioner. Parliament
determined the total amount of land tax to be raised from each county,
while the land tax commissioners decided the amount to be levied on

62.   Gloucestershire QS, Ephiphany, 1718.

each parish. Similarly, the window tax commissioners were responsible for raising the tax which was payable by every householder and by owners of certain specified buildings, according to the number of windows that they had. The commissioners of sewers were far older than any of the other bodies. Even before the Norman Conquest the inhabitants of low-lying and seaboard areas had been responsible for the erection of embankments and the cleansing of sewers to prevent incursions from the sea and to ensure that land did not become water-logged. A statute of 1427[63] gave statutory authority to the commissioners of sewers and set out their duties. This was extended by several further enactments until 1532, when 23 Hen. VIII, c. 5 directed that commissions of sewers were to be issued throughout the country to substantial persons nominated by the Lord Chancellor, the Lord Treasurer and the two Chief Justices of the King's Bench and Common Pleas respectively. It also laid down a property qualification which ensured that, except in urban areas, the commissioners were landowners, and it redefined their duties, which included the carrying out of repairs to certain bridges and other installations and the raising of necessary funds from local landowners. The commissioners were paid a salary. Holdsworth comments that the development of the commissioners of sewers was "very similar to the development of the Justices of the Peace"[64] and he quotes "the Judges and other professional lawyers who figure largely in the early commissions are, in the modern period, displaced by local residents, whose qualification is one of property."[65] The commissioners of sewers in rural areas were not finally abolished until 1930.[66]

Curbs on the justices' authority

As we have seen, the tight supervision of the justices' actions by the Council, which had characterized the Tudor period, had vanished by the eighteenth century, while scrutiny by the common law courts had become minimal.

Supervision was most apparent in the hearing of appeals at Quarter Sessions against decisions of one or more justices out of sessions. This was expensive, and many private appellants were deterred by the cost. Nevertheless, the hearing of appeals occupied a considerable amount of time at Quarter Sessions, although the majority of the appellants were those who had the most to gain and lose from the outcome and who could afford to pay, especially parishes which challenged

---

63. 6 Hen. VI, c. 5.
64. *H.E.L.,* vol. X, p. 205. Quoting Second Report of Royal Commission on Public Records, App. II, p. 99.
65. *Second Report of Royal Commission on Public Records,* App. II, p. 99.
66. Land Drainage Act, 1930.

settlement decisions and wealthy landowners who appealed against rate assessments. A further appeal did not lie beyond Quarter Sessions, but on the other hand the decisions of the justices both in and out of sessions could be challenged by various means in the common law courts, principally the King's Bench.

As already mentioned, the superior courts did not attempt to interfere in or to override the exercise by the justices of a discretion which they had been given by statute or by common law. In *R.* v. *John Reason,*[67] in which proceedings were taken on *certiorari* to remove an acquittal by the justices, the court ruled that it could not take action to secure the accused's conviction. It was said that:

> "The evidence given was entirely and exclusively for the consideration of the justices below, who were placed in the situation of a jury; and as they had acquitted the defendant, this court could not substitute themselves in the place of the justices acting as jurymen and convict him. That they could not judge of the credit due to the witnesses whom they did not hear examined, that they could only look to the form of conviction, and see that the party, if convicted, had been convicted by legal evidence."

The principle was laid down by Lord Mansfield in the leading case of *R.* v. *Young and Pitts*[68] in which he stated that the King's Bench had "no power or claim to review the reasons of Justices of the Peace, upon which they form their judgments ... But if it clearly appears that the justices have been partially, maliciously, or corruptly influenced in the exercise of this discretion, and have (consequently) abused the trust reposed in them, they are liable to prosecution by indictment or information; or even, possibly, by action, if the malice be very gross and injurious." Again in *R.* v. *Cozens*[69] Lord Mansfield said "No Justice of the Peace ought to suffer for ignorance, when the heart is right. On the other hand, when magistrates act from undue, corrupt, or indirect motives, they are always punished by this court."

Differences in the jurisdiction exercised by justices in and out of Quarter Sessions were also enforced by the higher courts. In *The Queen* v. *Bradley,*[70] Quarter Sessions had fined the overseers of highways £30 for not passiong their accounts. The decision was quashed because the statutory power to fine had been given, not to Quarter Sessions but to special sessions.

Holdsworth claimed that what he described as "this intelligent and

67.　　(1795) 6 T.R., p. 376.
68.　　(1758) 1 Burr, pp. 561-562.
69.　　(1780) 2 Dougl., p. 427.
70.　　1713, Sessions Cases, 11.

impartial control" was perhaps the "principal cause of the very considerable success of the eighteenth century system of local government and of the large measure of popular approval which it received."[71] The popular approval of the justices, at least by the end of the century, did not appear to have been as great as this may suggest, but the control exercised by the King's Bench and other courts undoubtedly had a salutary effect upon the conduct of the justices who took greater care than they would have done otherwise in exercising their powers. It also served a most useful purpose in guiding justices and helping them to avoid mistakes in law and procedure.

The scrutiny by the superior courts might be achieved by indictment, by prerogative writ or by a civil action or motion to quash an order. Whereas judgment on an indictment could be challenged by a writ of error, this was not available in the case of orders and convictions by justices in their summary proceedings, and in these cases the remedy was to proceed by writ of *certiorari* to question the justices' jurisdiction.[72] As proceedings by any of these methods was costly they were not resorted to very often (most reported cases were initiated in the name of the Crown), yet when action was taken, the courts applied the law very strictly, even in the interpretation of statutes which appeared *prima facie* to remove their control over the justices' courts. Thus in 1760 it was claimed that the Conventicle Act 1670 had removed the power to issue a writ of *certiorari* by providing that convictions under the Act should be finally determined by Quarter Sessions. It was held, however, that the common law courts still had power to issue the writ because the latter did not inquire into the merits of the case itself, but rather into whether the court of limited jurisdiction had exceeded its authority.[73]

In addition to calling in question some act done by the justices, it was also possible by writ of *mandamus* to compel them to exercise their jurisdiction or to discharge some duty if they failed to do so. As stated by Holt, CJ, in 1700, "where any court is erected by statute, a *certiorari* lies to it; so that if they perform not their duty, the King's Bench will grant a *mandamus*."[74] *Mandamus* was the normal means of ensuring that justices fulfilled their administrative duties in a proper manner. Where justices could be shown to have conducted themselves improperly they might be made subject to criminal proceedings and punished. Holdsworth cites examples of criminal proceedings being taken against justices in respect of acts done in the course of their duties. One of these cases illustrates the partiality of the JPs towards

71.   *H.E.L.*, vol. X, p. 249.
72.   See *R. v. The Inhabitants of Seton* (1797) 7 TR, pp. 373-374.
73.   *R. v. Moreley* (1760) 2 Burr, p. 1040.
74.   *Groenvelt v. Burwell* (1700), 1 Ld. Raym., p. 469.

members of their own class. In 1721, in a case alleging failure to take the oaths of allegiance, an information was granted against justices who refused to give the prosecutor a certificate which was required by statute in order that further proceedings might be taken at Quarter Sessions. Their reason was that "coming afterwards to understand the party was a gentleman of fashion and not suspected to be against the Government, lest a transaction of this nature should be an imputation upon him, they refused to give the prosecutor his oath of the service of such summons that the matter might go no further."[75]

The control exercised by the King's Bench and other courts, albeit on a somewhat limited scale, was of the greatest significance in two respects. First, it kept the justices within one unified legal system. Apart from the limited requirements of some Acts (such as the obligation to grant licences on certain fixed days) there was no set of statutory rules governing procedure at either Quarter Sessions or Petty Sessions, and practice differed from one county to another. In time they might well have developed totally different systems were it not for the overall control and unifying influence of the courts at Westminster. Secondly, it established a body of local government and administrative law which continued to be developed from then onwards and was applied to the new local government bodies of the nineteenth and twentieth centuries.

Assizes

The control over the justices' powers mentioned in the preceding paragraphs was exercised mostly by the courts at Westminster. Assizes still visited counties, usually twice a year, but the Judges no longer played as prominent a part in the affairs of the justices as they had done in previous centuries when they supervised much of the justices' administrative and judicial work and were also consulted on their appointment and dismissal. In addition to intervening in specific cases it had been customary for the Assize Judge to disseminate Government propaganda, to expound on matters of general interest and to discuss with the justices, most of whom did their best to attend Assizes, the numerous questions which were of current concern to them. In the eighteenth century the Assize Judges were no longer asked to advise on the appointment and removal of justices and less of their time was occupied with the justices' in their work. They might still, however, be required occasionally to disseminate information. For example, until 1787 the Government did not allow copies of Acts of Parliament to be distributed to the justices and therefore until then the

---

75.   *R.* v. *Newton* (1721) 1 Stra., p. 413. Cited Holdsworth, *H.E.L.*, vol. X, p. 247.

Judges explained the provisions of new enactments when they visited counties on circuit.

Fewer justices attended Assizes than they did previously, but it was usual for the Assize grand jury to be composed for the most part of justices who used this opportunity to voice their opinions on a wide range of subjects. It was also not uncommon for one or two justices to be included with the Judge in the commission of oyer and terminer. To an even greater extent than before the eighteenth century Assizes heard criminal cases with which Quarter Sessions could not or would not deal. This generally included the more difficult and important cases and all charges of murder, but many Quarter Sessions also left all except the more minor offences to be tried at Assizes. Some of the time at Assizes was taken up with litigation, particularly property disputes, which were entirely outside the jurisdiction of the justices.

From the beginning of the eighteenth century the Judges of Assize confined themselves almost entirely to their judicial work, and they were little concerned with the justices' administrative and executive functions in which they made virtually no attempt to interfere from 1688 onwards. In the judicial sphere, the control of the justices through the Assize Judges became closer after the abolition of the Star Chamber, but in spite of this the justices performed even their judicial work with a considerable degree of independence.

As before, there was no right of appeal to Assizes from the decisions of the justices at Quarter Sessions or Petty Sessions, but the justices continued to consult the Judges on various aspects of their work, and the guidance and advice given by the Judges played a major part in keeping the practice of the lower courts within the law.

The Assize Judges had ceased by the end of the seventeenth century to be a channel for the propagation of national policy. The Government now tended to use the Lords Lieutenant for this purpose. The Lords Lieutenant in turn would disseminate information through the justices and local officials.

This chapter, in describing the courts and other bodies through which the justices operated, has given an outline of the wide scope and variety of the functions that they performed during the period between 1689 and the great reforms of the nineteenth century. The following chapter describes in more detail the principal matters which occupied the justices' time. Most of these constitute an area where, in an increasingly critical environment, the justices were subject to mounting censure. This, coupled with the inability of the justices to adjust to the changing times, led to the major reforms which followed.

CHAPTER III

THE AGE OF INDEPENDENCE
POWER AND "DECLINE"
1689-1820

PART III - THE TARNISHED IMAGE

The extensive duties of the eighteenth century justices; Judicial; Finance; Militia; Highways; Police; Paupers and Vagrants; Gaols and Houses of Correction; Licensing; The Game Laws - Growing Criticism - Assessment of Blame

Extent of the Justices' Authority

SOME ACCOUNT HAS ALREADY been given of the duties performed by justices in and out of Quarter Sessions during the eighteenth century. It remains to provide a more exact indication of the extent of their authority in the era when this reached its maximum, and also to describe at greater length the principal ways in which they occupied their time.

The performance of the justices in most fields during the eighteenth century has been the subject of severe criticism. They might well have been deprived of their unique position much earlier had the opposition been better organized, but this did not become effective until the country was engulfed in the reforming zeal of the nineteenth century, when the justices' apparently invulnerable bastion was finally breached. In the meantime they carried on their business in general accord with the standards of the age.

The extent and diversity of the justices' authority from the Revolution onwards is reflected in the plethora of contemporary textbooks, some of which have already been mentioned. The most important work at the beginning of the period was that of Edmund Bohun whose *The Justice of the Peace, His Calling and Qualifications* was published in 1693. He, among others, recommended that every justice should keep a record of his acts and decisions, a piece of advice which was followed by only a minority of his readers. Bohun's work was highly informative, but he also reflected the political atmosphere of the time and recognized the rivalries in which the justices had become involved through party politics. Another manual written in this period was *The Office and Authority of a Justice of the Peace,* by William Nelson who was a Sussex JP. He was concerned at what he regarded as a decline in the quality of the commissions resulting from the appointment of men of inferior standing. "This Court of Justices of the Peace, which was once, as my Lord Coke observes, 'such a Form of subordinate Government for the Quiet of the Realm, that, if duly executed, no part of the Christian World had the like' hath been composed of such an unsuitable Mixture of men, that this became a Subject in Plays, and a Jest in Comedies." In 1745, Thomas Barlow published *The Justice of the Peace: a Treatise Containing the Power and Duty of that Magistrate,* and Sir William Blackstone's *Commentaries on the Laws of England* were published between 1765 and 1769. The Commentaries are a lucid exposition of the whole of English law and were not intended as a guide to the Justices of the Peace, but they naturally include a discussion of the law which the justices had to apply, and they also comment on the role of the justices themselves. The most outstanding and influential of all magistrates' textbooks was the Reverend Richard Burn's *The Justice of the Peace and Parish Officer,* first published in 1755 to which several reference have already been made. Its success is not surprising. It was comprehensive and met the needs of the lay justices of the eighteenth and nineteenth centuries, who required clear and extensive guidance in the multifarious duties they had to perform. Even the Judges of the King's Bench recognized its authority. In 1789 a case was submitted to the King's Bench in which a single justice had convicted a man for using a gun contrary to the game laws. The Judges were of the opinion that the records of the conviction gave insufficient evidence of the offence but, since it followed the model provided in Burn's manual they decided to consider the conviction as valid in law.[1]

Burn's manual describes in detail all the powers and duties of the justices and of the officers with whom they were involved and he sets them out alphabetically under headings. The full list, numbering 106 subjects in all, is to be found in Appendix III and it provides a striking indication of the wide scope of the justices' authority. By far the most lengthy item was "Poor" which accounted for one entire volume out of five by the time the 23rd edition was reached in 1820. The next longest title was "Excise and Customs," followed by "Game,," "Highways" and "Militia." Many of the other items mentioned occupied only a minimal amount of the justices' time, but there were many subjects, all of which have already been mentioned, to which the justices gave a great deal of attention during the era in which they reached the zenith of their power. The most time-consuming of these may be considered under the following nine headings (which do not coincide precisely with those set out in the list by Burn):

(1) Judicial; (2) Finance; (3) Militia; (4) Highways; (5) Police; (6)

---

1. *R. v. Thompson,* 2 TR 24.

Paupers and Vagrants; (7) Gaols and Houses of Correction; (8) Licensing, and (9) The Game Laws.

The justices exercised their powers under the first three of these without arousing noteworthy disapproval, but each of the remaining six gave rise to increasing criticism.

(1) Judicial Functions

A brief description of the justices' judicial work during this period, both in and out of Quarter Sessions, was given in the last chapter when describing the machinery through which they discharged their three-fold duties.

Quarter Sessions

As already explained, Quarter Sessions began to distinguish between judicial and administrative work from the early eighteenth century. They sat in public to deal with criminal cases but in a private room, often in a different building, for administrative business. Prior to 1689 an appreciable amount of time was spent in dealing with church offences, particularly absence from service on Sundays. By the 1730s most of these cases had been replaced by frequent accusations against alehouses and inns on the grounds that they were unlicensed or disorderly or allowed the playing of unlawful games. By far the largest group of offences tried at Quarter Sessions, however, was that of larceny in its various forms. Quarter Sessions still dealt at first instance with a number of other types of case, of which the most numerous were assaults, robbery, riots against the militia and a certain number of minor riots - mostly disturbances in villages occasioned by resistance to constables making arrests or to bailiffs making distraints. Difficult criminal cases were referred to Assizes which also dealt with all civil matters.

The justices' jurisdiction still extended to all crimes except treason and it was not until 1842 that Quarter Sessions ceased to be able to try cases of murder, but whereas they had regularly imposed the death penalty during previous centuries, by the eighteenth it was customary for these offences to be committed to Assizes. Cases of abnormal difficulty were also usually referred to the Assize Judges. This movement resulted in a substantial drop in the number of serious crimes dealt with at Quarter Sessions. The reduction became still greater with the notable increase in the number of statutory capital offences which occurred during the period. There were only some 50 of these in 1688 but more than 220 by 1820. A high proportion of those sentenced to death were under 21 and many were children. The supposed reason for increasing the number of capital offences was to deter offenders, but in fact it came to defeat its own object. There was a continuing rise in the number of crimes at all levels, while public revulsion against hanging for minor offences was reflected in the refusal of injured parties to prosecute and in juries, with the approval of Judges and justices, going out of their way to acquit. There were four times as many executions in the early seventeenth century as there were in 1750 when about 100 executions took place in a year. After the introduction of transportation on a large scale in 1719 an increasing number of prisoners under sentence of death were reprieved and instead transported to penal colonies. Transportation was an option open to Quarter Sessions as well as Assizes and was used frequently, especially as a means of avoiding the cost of maintaining a prisoner in custody, as we shall see later. Although Quarter Sessions no longer resorted to capital punishment they continued to impose brutal corporal sentences. Burning on the hand was still inflicted on thieves, and the most common sentence for theft was whipping. There are innumerable records of women as well as men, convicted of theft of items valued at less than one shilling, being sentenced to be stripped to the waist and whipped. Solitary confinement for long periods was also common. In following this penal policy the justices and the Judges were giving effect to the views held by most members of British society at the time, but the results were unimpressive. In several other European countries penalties were less severe yet the incidence of crime was lower.

Criminal procedure at Quarter Sessions remained the same as it had been in the past. After the delivery of the charge, the Grand Jury retired and considered what bills they should present. The trial jury later sat to try offenders against whom true bills were presented. There was usually a considerable interval between the deliberations of the Grand Jury and the subsequent trial, and this was normally occupied by the justices in dealing with miscellaneous matters, often of an administrative nature. All felonies still enjoyed the benefit of clergy and therefore, as Burn points out, where a statute created a felony and stated that the offender should suffer death "clergy lies notwithstanding, and is never ousted without express words."

The position in the eighteenth century may be summarized by saying that the judicial work was almost entirely criminal and that the more serious cases were normally tried at Assizes, while Quarter Sessions were engaged to a greater extent than before in hearing appeals against the decision of justices out of sessions, leaving the latter to handle the bulk of business at first instance. Most minor offences were tried summarily at Petty Sessions and some were still dealt with by a single justice.

Courts of summary jurisdiction

We have seen that Henry VII first granted justices the power to dispose of criminal charges summarily without recourse to a jury. In spite of opposition from the Judges and legal writers, this process continued, and still continues to this day. At the time of the Restoration, the number of offences triable summarily amounted to about 70. A hundred years later the figure was nearly three times as great. Parliament, with its majority of JP members, favoured the extension of the justices' powers of summary jurisdiction out of sessions, but it accepted that there was danger in leaving these powers unfettered. Therefore, when passing legislation extending summary trial they included provisions allowing a right of appeal to Quarter Sessions which, unlike *certiorari*, lay on questions of fact as well as law. Defendants were slow to avail themselves of this procedure, but before the end of the century it was being used more frequently than *certiorari*, notwithstanding the possibility that the justices hearing the appeal at Quarter Sessions might be influenced by a desire to support their colleagues in the court below. In this regard the system could also be criticized on the ground that a civil action would lie against a justice in respect of his wrong judgment or order only if the judgment or order were quashed. The protection afforded to the justices was increased by an Act of 1751[2] which required a plaintiff to give a justice one month's notice of intention to sue. Within this time the justice might escape liability by tendering amends. If, however, the plaintiff refused and continued with the suit he would lose his case and have to pay the justice's costs if a jury found that the amends were adequate. Under a further Act of 1804,[3] if the plaintiff's conviction were quashed, he could recover only the amount of his fine (if one had been imposed) plus two pence unless he could prove that the justice had acted maliciously or without proper cause. It is not surprising that the number of civil suits brought against justices seem to have been few in number except in Middlesex and Westminster.

Sentencing

Punishments imposed by the criminal courts remained much the same as they had been in the previous century except for the introduction of transportation on a regular scale in 1719;[4] but, as we have seen, there was a great increase in the number of offences which attracted the death penalty. These offences included destroying turnpikes or cloth in

2.   24 Geo. II, c. 44.
3.   43 Geo. III, c. 141.
4.   The earliest instance of transportation was in 1619 and the practice grew towards the end of the century when the old castles in which most prisons were situated ceased to be maintained.

the loom and even writing threatening letters and cutting down trees in an avenue. As mentioned above, most capital causes were transferred to Assizes, but Quarter Sessions still had the power to try them until 1842. The penalties imposed by Quarter Sessions were often extremely harsh. As late as 1830 Wiltshire Quarter Sessions sentenced a man to 14 years transportation for stealing a wooden plank valued at one shilling. A particularly unedifying feature of that case was that the stolen plank was the property of a local justice who sat on the bench which sentenced him. When imposing sentences for minor offences the courts continued to be obsessed with the need to deter others by giving as much publicity as possible to the humiliation of the offender. This was an essential element in the penology of the age and it had the full backing of Parliament. In the armed services the entire ship's company or military unit was paraded to witness the flogging of an offender and the same approach dominated civilian life. The stocks and the pillory were therefore still a frequently used option. So too was whipping and the sentence was usually accompanied with orders to ensure that it became a public spectacle. Thus at Chichester Quarter Sessions in 1757 a women was convicted of stealing five yards of cloth. Her sentence was to be stripped from the waist upwards, tied to the tail of a cart and whipped through the town between the hours of 11 am and 1 pm on a Saturday when the streets were likely to be most crowded.

It could well be inferred from these sentences that they emanated from the brutal character of the justices. Obviously such cruel treatment implies gross callousness on the part of the sentencers, at least by modern standards, but it was representative of the view currently held by most sections of eighteenth century society which claimed that the only effective way to stop crime was to impose harsh punishment on the criminal. It was assumed that a person who had been convicted of an offence must be subjected to such treatment that neither he nor anyone else who witnessed the execution of the sentence would offend again. The same sentiments were expressed whether the justices were dealing with a common thief or with workers indulging in industrial action. Churchmen as well as landowners subscribed to the view that harsh penalties were justified, indeed essential. As we saw in ch. I, the clerical justices tended to be as harsh as their colleagues in the sentences they imposed, even on workers who demonstrated against inadequate wages.[5] It would be a long time before this philosophy became unacceptable. There is ample evidence, however, to suggest that the great majority of justices did not impose the maximum sentence unless they were convinced that the criminal

---

5.   *Supra,* p. 35.

was not amenable to reform.6 Moreover, there were many instances of remarkably lenient sentences. It is clear that, when dealing with individuals whom they did not regard as hardened criminals, the justices took all the circumstances into consideration and usually imposed a sentence well below the maximum.

The sentencing of children even more than that of adults seems to modern eyes to have been excessively harsh. This was largely due to the fact that the law applied equally to all above the age of seven. Until 1847 children charged with indictable offences were tried at Assize and Quarter Sessions in the same manner as adult offenders and they were liable to receive the same sentence.7 In spite of this, there are many recorded instances of Quarter Sessions imposing light sentences on youngsters even when they appeared before them on successive occasions. The story of Moses Rose of Gloucester is a fairly typical example of how young criminals were treated by the justices in the early nineteenth century.

Moses Rose first came to the attention of the courts when he was aged 13. He was convicted of the theft of eight japanned trays for which he received a sentence of three months imprisonment, whereas the maximum sentence would have been two years imprisonment or transportation for seven years. In the following year he was charged successively with two further offences, but before the cases came to trial he was discharged by the Grand Jury who were dissatisfied with the *prima facie* evidence. A year later Rose was before the courts again charged with stealing. The sworn deposition makes it clear that this was a piece of professional shoplifting. He entered a small grocer's shop with a companion who distracted the shopkeeper by purporting to offer him some songs for sale. While the shopkeeper was attending to his friend, Rose stole half a pound of butter. When apprehended in a local beerhouse he attempted to get rid of the butter without this being detected. Having regard to his past record, the justices decided that they should impose an exemplary punishment, but even then the sentence was six months' imprisonment and whipping, which was well below the maximum sentence which could have been imposed. Two years after that Rose was again caught stealing, but this time he was tried at Assizes where the Judge sentenced him to transportation for life. He died a convict in Van Diemen's Land many years later.

One can always find examples on the other side, but these can almost invariably be related to an individual justice who was an exception to the general rule. These instances became fewer as Petty

6. Reference to *Criminal and Victim* by George Rudé, for example, demonstrates clearly that the maximum penalty was frequently not imposed.
7. The ages of young offenders which are given in court records at this time can be misleading. Compulsory registration of births was not introduced until 1837 and there was often no reliable evidence available of a young person's age.

Sessions assumed much of the role previously undertaken by a single justice. If the latter were insensitive, or even sadistic, he was kept in check by the majority of his colleagues. There were, of course, ways in which a vindictive individual justice could still vent his spleen, but usually he came to regret what he had done. There was the notorious Sir Thomas Throckmorton, a Gloucestershire justice, who was a chronic trouble-maker. He quarrelled with some of his colleagues and indulged in corrupt practices. There was an occasion when an old man who was taking a sugar loaf to Sir Thomas's house at Tortworth was asked what he was doing, and replied that he was going "to offer my candle to the devil." When this was reported to him, Sir Thomas avoided taking action which might enable his colleagues to intervene. He happened also to be a Deputy Lieutenant and at the next muster he pressed both the old man's sons into the army for the Low Countries where one died and the other paid heavily to buy his discharge. In consequence of his corrupt practices, Throckmorton was ultimately fined £2,200 by the Star Chamber and sentenced to imprisonment and public penance.[8]

Prosecutions
We have seen that the part played by constables in initiating prosecutions decreased during the eighteenth century. The justices themselves continued to make presentments, but a large numer of prosecutions came to be initiated by private individuals who hoped to benefit from a share of the fines in accordance with the provisions of various statutes. There was a further development during the century when Quarter Sessions were authorized in 1752 to pay allowances to prosecutors in cases of felony, the cost being borne by the county rate.[9] Later Acts extended these provisions to include witnesses, and in 1826 they were also made to cover misdemeanours.[10] The 1826 Act required Quarter Sessions to publish a scale of allowances after approval by a Judge of Assize, and most counties had done so by the early 1830s.

(2) Finance

Rates
Previous chapters have shown that from the time of the early Poor Law legislation, particularly the Act of 1601 (43 Eliz. I, c. 2 and c. 3), the justices in Quarter Sessions were authorized to levy an annual rate for the relief of poor prisoners and for the inmates of hospitals and almshouses. This was collected by the churchwardens and overseers

8.   Hawarde, *Reportes des Cases,* pp. 134-137, 243.
9.   25 Geo. II, c. 36.
10.   7 Geo. IV, c. 64.

and handed to the high constables and later to the treasurers.[11] The system was extended by further statutes, and by the eighteenth century rates were levied not only for poor relief but also for numerous other matters: highways and bridges, shirehalls and other county buildings, gaols and houses of correction, fees of Clerks of the Peace, and after 1853 their salaries. Money from the rates was also used to cover the cost of the constables in conveying prisoners vagabonds and military baggage. Payments were made to justices' clerks as well as to constables for executing the Militia Acts, and finally the rates also bore the cost of prosecutions of transportation and other sentences.[12]

Most rates were raised by the justices on a yearly basis, but sometimes special rates were levied to meet specific expenses. In the case of taxes payable to the national Government, such as land tax and window tax, the total amount for each county was fixed by the Government, but collection through the rate was left to the county authorities, and Quarter Sessions fixed the assessment for each hundred or parish. Although some Acts prescribed the manner in which rates were to be raised the justices generally were left with a large measure of discretion. Quarter Sessions decided the amount of the rate to be paid by each area which was then levied on the inhabitants in accordance with the property they owned, though it was assessed in different ways, sometimes in acreage, sometimes on rental value.

The law governing rates and their collection became so complicated that an Act was passed in 1739 "for the more easy assessing, collecting and levying of County Rates."[13] This remained the principal Act on rates until 1815 (55 Geo. III, c. 51). It replaced the multiplicity of separate rates by one general rate for most purposes. In the eighteenth century the normal procedure for the collection of rates was for the Clerk of the Peace or his deputy to issue warrants on behalf of Quarter Sessions to the high constables of each hundred, calling on them to collect their proportion of the total sum. The high constables divided the amount between the parishes in their hundreds, and this was collected by the parish constables and passed to the high constables. Where there was a poor rate it was collected by churchwardens and overseers who paid it to the high constables. The high constables handed over the money to the treasurers appointed by Quarter Sessions who were paid salaries, limited by the 1739 Act to £20 a year. The treasurers disbursed it as directed by Quarter Sessions to whom high constables as well as treasurers were accountable. Appeals against assessment lay to Quarter Sessions. No new rate might be imposed

11.   In 1844 (7 & 8 Vict., c. 33) the duty of collecting the county rate was transferred from the high constables to the newly established poor law guardians.
12.   An example of the levy of a rate is given in Appendix IV.
13.   12 Geo. II, c. 29.

until three-quarters of the money collected from the preceding rate had been spent.

The amount of the rate levied rose during the eighteenth century by as much as 15 times, and even more in some counties. This was due largely to higher expenditure on certain local requirements, such as highways and the poor, but at the end of the century a heavy additional demand arose from the wars with France which involved the expenditure of substantial sums on the militia, on raising men for the army and navy and for the maintenance of their families. Many justices protested that the cost of the war should be borne by national and not county funds.

Customs and Excise

An appreciable amount of time was spent by the justices in complying with the statutes relating to customs and excise. Evasion of the payment of duty was a common activity and during the Napoleonic Wars smuggling became a thriving industry. Goods imported, exported and carried coastwise were subject to duties set out in several Acts, the most extensive being that of 1787 (27 Geo. III, c. 13). Responsibility for collecting the duty rested with commissioners of customs. Alleged breaches of the regulations came before the justices who imposed penalties on the offenders. Special provisions applied to smugglers, and it was a felony for three or more persons armed with offensive weapons to attempt to smuggle goods. Persons charged with offences under the customs laws might be brought before a single justice on the information on oath of one or more credible witnesses. The justice then certified the information to one of the Secretaries of State who might order the offender to surrender within 40 days to a Judge of the King's Bench or to a JP, who thereupon committed him to gaol. The order was to be published and, if the offender failed to surrender in accordance with it, he was to be attainted of felony and dealt with accordingly.[14] The offence could be tried by the courts in any county.

Vessels, carriages, horses and cattle involved in the evasion of duty might be seized, subject to determination by two justices "whose judgment shall not be liable to any appeal or *certiorari.*"[15] The justices might also issue warrants for the sale of the items seized.

Excise matters, which still fell largely under an Act of Charles II,[16] were the responsibility of commissioners of excise whose head office was in London. Offenders against the excise laws were dealt with by the commissioners themselves in London but by two or more JPs in other areas. These might order fines and forfeiture and also impose

14.　　24 Geo. III, c. 4, s. 2.
15.　　8 Geo. III, c. 18.
16.　　12 Charles II, c. 24.

imprisonment "till satisfaction be made." As in the case of customs judgments, no appeal lay to Quarter Sessions nor elsewhere against a decision of the justices, except in certain types of case mentioned specifically in the statutes.

Annual licences were required by those selling a variety of goods. The principal of these were drinks (including tea, coffee and chocolate), bricks, tiles, candles, glass, leather, paper, salt, soap, sweets, tobacco and snuff. Duty was payable on each item sold.[17]

Under 19 Geo. III, c. 69, s. 32, any officer of customs and excise who "shall not use his best endeavours to seize any tea, coffee or foreign spirituous liquors ..." could be summoned to appear before a single JP "residing near where such officer shall make default." The justice might, on complaint, examine the officer and if he thought fit, transmit his findings to the Commissioners of Customs and Excise who might dismiss the individual from the service.

The enforcement of the customs and excise laws was an area in which one may observe a peculiar defect in the JP system in that the justices were often lacking in enthusiasm to uphold the law, and on occasions were positively obstructive. This was a weakness which was not likely to be found in whole-time professional magistrates deployed by the Government from the centre and whose concern would be to satisfy the authorities who had appointed them. Such officers would probably have had little regard for local feeling where this clashed with national policy. There were many instances, however, where Justices of the Peace were evasive in the implementation of the law on excise and tax payments. A similar attitude was to be seen among the justices in coastal areas who were faced with the activities of wreckers as explained later when discussing "Police".

Prices and Wages

The justices continued to have responsibility for regulating certain trades, but generally they were less involved in this sphere than before. They also became less concerned in the fixing of prices and wages. With the advent of the Industrial Revolution the level of wages became largely a matter for the employers and the workforce (giving rise to acute industrial unrest) and the fixing of rates by the justices practically ceased except in certain cases. The new economic climate mitigated against the justices' intrusion into the labour market and the Government came to regard the fixing of maximum prices and wages as undesirable and unnecessary. In 1756 an Act[18] was passed giving justices power to decide the level of wages to be paid in the wool

17.   See Burn, 18 ed., vol. II, pp. 44-286.
18.   29 Geo. II, c. 33.

industry, but in the following year this was repealed[19] on the ground that "it is found impracticable to form any general rate of wages which would be just, adequate and suitable to the several branches and circumstances of the said manufacture." The justices retained the power, however, to fix the price at which flour was sold by millers and bread sold by bakers.

It was in the same spirit of non-intervention that Parliament passed an Act in 1771 repealing earlier enactments against forestalling, engrossing and regrating.[20]

(3) Militia

Responsibility for the militia rested largely with the Lords Lieutenant and the Deputy Lieutenants, but the justices were also involved to an appreciable extent, partly because most DLs were also JPs and partly because a number of duties relating to the militia were placed upon the justices by statute.

The administration of the militia was in the hands of Lieutenancy meetings. Most of the work was done at divisional meetings which consisted of at least two DLs, but where two did not attend one DL and one JP might perform all the duties. These included the preparation of lists of those who were to serve in the militia and the swearing in and enrolling of the men. The cost of the militia was borne on rates levied by churchwardens or overseers on the inhabitants of the parish, subject to appeal to Quarter Sessions. Those who failed to attend training (28 days a year on dates fixed by the Lieutenancy) were to be brought before a single justice who might fine them £20, with up to six months imprisonment in default of payment. Billeting was the responsibility of the mayor, bailiffs, constables and "other chief magistrates and officers" or in default of these it could be done by a JP.[21] Annual reports on the names, numbers, ranks and times of training had to be sent to the Clerk of the Peace who transmitted them to the Treasury and the Receiver General. If the Clerk of the Peace did not receive an annual certificate showing that the militia had been raised, he reported the failure to Quarter Sessions, and the county was obliged to pay £5 for every man who was not raised. The JPs at the sessions assessed the rate upon the county. Justices could make orders for payment out of the poor rate of relief to families of those serving.[22] Subalterns who did not have estate that would qualify them for captaincy were entitled to a special allowance on taking an oath before

19. 30 Geo. II, c. 12.
20. 12 Geo. III, c. 71.
21. 26 Geo. III, c. 107, s. 78.
22. 35 Geo. III, c. 81.

a JP of their county.[23]

Deserters were to be taken before a single justice for examination. He might commit the deserter to the county gaol or house of correction to await disposal. He then forwarded an account of the proceedings to the county Lieutenancy meeting for subsequent trial by court-martial.[24] This was another example of there being no right of appeal against the decision of a justice, for it was declared that no order or conviction should be removed by *certiorari*, and no execution or other proceedings upon such order be superseded thereby.[25]

The militia was generally an inefficient and unreliable body. Its object was to act as a force for home defence within a restricted area. During the century it was often called upon to quell riots, as we shall see later in this chapter, but this was an area in which the regular army also played a part: in both instances the military were supposed to act in support of the justices in maintaining order.

Apart from giving orders to quell disturbances, the justices were concerned with the regular army and navy only to the extent of assisting in the drafting of recruits and in their transfer to ports of embarkation.

(4) Highways

The maintenance of highways could still be enforced by the presentment of a parish or of anyone else who had failed in their duty to maintain. The presentment could be made by a single justice on his own knowledge or by the Grand Jury, and the matter was then tried at Quarter Sessions and the inhabitants of the parish might be fined a substantial sum. This was, however, usually suspended for three months to allow the parish to carry out the repairs subject to inspection by one or more justices, who would issue a certificate if they found the work satisfactory. If the parish failed to do the work the fine was levied by the sheriff on the inhabitants and was handed to the surveyors or to someone else to be spent on the repair. As in previous centuries, there were some justices who rode about the countryside observing the condition of the roads and threatening presentment at the next Quarter Sessions if repairs were not carried out.

The justices' involvement in highways was extended by an Act of 1691[26] under which they were to hold sessions in January each year when they were to nominate surveyors of highways from lists submitted by the constables and inhabitants of parishes. Special sessions were also to be held every four months at which the justices

23.   35 Geo. III, c. 35.
24.   26 Geo. III, c. 107.
25.   *Ibid.*, s. 133.
26.   3 William and Mary, c. 12.

might levy a rate if they were satisfied that the highways could not be repaired without it. Another Act, of 1697,[27] empowered Quarter Sessions to enlarge highways and to compensate landowners who were affected.

The use of roads continued to increase during the eighteenth century, especially for the carriage of merchandise and for the passage of persons both on business and for pleasure. In particular, the upper classes travelled frequently to London or to one of the spas. There was a particular need to protect the highways from damage caused by the greater use of wheeled vehicles. All this added to the work of the justices in ensuring that the roads were kept in repair, a task in which they proved to be singularly ineffective. The justices blamed the state of the roads on increasing use by persons who had no connexion with the area, and they were reluctant to place the heavy burden of repair upon the inhabitants of their own neighbourhood. Their aim therefore was to restrict the use of highways rather than to make the passage easier. Parliament sought to meet the situation by passing as many as 18 General Acts in the course of some 70 years.[28] These Acts did little to place extra responsibility on the justices, which is not surprising as they still accounted for the majority of the Members of Parliament, but unintentionally the legislation added to the justices' burden because most of the Acts were confusing and much time was spent on their interpretation. For example, the justices were often required to decide whether the proper number of horses were being used to draw a vehicle and were suitably harnessed. The permitted number varied from one Act to another and according to the type of vehicle, its weight, the number of wheels, the character of the load and the circumstances in which it was being used, and the justices had a discretion to allow more horses to be used on steep hills than were permitted normally.[29]

A codifying Act was passed in 1766[30] which repealed all previous legislation, and this was replaced by another codifying Act in 1772[31] under which special highway sessions were to be held in the week after Michaelmas Quarter Sessions, and any two justices could hold such sessions whenever they thought fit. These special sessions would be held, for example, to appoint a new surveyor or replace one who had died during his term of office. Prior to the Michaelmas sessions the constables, churchwardens, surveyors of highways and householders assembled at the church to assess the parochial rate and to prepare a

---

27.   8 & 9 William and Mary, c. 16.
28.   For details see Webb *ELG: The Story of the King's Highway,* p. 81, note to p. 74.
29.   Burn commented that "if a person would know what number of horses or beasts in cart or waggon are allowed ..." he must look at ten different Acts passed at different times, "before he shall be sure that he hath found all which the law hath enacted concerning the same ...".
30.   7 Geo. III, c. 42.
31.   13 Geo. III, c. 78.

list of at least 10 persons having estates of not less than £10 value a year, or personal estate of £100 or a tenement of £30 yearly value. At the sessions themselves the justices appointed from this list one or more surveyors for the ensuing year. If the justices did not think that those in the list were suitable they might appoint others. Any refusing to serve forfeited £5. The justices delivered to each new surveyor a statement of his duties and each surveyor on appointment had to pay the justices' clerk a fee of one shilling.

The justices could also prescribe the manner in which a highway was to be repaired and could fix the time when this was to be done. They were also given power to widen or divert highways and footpaths and to stop up any that were found to be unnecessary. Further powers to stop and divert were given to them by an Act of 1815[32] which also provided for notice of the proceedings to be published in newspapers. The Act of 1697 allowed appeal to Quarter Sessions by persons damaged by the action of the justices. This remained the law until the Highway Act of 1835.[33]

Stopping Up and Diverting Roads and Footpaths
Before 1815 there was no legal means of stopping up either a highway or a footpath other than by writ of *ad quod damnum* issued by the Lord Chancellor, ordering the sheriff to summon a jury to inquire whether the proposed closure or diversion would be injurious to the public. If the jury returned a favourable verdict, Quarter Sessions could make an order. This was costly and the cases when the procedure was resorted to were rare. Until the end of the eighteenth century landowners had no desire to close the roads and footpaths which crossed their land and which were used almost entirely by farm labourers and by a few other local inhabitants; but as the urban areas increased, the townsfolk spread out into the adjoining countryside and were regarded as a nuisance by those over whose land they wandered. The landowners, many of whom were justices, took action by placing physical obstructions across the paths and by erecting signs threatening dire consequences if anybody passed along them. There was no statutory authority for them to do this and therefore, as might be expected, the landed gentry in Parliament secured the passage of a Bill in 1815 which gave power to any two justices acting summarily to close any footpath which they considered to be unnecessary, subject to appeal to the next Quarter Sessions. There is no doubt that many justices exercised these new powers in their own interest and in that of their friends. They regarded the Act as having been passed purely for

32.   55 Geo. III, c. 68, s. 2.
33.   5 & 6 William IV, c. 50.

their own benefit, which in a sense it was, as those responsible for introducing the legislation and securing its passage, against radical opposition, looked upon it in this light. There were no complaints during the eighteenth century and earlier about the way in which the justices used their powers to stop up or divert a highway, but they became numerous and clamorous during the nineteenth century when it was alleged that the justices regularly abused their authority to stop up or divert all types of public thoroughfare, and that it was extremely difficult to have the orders quashed at Quarter Sessions. The reputation of the Justices of the Peace was brought into disrepute by many of their number who used their new statutory powers purely for their own advantage.

Turnpike Roads

In spite of the new statutory provisions, the state of the roads remained deplorable, partly because of the failure of the justices to implement the legislation. The need to improve communications led to the construction of canals and of turnpike roads. The latter were under the control of Turnpike Trusts which improved and maintained the road surfaces and were authorized by local Acts of Parliament to recoup their expenses by levying tolls. The idea of making the users of the roads pay for the cost of maintenance met with the full approval of the justices and most of them became members of a Trust, some serving on more than one simultaneously. This could take up a considerable amount of time, especially if, as often happened, they had to travel long distances to attend meetings. An additional burden to the justices was the need to deal with outbreaks of violence which occurred frequently when local people who objected to the turnpikes would tear down the gates and the houses of the keepers.

As already mentioned, the first of the Turnpike Trusts was legalized in Cambridgeshire in 1663, and in the last half of the seventeenth century Parliament accepted the petitions of a number of counties and passed local Acts enabling Quarter Sessions to erect gates and levy tolls whose proceeds were to be spent on improving and maintaining specified lengths of roadway. In most cases the result was not entirely successful owing to local opposition and to the ease of evasion. The idea of the turnpike road, however, (the term was first used in an Essex Act of 1695)[34] was attractive to the Government and Parliament as well as to the justices, and from 1706 onwards numerous Acts were passed establishing new statutory bodies to levy tolls and maintain highways and which were quite distinct from Quarter Sessions. Whereas the previous bodies of this kind were composed solely of JPs, the Trusts were made up of persons named in the Acts, most but not

34.   7 & 8 William III, c. 9.

all of whom were justices. Subsequent vacancies were filled by co-option. Almost every justice served on at least one Trust. Regular meetings of the trustees were held quarterly, but they often met more frequently.

Although the Trusts had powers to construct and maintain highways, this did not relieve the parishes of their obligation to repair the same road if it was defective, and the Trust surveyor had authority to employ statutory labour for a number of days per annum, the period being sometimes specified in the Act and sometimes left to the Trust subject to appeal to two justices in petty or special sessions. The trustees also had authority to arrange with parishes for the payment of an agreed amount to be raised on the rates by the parish surveyor in lieu of statutory labour.

The Turnpike Acts usually limited the Trusts to periods of 21 years. It seems to have been assumed that within this time the roads would have been put into a condition which would make it reasonable to dispense with the turnpike and to return to the previous system of maintenance. With this in mind Parliament usually provided that if all the debts were paid and the road was in a satisfactory state, the justices might terminate the provisions of the Act before it expired. The legislature, and its numerous JP members, however, soon came to the opinion that the need for turnpikes did not vanish, as had been expected, within 21 years. By the 1720s the turnpikes were well established, and by 1727 a number of general enactments had been added to the local Acts for dealing with turnpike roads. These included provisions raising the penalty for destroying turnpike gates and houses from whipping with three months' hard labour to death.[35] The law on the subject was consolidated in a comprehensive General Turnpike Act of 1773[36] and in a further Act of 1822.[37]

Between the 1750s and 1780s there was a tremendous improvement in highways and by the end of the century most of the larger towns and industrial centres were linked by turnpike roads, though this amounted to only about a sixth of the total mileage of highways in England and Wales. There was a good deal of corruption in the administration of some of the less important turnpikes, but generally speaking the system was a success and it might have been assumed that it would have had a long future ahead of it. The turnpikes were driven out of business, however, in the nineteenth century by the railways, and the management of the roads reverted largely to the local authorities, though these were the new elected bodies in which the JPs were no longer concerned. Until then, the local justices who were trustees

35. 18 Geo. II, c. 20.
36. 13 Geo. III, c. 84.
37. 3 Geo IV, c. 126.

played a prominent part in the operations, often taking the lead in promoting schemes for general improvement. There were other occasions, but apparently less frequent, when justices acted in their own interests with adverse effect.

(5) Police

Arrangements for policing the country remained the same as they had been since Tudor times, and responsibility for detecting and apprehending criminals and for bringing them to trial, and also for quelling disturbances, continued to rest with the justices, supported by constables and to an increasing extent by the military.

The detection and arrest of offenders presented similar problems to those encountered in previous centuries, and the pattern of crime remained largely the same, but certain offences came to the fore. The towns were infested with pickpockets while highwaymen became a menace to travellers on the roads. In some instances the justices' difficulties increased in consequence of the obligation to enforce rigid new laws. This was particularly so in cases where the sympathy of the local population lay with the offender and where the justices themselves were loath to intervene, such as those relating to customs and excise. This often arose in coastal areas where the justices were required to suppress the smuggling trade which boomed after the outbreak of the wars with France, and where the smugglers were supported by a substantial number of the population. In addition to this the justices near the coasts had long been bedevilled by the custom of wrecking. The inhabitants of islands and of coastal areas of the mainland regarded the looting of shipwrecks as perfectly legitimate, and indeed relied upon it as a way of supplementing their meagre supplies. As the number of wrecks grew with the increase in merchant shipping the local justices, who tended to sympathize with the wreckers, were hard-pressed to salve their consciences, not only when administering the criminal law but when called upon to aid the owners of the ships and their cargoes.[38]

The greatest increase in the burden thrown upon the justices arose from the industrial unrest which was an integral part of the huge expansion in trade and industry that occurred from the latter part of the eighteenth century onwards. The justices had always been responsible for quelling local riots which erupted fairly frequently during previous centuries. Mostly these were small outbreaks of disorder arising from attempts by constables to make arrests, but sometimes they were demonstrations by discontented labourers, and it

---

38.   For an example see "The Wreck of the Hornby Brig," *The Justice of the Peace* journal, June 13, 1987, p. 379.

was the latter which increased in scale with the Industrial Revolution. Large numbers of workers congregated in or near urban centres to air their grievances, presenting a real or a supposed threat to the peace, and sometimes the gathering terminated in a full scale riot. The forces normally at the disposal of the peacekeepers were totally inadequate to deal with these events and the justices were obliged to rely increasingly upon the military, either the militia or the national army. To strengthen their arm, the Riot Act of 1715, which re-enacted much of an earlier Act of 1549, was passed. This made it a capital offence for a crowd of 12 or more persons to remain together for more than one hour after a justice had read a proclamation specified in the Act ordering them to disperse. The principal object of the Act was to enable the military to break up a crowd by force, but it was not always implemented effectively. Doubts were expressed as to how long the troops must wait before they intervened and as to whether they were obliged to obey orders from the justices or whether the latter's reading of the proclamation merely enabled them to act at their discretion. Public sympathy, and sometimes that of the troops themselves, usually lay with the rioters, and both the army and the justices ran the risk of revenge. There was the famous case of Captain Porteous who, in 1736, was sentenced to death for firing on a crowd in Edinburgh, but before his execution the mob broke into the prison and lynched him.[39] Likewise, the justices might have their homes destroyed by the mob. Several examples of this occurred during the Gordon Riots in 1780. On the other hand, the justices were severely criticized if subsequent events suggested that the violence did not justify the use of the military. More often than not the justice, having arrived at the behest of a constable or sometimes a military commander, experienced difficulty in deciding what action, if any, he should take, and if he hesitated too long he was censured for failing to perform his duty. One well known incident of this kind, which was to figure prominently in political propaganda, became known as the "massacre of Peterloo." In August 1819 a large demonstration was held in an open space in Manchester called St Peter's Field. The authorities had ample notice of the event through the wide advance publicity which had been given. Accordingly 12 JPs assembled in a building overlooking the area in which the demonstration was to take place, while detachments of yeomanry and infantry were stationed nearby. After speakers began to address the crowds, but before serious disturbance had developed, the Riot Act proclamation was read, the justices ordered the yeomanry to charge and a number of persons in the crowd were killed. The justices,

39.   Many of those who became senior commanders later in their careers had had experience of quelling riots when they were junior officers. James Wolfe, for example, the general who captured Quebec, exercised one of his first commands when he was called upon by the Bristol justices to quell rioting by the weavers of the Stroud area in 1756.

who included three clergymen, were severely censured in Parliament and elsewhere and in general their reputation suffered considerably from this event which occurred at a time when the whole system of lay magistrates was falling into disrepute. So far as the twelve Peterloo justices were concerned, they were exonerated by the Government which, as a matter of policy, supported the justices upon whom they were still obliged to rely as police authority. The Home Secretary, Lord Sidmouth, thanked them on behalf of the Prince Regent, though he commented that it was government policy to support the justices when they performed honest and reasonable acts without inquiring too closely into the merits of each case.

After the Gordon Riots in 1780 there were calls for the establishment of a police force, but when, as we shall see in the next chapter, the Government introduced a Bill in 1785 to set up such a body for London and Westminster it was defeated. London did not get its police force until 1829 and it took another 30 years for the rest of the country to follow.

(6) Paupers and Vagrants

The Poor
The administration of the Poor Law, which was at its height by the end of the eighteenth century, occupied the largest portion of the justices' time, even though the day-to-day work was conducted by the overseers. It was generally regarded as the most important and difficult part of the justices' work apart from keeping the peace. It involved Petty Sessions and justices sitting alone as well as Quarter Sessions. Some Quarter Sessions were occupied for half of their time in these matters, and individual justices might be involved almost every day in settling disputes. For a hundred years before the Poor Law reform of 1834, the cost of its administration, which rose throughout the period, was greater than that for all the rest of local government together. A Parliamentary report of 1813 showed that poor relief during the previous year had amounted to £6,656,000, and that in addition removals and law charges came to £324,957.[40] There was a sharp rise towards the end of the eighteenth and in the early nineteenth century. In 1740-1750 the average cost was £689,971, for 1783-1785 it was £1,912,241 and for 1803 it was £4,077,891. The amount varied with each parish. Thus, in the Gloucestershire village of Micheldean, which was typical of many, it rose during the last half of the century from £50 a year to over £500 for a population of less than 600. In Blockley, with a rather larger population, the cost had risen from £120 in 1695 to £748 in 1795; by 1815 it had reached £1,291 and by 1830 £1,670. Four

40.   Sir G. Nicholls, *History of English Poor Law* (1904) vol. 2, p. 165.

years later the rates were greatly eased by the Poor Law Amendment Act, 1834.

The duty to relieve the poor fell primarily upon the overseers while it was the justices' duty to ensure that they performed their functions satisfactorily. This is shown clearly by the innumerable directions of Quarter Sessions contained in the Order Books. For instance:

"Little Walsingham overseers to pay 12d a week towards maintenance of Ralph Hambling. If they refuse, to be bound over to next sessions."

"Taverham overseers to provide a habitation for John Howard, a very poor old man. Otherwise, attachment against them."[41]

The overseers were able to pay sums of money to the sick and infirm to enable them to obtain necessities such as fuel. Where necessary they could also call upon people in the neighbourhood to take care of them for a fee. The sums paid by the overseers for these purposes had to be approved by Quarter Sessions to whom the overseers were required to submit their accounts. The following extract from Essex Quarter Sessions records of 1748 is typical of many:[42]

May	John Parker to buy wood	6d
	Paid widow Hasler to look after John Parker	2.0
June	Paid Thomas Johnson for a coffin for John Parker	6.0
	Paid the Church Clerk his fees	3.6
	Paid widow Hasler for looking after John Parker	2.0
	Paid widow Hasler and her sister for sitting up and looking after John Parker	3.0
	Paid Mrs Prior for sitting up with John Parker	1.0
	Paid widow Hasler for taking affidavit for John Parker	1.0
	Paid Arthur Clark for beer the woman had that sat up with John Parker and the men that carried him	3.0
Nov	Paid Mr Rix to bury John Parker	2.0

The eighteenth century Poor Law was still based on Tudor legislation, particularly the Acts of 1597 and 1601, with its threefold

41.   Norfolk QS Order Book, 1650-1657, paras. 283, 218.
42.   Essex RD, D/P 1/12.

approach: the relief of the aged and impotent poor; the setting of able-bodied poor to work, including the apprenticing of children; and the suppression of rogues and vagabonds. The cost was covered by a rate levied on the inhabitants of each parish and assessed by two justices (one of the *Quorum*) living in or near the parish or division. Appeals against assessment lay to Quarter Sessions who might quash or amend the rate. The overseers levied the rate with power to distress on a warrant from two justices (one of the *Quorum*).

Although trade and industry increased rapidly towards the end of the century, agriculture remained the largest employer of labour, but the conditions of the working population in rural areas deteriorated as a result of enclosures and of the ending of home industries. Wages did not keep pace with the rising cost of living and far larger numbers than before applied for assistance. There was little uniformity in the rates of relief. This was usually governed by the price of flour or bread which fluctuated, and some overseers were more generous than others while the justices, to whom an applicant might appeal, varied even more widely. A pauper might appeal to Quarter Sessions or to a single justice; the latter being the most usual course. On these occasions the justices often showed a remarkable degree of compassion and overrode the overseers, though in so doing they undermined the overseers' authority and thereby weakened the system.[43]

Workhouses and Houses of Industry

The Elizabethan Act (43 Eliz., c. 2) of 1601 had provided for the poor to be given flax, hemp, wool and other materials, presumably to enable them to carry out productive work in their own homes, but although the justices and the overseers were expected to supervise the work they were given no power to acquire or erect premises in which it could be carried out. By the end of the seventeenth century the general practice was merely to provide outdoor relief to any who seemed to be destitute. This led to a steady increase in the cost and a consequential rise in the rates.

The answer seemed to be to set the able-bodied poor to profitable work in supervised institutions. For a long time many villages had maintained poorhouses which were little better than shelters with no provision for food, but near the end of the seventeenth century an enthusiastic movement began to provide the poor with paid work which they were compelled to undertake. This took the form of providing workhouses, one of the earliest of which was opened in Bristol under a Local Act of 1696, which provided for a workhouse to be erected and maintained at public expense. It was to house both

43.   Under an Act of 1722 (9 Geo. I, c. 7) a justice could not overrule the overseer unless the pauper swore on oath that there were reasonable grounds for relief and the justice heard the case of the overseer as well as that of the pauper.

those who, through age and infirmity, were unable to work and also the able-bodied who would be forced to work and would be provided with tools and materials for this purpose. Parents unable to maintain their children could send them to the workhouse where they would be instructed in work and discipline and ultimately apprenticed. The whole operation was to be under the management of a Corporation of the Poor consisting of the mayor, aldermen, churchwardens and four persons elected at a public meeting of the inhabitants of each ward. It was stated in the Act that these arrangements would free the magistrates of the daily trouble they had about settlement.[44] Between 1696 and 1712 thirteen other towns obtained Local Acts enabling them to establish similar institutions. In practice the workhouses differed from one area to another according to the views taken as to their purpose, and they varied from a means of providing profitable employment to a house of correction or a hospital for the sick.

In 1723 a General Act enabled parish officers to hire premises and maintain them as workhouses. Later Acts allowed parishes to combine to establish a joint workhouse. The same idea was behind the creation of "houses of industry," the earliest of which was established in Suffolk by a group of substantial citizens including several JPs. In 1756 they obtained a Local Act which established a new Poor Law authority comprising twenty-eight parishes in two hundreds. The authority, called the Incorporated Guardians of the Poor, was empowered to operate the Poor Law and to erect a building. Overall responsibility was entrusted to all JPs in the area together with all freeholders and leaseholders of land above a specified value and all local rectors and vicars. These elected a number of directors and acting guardians in whom the management was placed. In 1783 Shrewsbury obtained a Local Act to set up a house of industry under the control of all owners of freehold worth £30 a year and all inhabitants rated at £15 a year. These appointed a number of officers and also elected twelve directors of the poor who were in charge of the direction of the project. One of the advantages of these schemes was that they enabled several parishes to combine in the creation of a workhouse, and they reduced the number of settlement disputes between parishes. An unforeseen result was that paupers were reluctant to seek assistance for fear of being subjected to the régime in the new institutions, and the number of claimants for relief was therefore reduced.

None of the Local Acts relieved the JPs of their responsibility for supervising the Poor Law, and the directors and acting guardians were obliged to submit their accounts to Quarter Sessions; yet in practice they acted at their own discretion and without interference from the

44.   7 & 8 William III, c. 32.

justices. At the same time, the parish officers took their orders from the new directors and acting guardians who could fine them for failing to perform their duties as the justices had done previously.

For a time the new institutions, which were virtually independent and which were copied in a number of areas, thrived and met with general approval, at least from the upper classes. They did not, however, achieve the high hopes of their founders and they ultimately fell into disrepute. In practice, the management of the houses of industry came to be left in the hands of officials, the directors and acting governors not taking the trouble to attend meetings or to visit the houses. Moreover, outdoor relief continued to be paid and it increased as parishes came to realize that it was cheaper to proceed in this way instead of maintaining people in work in the houses. Consequently the poor rate was not reduced as had been expected. The poor themselves preferred relief instead of being dragooned into the institutions. In some places they broke into open rebellion, demanding a return to the old system, but they were soon crushed by the military.

The houses also proved to be breeding grounds of epidemics. They were insanitary and lacking in accommodation. There was also much promiscuity and the houses were the scene of great cruelty by the contractors to whom they were farmed out and who underpaid those who worked for them. To meet this the justices would order the overseers to pay the workers an additional sum to make up the difference between the wage they received and the minimum standard.

The shortcomings of the institutional system could be blamed on lack of effective control. The resident governors were left free to exploit the inmates to their own advantage and the directors failed to exhibit the interest taken by the Justices of the Peace in the bodies for which they were directly responsible. The creation of these new authorities was, however, of great significance for the future of the JPs because from them was derived a new type of local authority which may be said to have provided the prototype for the democratically elected bodies with a full-time, salaried bureaucracy which took over the administrative functions of the county justices a hundred years later.

The Speenhamland system
The most momentous intervention by the justices themselves, although one which ultimately collapsed, was at Speenhamland in Berkshire. As in previous centuries poor harvests invariably caused great distress among the labouring classes. In 1794 the harvest was a fifth below the average for the previous three years with the result that the price of corn almost doubled while, as usual, wages did not rise in proportion.

In January 1795 Berkshire Quarter Sessions decided that the poor rate should be used to augment wages and they summoned a meeting of all the county justices and certain other persons to decide upon the details of the new scheme. This historic meeting was held at the Pelican Inn at Speenhamland in May 1795 at which a new system was adopted. It was confirmed that the justices would not use their statutory powers to fix minimum wages. Instead, the overseers were to be ordered to supplement wages when the price of bread rose by a certain amount, the scale varying according to the size of the family whether or not they were legitimate.[45] One of the objects of this well-intentioned scheme was to save the poor from the degradation of the workhouse. It proved to be misguided. Had the justices exercised their powers to fix minimum wages the cost would have fallen upon the employers who benefited from the rise in prices, but the Speenhamland system was largely the cause of the huge increase in the cost of poor relief which fell on the ratepayers.

It was a feature of the eighteenth century that, in the absence of statutory rules, Quarter Sessions frequently adopted regulations drawn up by the justices in another county, and the Speenhamland system was quickly followed in most other parts of the country, except in the north. It is clear that the justices were deeply concerned by the plight of the poor and were anxious to take all reasonable steps to mitigate it. At first the scheme seemed to be a satisfactory solution to the problem, but in the course of time it became apparent that the situation had become worse. Farmers kept wages low, knowing that they would be made up from public funds, while labourers, realizing that they and their families would always be supported, made little effort to work. Pauperism throughout the country became worse than ever. The justices' well-intentioned ideas came to be criticized as being those of members of the employing classes who were reluctant to raise wages when it might be difficult to reduce them later, but there is no evidence that this charge was justified.

The Speenhamland experiment was not entirely original as there had been previous occasions when cash payments were made to able-bodied persons whose wages were insufficient to suport their families, but it was a turning point in the patterns of poor relief leading to the major reforms of 1834.

Poverty caused by Natural Disaster
People who were comfortably off were sometimes reduced to poverty

45. It was agreed that: "when the gallon loaf of seconds flour weighing 8 lb. 11 oz. shall cost one shilling, then every poor and industrious man shall have for his own support three shillings weekly, either produced by his own and his family's labour, or an allowance from the Poor Rates, and for the support of his wife and every other of his family one and sixpence." The rate was to vary according to the price of the gallon loaf.

suddenly by having their homes and all their possessions destroyed by fire. Such destruction was a frequent occurrence in the time of timber houses and no fire-fighting services. On these occasions the person who was left destitute would apply to the justices for relief and in the case of small amounts Quarter Sessions would order the county treasurer to make a payment. In more serious cases the sessions would certify the genuineness of the claim to the central government which would authorize application for help on a wider scale. Instances of both these sets of circumstances are to be found in many Quarter Sessions records from the seventeenth century and earlier. For example, in the Norfolk Quarter Sessions Order Book of 1650-1657, compiled during the Commonwealth, we find (para. 779): "Bridget Durrant lost near £40, and her grandchild burnt, proved by oath of John Curby of Antingham. Court allowed her 20 nobles, to be paid by Treasurers ..." In the case of a large amount an order reads (para. 745): "Petition of John Cooke, of Waiborne, yeoman, attested by Chief Constables of Hold, and Minister and Chief inhabitants of Waiborne. Houses burnt by dreadful fire March 27 last, and goods destroyed. Loss of least £300, he and family ruined if no relief. Asks recommendation to His Highness for letters patent for asking the benevolence of well disposed persons, as usually done in like cases. Granted."

Apprenticeship
We have seen that the justices were responsible from Tudor times for apprenticing the young and for settling disputes between apprentices and their masters. County archives contain large numbers of records of apprenticeship orders and of disputes, the latter often involving charges of assault which were examined in detail by the justices and which occupied a substantial amount of time at Quarter Sessions.

The apprenticeship system was open to abuse on a considerable scale and there were undoubtedly many cases in which great suffering occurred. The possibility of a child being apprenticed to a cruel employer was illustrated vividly by Dickens in ch. III of *Oliver Twist* when Oliver was saved by the two justices from a harsh fate, though both of them cut uninspiring figures. It is clear nevertheless from the orders which have been recorded that in a large proportion of cases the justices' inquiry was reasonably thorough and that they refused to make an order if they were not satisfied with the integrity of the prospective master. There were also very many cases in which, after the apprenticeship had begun, the master's conduct was unsatisfactory and the justices therefore discharged the apprentice. During the Civil War many apprentices served in one or other of the opposing armies, and in some cases their masters refused to accept them back into service at the end of hostilities. Such cases were referred to the justices who usually ordered the master to receive the apprentice on pain of attachment for contempt.

Settlement

Until 1834 the settlement of paupers was governed by the Act of Settlement and Removal of 1662, under which any person likely to become chargeable to the poor rate was made to reside in the parish where he was 'settled' which was usually his birthplace, and if he were found elsewhere he was forcibly sent back to his place of origin. The reason behind the Act, which is clear from the preamble, was that previously paupers tended to move away from the less generous parishes to those where they were likely to be treated more bountifully. Under the law, enforced by the justices, tens of thousands of poor persons were compulsorily moved every year from one poor law area to another. Pregnant women were turned out of the parish so that their children should not be born there and so establish a settlement right. Cottages might be destroyed to prevent them being occupied by potential paupers. One of the worst aspects of settlement cases was that they could break up families and disperse the children among different parishes.[46] As we shall see in the following chapter, many of these homeless people ultimately found their way to London, where they were able to remain because of the lax administration of the Poor Law in that area. In most counties the authorities showed concern for the aged and infirm, but they treated the able-bodied poor with great harshness.

Under s. 1 of the 1662 Act the churchwardens or overseers in any parish could complain to a single justice within 40 days after a person came "to settle in any tenement under the yearly value of £10" in the parish, and the justice could then issue a warrant to bring the party before him for examination. It then required two justices, however, (one of the *Quorum*) to order the removal of the individual to the parish where he was last legally settled. If he failed to comply, a single justice might send him to a house of correction to be punished as a vagabond (s. 3). There was a right of appeal to Quarter Sessions against the ruling of the two justices. It was common practice for the parish to which the pauper was to be sent to lodge an appeal, and

46. The Rev. F.E. Witts, recorded in his diary on April 27, 1821: "The overseer at Halling brought up two gypsies, casual poor in their parish in order to their being examined to their settlement. Lock the husband swore that he was born under an oak on Halling Down as he had heard from his mother, being an illegitimate child and knowing nothing of his father: also that he was recently married to his wife Mary with whom he had cohabited 20 years, having by her six children. It seems that the Parish of Halling has little or no chance of proving him settled elsewhere. On examining the woman, she swore all the children to be Lock's - Lucas and Adam born like their father in the parish of Halling - Eve at Cold Ashton - Sarah at Brimpsfield - Temperance at Hawkesbury - Joanna at Cranham. The law was strictly interpreted and removal orders were made in respect of the last four children, sending them to their respective birth places." Hawkesbury and Cranham appealed against the order but it was upheld at the Trinity Quarter Sessions.

many were successful. An example is to be found in Appendix IV.

Anyone who unlawfully returned to the place from which he had been removed by order of two justices was deemed to be an idle and disorderly person, and any one justice (on his own view, or the individual's confession, or on the oath of one credible witness) might commit him or her to the house of correction to undergo hard labour for not more than one month.[47] If the churchwardens or overseers of the parish to which the person had been removed refused to receive him and to provide work for him, any justice of the division was to bind them over to appear at Assizes or Quarter Sessions to be indicted for contempt.[48] Under a later Act[49], if any churchwarden or overseer refused to accept a person in accordance with a warrant of two justices, a single justice could order the offender to forfeit £5 to be used for the poor of the parish or town from which the person was removed. Failing payment, the justices might commit the offender to the common gaol for 40 days.

The Act of 1662 enabled justices to remove persons who were likely to become chargeable on a parish, but this provision was repealed by an Act of 1795[50] which enacted that no person might be removed from the parish which he inhabited to the place of his legal settlement unless he became actually chargeable "to the place where he shall inhabit." If, however, any person convicted of larceny or other felony, or deemed a rogue, vagabond, or an idle or disorderly person, or who appeared to two justices where he resided to be a person of evil fame or a reputed thief, he was to be considered a person actually chargeable within the meaning of the Act and might be removed to his place of settlement. The same provision applied to an unmarried woman with child.

The thought uppermost in the minds of the ratepayers of each parish was the avoidance as far as possible of any increase in the poor relief which the parish had to pay. It was for this reason that so many inter-parish settlement disputes came before Quarter Sessions, and where it was not possible to throw the burden onto another area steps were taken to see that private individuals were made to support their relatives if they had sufficient resources. Thus:

"Petition of Cley Inhabitants. Robert Woodwell died poor leaving a widow and four children chargeable. Their grandfather, John Woodwell, lived at Trowse with an estate of £30 a year, and should contribute. Ordered, he is to pay Cley overseers 2/6 a week."[51]

47.   17 Geo. II, c. 5, s. 1.
48.   13 & 14 Charles II, c. 12.
49.   3 William III, c. 11.
50.   35 Geo. III, c. 101.
51.   Norfolk QS Order Book, 1650-1657, para. 412.

Rigid application of the law of settlement could have resulted in employers being unable to obtain labour even when there were unemployed persons seeking work eslewhere. To meet this situation, 8 & 9 William III, c. 30, provided that where a person was unable to find work in his own parish, he might seek it in another parish if he obtained a certificate from the overseers, attested by two or more "credible witnesses" and subscribed by two JPs. The certificate was to be presented to the overseers of the parish into which the poor person moved. Only if he or his family asked for relief or became chargeable to the new parish could he be returned to his former parish which issued the certificate.

The determining of settlement disputes was one of the most difficult and time-consuming tasks of the justices, and Poor Law settlement removal orders are among the most numerous of the county documents which survive from this period.

There were various different grounds on which a settlement decision might be made. The following orders recorded in the Norfolk Quarter Sessions Order Book 1650-1657, were based on (1) birth; (2) parentage; (3) apprenticeship; (4) service; (5) residence.

(1) "Margaret Turner, taken as a vagrant, punished and sent to Hocholde ..., last place of abode. Inhabitants complain, showing she was born at Stanforde. Ordered to be sent to Stanforde to be provided for (para. 158).

(2) Petition of Saxlingham Thorpe Inhabitants. Ann, wife of Robert Legate, settled at Hempnall by Sir William Doyley, Kt., and Edward Ward, Esq. Came to house of her mother, widow Hellinge, at Saxlingham, and gave birth to a child which is likely to prove chargeable. Ordered, Ann and her child be put to town of Hempnall (para. 472).

(3) After hearing counsel for parishes of Hempstead and Edgefield, ordered, Philip Browne to be settled at Hempstead, 'for that it appeared to this court that the master to whom the said Browne was put unto was nothing worth nor capable to take an apprentice, and that one of the towne of Hempstead was also p'sent upon the agreement made betweene the said Master and the said Browne' (para. 623).

(4) Ann Catton to dwell with her master William Bircham of Snettisham for term retained for. Snettisham thereafter to be responsible for her (para. 140).

(5) John Howard to be sent to Taverham, last place of abode, to be settled. Overseers to allow him 12d p.w." (para. 144).

Sometimes Quarter Sessions attempted to avoid making a settlement order by putting pressure on an employer who had brought a pauper to a parish. Thus Norfolk sessions directed that: "Francis Turner of Ringland to pay Bintry overseers 6d a week for 10 weeks for bringing there some poor people likely to become chargeable" (para. 330).

Rogues and Vagabonds

Vagrancy was closely allied with the Poor Law under the Tudor legislation, which continued to apply until the second decade of the eighteenth century. While the aged and impotent were to be relieved and the able-bodied given work, rogues, vagabonds and sturdy beggars were to be whipped and sent to the place where they had last dwelt for a year, where they were to be made to work in a house of correction. During the eighteenth century the problem of vagrancy aroused considerable interest in Parliament as well as in the countryside, and a number of further Acts were passed which extended the justices' duties. The first of these Acts, passed in 1713[52] enlarged the list of those described as rogues and vagabonds and defined more clearly the procedure to be followed by the justices. They were given power to impose severe punishment when dealing with dangerous rogues, and even more severe in the case of rogues who were both dangerous and incorrigible. The justices were also empowered to apprentice vagabonds or to put them to service in Great Britain or in the plantations for seven years.[53] If a parish failed to set rogues and vagabonds to work it was to be penalized by the justices, and so too were the masters of ships who brought such rogues into the kingdom from Ireland, the Isle of Man, the Channel Islands and the plantations.

The 1713 Act was superseded by one of 1740 which was quickly replaced by the more extensive one of 1744[54] which divided vagrants into three categories: (i) idle and disorderly persons; (ii) rogues and vagabonds; and (iii) incorrigible rogues. Each category was to be treated differently. The Act also required justices to make "a general privy search in the night" for rogues and vagabonds in their divisions at least four times a year. Vagrants apprehended at this or at any other time were to be sent to the houses of correction or publicly whipped. They could then be sent to their place of legal settlement. An Act of 1752[55] gave the justices power to examine persons alleged to be rogues and vagabonds as to their places of settlement and means of livelihood, and to commit them to prison for six days if they could not show that they had lawful means of livelihood or could find a householder to answer for them. Any able bodied person who had no means of

52. 11 Anne, c. 26.
53. 13 Geo. II, c. 24.
54. 17 Geo. II, c. 5.
55. 25 Geo. II, c. 39, s. 12.

support was ordered to find employment on pain of imprisonment. Thus Mary Plumstead of Elmeham in Norfolk was ordered to "find herself a master within one month or to be sent to Walsingham H. of C. to remain there till hired."[56]

The Act of 1744 (s. 20) also gave justices power to confine lunatics and to take any of their property to pay the cost of their maintenance. Under a later Act arrangements were made for licensing and controlling madhouses. In the country this was done by Quarter Sessions, but in London and Middlesex by a committee elected by the College of Surgeons.[57] A further provision of the 1744 Act gave the justices power to enlist male vagabonds and incorrigible rogues in the army or navy.

The justices devoted much of their energy towards dealing with vagabonds but without any conspicuous success. Their numbers and the problems they created were as great as ever. This was, however, one of the areas in which the justices came to show a humane approach in the discharge of their duties. Towards the end of the century they were clearly less willing to impose sentences of whipping or imprisonment. Instead, they adopted a procedure whereby the vagrants were returned to their own parishes without punishment so long as they complied with the justices' orders.

Justices blamed for harshness of the System

It has been suggested that in the administration of the Poor Law in general during the eighteenth century the former paternalism of the justices vanished.[58] It is true that the Poor Law was administered harshly during this period and that in settlement cases justices were often motivated by a desire to relieve their own parish of financial liability, but in fairness it should be added that the behaviour of the justices was characterized by innumerable acts of compassion and philanthropy. It was the system rather than those who administered it that was at the root of the evil. The justices clearly regarded themselves as having a responsibility for the less fortunate members of society, but this was sometimes clouded by their own interests as employers and landowners.

(7) Gaols and Houses of Correction

Gaols

Until the end of the seventeenth century gaols were the responsibility

---

56. Norfolk QS Order Book, 1650-1657, para. 624.
57. 14 Geo. III, c. 49, made perpetual by 26 Geo. III, c. 91.
58. See D.L. Keir, *Constitutional History of Modern Britain since 1485,* Black, 7th ed., 1964, p. 313.

of the sheriffs, except for those which were privately owned under franchises. In both cases the management of the gaols was in the hands of gaolers who sought to make a profit, mainly from fees charged to the prisoners. The gaoler merely paid a fixed rent for his office which could be bought and sold.[59] Prisoners had to pay a fee on admission to the prison and when they were released, which meant that many remained in prison even when they were entitled to be discharged. While in custody prisoners could obtain special treatment in a number of ways by paying to the governor or keeper fees set out in a tariff which varied according to the prisoner's status. The tariff for Durham prison in the eighteenth century, which was similar to that of most other prisons at the time, contained the following items:[60]

For lodging with a bedfellow in the Common Chamber each Prisoner for every week	1s 6d
For every Prisoner in Execution for debt or damages for his freedom from Irons for every pound	2d
Of every Prisoner from the Court of Chancery as above in Commission for the like freedom not exceeding	10s
For Chamber Rent and Lodging: For Lodging with a Bedfellow in an other Chamber save the Common Chamber of each Prisoner for every week	2s 4d
For Lodging in that Single Bed in that Common Chamber without admittance of a bedfellow for every week	3s 6d
Out of which Rates Abatement shall be made to every Prisoner that findeth his own bedding Bedcloaths and Sheets and admitting a bedfellow with him for every week	6d
For Diett of Prisoners	
of every Knight not exceeding for every week	10s
of every Esquire or Gentleman not exceeding for every week	7s 6d
of every Yeoman Artificer or Labourer not exceeding for every week	6s
For wine ale beer or brandy at the common prices generally used in the Town.	

Large profits were also made from the more affluent prisoners who

59.   The practice of buying and selling the office was abolished by 3 Geo. I, c. 15.
60.   Durham RO, Baker MS, p. 156.

could afford to pay for bedding, food and even separate and comfortable quarters. In most counties the level of fees had been approved at some time by Quarter Sessions.[61] Most gaolers were unscrupulous sadists who had no concern for those in their charge and who were ready to increase their takings by extortion and to appropriate donations sent by benefactors for the relief of poor prisoners.

The sheriffs hardly ever visited prisons and there was no supervision of the condition of the prisoners which was appalling, both sexes and all ages being herded together in squalor in overcrowded, unheated, unventilated and lice-ridden cells. There was also no distinction between the treatment of convicted criminals and those awaiting trial.

The justices were not concerned with the administration of the gaols until the eighteenth century. They were enabled to build and repair gaols, and impose rates to cover the cost, by an Act of 1700.[62] Until then there were no purpose built gaols. Some were still situated in old and decaying castles like those in Gloucester, Lancaster and York. In Reading the gaol was no more than a few rooms in a public house. The justices had no control, however, over the management of the gaols until 1729, when Quarter Sessions were empowered to fix the maximum fees charged by gaolers,[63] and 1759 when they were given powers of management.[64] These two Acts were passed following an inquiry by the House of Commons into the management of the Fleet and Marshalsea prisons in 1729 which disclosed appalling abuses and cruelty by the gaolers.[65] In 1759 Parliament provided that creditors who put their debtors in prison might be required to allow them four pence a day for their maintenance (32 Geo. II, c. 28) but few debtors seem to have benefited from this. In 1774 the justices were given power to have both gaols and prisoners cleansed with a view to reducing the fatal gaol sickness which claimed the lives of Judges and advocates as well as of the prisoners themselves. The Act[66] which was declared to be "for preserving the health of prisoners in gaol and preventing the gaol Distemper," required the JPs in Quarter Sessions in England and Wales to order that the walls of rooms in which prisoners were confined should be scraped and whitewashed at least

61. John Howard's report on Gloucester Prison showed that the gaoler received a salary of £10 a year but was also entitled to charge £1.0s.10d. from debtors, 17s.8d. from felons at Assizes, 13s.4d. from felons at Quarter Sessions, and £6 for transporting prisoners. He also had a licence to sell beer to the prisoners. From 1783 Quarter Sessions forbad the gaoler to sell liquor and to permit gambling, under a penalty of £10 or three months imprisonment. To offset his loss of income his salary was raised to £60.
62. 11 & 12 William III, c. 19, continued by 10 Anne, c. 14, and made perpetual by 6 Geo. I, c. 19.
63. 2 Geo. II, c. 22, s. 4.
64. 32 Geo. II, c. 28, s. 6. In 1772 they were given power to appoint prison chaplains (13 Geo. III, c. 58).
65. HC Journals (1729), vol. XXI, p. 274.
66. 15 Geo. III, c. 59.

once a year, to be "regularly washed and kept clean and constantly supplied with fresh air, by means of Hand Ventilators or otherwise," and two rooms in each prison were to be set aside for sick prisoners, one for men and one for women. Each prison was to have a warm and cold bath, "or commodious Bathing Tub," and prisoners were to be ordered to be washed in the baths or tubs before they left the prison for any purpose. The justices were also to appoint a surgeon or apothecary at a stated salary to attend each gaol or prison, and he was to report to the justices on the state of the prisoners at each Quarter Sessions. The justices were further required to make such orders as they thought fit to have the courts of justice properly ventilated and to preserve the health of the prisoners. The cost of all these operations was to be defrayed out of the county rates in so far as the counties were concerned, and out of "Public Stock or Rates of such Cities, Towns corporate, Liberties" etc., in respect of gaols belonging to them. The justices' powers and duties were extended further by an Act of 1783.[67]

These statutes were largely permissive, and there was no power vested in a Minister to ensure that the justices complied with them. Consequently the justices, who for the most part did not show much enthusiasm for their new duties, were slow to exercise them. The reason for their reluctance seems to have been due partly to a desire to avoid increasing the burden which would fall on the rates, partly to the fact that they already had enough tasks to perform and partly to the unpleasantness of visiting prisons and the danger to their health which this entailed. There were, however, exceptions and a number of individual justices took their duties seriously from an early stage, visiting prisons notwithstanding the danger and bringing the scandalous conditions to the notice of their colleagues who, in most of these cases, took action to bring about improvements.[68]

In the 1770s John Howard began his investigation of the prison system. He was himself a high sheriff (of Bedfordshire in 1773) and had his interest aroused during his term of office when he was one of the few sheriffs who visited a prison. Thereafter he campaigned tirelessly and his revelations in his *The State of the Prisons*, first published in 1777, made a deep impression on the public and Parliament. Although he was never a JP, he recommended that the whole administration of the prisons should be assigned to Quarter Sessions who were to employ gaolers and other staff as salaried servants. After a long campaign, most of his proposals were

---

67.   24 Geo. III, c. 54.
68.   Several instances are cited by the Webbs, beginning with the Rev. George Botts of Suffolk in the 1760s and including the Rev. Henry Zouch, mentioned earlier, who was responsible for the complete reorganization of the county gaol at Wakefield. *ELG, English Prisons under Local Government*, pp. 54-55.

implemented during the latter part of the century and, although the sheriffs retained some nominal authority over gaols, the entire administration was placed for all practical purposes under the justices.

A number of justices were inspired by Howard's work to initiate reforms in their own counties without waiting for national legislation. The Webbs attribute this movement to the additional pressure which was placed on the prisons when transportation of convicts ceased at the beginning of the American War of Independence. It is true that in 1776 the condition of the prisoners was made even worse, if that were possible, by the removal of transportation as a sentencing option when the War of Independence broke out and it became impossible to send convicts abroad until transportation to Australia began in 1787. As a temporary expedient the Government established national prisons by converting some old ships to provide convict accommodation, but this was not sufficient to relieve the pressure appreciably on the existing prisons, and most counties were obliged to spend money on expansion.

This does not appear, however, to have been the only reason why justices began to play an active part in improving the prison system. There were many who were clearly inspired by a genuine desire to alleviate the lot of the inmates. One sees conspicuous examples of this in the 1780s and 1790s, particularly in Lancashire, Norfolk, Suffolk, Sussex, Wiltshire and the West Riding. In a few instances prominent members of the nobility took the lead among the justices. As mentioned earlier, the Duke of Richmond, Lord Lieutenant of Sussex, was instrumental in having new types of prison, with separate confinement and productive work, built at Horsham and Petworth. The most outstanding prison reformer among the justices, however, was Sir George Onesiphorus Paul of Gloucester. Paul was foremost among the pioneers who carried into effect the reforms advocated by John Howard. Indeed, they would probably have been implemented much later than they were had it not been for his efforts. In his earlier years Paul gave every indication of being a typical fun-loving country gentleman. He had inherited a baronetcy and a substantial fortune from his father who was a successful clothier. Having been educated at St John's College, Oxford, he went on a lengthy grand tour of Europe where he squandered much of his money, but he also acquired a substantial library and became a member of the Dilettante Society. He was a gambler and on his return to England became a racehorse owner. In 1780 he became high sheriff of Gloucestershire and, having spent a good deal more of his wealth on the dinners and entertainments involved in his office, he suddenly abandoned his irresponsible way of life. He made his first attempt to initiate prison reform when, as foreman of the grand jury, he addressed the Gloucestershire Lent Assizes in March 1783. He called attention to the unacceptable state of the existing gaol and urged that a prison service as advocated by Howard should be introduced. He was now a Justice of the Peace and he continued to press his argument at Quarter Sessions and at public meetings and he soon persuaded many of the leading men in the county to support him. Within a few months it was decided to press for a Private Act of Parliament to establish a new county gaol and five bridewells on lines proposed by Paul.[69] The Bill was entitled "An Act to enable JPs to build and repair gaols in their respective counties." After some delay and amendment it was introduced in Parliament and passed in 1785[70] under the title, "An Act for Building a New Gaol, a Penitentary House, and certain New Houses of Correction, for the County of Gloucester, and for regulating the same." The Act enabled the county to build a new gaol and four model houses of correction at a cost of nearly £50,000. The gaol was placed under the control of commissioners. All county justices were commissioners and in addition any holder of land to the yearly value of £250 was qualified to become a commissioner. Paul himself usually chaired the meetings. The new gaol was completed in 1791 and the prisoners were moved in July.

The staff of the new gaol included a surgeon, a chaplain, a matron for the female prisoners, a turnkey, a taskmaster to supervise the prisoners' work and a number of lesser officers. Prisoners were subjected to hard labour, but were provided with a good daily meal, clothing, bedding and fresh air and exercise, and they were visited regularly by the governor, chaplain and surgeon. The building was heated. Chains and brutal punishments were abolished. Emphasis was placed on the need to prevent intercourse between prisoners and for this purpose each prisoner had a separate cell. In the regulations for the gaol which were drafted by Paul he greatly improved on those proposed by Howard and also on the provisions of the 1974 Act.

Although Paul was the outstanding Justice of the Peace in the field of prison reform there were other individual justices in various counties who proved to be dedicated to the same principles. At the beginning of the nineteenth century, one of these, James Neild, toured the prisons throughout Britain in the manner of John Howard. Gradually a number of counties followed the example of Gloucestershire, but there was no movement in Parliament for further reform until interest was awakened by Sir Samuel Romilly in 1810 which ultimately led to the passing in 1823 of a major Act for prison reform at the instigation of the Home Secretary, Sir Robert Peel.

Houses of Correction
Unlike gaols, houses of correction were always the responsibility of the

69.   Gloucestershire RO, Q/SO 10, Order book pp. 205-208.
70.   25 Geo. III, c. 10.

Justices of the Peace since they were initiated by the Tudors as part of the system of poor relief. As we have seen, the houses of correction, which were built and maintained by the justices and were entirely under their control, had been introduced as reformatories for the able-bodied poor who refused to work, and they were quite distinct from the gaols, which might be used for punishment but were occupied by even larger numbers of debtors and those awaiting trial.

After 1688, in the absence of any guidance and supervision from the Privy Council or elsewhere, the justices tended to lose sight of the concept of houses of correction as places of work and reformation, and gradually there came to be little difference between these institutions and prisons. The normal practice was for the unemployed poor to be given small money payments or relief in kind, but in the case of sturdy rogues and vagabonds they were committed to a house of correction, where the master was given absolute discretion to use them as he pleased. This change of approach was encouraged by an Act of 1720[71] which empowered the justices to commit vagrants and persons charged with small offences, and also persons unable to find sureties, either to a gaol or a house of correction. This was a complete reversal of the initial object of the houses of correction which was to provide places of employment for the unemployed poor and not to inflict punishment. In the eighteenth century the practice was to force the inmates to work under punitive conditions, some of the proceeds of their labour being used to defray their keep and the rest to supplement the master's salary. In this way the houses of correction ceased to be a drain on county resources and could be left largely to run themselves. The justices therefore tended to forget about them and in most areas the supervision was minimal.

The Act of 1744[72] gave the justices power to build, enlarge or hire buildings if a presentment were made by a Grand Jury at Assizes or at general or Quarter Sessions that there was a need in the county for houses of correction, or additional ones. Quarter Sessions could nominate one or more justices to inspect an institution and report to the next sessions who were to make such orders as they thought fit for the treatment and discipline of the inmates. This seems, however, to have had little effect and in most counties there was hardly anything to distinguish the houses of correction from the gaols.

(8) Licensing

Long before the eighteenth century various statutes had placed upon the justices the duty of authorizing persons to indulge in certain trades or other activities. The most important of these was the licensing of

---

71.   6 Geo. I, c. 19.
72.   17 Geo. II, c. 5, s. 30.

sales of intoxicating liquor, which dated from Tudor times. Before turning again to this part of the justices' work it needs to be noted that two other licensing functions were given to them for the first time during the period from 1689 to 1820. In 1689 itself, as already mentioned, the Toleration Act required Quarter Sessions to license non-conformist meeting houses. In 1737, the Playhouse Act required every play in a theatre and also every actor to have a licence from the Lord Chamberlain who was responsible for censorship. Enforcement of the law fell upon the justices. This Act, which was not repealed until 1968, was at least partly a reaction of Walpole to the satirical attack on his Government by Henry Fielding who became a Bow Street Magistrate. The justices' involvement was extended by a further Act of 1788.[73] It was not uncommon for Quarter Sessions to issue warrants prohibiting plays. Thirdly, by an Act of 1773[74] private lunatic asylums had to be licensed by Quarter Sessions, and two justices and a physician appointed to inspect them. In 1808 the justices themselves were empowered to set up asylums.[75]

We have seen that the Justices' responsibility for alehouses began in 1503 when an Act of Henry VII authorized them to suppress disorderly houses, and in 1551-52 they became responsible for licensing the sale of intoxicating liquor when two justices were given power to grant licences to alehouse keepers from whom they took recognizances to prevent drunkenness and unlawful games and to maintain order. These provisions did not extend to the sale of spirits, and even in the case of ale they were applied very laxly by the justices from the time of the Restoration. This laxity continued during the eighteenth century, in spite of a number of new Acts which extended their responsibility. In 1729 an Act[76] decreed that no one might sell spirits by retail to be consumed on the premises unless they had been licensed in the same way as alehouse keepers. Another Act of the same year[77] had imposed new duties on spirits and required retailers to obtain a licence at £20 a year. It also prohibited the sale of spirits in the streets. In spite of these restrictions, the sale of spirits continued unabated and in 1736 the Gin Act[78] imposed a new licensing system whereby, in addition to the justices' licence, an additional excise licence costing £50 a year was required. This measure also proved ineffective and was replaced in 1743[79] by another, which retained both licences but reduced the excise licence to £20. This was extended to beer in 1808.[80] More will be said about gin licensing in the next chapter

73.   28 Geo. III, c. 30.
74.   14 Geo. III, c. 49.
75.   48 Geo. III, c. 96.
76.   2 Geo. II, c. 28.
77.   *Ibid.*, c. 17.
78.   9 Geo. II, c. 23.
79.   16 Geo. II, c. 8.
80.   48 Geo. III, c. 143.

when referring to conditions in the London area. The justices were not concerned with the grant of the excise licence, whose object was principally to raise revenue, but it was they who were responsible for seeing that the system was properly operated. They, and not the excise authorities, decided whether a public house might be opened for the sale of beer and spirits. In 1751 the justices were given power to search for and seize spirits in gaols, workhouses and houses of correction, and they were protected against actions for damages and writs of *certiorari.*

The justices had a very wide discretion in the granting or refusing of licences, and because of this the higher courts would not interfere unless there was clear evidence of bias or malice.[81] The exercise of the justices' powers was, however, subject to certain statutory restrictions. Under an Act of 1751, a licence could not be granted to anyone who occupied a tenement valued at less than £10. Licences to sell spirits for consumption on the premises could be granted only to those who kept and who lived in taverns, victualling houses, coffee houses or alehouses and not to grocers, chandlers, keepers of brandy shops or distillers.[82] Moreover, no one could be granted a licence unless he produced a certificate from the local parson and the majority of the churchwardens or from three or four substantial local householders that he was "of good fame and of sober life and conversation."[83] The Act of 1753 which contained these provisions was of particular interest to future generations of justices in that it was the origin of "Brewster Sessions." The justices were to exercise their licensing powers at special sessions of the Justices of each division held annually on the first day of September or within 20 days thereof. A licence was to be granted for one year only at the end of which time it had to be renewed. Brewers, distillers and maltsters were disqualified from acting as justices in any matters relating to licences of beer or spirits.

In the earlier part of the eighteenth century the justices were generally lax in their administration of the licensing laws.[84] Apart from the "Trading Justices" in Middlesex, described in the next chapter, who made a profit out of their operations, the justices in most counties made little effort to see that licensed premises were properly conducted and they granted licences indiscriminately. In some places they signed the licences in blank and left it to their clerk to complete and issue them, the clerk receiving a fee for his pains. Licences were

---

81. *R.* v. *Williams and Davies* (1762) 3 Burr., p. 1317. It was recognized that they had a complete discretion in the grant of licences but if they acted corruptly they could be prosecuted. Thus in 1765 two justices of Corfe Castle were committed to prison for a month and fined £50 each for refusing to grant an alehouse licence to an innkeeper because he had voted for a candidate for Parliament to whom they were opposed. *R.* v. *Hann and Price,* Burr., pp. 1716, 1786.
82. 16 Geo. II, c. 8; 17 Geo. II, c. 17.
83. 26 Geo. II, c. 31.
84. The Webbs give a full account of the justices' failure to perform their duties in *The History of Liquor Licensing in England,* pp. 33–41.

granted to almost anyone who applied, and once granted they were seldom withdrawn. It is not surprising that the consumption of beer and ale assumed spectacular proportions.[85]

The various statutes already described made little difference to the general picture. The number of alehouses multiplied and the Government was generally well pleased with the operation of a system which increased its revenue. All this suddenly changed, however, towards the end of the century with a move against vice and immorality initiated by Wilberforce with the backing of the Queen. For a time the country was swept with a movement to raise moral standards, particularly of the lower orders. In 1787 there was a Royal Proclamation against vice and immorality, copies of which were sent by the Home Secretary to justices throughout the country, among whom there was a ready response. Among the steps taken by the justices was the laying down of rules for granting licences and for the conduct of licensees. Licence holders who did not comply had their licences withdrawn, and the number of alehouses was substantially reduced. In many places there was early closing and Sunday closing. In most areas the total number of licensed premises was reduced wherever existing facilities were thought to be excessive. Whether the justices were strictly able in law to impose these conditions is open to some doubt, but they seem to have done so with impunity. Clearly, the statutes gave them a wide discretion and, as already noted, the higher courts were reluctant to intervene.

In consequence of the new activity by the justices, the consumption of alcohol was reduced, the condition of the licensed houses and the behaviour of those who frequented them was greatly improved and the incidence of crime was lowered.

The tide changed once more after the beginning of the nineteenth century when the justices seemed to have lost interest again in licensing, but were subject to increasing public criticism for the way in which they did or did not perform their duties.

Among the most prominent critics of the justices were the Radicals who objected to working men being deprived of their living by the arbitrary action of unrepresentative magistrates. It was claimed that an alehouse keeper, unlike any other tradesman, having invested all his worldly wealth in licensed premises, could be deprived of everything at the whim of a magistrate whose motives as often as not were questionable. Objection was also taken to the acquisition of public houses by large firms of brewers and distillers, and it was alleged that this was the result of a policy adopted by the justices. Parliamentary

---

85. The Webbs calculated that 36 gallons of beer were consumed each year for every man, woman and child in the population, an average consumption per head which has never been equalled. *Ibid.,* p. 17.

inquiries in 1816 and the following year showed that a large percentage of licensed premises were owned by brewers, and the committee condemned this because of "the restricted power which the public at large possess of employing their capital in the trade of victualling houses."[86] It was claimed that the justices had allowed public houses to fall into the hands of a small ring of wealthy and powerful brewers who were likely to conspire together to raise prices; a prospect which was anathema to Adam Smith and the growing circle of free traders. The justices were also criticized generally for refusing to grant new licences and for arbitrarily withdrawing old ones.

The reputation of justices throughout the country also suffered unfairly from the publicity given to the corrupt justices in Middlesex (described in the following chapter). The report of a House of Commons Committee into the obvious shortcomings of the Middlesex justices in all aspects of their work was generally assumed, wrongly, to apply to commissions throughout the country, and the achievements of licensing justices during the short spell after 1786 was totally ignored.[87] Much of the evidence submitted to the House of Commons committee came from unsuccessful applicants for licences and from those who had experience of the corrupt justices in Middlesex, especially those in the Tower Hamlets. The recommendations contained in the committee's report amounted to the removal of the justices' long-standing power to withdraw licences and to impose conditions upon licensees. The justices' function was therefore to be confined to deciding whether an applicant was of good character, in which case a licence would automatically be granted to him. There was no question of limiting the number of licensed premises to suit the area.

The report received widespread publicity and acclaim. No one spoke out on behalf of the justices and it was widely assumed that they deserved all the vilification which had been heaped upon them. This was an outstanding instance of the undoubted defects of the Middlesex justices being wrongly attributed to those in the rest of the country.

The reaction of the justices themselves was to abandon what little remained of the firm policy adopted after 1786. There were fewer withdrawals of licences and less rigid conditions were imposed on licensees. There was, however, some restriction on the number of public houses in each village, largely in deference to the views of the public in the area.

We shall see in ch. V that the almost hysterical attitude towards the licensing powers of the justices which followed the publication of the House of Commons Committee's report in 1817, led to the passing

86. Report of the House of Commons Committee on Public Brewers, p. 1818.
87. Select Committee on the Police of the Metropolis, 1817.

thirteen years later of the Beer Act[88] which removed entirely from the control of the justices all premises which sold only beer. This disastrous Act would not be repealed until 1869.

(9) The Game Laws

We come finally to the application of the game laws which have probably received more execration than any other branch of the justices' functions. Not only was there abhorrence among contemporaries but the justices' behaviour has long been regarded by historians as synonymous with tyranny.

In 1828, Henry Brougham, who later became Lord Chancellor, delivered a devastating attack on the justices in a speech in the House of Commons which was directed particularly towards their administration of the game laws. He said, "There is not a worse constituted tribunal on the face of the earth, not even that of the Turkish cadi, than that at which summary conviction on the Game Laws takes place; I mean a bench or a brace of sporting magistrates."[89] In *Tom Jones*, Fielding wrote that "Many justices of the peace suppose they have a large discretionary power, by virtue of which under the notion of searching for and taking away engines for the destruction of game, they often commit trespass, and sometimes felony, at their pleasure."[90] It was claimed in the earlier nineteenth century that one in every four prisoners in English gaols was an offender against the game laws.

This view of the eighteenth and nineteenth century JPs has persisted into the twentieth century. The Webbs, writing in 1906, concluded that "In the hands of the country gentleman of the eighteenth century, and still more of the beginning of the nineteenth century, Game Laws became, it is clear, an instrument of terrible severity, leading, not infrequently, to cruel oppression of individuals of the 'lower orders' suspected of poaching."[91] The Webbs were prepared to qualify this condemnation only to the extent of saying that "It is characteristic of the English country gentlemen that it was not to the love of money that their judicial impartiality and intellectual integrity succombed, but to their over-mastering desire to maintain their field sports and protect the amenity of their country seats."

As already mentioned, there was little contemporary opinion which was not biased and later writers like the Webbs had scant unprejudiced material on which to base their conclusions. Most of the sources were

88.   11 Geo. IV and 1 William IV, c. 64.
89.   Hansard N.S., vol. XVIII, p. 166. February 7, 1828.
90.   *Tom Jones*, Bk. XII, ch. IX.
91.   *ELG, The Parish and the County*, p. 598.

pamphlets and periodicals, Parliamentary papers and debates and works of fiction, almost all of which were heavily biased against the game laws and those who administered them. Later writers, however, have continued to condemn the justices for their application of these laws. J.L. and Barbara Hammond in 1948 wrote that the laws spilt the blood of men and boys "for the pleasure of the rich," and in 1976 B.A. Holderness described them as "a classic example of class selfishness."[92] Most other historians continue to take the same view, even though they have no doubt studied the many documents which have only become accessible since the middle of the present century. The wealth of records which are now available reveal an intriguing picture and they enable us to form a more accurate judgment than was possible previously.

There were undoubtedly shocking cases which, as instances of the behaviour of certain individuals, fully support the adverse comments cited above. One of the most notorious of these occurred in 1822. A farmer who was coursing hares on his own tenanted land with the permission of his landlord was summoned by the gamekeeper of the adjoining landowner who was the Duke of Buckingham, a Justice of the Peace. He was brought before the Duke who sat alone in his private residence and who convicted him on the evidence of the keeper supported by another of the Duke's keepers. The Duke refused to allow the farmer to bring an attorney to defend him, nor would he permit a friend to take notes. The Duke announced that if "he uttered one impertinent word there was a Constable in the room to take him to gaol or the stocks."[93] It seems probable that this case inspired Brougham's remarks in 1826, quoted above, and it is questionable whether Brougham had much other evidence on which to base his assertion. There were other instances of thoroughly reprehensible behaviour by individual justices, but on the other hand there is now ample evidence of a rather different story in so far as the majority of the justices was concerned. It should also be noted that, contrary to what is generally supposed, those who engaged in poaching were not always poverty stricken labourers who did so to save themselves and their families from starvation, though this was often the case. There were many instances of organized gangs who killed and stole deer and game to sell for profit. There were also groups, sometimes composed of young bloods from the gentry themselves, who poached, usually with greyhounds, purely for sport.[94] Before, however, considering the extent

---

92. J.L. and Barbara Hammond, *The Village Labourer* (new edn, London, 1948), p. 184; B.A. Holderness, *Pre-industrial England: economy and society, 1500-1750* (London, 1976), pp. 43-4.
93. Sir Spencer Walpole, *History of England*, vol. i., p. 159. Quoted by Webb, ELG, *The Parish and the County*, p. 599.
94. For example see F.G. Emmison, *Elizabethan Life: Disorder*, Essex County Council publication (1970), p. 236.

to which criticism is justified let us first look at the eighteenth century game laws which the justices were empowered to administer.

We have seen that hunting in royal forests was forbidden from the Norman Conquest and that severe laws were applied in early times, but their severity was mitigated in 1225 by a statute of Henry II under which "no man from henceforth shall lose either life or limb for killing our deer." At first, statutory prohibition of hunting applied only to royal land, but from 1389 no one who was not in the higher ranks of society was allowed to hunt anywhere. An Act of that year[95] provided that no one might keep dogs or use ferrets, nets or other "engines" to take deer, hares, conies or "other gentlen's game" unless he were a layman with lands or tenements of the value of 40 shillings per annum or a beneficed clergyman with income of £10 a year. The property qualification was raised to £100 per annum in 1671,[96] except for the heir of an esquire or person of higher degree. The effect of this Act was to make hunting the exclusive privilege of the landed gentry whom it placed on virtually the same level as the King so far as the sport was concerned. The only restriction on the gentry was that they were subject to the law of trespass if they hunted on someone else's land without permission. In order to curb unnecessary proceedings for trespass, however, another Act of 1671 provided that plaintiffs in such cases could not be awarded full costs unless they could show that the damage exceeded 40 shillings, which was seldom the case.

As the qualification for a Justice of the Peace was raised to £100 in 1732 it meant that thereafter every justice was qualified under the Game Acts. This was the beginning of the monopoly in hunting enjoyed by the gentry throughout the following centuries. Only those in the upper levels of the social structure were entitled to enjoy the pleasures of hunting or to benefit from what was caught. Everyone else, which meant the vast majority of the population, was excluded. Class exclusiveness had also been extended by an Act of 1541[97] which made it illegal to keep a gun or crossbow unless the person had lands, tenements or hereditaments to the value of £100 or was a peer, knight, esquire, gentleman, yeoman or the servant of a peer. An Act of 1603 extended the qualification to persons having copyhold to the value of £30 per annum, or goods or chattels valued at £200. Further Acts on the same lines were passed in 1605, 1609 and 1671.

From the Revolution onwards the Game Acts were complicated and were being continually repealed and re-enacted with amendments, and the justices themselves and their clerks seem to have had some difficulty in interpreting them. Moreover, different Acts applied to different types of game and there were also marked differences

95.   13 Richard II, St. 1, c. 13.
96.   22 & 23 Charles II, c. 25.
97.   33 Henry VIII, c. 6.

between pursuing game on enclosed and on unenclosed land. The most serious offences were those involving the killing of deer, while slightly less severe penalties applied to the taking of pheasants, partridges, moorfowl, hares and rabbits. Foxes, badgers and otters were classed as vermin and were not protected. Hunting by night was treated as a more heinous offence than if done by day, and the Acts applied the most severe penalties in these cases, especially from the 1770s.

The period during which there was the most prolific legislation on the subject lay between the Restoration and 1831, when the Game Reform Act brought the era to an end. During this time no less than 54 principal Acts relating to the game laws were passed. In view of the constantly changing statutory provisions it is impossible to give a clear picture of the law during this period, but the following is an outline of the most significant statutes, followed by an assessment of the harshness of the penalties which they enabled the justices to impose.

At the time of the Restoration, anyone hunting deer on enclosed ground without the consent of the owner could be imprisoned for three months and fined £10 or treble the damage, plus costs. The use of dogs, snares, nets or other "engines" to take other game involved a penalty of three months' imprisonment and a fine of 20 shillings per creature taken. In addition there were various fines, with imprisonment in default, for hunting game out of season. There were additional penalties for hunting at night or in disguise. Hunting deer at night had been a felony since 1485 and a capital offence, while taking game birds involved a fine of 10 shillings for each partridge and 20 shillings for each pheasant, with one month's imprisonment without bail in default. The hunting of conies was restricted only on enclosed land, when the penalty was three months' imprisonment with £10 fine or treble damages. There were also restrictions on buying and selling game where the penalties were purely monetary; in the case of deer the amount was 40 shillings per deer. For persons convicted of stealing eggs the penalty varied according to the species of bird, being one year's imprisonment with a fine of 20 shillings per egg in the case of cranes or bustards, and a fine of 20 shillings per egg or three months' imprisonment in default for stealing the eggs of partridges and pheasants.

One of the principal grounds for criticism of the justices' application of the game laws was that these cases could be dealt with by a single justice sitting in his own parlour. This was part of the general process of devolving jurisdiction from Quarter Sessions to individual justices which was already to be seen in the seventeenth century and which was obviously open to abuse. Until the Restoration, charges of stealing deer had to be brought before Assizes or Quarter Sessions, but poaching game could be dealt with by two justices on the oath of two credible witnesses. Under an Act of 1661,[98] however, a poacher charged with stealing deer might be convicted by a single justice on the oath of one credible witness.

In 1671, the Act[99] mentioned earlier recognized the development of game shooting as a pastime for the landed gentry by providing that lords of manors and others not under the degree of esquire might authorize one or more gamekeepers to preserve the game on their land, with power to seize dogs, "engines," etc., and any game which had been taken by poachers. The gamekeeper might also search houses of suspected persons without a warrant. Under an Act of 1693[100] the gamekeeper was indemnified from prosecution if he killed a night poacher in the course of performing his duties. The power to appoint gamekeepers was limited, however, by an Act of 1711[101] to one keeper per manor at any one time. The names of the keepers were to be registered with the Clerk of the Peace who was to issue a certificate for a fee of one shilling. Later, as gamekeeping developed, an Act of 1784[102] laid down that a certificate with a stamp duty of 10s.6d. must be taken out annually by each gamekeeper, a requirement which was not repealed until 1949 although the rate of duty was raised on several occasions in the meantime. The keepers were protected by the law which imposed heavy penalties on poachers who assaulted them, this being one of the few instances where transportation was decreed for first offenders (in the case of poachers hunting deer).[103] Soon the landowners recognized the need for legal control over their keepers and, under several Acts between 1718 and 1802, various penalties from fines to imprisonment and transportation, could be imposed on keepers for taking and killing deer without permission.[104] Under an Act of 1707 a gamekeeper could be sentenced to imprisonment for three months with hard labour for selling or disposing of game without the consent of his master.[105]

The harshest penalties could be imposed in respect of poaching by night. An Act of 1772 contained drastic provisions for the treatment of armed poachers hunting deer at night. If armed with swords, firearms or other offensive weapons in any enclosed ground they were subject to the death penalty without benefit of clergy.[106] The penalties for taking game birds were less severe. In 1773 it was enacted that anyone knowingly and wilfully killing, taking or destroying, or using any gun, dog, snare, net or other "engine" with intent to kill, take or destroy

98.   13 Charles II, St. 1, c. 10.
99.   22 & 23 Charles II, c. 25.
100.   4 & 5 William and Mary, c. 13.
101.   9 Anne, c. 25.
102.   24 Geo. III, sess. 2, c. 43.
103.   (1737) 10 Geo. II, c. 32; (1827) 7 & 8 Geo. IV, c. 27.
104.   5 Geo. I, c. 15; 16 Geo. III, c. 30; 43 Geo. III, c. 112.
105.   5 Anne, c. 14.
106.   13 Geo. III, c. 80, s. 1.

game between 7 pm and 6 am from October 12 to February 12, and between 9 pm and 4 am from February 12 to October 12, might be convicted by one or more justices on oath of one or more credible witnesses. The penalty for a first offence was a fine of between £10 and £20, and for a second offence between £20 and £30. For subsequent offences one or more justices might commit the offender to gaol or house of correction until the next Quarter Sessions where, on conviction, he might be fined £50. Only if the fine were not paid did the justices have power to order imprisonment for between six and twelve months and whipping. This Act also contained provisions for dealing with a convicted offender who lived in another area to the one in which the offence was committed. The justice or justices before whom information or indictment was made were enabled to pursue him by warrant endorsed by a justice in his place of residence and executed by the constable. Under an Act of 1800[107] two or more persons found on private land between the hours of 8 pm and 6 am from October 1 to February 1 or from 10 pm to 4 am from February 1 to October 1 and having with them a gun, net, "engine" or other instrument to destroy, take or kill game and anyone found with an offensive weapon assisting such persons might be arrested by the owner and his employees and taken before a justice who might deal with them as rogues and vagabonds within the meaning of 17 Geo. II, c. 5 (see above, p. 102).

A number of Acts dealt with the selling of game, with the destruction of fences and walls around parks and with hunting on Sundays or at Christmas. Almost all of them laid down fines as the punishment for first offenders, but imprisonment was to be imposed in respect of subsequent offences or in default of payment of the fine.

Space does not allow a detailed account of all the enactments relating to game which were passed during the 150 years from 1689. Many of them repealed and re-enacted earlier statutes with amendments. This enormous amount of legislation which restricted the taking of game in favour of the landed gentry may well be taken to indicate a tyranical attitude on the part of members of this class who, as Members of Parliament and as Justices of the Peace, were instrumental in making the laws and in enforcing them. It cannot be denied that an excessive amount of Parliamentary time and energy was expended on these measures, and it seems obvious that many of the justices and their associates were obsessed with the preservation of their sporting rights. This being so one might have expected that the Acts passed by Parliament would have empowered the justices to impose savage penalties, and this is indeed the impression which

---

107.   39 & 40 Geo. III, c. 50.

seems to have been formed by many historians. It is questionable whether this judgment is justified.

In the first place, many seem to have been under the impression that infringement of the game laws was a capital offence. This is what might have been expected if the laws had been based on a tyranical approach, but in fact the death penalty could be imposed only upon persons who hunted certain types of game by night on enclosed ground and who were disguised and armed with lethal or offensive weapons. In no circumstances could the death penalty be imposed for offences relating to the taking of pheasants, partridges, hares and other game. Moreover, capital offences were tried before Assizes and no longer before the JPs at Quarter Sessions.

The view has also been widely held that transportation was used as a regular punishment for even minor offences. In fact there were few offences for which it was, or could, be imposed on first conviction. Under a number of Acts transportation was an option for second and subsequent offences, but the following were the only ones for which it could be imposed for a first offence. Under an Act of 1719[108] seven years' transportation was the penalty for killing or wounding deer on enclosed ground, but this was replaced in 1775[109] by a fine of £30 or imprisonment for one year. Thereafter, transportation could be ordered only for subsequent offences. Under an Act of 1816[110] the penalty for a first offence of protecting or assisting night poachers of game was seven years' transportation or such other punishment as might be inflicted for a misdemeanour. Under an Act of 1828[111] three or more persons, of whom any were armed, who hunted in groups at night might be transported for seven to 14 years or imprisoned with hard labour for a maximum of three years. In 1764 an Act[112] decreed that the penalty for hunting conies was to be seven years' transportation, or alternatively a fine, whipping or imprisonment at the discretion of the court. This was extended to a maximum of fourteen years' transportation by an Act of 1827.[113] In 1737 an armed assault on a gamekeeper in grounds where deer were kept was punishable with seven years' transportation. This was extended by the Act of 1827 to allow justices the alternative of imprisonment for up to two years with three whippings.

Large numbers of offenders against the game laws were sentenced to imprisonment and it is true to say that a substantial proportion of the prisoners in the eighteenth century gaols were there under sentences for infringement of those laws, in spite of the fact that under

108.   5 Geo. I, c. 28.
109.   16 Geo. III, c. 30.
110.   56 Geo. III, c. 130.
111   9 Geo. IV, c. 69.
112.   5 Geo. III, c. 14.
113.   7 & 8 Geo. IV, c. 29.

most statutes imprisonment could not be imposed for a first offence. This in itself gives the impression that the justices were bent on imposing the harshest penalties. In fact, most of those sentenced to imprisonment had been convicted on more than one occasion and the reason why so many repeatedly broke the law was because they regarded poaching as a legitimate means of augmenting their meagre diet, and even of avoiding starvation. They did not regard poaching as wrong, and they bitterly resented the attempts of landowners to take from them what they regarded as their rights. There were also many such people who were in fact sent to prison on first conviction because they could not, or would not, pay a fine. So far as the legislation was concerned, there were only a few circumstances in which imprisonment, other than in default of payment of a fine, could be imposed for a first offence. One exception to this was the Act of 1800[114] whereby groups of two or more persons who hunted game at night might be committed to a house of correction for up to six months with hard labour. The maximum was increased in 1825 to two years, and the offender could also be made to serve in the navy or army.[115] Those who, at night, destroyed pales or walls around parks could be sentenced to three months for a first offence.[116] This was reduced in 1776 to a fine of £30 for the same offence by day or night, imprisonment being available only in default of payment. Under an Act of 1692 those who burnt heath and certain other plants between February 2 and June 24 were to be committed to a house of correction for from ten days to one month with whipping and hard labour.[117] As already mentioned, a gamekeeper who sold game without consent of his master could be sentenced to imprisonment for three months with hard labour.

The accusations against the justices are twofold. It is alleged that, with their influence in Parliament, they secured the passage of savage legislation to protect their private interests and, having obtained these powers, they exercised them as justices in a ruthless manner. As to the former, we have seen that most of the statutes gave the justices power to impose only a fine for a first offence and that even in the case of subsequent offences the penalties were not outstandingly harsh when judged against the criminal law in general at that time. It should be noticed that, instead of steadily increasing the severity of the available sentences as the century proceeded, there were occasions when existing statutes were modified. Thus, in 1769, under 10 Geo. III, c. 19, the taking of game at night involved imprisonment for three to six months for a first offence and six to twelve months for a second

114. 39 & 40 Geo. III, c. 50.
115. 5 Geo. IV, c. 69.
116. 3 & 4 William and Mary, c. 10.
117. 4 & 5 William and Mary, c. 23.

offence plus, in each case, a public whipping. As we have seen, however, this was repealed three years later and replaced by an Act (13 Geo. III, c. 80) under which the penalty for a first offence was a fine of from £10 to £20 and for a second offence £20 to £30 with imprisonment for three months in default. For a further offence the penalty was a £50 fine, and only in default could the justices at their discretion order the offender to be whipped. In 1691 an Act[118] provided for three months' imprisonment to be imposed upon any found guilty of a first offence of destroying pales or walls around parks by night. In 1776, however, this was replaced with a fine of £20, and imprisonment could be imposed only in default of payment. In 1802 it was enacted by 42 Geo. III, c. 107, that gamekeepers hunting deer or unenclosed ground in their own charge but without permission should be fined £100, with six months' imprisonment in default and seven years' transportation for subsequent offences; but an Act of 1811 (51 Geo. III, c. 120) allowed the justices to mitigate the fine to not less than £20.

The accusation that the justices secured the passage of legislation giving them tyrannical powers over those who interferred with their sporting pleasures is therefore not convincing. As regards the sentences which they imposed under this legislation, it must also be recognized that these sentences fell well short of the maxima allowed by the Acts. There are numerous recorded instances of justices in the eighteenth century who mitigated fines of first offenders including those convicted of night poaching. The penalty was usually a moderate fine, the example in Essex set out in Appendix IV below being fairly typical. In another Essex case county justices adjourned a trial in order to urge that the prosecution should be dropped. Although the evidence warranted a conviction they wrote to the prosecutor that there was "such an absence of any aggravating circumstances and such a want of deciding Poaching intentions ... that they thought it best to set before you these particular circumstances" in the defendant's favour.[119]

One may, of course, take a cynical view and say that in the case of poaching offences the justices exercised leniency in the hope that the accused would help to identify others, especially receivers of stolen game. No doubt there is some truth in this. In 1707 the Act (5 Anne, c. 14, s. 3) empowered justices to grant immunity from punishment to any offender against the game laws who informed on a trader. On the other hand there were many instances where this does not appear to have been the sole motive for a humane approach. It was certainly rare for the maximum penalty to be awarded, and there were many instances where the justices seem to have been surprisingly lenient.

118. 3 & 4 William and Mary, c. 10.
119. Essex RO, D/D Av. C. 8.

These facts were not realized until recently and, until then, it was generally supposed that the justices habitually acted as ruthless and vindictive despots, incensed by the prospect of anyone who might interfere with their enjoyment. Not only has a great deal of information become available in recent years, but it has now been carefully analysed, particularly by P.B. Munsche in his scholarly work, *Gentlemen and Poachers. The English Game Laws, 1671 to 1831.*[120] Munsche cited cases where the justices regularly reduced the fines on those they convicted of game law offences by as much as a half of the maximum allowed by statute, and generally showed humanity towards the accused defendant.[121] He also gives as an example the mid-century justices in Wiltshire who used their powers of summary conviction to commit only a very few poachers to prison.[122] The Webbs' charge that the justices were grossly partisan is examined by Munsche in ch. 4 of his book, and he concludes that it "is, at best, ambiguous. Examples of 'grossly partial' treatment of suspected poachers can be found, but so can examples of impartial, scrupulous and even merciful judgment."

Munsche's work contains a comprehensive analysis of all the game laws between 1671 and 1831, and reveals the "tyrants" of the eighteenth century in an entirely new light. Research among the newly available material certainly confirms his conclusions which are that, "while JPs cannot be totally acquitted of the charge of biased judgments, the latter were becoming less likely by the early nineteenth century, the very period in which the largest number of persons were being tried for offences against the game laws."[123] There are plenty of examples of leniency and it is significant that Parliament itself contemplated removing night poaching cases from Quarter Sessions to Assizes on the ground that the justices were too lenient.[124]

The justices were not without some supervision in the exercise of their duties and this extended to the game laws, although there are not many examples to be found. In 1726 a civil action for false imprisonment was brought by one Hill against a justice called Bateman and the constable who had committed him to prison on Bateman's warrant. Hill was charged with destroying game and in such a case the justice should have ordered a fine and the levy of the penalty on his goods. It was held that an action lay against Bateman. As regards the constable, the ruling was that the justice's warrant was a sufficient justification for his action, though this could not be the case where the justice issued a warrant in circumstances which were clearly out of his jurisdiction.[125]

120. Cambridge UP (1981).
121. *Ibid.*, p. 96.
122. *Ibid.*, pp. 100-101.
123. *Ibid.*, p. 163.
124. Parliamentary Debates, First ser. XXXV, col. 339.
125. *Hill v. Bateman and Another*, 1726, Sessions Cases, 99.

It cannot be denied that the justices had a class interest in enforcing the game laws. There are also plenty of instances in which they applied the laws ruthlessly. Considering, however, that they were acting in their own interest, it is surprising that in the vast majority of cases they seem to have acted with restraint and that often they exhibited a considerable degree of leniency and understanding. One must recognize that almost all contemporary comment was biased and was adduced by those who, on principle, disapproved strongly of the justices and of their functions. These one-sided comments have not stood the test of examination in the light of the facts which have recently been revealed.

The manifest defects of the Justice of the Peace system in administering the game laws arose from the system itself. It was entirely under the control of men who were, at one and the same time, legislators, prosecutors, judges and juries in causes in which they themselves had a strong personal interest. Although some succumbed to the temptation to take full advantage of the situation, the majority deserve at least some credit for managing to adopt an approach which was not excessively partisan.

Conclusion

In this and the previous two chapters we have examined the local government of England and Wales during a period when it was under the almost unfettered control of the Justices of the Peace. In this period the justices came to exercise an authority which dominated the national as well as the county scene and went far beyond what would normally be expected of magistrates and local administrators. They had achieved this position because they and the rest of the country gentry of whom they were the leaders had revolted with total success against the King and his Council in the Glorious Revolution of 1689, and thus secured freedom from all central control. The relationship between them and the national Government became one of free consultation and co-operation, political and social power being centred in the country landowners. This was particularly noticeable during the period of Whig hegemony when the authority of the Whig oligarchy was limited locally by the power of the justices, supported by the other squires, who were mainly Tory. So strong was the position of the justices that it was they who influenced Government decisions on many matters and not the Government which controlled them. This state of affairs continued throughout the eighteenth century until, in the nineteenth, under the influence of the Industrial Revolution, the autocratic rule of the rural aristocracy was supplanted by democratic

Government at both national and local level.

The justices who governed the country during this period have been the subject of many vituperative epithets both in their own age and subsequently. Historians have depicted them as corrupt and incompetent tyrants, and even some of their own supporters have regarded them as benevolent despots. Is this judgment justified?

There can be no doubt that the justices adopted a harsh policy of class distinction. They were hard on the lower classes and shamelessly lenient towards their own. The propertied members of society were allowed to behave with impunity in a licentious manner which would have been visited with dire punishment if indulged in by their inferiors. There was also a tendency to favour supporters of one's own political party. Again, there was an obvious susceptibility to the pressure of their personal interests, which was particularly evident in the stopping-up of thoroughfares and the application of the game laws. There were also isolated examples of sadism, narrow-mindedness, overweening ambition and incompetence, and any body of persons which contains individuals of this nature deserves disapprobiation. Yet there can be no doubt that, except in Middlesex and Westminster, the number of inadequate Justices was far outweighed by those who did not exhibit these defects, and many of the characters who figured prominently in the minds of critics were creatures of fiction who added spice to the pages of the novelists. The real life characters resembling Throckmorton and the Duke of Buckingham appear to have formed only a very small proportion of the total number of justices in this era. It must also be recognized that much of the invective was inspired by a determination to discredit an outdated system. It was not difficult to find examples to support this campaign which ignored anything on the credit side.

An increasing source of complaint was the growing weight of local taxation, for which the justices were responsible. Those who were not justices resented the ability of Quarter Sessions, a wholly unrepresentative body, to raise the rates at the expense of the rest of the county. It cannot be denied, however, that the expenditure was necessary. Indeed, it may be said to the justices' credit that they themselves paid their share of the rates and the money was spent not only on maintaining common services such as highways which benefited the justices as members of the community, but also large sums were expended on poor relief, lunatic asylums and gaols and houses of correction. The self-interest of the justices was curiously absent when it came to spending money on improving the lot of the rest of the community.

The justices were severely censured for having introduced payments to paupers from the rates in aid of wages; yet at the time members of the Government and public opinion generally approved of what they had done. Later, when the disastrous effects of this policy were recognized and it was abandoned by the justices, they were attacked with equal ferocity.

By then, however, the climate had changed and any merits that the justices may have had were totally ignored in the critical atmosphere which spread throughout the country after 1815. As we shall see in ch. V,[126] they could do nothing right in the eyes of the public or of most of the politicians and, even when they acted with the best of motives, it was, in the words of the Webbs, "imputed to them as a crime." [126]

As to the charge of incompetence, there is no evidence to support this as a general rule. It obviously applied to certain individuals, but so far as the whole body of justices were concerned they were capable and intelligent and showed notable ability at least in discharging those of their duties which they found congenial. Unfortunately, there were some in which they showed little interest, either because of the nature of the work itself or because it involved travelling a long distance from their home. Consequently, administration was allowed to fall into arrears, but this was not due to the justices' ineptitude. It was certainly a defect in the system, but it arose largely from the justices being over-burdened and from the absence of any central control and supervision of their work.

The loud outcry against the justices who stopped-up thoroughfares for the benefit of themselves and their friends was probably fully justified. It was typical of the arrogance of those who governed the counties that they should have interpreted the highway legislation as having been passed in the interest of the landowners, whereas its clear intention was that stopping-up and diversion should be carried out only in the interests of the community.

There was also some substance in other charges brought against the justices, as in respect of their responsibility for policing, gaols and licensing, but in most cases there were strong mitigating circumstances and sometimes the accusations were ill-founded. In the discharge of their police duties, and particularly in the suppression of riots, the justices were attacked from both sides. They were said to be both ineffective and too harsh. Ineffectiveness usually arose from the absence of any justice in the vicinity of the disturbance. Time after time constables had to travel considerable distances in search of a justice and, when one was finally found, he might arrive on the scene too late. If he acted too precipitately he would certainly be censured. Whatever he did was wrong in the eyes of the critics. There was a growing need for a standing police force which could act swiftly and

126. *ELG, The Parish and the County* pp. 594-595.

effectively in an emergency.

The condition of the prisons was a scandal for which all those concerned must take the blame. Some of the justices themselves, however, were among the leaders of prison reform and the substantial improvements which took place owe much to them. Criticism should be confined to the justices in those counties which did not follow the reforming lead of Gloucestershire and some other counties.

Criticism of the justices' performance in the licensing field was based on the claim that licences were issued in an arbitrary manner, and above all that the justices' policy further enriched the already wealthy brewers and ruined the poor keepers who lost their licences. In the prevailing spirit of free trade it was maintained that the sale of liquor should be left to supply and demand which, it was said, would lead to just the right number of alehouses to suit the population in each area. The fact that when such a system was later established it proved to be disastrous and had to be replaced by one which was again supervised by the justices and which continues to the present day is a vindication of the justices' performance.

It has also been said that the quality of those appointed to the commission in the eighteenth century deteriorated. If this is intended to mean that a larger proportion of the justices were drawn from families which had only recently become accepted by the landed gentry it is true, but it is totally wrong to say that there was a lower standard of ability, integrity and conscientiousness among those appointed to the commissions. In this respect those who had recently risen in the social scale tended to make the most effective and public-spirited magistrates. Much of the strength of the magistracy during this period lay in those justices who were members of newly established families which had made their fortune through trade in the city areas, particularly London, and had moved into the country and bought substantial estates. They were by nature energetic and enterprising and were keen to play an active part in the local Government of their new areas. They and the clerical justices were often seen to be doing the lion's share of the work, and it was they who introduced much of the enlightened approach to social problems which emerged during the latter part of the century. A genuine attempt was made by the Lord Chancellors, the Lords Lieutenant and others concerned in the appointments, to chose only those who were most suitable for the office and, although the final choice tended to be based primarily on property and political affiliations, there is ample indication that the overall quality of those serving on the commissions at the end of the century was distinctly higher than it had been at the beginning. This was particularly noticeable among those who took the lead at both Quarter Sessions and Petty Sessions. In the words of the Webbs: "In nearly all cases, the squires and clergymen who filled the Commission seem to have had an instinct for choosing, as chairmen and trusted administrators, men of remarkable incorruptability and public spirit."127

Incorruptability is a point which needs to be emphasized on the credit side. Apart from those in the metropolitan area, the justices were seldom accused of corruption. This is not surprising as they did not owe their livelihood to their office. They were wealthy men to whom it mattered not whether they derived any profit from the work they did, and they would have been scrupulously careful to avoid the social stigma and degradation which such a charge would have brought upon them. There were indeed some exceptions, but they seem to have been extremely few in number, and in those cases of which records survive, their activities appear to have been closely proscribed by their colleagues. At no time did such an individual reach a position of any significance in a county. To quote the Webbs again, "The faults of which the justices ... were accused, are ... in themselves testimony to the freedom of the Rulers of the County from personal corruption, and evidence of a quite remarkable disregard among them of their direct pecuniary advantages."128

Mention has been made of some of the justices who went out of their way to help the needy inhabitants of their respective areas. For every tyrant among the justices there were dozens who were ready to act as guides and counsellors to the more humble citizens, and although the cynical comment may be made that this could have been done to enhance their local image, there is no evidence of such an incentive, and it is clear that these activities were of great benefit to the community. Innumerable examples are to be found of justices who did not figure prominently in the conduct of magisterial affairs and who did not play a lead in major reforms, but who took steps, in various minor ways, to help the less fortunate members of society. Typical instances are to be seen in Gloucestershire, where the Reverend Charles Coxwell gave two of his cottages to house the poor, and Thomas Estcourt fitted up a farmhouse and appointed a woolworker at a salary of £35 who was to instruct children in spinning, their products being sold for the benefit of the institution and with no profit to himself.

We have also seen that, contrary to popular belief, the justices did not indulge regularly in imposing harsh sentences. Quite apart from sentencing, however, which was often influenced by genuine clemency, as in the case of Moses Rose, it is evident that the justices were guided by compassion when performing other duties inherent in the administration of the criminal law. Thus, in 1796, Ann Read was

127. *Ibid.*, p.372.
128. *Ibid.*, p. 581.

apprehended on a charge of felony and committed to Chelmsford gaol. It was subsequently ordered that she be discharged and sent back to her place of settlement. The usual practice was for discharged prisoners to find their way home on foot, but Ann Read was lame, and accordingly the justices, in ordering the keeper of the gaol to release her, also directed that she be conveyed at public expense to her village and handed over to the churchwarden and overseer of the poor.[129] Numerous similar cases are to be found in many county archives.

Reading the private papers of Justices of the Peace during this period one is often struck by their enlightened and humanitarian view. One must, of course, accept the possibility that the letters and documents which have come down to us were written by the more enlightened elements on the commissions who may well have been in a minority, and there are certainly indications in some of the letters that the writers' colleagues were less enthusiastic than themselves. Yet one also gains the impression that the more progressive justices usually found a fairly receptive audience at both Quarter and Petty Sessions, and that the JPs exhibited greater public awareness and a stronger inclination to solve current problems than the average member of contemporary society. At the same time, service on the Commission of the Peace made the justices more aware of the shortcomings of the existing system and of the misery which these caused.

Passing judgment upon the Justices of the Peace of the eighteenth and nineteenth centuries must vary according to whether one is assessing the justices themselves or the system. So far as the justices were concerned, there is good reason to conclude that, apart from those in the metropolitan area and a small number of individuals elsewhere, their performance was all that could reasonably have been expected of them in the circumstances of the time. It is not surprising that they should have been lax in discharging some of their duties, considering the great volume of work which was placed upon these part-time, unpaid and untrained magistrates. In spite of this, the great majority took their office seriously and showed dedication to the task and to the population for whom they were responsible. There is certainly no convincing evidence that the legendary hubristic, tyrannical JP existed in more than an insignificant minority and, far from being ignorant and incapable, the majority gave abundant indication of being above average in intelligence and competence.

The shortcomings of the Justices of the Peace lay therefore in the system which they were required to operate rather than in the character and behaviour of the men themselves. Most of what has been said above has applied mainly to the justices as individuals. It is a different matter when one comes to analyse the Justice of the Peace

---

129. Order of March 14, 1796 by John Judd Junior, Justice of the Peace. Essex RO, D/P 1/13/1.

system. This had been effective in previous generations, but it could no longer cope with the increased pressure of the changing world and with the work which had become far too great in volume and complexity. The justices had neither the ability nor the time to handle the problems arising from every aspect of the new political, social and above all economic climate which had been created by radicalism, by a rapidly growing working population and by the whole ambit of the Industrial Revolution. Public opinion was against them because the world was imbued with an atmosphere in which the old, established systems became unacceptable and had in principle to be replaced with new institutions which were in accord with the spirit of radical reform. In the nineteenth century emphasis came to be placed upon democratically elected bodies, and to the supporters of the new political philosophy the concept of Government by the lay magistracy was anathema. Not only were the justices appointed nominally by the Crown, but in fact they had become a self-perpetuating oligarchy. It was but natural that the politicians and others who were imbued with the new progressive spirit should distort the truth in order to further their cause, and in so doing they heaped much undeserved odium upon the justices as individuals rather than upon the outdated system.

The Justices of the Peace at the beginning of the nineteenth century did have many shortcomings, especially by the critical standards of the twentieth century, and in performing their multifarious functions they often fell far short of the ideal. It should be acknowledged, however, that until then the government of the country under their rule had been a remarkable achievement which could only have been attained by the dedicated endeavours of many intelligent and public-spirited men. Until the eighteenth century, the justices had, with but few exceptions, discharged their unique functions remarkably effectively, and almost certainly with greater success than would have been achieved by the only possible alternative at that time - the salaried official who was to be found in other countries. Such officials would no doubt have been more expedient from the Government's point of view, as they would have implemented national policy without question and would have avoided showing personal animosity through fear of dismissal. They would not have indulged in stopping up thoroughfares for personal motives, nor would they have allowed themselves to be swayed unduly by the sentiments of their neighbours or by sympathy for those who infringed the law, as in the case of breaches of the excise regulations. To judge by experience on the Continent, however, the Royal official would have been open to bribes and would have lacked a close understanding of the way of life and the needs of the inhabitants of his district. Least of all would he have had any inclination to go beyond the bounds of duty and to help those whose lot was worse than his own. In contrast to this, the justices were incorruptible, well informed on local issues and dedicated to the interests of the community, and also capable of resisting any improper pressure from a Government which was still largely autocratic. Sydney Smith, referring to the licensing of alehouses, asked:

"What in truth could we substitute for the unpaid magistracy? We have no doubt but that a set of rural judges, in the pay of government, would very soon become corrupt jobbers and odious tyrants, as they often are on the Continent. But the magistrates, as they now exist, really constitute a bulwark of some value against the supreme power of the state."

In comparing the situation in England with that in Continental countries, it is pertinent to observe that one of the most marked differences was the ready assumption of responsibility by the English gentry, whereas in other countries there was a reluctance to do so, especially in France (though this may have been due more to pressure from the King than to disinterest on the part of the gentry). Norma Landau sums up the position by saying: "On the Continent, the elite fled from their estates, preferring the pleasures of the court to the burdens of local leadership. In England, the elite accepted the obligations inherent in their social status."[130]

In the nineteenth century the Justices of the Peace were at last unable to meet the challenge of a rapidly changing world and to adapt themselves to the new climate as they had done in the past. The principal weaknesses lay in an insufficient infrastructure, in the lack of supervision and control and in the loss of public confidence in what had come to be regarded as an undemocratic system. The first two of these might have been overcome by introducing a system similar to that which was in fact adopted in the later nineteenth century with the establishment of a local Government bureaucracy, coupled with effective supervision of local administration by ministers and government departments. Something of this kind had indeed already been introduced. We have seen that for some time the increased demand for public services had been too great to be met by the traditional method of administration through the courts, and already a number of new *ad hoc* bodies had been created, for which the justices were responsible and which they no longer controlled through medieval judicial machinery.

As regards Government supervision of the JPs, it may be noted that this had operated very effectively before the Revolution, especially in Tudor and early Stuart times. The Privy Council at its best provided an exceedingly efficient means of supervising all the functions of local

130.   *The Justie of the Peace 1679-1760.* (1984). Univ. of California Press.

Government and ensuring that they were performed satisfactorily and in the public interest. There were occasions when the Council, inspired by able members like Burghley and Francis Bacon, showed great insight and initiative in providing the justices with guidance and inspiration in solving the numerous problems with which they were confronted. There were moreover occasions, of which the prime example was the threat of Spanish invasion under Elizabeth, when no concerted action would have been taken by the country as a whole had it not been for the driving force of the Council and the firm and concise directions which it issued through the justices on a nation-wide basis. Supervision and guidance, and where necessary support, by the Council and the Star Chamber had made local government through the justices singularly effective. The revival of something of this kind might have proved efficacious in the nineteenth century had it not been for the universal opposition to any body which was not based upon the principle of representation and popular election.

It is reasonable to conclude that the demise of the local government role of the Justices of the Peace in the nineteenth century was inevitable because of the political philosophy of the new age, rather than because of the shortcomings of the men who held this ancient office. It is interesting to note that when the final blow fell with the establishment of county and district councils in the 1880s, a contemporary historian (F.W. Maitland, who admittedly was inclined to be effusive in his praise) lamented the change which was about to take place and wrote of the Justice of the Peace:

"As a governor he is doomed: but there has been no accusation. He is cheap, he is pure, he is capable, but he is doomed: he is sacrificed to a theory on the altar of the spirit of the age."

CHAPTER IV

STIPENDIARY MAGISTRATES

Collapse of the Justice of the Peace system in the metropolitan area - Creation of the Bow Street Police Office - Introduction of Stipendiary Magistrates - Extention piecemeal beyond London - Final establishment of a national Stipendiary Magistrate system co-extensive with that of the lay justices

The metropolitan area

DURING THE EIGHTEENTH CENTURY, the office of Justice of the Peace, although subject to increasing criticism, remained generally acceptable to the majority of the population, or at least to that section which dominated both national and local affairs. There was, however, a striking exception in the case of the justices for the metropolitan area around London where "decline" is inadequate to describe the wholesale deterioration in the type of persons who held the office and in the manner in which they discharged their duties.

The system of maintaining law and order through JPs was well suited to a rural community as it still existed in most counties of England and Wales, but it was clear from the beginning of the century that this did not operate effectively in a heavily urbanized society. The problem was largely confined to Middlesex where the metropolitan area of the capital had spread over a considerable part of the county. Here two factors were paramount in leading to the deterioration; the unwillingness of men of stature and integrity to serve as justices and an overwhelming increase in the volume and seriousness of crime. The problem was not so grave in those urban areas which were parts of cities and boroughs and where the justices, although far from ideal, were persons of local standing with a sense of civic responsibility and had not sunk to the debased level of those in Middlesex. In the city of London a fairly high standard was maintained by the Lord Mayor and aldermen who conducted the city courts, but there was a marked contrast in the adjoining county of Middlesex which had ceased to be dominated by the leading, landowning gentry, and where the commission came to be filled by men of less degree who had secured appointment by various means, often for political or financial services. They came to be referred to as "trading" or "basket" justices, the baskets being receptacles in which gifts were placed.

The situation had been aggravated by the Government's policy of removing political opponents from the commissions and replacing them with supporters. The attitude of the new justices towards their office was totally different to that of the county squires. The latter, for all their faults, had a strong sense of responsibility and jealously maintained the reputation which had been acquired by their predecessors. The Middlesex JP, on the other hand, had a commercial approach to life and instinctively regarded any office he occupied as a means of acquiring monetary gain. This became increasingly possible with growing opportunities to charge fees for magisterial work. We have seen that from the fifteenth century justices were entitled to fees for certain services such as granting alehouses licences, but these were regarded as of little significance by the wealthy landowners who then constituted the county commissions, and in many cases the proceeds were allocated to charitable purposes. By the eighteenth century, however, the circumstances in which fees might be charged were increasing, and an unscrupulous justice had ample opportunity to derive a considerable income from this source. The Middlesex justices abandoned all charitable thoughts and began to keep the fees for themselves. An example of this trend was provided by an Act of 1745 which imposed a fine on anyone who uttered a swear word (graduated from one shilling for a labourer to five shillings for a gentleman). This could be imposed summarily by a single justice. The proceeds were intended for the poor but were purloined by the justices who increased their income by encouraging false accusations or even by claiming falsely that they themselves had heard someone swear. They were prepared to adopt other corrupt practices for their own ends; for example, they had long been entitled to a fee for granting bail, but some of those in Middlesex sent out constables to arrest every person found on the street at night from whom a bail fee might be extracted. Again, there were some who demanded bribes for licensing public houses and others who obtained protection money from prostitutes and brothel keepers. A number of examples of the misbehaviour of Middlesex justices are to be found in the minutes of Quarter Sessions and sometimes the sessions petitioned for the removal of a justice from the Commission.[1]

The behaviour of Middlesex justices naturally became the butt of contemporary drama and literature. Many instances are to be found in the works of Fielding, Gay and Smollett. Earlier examples were depicted in *Hudibras* by Samuel Butler who was himself clerk to several of the landed gentry and as such acted as Clerk to the Justices. Although these were fictitious they reflected public recognition of the

---

1. In 1777 Middlesex Quarter Sessions even set up a committee to inquire into the behaviour of certain of the county justices who had "grossly misbehaved themselves in the execution of their office." (Quarter Sessions Minutes, December, 1777). At least one justice was removed as a result of the committee's report. Some striking examples of misbehaviour by Middlesex justices are given by the Webbs in *ELG, The Parish and the County*, pp. 330-1.

serious defects of magistrates in this area. These were the subject of abrasive criticism by serious writers throughout the eighteenth century. Thus in 1709, Dean Jonathan Swift wrote:

"There is one abuse in this town which wonderfully contributes to the promotion of vice; that such men are often put into the Commission of the peace whose interest it is that virtue should be utterly banished from among us; who maintain, or at least enrich themselves by encouraging the grossest immoralities; to whom all bawds of the ward pay contribution for shelter and protection from the laws. Thus these worthy magistrates, instead of lessening enormities, are the occasions of just twice as much as there would be without them."[2]

In May, 1780 Edmund Burke said in the House of Commons that the Middlesex justices were generally "the scum of the earth; carpenters, brickmakers, shoemakers, some of whom were notoriously men of such infamous character that they were unworthy of any employ whatever, and others so ignorant that they could scarcely write their own names."

It was these corrupt and incompetent individuals who were responsible for keeping the peace and for apprehending and examining the ever-increasing numbers of criminals. They were obliged to rely upon the unpaid parish constables, as in other counties, and upon night watchmen who, since 1640, had patrolled the streets but who were so ill-paid that no able-bodied man would consider undertaking the job. On top of this, a race of unscrupulous solicitors emerged in Middlesex who made fortunes from defending law-breakers and securing their release by outwitting the ignorant justices who were neither lawyers themselves nor had legally qualified clerks to advise them. It is not surprising that the justices failed abysmally in the performance of their task and that the situation deteriorated to a state bordering on anarchy.

Lawlessness became an even greater menace to society in the eighteenth century than it had been before. Among the causes was the Poor Law under which the homeless and destitute were driven from parish to parish and finally arrived in London and other cities where they immediately joined the gangs of criminals whose numbers were also swollen by disbanded soldiers and sailors. All contributed to the appalling squalor of the overcrowded metropolitan area. The problem was exacerbated for a time by an unlimited supply of cheap gin. Whereas ale was sold mostly in inns and taverns which were licensed and controlled by the justices, the sale of spirits was unsupervised. The

2. *A Project for the Advancement of Religion and the Reformation of Manners,* p. 15.

Government tried to introduce a licensing system for spirits in 1727, but withdrew it in 1733 at the demand of the wheat-growing landowners. An attempt to reintroduce it in 1736 met with defiance and the justices were mostly impotent in enforcing the law. The destitute classes resorted to the consumption of vast quantities of cheap gin as a form of escapism, with serious social consequences.

As the forces of law and order became ineffective the criminal classes reaped a rich harvest from the growing affluent classes. Highway robbery on the roads leading to the greater cities was in its heyday and even enjoyed a certain amount of glamour. Inside the towns the street robbers, from pickpockets, many of whom were children like Dicken's Artful Dodger, to large gangs of cut-throats, operated almost with impunity. Smollett wrote: "Thieves and robbers are now become more desperate and savage than they have ever appeared since mankind was civilized."

Were it not for the introduction of the Tyburn Ticket and of the financial rewards for successful prosecutions mentioned earlier, it is probable that few of the urban criminals would ever have been brought to justice. As it was, a number were convicted and hanged, but the system led to the rise of professional "thief takers" who made a living from prosecutions, and many of whom had sinister backgrounds and were deeply involved in the underworld.

The need to devise a far more effective method of dealing with criminals had become acute, but it would be well into the nineteenth century before a solution would be found in a system of whole-time, legally qualified magistrates and an independent, professional police force. In the meantime we can see a series of moves forwards and backwards resembling the vicissitudes of the keepers and early justices of the fourteenth century. In considering the development of the stipendiary system in the metropolitan area it is interesting to note that the Government, far from taking the lead, consistently dragged its feet over the issue for fear of being accused of unjustified interference, and until well into the nineteenth century it was a small number of the Middlesex justices themselves who piloted the way forward. These were public-spirited men, contemptuous of their fellows, who came to establish a new peace-keeping and criminal justice organization centred on a private house in Bow Street. From there they began to operate in 1740, and there, apart from a short move in 1880 to state-owned premises in the same street, their successors are to be found today.

The county of Middlesex included Westminster, and for a long time there was one commission for the whole area, but in 1618 the City and Liberty of Westminster were granted a separate commission, probably with a view to enabling the Government to exercise more direct control over the justices in the area surrounding the Houses of

Parliament. A number of the Westminster justices were also appointed to the Middlesex Commission, for otherwise their warrants could not be executed throughout the county unless endorsed by a Middlesex JP. These arrangements made little difference to the quality of the justices which was equally low on both commissions.

Long before the scandals of the "trading" justices had aroused public indignation a peculiar type of magistrate began to appear on the Westminster and Middlesex commissions. This was the "court justice" who was specially chosen by the Government to combine the role of policeman and judge with that of courtier and spy. Their task, in addition to that of an ordinary JP, was to consult with the authorities about the maintenance of order in the capital and with special regard to the security of the Sovereign. Very little is known about the origin of this office which probably began in the sixteenth century. There is evidence that these justices received some payment from the Government for their services and in the eighteenth century some of them developed a role in which one may see the origin of the system of stipendiary magistrates.

As the reputation of the Middlesex and Westminster justices deteriorated, men of the right quality became increasingly reluctant to undertake the office, but there were a few exceptions. One of those who held the office of court justice in the mid-eighteenth century was Thomas De Veil who is often regarded as the immediate ancestor of the chief magistrate at Bow Street, though no such office was officially recognized until long after his time. The room of the present chief metropolitan magistrate contains a plaque which shows De Veil as the first holder of the office, and during his lifetime he was sometimes referred to as the principal magistrate at Bow Street, but his official position was never more than that of any other justice on the Middlesex and Westminster Commissions. What distinguished him from his fellows were the efforts he made to improve the office of magistrate and the steps he took to make its work effective, including the establishment of the first full-time magistrate's office and courtroom.

De Veil, who was born in 1689, is generally regarded as having been one of the "trading" justices, but there is no convincing evidence to support this. He took fees but, as far as we know, these were all ones to which he was legally entitled and he did not accept bribes. He also received at least one grant of £250 from the Treasury, in a similar manner to the previous court justices who were remunerated for special services. In a book which he wrote for the guidance of his fellow justices, De Veil wrote: "As to justices' Fees or Perquisites, the best rule is to observe strictly the Oath of Office; which tells you what you may safely take yourself, or suffer your clerk to receive for you; which last method is best suitable to the dignity of that Honourable

Station."[3] Nevertheless, it would appear from the memoirs (mentioned later) of Henry Fielding who succeeded him that his interpretation of what was legitimate may have been more liberal than that of his successor. He was certainly far from perfect. He was a flamboyant character, vain, arrogant and extravagant, and his morals left much to be desired even by contemporary standards.

De Veil was the son of an emigré Huguenot minister and therefore his family background was far removed from that of the landed gentry who constituted the basis of most county commissions. He served in the army, rising from the ranks to become a captain and was later made a colonel in the militia. In 1729 he was appointed to the Middlesex and Westminster commissions and immediately set up an office in Leicester Fields, from which he moved, via Soho, to Bow Street in 1740. He sat regularly at Middlesex and Westminster Quarter Sessions but never became chairman, and it was as a police officer and detective rather than as a Judge that he gained an outstanding reputation.

De Veil developed a police system centred on his office in Bow Street[4] and he achieved considerable success in detecting and apprehending criminals. He was also a man of great courage and initiative and scored some spectacular achievements in quelling riots and maintaining order. He dealt effectively with situations which arose during the Jacobite rising of 1745. He was frequently to be seen attempting, usually successfully, to read the proclamation under the Riot Act, and although on these occasions he was often obliged to rely upon the constables, he might also find himself, like other justices, with a body of troops at his disposal. It was generally assumed, however, that a justice could not call upon the military unless he had first read a proclamation under the Riot Act and the mob had then failed to disperse within one hour. In 1745 he was placed in charge of a mixed body of troops and constables which was sent to arrest the Jacobite, Lord Dillan, at his home in Hertfordshire. To enable him to carry out these extended operations he had been appointed also to the commissions for Hertfordshire, Essex, Surrey and the Tower of London.

The Government and the public came to regard De Veil with respect and he was consulted on a number of matters concerning law and order and the security of the realm. He was knighted in 1744 and died in office in 1746. He remained to the end a JP with no more official standing than his colleagues but he had established a precedent which was followed and developed. All of his successors occupied in turn the house in Bow Street (rented from the Duke of Bedford for

3.   Sir Thomas De Veil, *Observations on the Practice of a Justice of the Peace*, p. 19.
4.   For a description of the Bow Street premises and an account of their earlier occupants see Anthony Babington, *A House in Bow Street*, (1969) London.

£10 a year) in which he had converted the ground floor into permanent offices and a courtroom and where he laid the first foundations for an effective police and magisterial system for the metropolis. His term at Bow Street marked the beginning of the transitional stage between the "trading" justice and the professional stipendiary magistrate.

The unique position which De Veil had established did not vanish at his death. After a brief interval it was revived and extended by Henry Fielding, the author and playwright, who was appointed to the Middlesex commission in 1747 and to that of Westminster in 1750, becoming chairman of Middlesex Quarter Sessions in 1749. He was to have a profound influence upon the development of the magisterial system in the London area. Although he was the son of an impecunious army officer, Fielding, who was born in 1707, was well connected. His maternal grandfather had been a King's Bench Judge and his father was the brother of the Earl of Denbigh. He himself had several friends in the Government who were probably responsible for securing his appointment as a justice in order to provide him with an income, as he was at the time in financial straits. Fielding, however, was so scrupulously honest that he would accept only those payments which were clearly proper, and consequently, according to his own account,[5] his receipts dropped from the £500 a year of his predecessor to barely £300, out of which he paid the salary of his clerk.

> "I had not plundered the public or the poor of those sums which men, who are always ready to plunder both as much as they can, have been pleased to suspect me of taking: on the contrary, by composing, instead of inflaming, the quarrels of porters and beggars (which I blush to say hath not been universally practised) and by refusing to take a shilling from a man who most undoubtedly would not have had another left, I had reduced an income of about five hundred pounds a year of the dirtiest money upon earth, to little more than three hundred pounds; a considerable proportion of which remainded with my clerk."

It was only the occasional receipt of proceeds from his books - never very great during his lifetime - which kept him solvent. He also received some small, occasional payments from the Government's Secret Service Fund. It would seem that he deserved every penny he received because of the volume as well as the quality of his work. His memoirs indicate that he often sat for sixteen hours a day, and there is reason to believe that sometimes he sat up all night taking depositions.

---

5. *The Journal of a Voyage to Lisbon,* Works X, 1806 edn., London, p. 197. In *The Journal* Fielding refers to his office as being that of "a principal justice of the peace in Westminster," but there was no official recognition of this.

In 1748 Fielding moved into De Veil's old home in Bow Street, probably because of the court and office accommodation which it already provided, and immediately began improving the services which his predecessor had begun. His task was made somewhat easier by the fact that he had been called to the Bar by the Middle Temple in 1740 and had gained experience in practice on the Western Circuit. He set a high standard of personal integrity and fairness and his determination to improve the quality of the magistracy reflected views which he had held long before he became a justice himself. His satires painted a highly disparaging picture of the JPs in his day, Justice Squeezum being a striking example of the worst type of "trading" justice - ignorant, avaricious, depraved and corrupt.

Fielding was an outspoken critic of the criminal law and procedure in general and he was constantly urging reforms. Some of his proposals led to enactments by Parliament. An example of this was an Act of 1752 which gave the court power to allow the costs out of public funds of a poor prosecutor who obtained a conviction for felony, and in 1754 a similar power was granted to award costs to witnesses. He was also instrumental in bringing music and dance halls under the supervision of the justices and in increasing their authority over gaming houses and brothels.

Fielding's term of office coincided with a period of particular violence and to meet this he introduced a body of peace-enforcement officers who came to be known later as the "Bow Street Runners." At that time Westminster was divided into nine parishes with a total of about eighty constables and 300 watchmen who were incapable of dealing with the numerous gangs of criminals. Fielding therefore recruited a small group of volunteers, all of whom had served as constables, and formed a squad under the command of one Saunders Welch who had served for some time as High Constable of Holborn and who was later to become a Bow Street justice himself. These men were often referred to as "thief takers" but they were very different from the disreputable ruffians to whom the term had previously been applied. They were all dedicated to their work and took a pride in maintaining a high standard. They were held in constant readiness and could be called upon at short notice whenever a crime had been committed. They did not wear a uniform and were normally armed only with a baton. In spite of this, and their small number - six men in all - they were conspicuously successful in breaking up the criminal gangs who mostly proved incapable of adjusting to the new phenomenon of trained, experienced and resolute officers. As far as is known these officers received no salary but they were paid substantial rewards from successful prosecutions.

The policing part of a justice's functions included detection as well as the apprehension of offenders, but before Fielding's tenure of office there was nothing which resembled criminal investigation as it came to be understood in the nineteenth and twentieth centuries. De Veil had attained notoriety as a skilful examiner during his inquiries into alleged offences, but Fielding developed a technique which placed him among the leading precursors of the modern detective. He endeavoured to enlist the support of the public, and almost weekly a notice appeared in local newspapers appealing to those who had suffered robberies or burglaries to send the fullest possible details immediately to him at Bow Street. He would then examine witnesses and possibly instruct his "thief takers" to try to obtain further evidence. In the course of time the "thief takers" themselves became highly skilled in detective work and, with the approval of the justices, would offer their services to victims of crimes who were prepared to pay them for their investigations. At the same time, records of criminals and their activities began to be kept at Bow Street and could be consulted by justices throughout the country. By the time Fielding retired, shortly before his death in 1754, a fairly sophisticated system had evolved.

It will be seen that, as in previous centuries, the justice played the leading role at every stage of the criminal legal process. As soon as a crime had been committed he, either personally or through his subordinates, would search for clues and examine witnesses. Having considered all the evidence, he would make an arrest and interrogate the prisoner. Finally, at his discretion, he would either discharge the prisoner, sentence him to punishment or commit him to custody pending trial by jury. The work at Bow Street became so heavy under Fielding that a single justice was no longer able to discharge it in the manner he prescribed. He tried, unsuccessfully, to persuade the Lord Chancellor, Lord Hardwicke, to appoint his clerk, Joshua Broyden, to the commission to assist him, but in 1750 his half-brother, John, was appointed to the commission for Middlesex and in 1751 for Westminster and became his assistant.

Henry Fielding served at Bow Street for only six years, but his influence on the development of the system which led to full-time stipendiary magistrates was considerable. He brought to his office a reputation which was alien to justices serving in urban areas at the time and this led to the acceptance of the Bow Street office on a permanent basis as the centre of police administration. His service as a magistrate was equally important because of the coincidental advances which were made under his leadership in the detection of crime and the elimination of criminals. The origins of the police detectives and constables of the twentieth century may be found in his "thief takers" who developed into remarkably efficient detectives and peace-keeping officers.

Henry Fielding was succeeded by his half-brother, John, in 1754. John, who was 14 years younger than Henry, had been totally blinded as the result of an accident at the age of 17 while serving in the Navy. In spite of this he proved to be an outstanding magistrate, and indeed turned his physical defect to his advantage by conveying the image of impartial "justice" sitting blindfolded. He continued his brother's work in improving the efficiency and standing of his office and like him he maintained a high level of integrity. His blindness did not deter him from visiting the scene of a crime to carry out his own inquiries, and he was remarkably skilful in detecting criminals and in examining witnesses. His success in breaking up gangs of robbers led to a noticeable reduction in street robberies. It was said that most of those who succeeded in escaping his police officers left London to carry on their criminal activities under easier conditions elsewhere, and accordingly Fielding initiated a weekly bulletin giving descriptions of criminals who had departed from London which was circulated to all parts of the country. The publication came to be called *The Hue and Cry* and after 1829 it became the *Police Gazette.* In turn, justices in other areas sent to Bow Street particulars of those who had "escaped justice" in their own counties, together with a warrant for their apprehension which could then be forwarded to wherever it might be required. A kind of clearing-house, in conjunction with the permanent criminal records, was therefore established at Bow Street for all criminal activity throughout England and Wales. Fielding clearly did not regard himself as being circumscribed by the limited area of his own commissions and his assumption of the role of a national police authority with the mantle of chief magistrate for Westminster went unchallenged.

The magistrates at Bow Street were mostly concerned with the suppression of crime while administrative matters were left to the other justices, but there were exceptions. John Fielding's accounts, which are preserved in the British Museum, contain items for checking street lighting. This may, however, have been regarded as ancillary to the enforcement of the criminal law because the new lighting system was intended primarily to reduce the number of robberies. Fielding was also involved in suppressing plays under the new censorship law, but he seems to have acted only at the personal request of the Lord Chamberlain.

John Fielding, like his brother, held enlightened views on the treatment of offenders. An example of this was his aversion to sending boys to prison where they were likely to be corrupted rather than deterred from further crime. He urged that homeless urchins, who might become young criminals, should be given the opportunity to serve at sea, and under his influence a charitable organization was created for this purpose. His compassion was illustrated by his attitude towards prostitutes. He claimed that most of those in London brothels were between 12 and 18 years of age and he proposed a scheme for saving young girls from prostitution and for reforming those who had already become prostitutes.[6]

The need for at least two justices at Bow Street was greater than ever, and when John Fielding took over from his brother, the role of assistant magistrate was assumed by Saunders Welch, the former high constable and commander of the "thief takers," a man of outstanding ability and impeccable character who had been appointed to the Middlesex and Westminster commissions in 1755. Welch had been a close friend of Henry Fielding who had strongly recommended him to the Lord Chancellor for appointment as a JP. Unfortunately, he and John Fielding had difficulty in working together. Their views differed in a number of respects and, being both men of strong character, they could not be reconciled. Consequently, Welch set up a subsidiary office, first in his own house in Long Acre and thereafter in Letchfield Street. There were then three magistrates' offices in Westminster, one in Bow Street under Fielding which dealt with the more serious cases, one at Letchfield Street and one at the Guildhall manned by the other justices in rotation.

Neither Fielding nor Welch indulged in any corrupt practices. They took fees, but only those to which they were strictly entitled by law. This source of income was totally inadequate to defray the cost of the expanding police system, which included the publication of regular press notices explaining current trends in criminal activity and seeking the public's co-operation in correcting them. In 1755, Fielding and Welch submitted a joint proposal to the Government that they should be paid salaries for their services. The Government agreed that they should each receive £200 a year from the Secret Service Funds, which was increased to £400 for Fielding in 1756; but it would seem from correspondence between him and the Secretary of State that payment was allowed to fall into serious arrears. Fielding also received £30 a year from the War Office for dealing with deserters.[7]

Neither John Fielding nor Welch were legally qualified and they soon became aware of the disadvantages this could place upon magistrates in their position, especially when they had to deal with unscrupulous solicitors. Fielding therefore proposed in 1758 that the principal magistrate should be legally qualified, preferably a barrister, but it would be another 50 years before the Secretary of State, who,

6. Both schemes were adopted. The first, called the Female Orphan Asylum, was in Lambeth and trained girls between twelve and fifteen years of age to be domestic servants. The second was the Magdalen Hospital in Lambeth which attempted to reform confirmed prostitutes. Fielding became a governor of both institutions.
7. PRO War Office Records, Secretary of State. Misc. 1763.

until 1949, was the Minister responsible for the appointment of stipendiary magistrates, began as a matter of policy to appoint only members of the Bar of at least three years' standing.

The most severe test of the peace-keeping machinery came in 1780 when the capital was paralysed by the mob instigated by Lord George Gordon, ostensibly as a protest against legislation which removed certain disabilities from Roman Catholics. Fielding was on his death bed and unable to take any part in suppressing the outbreak, but it is unlikely that he could have succeeded in quelling it. The situation became completely out of hand, the business of Parliament was interrupted and enormous damage was done to property. The civil power proved to be ineffective and order was finally restored by a full scale military operation conducted by the army. The rioters were then taken before military courts martial instead of the civil courts.

The riots proved beyond doubt the inability of the existing peace-keeping system to deal with large scale outbreaks of disorder, and attention was focused on the need for major changes. There continued, however, to be strong opposition to any reform. This came from many quarters and not only from the lay justices themselves who might have been expected to oppose the introduction of a stipendiary system. There was revulsion among the public in general against any increase in the Government's powers, and it was assumed that this would be the outcome of the appointment of professionals who relied on the Government for their pay. In 1785, the Government introduced the London and Westminster Police Bill which sought to introduce a system of stipendiary magistrates throughout the metropolitan area, including the City of London, and also a professional police force under the control of three commissioners appointed by the Government. It was strongly opposed on the ground that it was unnecessary to replace the long-established system and there was a general fear of the arbitrary powers which the three commissioners were expected to exercise. Among the Bill's opponents were the Lord Mayor and aldermen of the City of London who comprised the magistrates for the City. They claimed, with some justification, that the proposed provisions ought not to apply to them because they were not open to the same criticism as the justices in the neighbouring areas of Middlesex and Westminster. The Bill was dropped and the position remained the same except that the corruption of the Middlesex justices became even more apparent than before.

In 1792 a Bill on Middlesex and Surrey justices was introduced by a private Member, Francis Burton, who referred to "the blessings which this country enjoys from the fair administration of the important office of a Justice of the Peace. In London, however, the case is different and, excepting the office in Bow Street and the administration of the magistracy in the city ... these blessings are inadequately, if at all experienced." The Bill, which had Government backing, was passed in the teeth of fierce opposition from the Whigs, led by Fox and Sheridan, who claimed that it increased Crown patronage and they argued that as the existing JPs were unpaid they were under no obligation to the Government and therefore could have "no interest in perverting the law to oppression." The Act began by reciting that:

"Whereas a due and regular attendance of fit and able magistrates at certain known places and stated times, in such parts of the counties of Middlesex and Surrey as lie in and near the Metropolis, and a vigilant and steady administration of the laws by them is requisite to the maintenance of peace and good order throughout the parts aforesaid ..."

The Act differed from the Bill of 1785 in that it did not extend to the City of London and it did not create police commissioners. Nor did it apply to the existing establishment at Bow Street, but it copied the latter by creating seven other Public Offices[8] on the same lines, each with three stipendiary magistrates, appointed by the Home Secretary on behalf of the Crown at annual salaries of £400, paid out of the Consolidated Fund. The Bow Street magistrates continued to be paid, at the same rate,[9] from the Secret Service funds. All fees were to be paid over to a Receiver and none were to be taken by any of the magistrates except for licensing and certain other work. Each office had its own force of not more than six constables paid at 12 shillings a week and their work was similar to that of the Bow Street Runners. The Home Secretary was responsible for buildings and equipment, except in respect of the Bow Street office which continued to be held on a personal lease by the senior magistrates until 1842. It is curious that none of the statutory provisions applied to Bow Street where magistrates and constables remained entirely independent. The Bow Street force was strengthened by an armed foot patrol, appointed by the senior magistrate and paid two shillings and six pence a night (five shillings for officers) who patrolled the streets and the roads leading into London, and by a mounted patrol which was a para-military, uniformed and well armed force which operated in Essex, Kent and Surrey as well as in Middlesex and was highly successful in curbing the activities of highwaymen. The mounted patrol members were paid 28

8. Situated at Great Marlborough Street, Queen's Square, Holborn, Finsbury Square, Whitechapel, Shadwell and Southwark. The last of these was in Surrey, the others in Middlesex or Westminster. In 1800 an eighth office was opened in Wapping.
9. The senior Bow Street magistrate received an additional £300 "in lieu of fees, emoluments, etc." The salaries were raised in 1821 to £600 and in 1825 to £800, and finally to £1,200 (chief magistrate, £1,400) in 1839.

shillings a week.[10]

The 1792 Act was aimed at improving the policing of the metropolitan area, and it was confined to the establishment of police magistrates' courts. A serious defect in the legislation was that it left most of the administrative business in the hands of the corrupt "trading" justices.

John Fielding had died in 1780 and was succeeded by another efficient magistrate, Sir Sampson Wright, who had already served at Bow Street for some years. Many of those appointed under the 1792 Act, however, were of poor quality, having previously been "trading" justices in Middlesex and Westminster and who continued to take fees as well as their salaries. In most cases they had secured appointment by patronage and jobbery. There were, however, some outstanding exceptions, such as Patrick Colquhoun, who had served on the Middlesex commission for some years before being appointed under the 1792 Act. His *Treatise on the Police of the Metropolis* had considerable influence upon the creation of a metropolitan police force which was finally established by an Act forced through by Sir Robert Peel against strong opposition in 1829. Under this Act,[11] control was given to two new justices who had no judicial duties and were required to devote the whole of their time to police work. They later became Commissioners of Police with their headquarters at Scotland Yard, but they continued to be justices until the two offices were finally separated by the Administration of Justice Act 1973.

In 1838 Peel was instrumental in the appointment of a Select Committee of the House of Commons which recommended that the police offices should be reorganized, that the magistrates' salaries should be improved and that the stipendiary system should be extended throughout the metropolitan police district. On the latter point the Committee said:

"At present, the district of the Metropolitan Police, under 10 Geo. 4, c. 44, extends a considerable way beyond the Police Office districts, whence the inconvenience arises of the Police being obliged to take a number of the charges before the County Magistrates, at their Petty Sessions."

The Committee also pointed out that the Central Criminal Court district extended even beyond that of the police and that it would therefore be advantageous if all three districts were to coincide. Following the presentation of the Committee's Report the police

10.   The foot patrol was composed of 68 men divided into 13 parties. The mounted patrol comprised 52 men and two inspectors.
11.   10 Geo. IV, c. 44.

district was extended by the Metropolitan Police Act 1839 to coincide with that of the Central Criminal Court and under the Metropolitan Police Courts Acts 1839 and 1840 police court divisions were created to cover such parts of the police district as were sufficiently populous to justify the existence of such courts.

The Metropolitan Police Court Act 1839 finally crystalized the judicial side of the metropolitan magistrates' work and it replaced the justices' offices with what were to be called "police courts," a term which would be retained for the next hundred years. The office of Chief Metropolitan Magistrate received official recognition, at an annual salary of £1,400, and the Home Secretary was given power to appoint a maximum of twenty-seven magistrates, all of whom had to be barristers, each at a salary of £1,200 a year. Thereafter these stipendiaries dealt with almost all criminal work while administrative functions continued to be performed by the JPs who sat in different buildings to the stipendiaries and were served by different staff. This division of responsibility was to continue until the 1960s, by which time virtually the only work left to the JPs was licensing (the rest having been transferred to the council of the new county of London which was established in 1888), though by then they had acquired a new type of jurisdiction in cases relating to juveniles. This will be referred to later, but it is relevant to mention here that it provided the first indication of a drawing together of the two types of magistrate. When juvenile courts were established in 1908, those in London were composed solely of a stipendiary sitting alone. In 1920 the Juvenile Courts (Metropolis) Act provided for juvenile courts to consist of a metropolitan magistrate and two lay justices, "of whom one shall be a woman." From 1933 some juvenile courts in the area were composed of three lay justices with no stipendiary, and between 1945 and 1950 the stipendiaries did not sit in the London courts at all. Thereafter a small number joined the juvenile court panel and sat, sometimes with lay justices and sometimes alone.

Under the Acts of 1839 and 1840 new metropolitan magistrates' divisions could be created by Order in Council, and as the built-up area spread the Home Secretary considered the creation of additional divisions from time to time. In 1840 the chief magistrate was asked whether a police court should be established for the districts of Tottenham, Edmonton, Woodford, Hampstead and Highgate. He found that the number of cases arising in these neighbourhoods was so few that there would not be sufficient work for a "resident magistrate." In 1853 the chief magistrate was again asked to inquire whether a police court should be set up in the district of Stratford and Beacontree, but again he reported that the work would not warrant such an arrangement. The following year inquiries were made into the possible establishment of a court for the districts of Finchley,

Hampstead and Edmonton, but it was concluded that, although such a step would probably become necessary in the not too distant future, in the meantime the cost of the additional court would not be justified. In fact no steps were taken during the next 25 years to extend the police court area notwithstanding the considerable growth of housing and population which added to the congestion and, in the opinion of many authorities including Parliamentary Committees, created an urgent need for more magistrates. One of the obstacles in the way of extension was the view held by many Members of Parliament that expenditure on the stipendiary courts in the metropolitan area should come from the rates, as in other parts of the country, and not from national funds. There was also a reluctance to increase the statutory maximum of twenty-seven magistrates, and although there were only 25 magistrates at this time it was thought that two vacancies should be kept open in case a need should arise to increase the number of posts in the existing area. Consequently, the only changes that were made until well into the twentieth century were small adjustments to the metropolitan police court district which did not involve the appointment of additional magistrates. In 1900, part of the borough of St Pancras, which was outside the district, was brought within its boundaries because the lay justices who had previously functioned there lost their court house and had nowhere to sit. In 1905, on the other hand, the district was reduced in size to exclude parts of Middlesex which had previously been within the district, and thereafter the area of the metropolitan stipendiary magistrates was limited to that of the new county of London less Hampstead. Previously, in 1892, the parishes of Wimbledon, Merton and Barnes had been transferred to the Surrey justices thus bringing the boundary of the metropolitan stipendiaries on the south side of the river into line with the county of London.

The only additional stipendiary appointments in the London area during this period were in the boroughs of East and West Ham which petitioned successfully for stipendiaries to be appointed under the Municipal Corporations Act 1882 and paid out of local funds. It was not until 1928 that congestion and delay finally led to the appointment of additional metropolitan magistrates bringing the total to the maximum of 27. The statutory maximum was raised to 35 by the Metropolitan Magistrates Courts Act 1959, to 40 by the Administration of Justice Act 1964 and to 60 by the Administration of Justice Act 1973.

It became usual for the metropolitan stipendiary magistrates to be appointed by name to the Commission of the Peace for adjoining counties so as to enable them to deal with cases arising short distances beyond the London boundary. This practice was confirmed by the Administration of Justice Act 1964 (s. 10(4)) whereby each magistrate became a Justice of the Peace *ex officio* for the counties of Essex, Hertfordshire, Kent and Surrey, and for each of the five London commission areas, but this did not entitle him to sit as a member of Quarter Sessions for any of those areas.

It was assumed that the 1792 Act, by drastically reducing the fees which JPs and their clerks might take, would throw the lay justices out of business and that therefore there was no need for the Act to deprive them expressly of the right to hold courts. Some of them, however, resolutely continued to do so and they were supported by a ruling of the High Court which declared that they might legally do so.[12] The result was a hybrid system of stipendiaries and lay JPs, which was bequeathed to the county of London when this was created in 1888. (This did not apply to Hampstead where there were no stipendiaries). The two systems had entirely different staffs and court buildings and were separately financed. One of the disadvantages of this arrangement was that it gave the prosecution a choice of tribunal. In the twentieth century the police brought virtually all their cases before the stipendiaries which meant that these did the lion's share of the criminal work, but most local authorities took their prosecutions (especially those relating to Public Health, Weights and Measures, Education and Shop Acts) to the justices who also sat in the domestic and juvenile courts and did the whole of the licensing business.

In 1936 the Home Secretary appointed a Departmental Committee under the chairmanship of Sir Alexander Maxwell to examine all the courts of summary jurisdiction in the metropolitan area. The Committee recommended[13] that the courts of the stipendiaries and lay justices should be amalgamated. This was not immediately implemented because of the war but the proposal was revived in the 1950s when pressure on the stipendiaries increased and when, following the implementation of the recommendations of the Royal Commission of 1946, it was considered that the standard of the lay justices had improved to a point where it was right to entrust them with full jurisdiction. In 1960 an Interdepartmental Committee was appointed jointly by the Home Secretary and the Lord Chancellor under the chairmanship of Judge Aarvold[14] to consider what steps should be taken to implement the recommendations of the Maxwell Committee. Their proposals, published in January 1962,[15] were embodied in the Administration of Justice Act 1964. This confirmed the integration of the stipendiary and lay justice systems and

12. *Dodson v. Williams* (1894) 10 *Times Law Reports* 211.
13. Report of the Departmental Committee on Courts of Summary Jurisdiction in the Metropolitan Area. HM Stationary Office publication, out of print.
14. Judge Aarvold was Common Serjeant of the City of London. He became Recorder in 1964 and was knighted in 1968. The author was a member of this committee.
15. Report of the Interdepartmental Committee on Magistrates' Courts in London, 1962 (Cmnd. 1606).

empowered the London justices to exercise the same jurisdiction as those in the rest of England and Wales. Greater London[16] was divided into five commission areas, excluding the City of London, and it was only in the centre or Inner London area that stipendiary courts were held. Within this area domestic proceedings were heard by courts composed either of a stipendiary as chairman with two lay justices or of two or three lay justices, or if this was not practicable a stipendiary might sit alone. Juvenile courts in Inner London were composed of magistrates drawn from a panel of stipendiaries and lay justices appointed by the Lord Chancellor who also appointed the chairmen (before 1964 these appointments were made by the Home Secretary). Each juvenile court consisted of three magistrates (one normally being a woman), but if lay justices were not available it might consist of a single Stipendiary.[17] Apart from these special provisions which applied to domestic and juvenile cases virtually all magisterial work in Inner London could be disposed of by a court composed of either a stipendiary or lay justices and only a few subjects such as fugitive offenders were reserved exclusively to the stipendiaries.[18] The only significant difference which remains between stipendiaries and lay justices is that the former may sit alone whereas for most purposes at least two justices are required to constitute a court.

The administration of the new combined system in Inner London was placed in the hands of a committee of magistrates, similar to a magistrates' courts committee elsewhere but composed equally of stipendiaries and lay justices. The chairman of this committee was at first the chairman of Inner London Sessions, but when all Quarter Sessions were abolished in 1971, the Courts Act of that year provided that the Chief Metropolitan Magistrate should be chairman *ex officio* of the committee. The chief magistrate did not, however, have any other authority over the lay justices, who had their own bench chairmen, while among his professional colleagues he remained only *primus inter pares* with certain powers to allocate work.

The Aarvold Committee's recommendations were based on the assumption that the London courts of summary jurisdiction would be housed in joint buildings in which there would be court rooms for both stipendiaries and lay justices with a common staff. Until then the stipendiaries had sat in their own buildings but the justices' courts

16.　The county of London had been transformed into the much larger area of Great London by the London Government Act 1963.
17.　Further details of juvenile courts in the twentieth century are given in ch. IX.
18.　The Administration of Justice Act 1964 provided (s. 9(1) & (3)) that in the Inner London area the jurisdiction conferred on Justices of the Peace by any enactment, by their commission or by common law should be exercisable both by metropolitan stipendiary magistrates and by JPs. In addition, the lay justices might exercise the jurisdiction conferred on metropolitan stipendiaries by any enactment except: (a) the Extradition Acs 1920-1935; (b) s. 40 of the Pawnbrokers Act 1872; (c) the Fugitive Offenders Act; (d) s. 28 of the Pilotage Act 1913; and (e) s. 25 of the Children and Young Persons Act 1933.

were held mostly in town halls[19] under arrangements made for them by the London county council. This was open to criticism on the ground that much of their work involved the enforcement of payments due to the local authorities. The concept of combined court accommodation was accepted by the Government, but financial restraints retarded the construction of custom-built courthouses for the next two decades.

The Maxwell Committee had recommended that the courts which had previously been referred to as "metropolitan police courts" should be called "metropolitan magistrates' courts," and likewise the "metropolitan police magistrates" should become "metropolitan magistrates." These terms were adopted in subsequent legislation.

Beyond the metropolitan area

The developments described so far in this chapter applied only to the metropolitan area around London. Elsewhere, although similar problems arose, they were not as acute because the quality of the JPs was generally higher and the incidence of crime somewhat lower than in Middlesex and Westminster. Nevertheless, the precedent set by the reforms in the latter area were soon the subject of debate in other parts of the country and in some places the conclusion was reached that they too should have the services of stipendiary magistrates. In all of these instances, however, when they finally came about, the stipendiary appointments were ancillary to and did not replace the unpaid JPs.

The reason for this difference was that, whereas the existing provincial JPs were mostly thought to be acceptable, they were too few in number to handle the vastly increased work unaided. In the boroughs, the number of persons who could exercise the functions of a magistrate were limited by the charter. In the numerous new urban areas which had not yet become boroughs the work was done by men on the commission for the county, but as we have seen there was strong aversion on the part of the existing county justices and of the Lords Lieutenant towards the appointment of justices who were engaged in trade and industry. Consequently, few JPs were appointed who lived in, or were willing to sit in, the urban areas and, as the population, and with it the work of the courts, increased with the industrial revolution, there were too few justices in the towns to dispose of the burden. Stipendiaries were therefore introduced to assist the justices in the disposal of criminal business and to expedite the trial of cases.

19. By 1960 lay justices were holding regular courts in three metropolitan magistrates courts' buildings. While doing so they were exempt from the restrictions imposed by the County of London justices (Jurisdiction) Order 1957 and had jurisdiction over all cases except those reserved by statute to metropolitan magistrates.

In these circumstances the reforms were introduced piecemeal where they seemed to be most required and not under a general Act which enforced the new system universally. The first provincial stipendiary magistrate was appointed in Manchester under a local Act of 1813, which expressly stated that there were too few justices to cope with the increase in work and that the problem should be solved by the appointment of a magistrate who should be remunerated "for his trouble." In 1835 the Municipal Corporations Act, s. 99, enabled any borough to petition the Home Secretary for such an appointment. This was replaced with similar provisions by the Municipal Corporations Act 1882, s. 161. The stipendiary, who was to be appointed by the Crown, had to be a barrister of not less than seven years' standing. He was to be paid by the borough such sum as the Crown might from time to time direct, but this was not to exceed the amount mentioned in the petition. The salary therefore depended largely upon the borough council and varied from one borough to another. Whenever a vacancy occurred, it could be filled only if the borough submitted a further petition. There was no statutory retiring age (except under a local Act in Salford where it was 72), though in the earlier part of the twentieth century the Home Secretary required an undertaking to retire at 70 as a condition of appointment. There was also no pension.

The 1835 and 1882 Acts applied only to boroughs, but another general Act - the Stipendiary Magistrates Act 1863 - extended the provisions to other urban areas with populations of not less than 25,000, though the barrister so appointed needed to be of only five years' standing. In fact no appointment seems ever to have been made under this statute. On the other hand, it remained possible for stipendiaries to be appointed under local Acts and several were created in this way, both for boroughs and other areas.[20]

Under these various provisions stipendiaries were not necessarily appointed where they were most needed but only where the local authority wished to have them; often for reasons of prestige or because the council were on bad terms with their justices. Moreover, it did not follow that once an area had obtained a stipendiary it would necessarily continue to petition for further appointments when vacancies occurred. A number of authorities declined to ask for replacements, most noticeably between 1949 and 1977 when the number of stipendiaries outside London dropped from 17 to 11 while

---

20.   Chatham and Sheerness Stipendiary Magistrates Act 1867; Merthyr Tydfil Stipendiary Acts 1843, 1868, 1894, 1907. Pontypridd Stipendiary Act 1920. Manchester Division and Borough of Salford (Stipendiary justices) Act 1878, separating Salford from the Manchester Division. Stafford Potteries Stipendiary Acts 1839, 1871, 1895. South Staffordshire Stipendiary Act 1899. Merchant Shipping Act 1867, s. 12; if the harbour-master of Holyhead was placed on the Commission of the Peace he had the powers of a stipendiary magistrate.

the lay justices, whose popularity was increasing, rose by nearly 50 per cent.[21]

A national system

This inconsistent system came under the scrutiny of the Royal Commission on Justices of the Peace of 1946-48, who condemned it on the ground that whether a locality had a stipendiary or relied entirely upon lay justices did not depend upon the nature of the work in the locality.[22] They pointed out that Bradford and Hull had stipendiaries whilst Sheffield and Bristol did not and that some county divisions of Glamorgan were included in the area served by a stipendiary while other comparable divisions relied upon lay justices. Nevertheless, the Commission recommended that the system whereby the initiative rested with the local authority should be retained subject, however, to a number of innovations, most of which were implemented in the Justices of the Peace Act 1949, under which a stipendiary might be appointed for a borough, for the whole or part of a county or for a joint district comprising both. The Act provided that the Lord Chancellor, instead of the Home Secretary, should recommend appointments to the Crown and that no stipendiary should be removed from office save on the Lord Chancellor's recommendation.

The Act made solicitors as well as barristers eligible for appointment, both as a provincial and as a metropolitan stipendiary magistrate; in each case they had to be of seven years' standing. This followed the recommendation of the Royal Commission who were impressed by evidence that some solicitors, especially those who had practised regularly in magistrates' courts, were as suitable for

21. In 1946, when the Royal Commission on Justices of the Peace was appointed, the provincial stipendiary magistrates appointed under the Municipal Corporations Acts 1935 and 1982 and under local Acts were as follows; with their salaries:

Birmingham	£1,600
Bradford	£1,500
Cardiff	£1,250
East Ham	£650
Huddersfield	£1,200
Kingston-upon-Hull	£1,500
Leeds	£1,705
Liverpool	£1,250
Manchester	£1,500
Merthyr Tydfil	£1,200
Middlesborough	£1,500
Pontypridd	£1,500
Salford	£1,000
Staffordshire Potteries, Stoke-upon-Trent	£1,250
Staffordshire South, Wolverhampton	£1,400
Swansea	£1,500
West Ham	£1,000

22. Report of the Royal Commission on Justices of the Peace 1946-48 (Cmd. 7463) para. 230.

appointment as barristers.[23] The Lord Chancellor attempted to apply a policy of appointing only persons who were in active legal practice, but the number of suitable candidates fell as the need for more appointments to meet the growing workload increased. This was due, in the case of barristers, to the fact that a stipendiary appointment was becoming less attractive both financially and from the point of view of status, while the solicitor applicants, though fairly plentiful, were not thought to be of the standard required. This led to a new innovation whereby appointment was opened to persons who were not in practice before the courts but were engaged in other forms of legal work; the most numerous being justices' clerks.[24]

Although the Act made the Lord Chancellor responsible for the appointment and removal of stipendiaries, it gave the Home Secretary authority to fix their salaries, after consultation with the local authority and subject to a maximum which must not be greater than that of a metropolitan magistrate. In the nineteenth century the salaries of the metropolitans were the same as those of County Court Judges. The Chief Metropolitan Magistrate was paid a small increment which, by 1949, was £300 above the £2,000 paid to a magistrate or County Court Judge. At that time a High Court Judge's salary was £5,000. The office of County Court Judge had been established in 1846, the idea being that he would handle the work in the lowest tier of civil courts as the magistrate did in the criminal law hierarchy. This continued to be the accepted principle for a hundred years, but in the 1950s the Judges began to move ahead of the magistrates when they were given jurisdiction to deal with undefended divorces. They increased their lead as their jurisdiction was further extended and when, in 1972,[25] they were merged in the new office of Circuit Judge, who exercised criminal as well as civil jurisdiction, they were placed on the same level as the Chief Metropolitan Magistrate, with the other magistrates well below.[26] At that time the provincial stipendiaries were not included in the national salary structure because their appointment and salary level were still matters for the local authorities, subject to the Home Secretary's approval. For the previous 20 years successive Lord Chancellors had taken the view that the appointment and terms of service of provincial stipendiaries should be brought into line with those of the metropolitan magistrates, but they always met with strong opposition from the local authorities who cherished their existing rights even though most of them did not exercise them. An opportunity to force through a change occurred in 1973 when, following local

---

23. The first provincial appointment of a solicitor was Mr. L.M. Pugh in Huddersfield in 1957 and the first metropolitan was Mr. L.E. Barker in 1960.
24. For a fuller account see Thomas Skyrme, *The Changing Image of the Magistracy*, pp. 187-8.
25. Courts Act 1971.
26. Circuit Judges were paid £9,750 per annum and magistrates £8,350.

Government reorganization, it was deemed desirable to abolish all Commissions of the Peace for areas other than counties. Under the Administration of Justice Act 1973 the existing Acts were repealed and the Lord Chancellor became responsible for the appointment and removal of all provincial as well as metropolitan stipendiary magistrates. Section 2 provided that all whole-time stipendiary magistrates were to be appointed by the Queen on the Lord Chancellor's recommendation, to hold office during Her Majesty's pleasure, and that they should not be removed from office except on his recommendation. They were to be JPs for the area in which they served. Those appointed had to be either barristers or solicitors of not less than seven years' standing.

Under s. 9 of the Act the salaries of all stipendiaries were to be determined by the Lord Chancellor with the consent of the Minister for the Civil Service, and from then onwards every stipendiary, both metropolitan and provincial, was paid the same, with the sole exception of the Chief Metropolitan Magistrate. From 1973 the salaries of members of the lower judiciary, as well as those of the higher, lay within the remit of the Top Salaries Review Body - an independent body established in 1971, which advised the Government on the level of salaries of senior members of the Civil Service and senior officers of the Armed Forces as well as of the Judges. The following 15 years covered a period of high inflation which was reflected in substantial increases in the salaries of all members of the judiciary. By 1978 stipendiary magistrates received £11,958; Circuit Judges and the Chief Metropolitan Magistrate, £13,208; High Court judges, £18,883. By 1990 they had risen to: stipendiary magistrates, £44,300; Circuit Judges and Chief Magistrate, £54,000; High Court Judges, £77,000.

Stipendiary magistrates were, and remained, under certain disadvantages as regards their superannuation rights when compared with most other members of the judiciary. In the first place, metropolitan magistrates had always been obliged to serve for 20 years before qualifying for the full rate of pension, which was half their finishing salary (provincial stipendiaries became eligible to receive pensions for the first time under the Justices of the Peace Act 1949) whereas County Court Judges and later Circuit Judges did so after only 15 years service. At first this difference was fortuitous, but by the 1960s it was the result of the inability of the Lord Chancellor's Department and the Treasury, and later the Civil Service Department, to agree upon the length of the qualifying period. In consequence this differentiation between stipendiary and other judicial officers continued indefinitely and was a disincentive to recruitment to the magisterial bench. There was also a difference in the age at which a stipendiary and a Judge had to retire, which was a further source of grievance. At first there was no statutory retirement age (except for the stipendiary at Salford where it was 70) but from the early twentieth century the Home Secretary informed each metropolitan magistrate on appointment that he would be required to retire at the age of 70; whereas County Court Judges could remain in office to 72. In 1946 there were some stipendiaries still serving who had been appointed before this requirement was introduced; two of these were then aged 79 and one 77.[27] The 1949 Act (s. 33(1)(a)) imposed compulsory retirement on every stipendiary, metropolitan and provincial, at the end of the completed year of service in the course of which he attained the age of 72 (the Royal Commission had recommended seventy-five in line with their proposal for lay justices). Some 20 years later, however, the ire of the stipendiaries was roused when the Justices of the Peace Act 1968, s. 2(2), reduced this to 70, whereas County Court Judges continued to serve until 72. Magistrates only were within the scope of the Act and it could not therefore have been applied to the Judges in any event, but it was the intention of the then Lord Chancellor, Lord Gardiner, to introduce further legislation applying the same age limit to other members of the judiciary. However, the Labour Government went out of office before this could be done and the new Lord Chancellor, Lord Hailsham of St Marylebone, who saw some merit in longer judicial service, was instrumental in partly restoring the position of the stipendiaries by including a provision in the Administration of Justice Act of 1973 (s. 2(5)) enabling them, with the Lord Chancellor's approval, to remain in office until the age of 72. In the meantime, the Courts Act 1971(s. 17(1) (2)) had provided for Circuit Judges to serve until the end of the completed year of service in the course of which they attained the age of 72, but the Lord Chancellor was empowered to extend them further, at his discretion, to 75.

As we shall see in ch. VI, the first woman lay justice was appointed in 1920, but it was not until a quarter of a century later that the first woman was appointed as a stipendiary magistrate. She was Miss Sybil Campbell who, when she became a metropolitan magistrate in 1945, was the first woman to join the professional judiciary. She was also one of the first women barristers, being called by the Inner Temple in 1922. The delay in making such an appointment can be accounted for almost entirely by the lack of female candidates, which in turn was due to the very small number of women practitioners who were far outnumbered by their male colleagues and whose practices suffered from sex-discrimination by many of the litigating public. Miss Campbell encountered the same attitude when she reached the bench, and this

27.   Report of Royal Commission 1946-48, para. 237.

was largely responsible for the reputation which she gained of imposing stiffer penalties than her fellow stipendiaries. By the time she retired in 1961, however, her reputation was one of toughness with fairness.[28]

From 1973 there was a co-ordinated national system of stipendiary magistrates for the whole of England and Wales. Under the new Act the Lord Chancellor could appoint one or more stipendiaries in any commission area where he thought they were required. He was also authorized to direct them to sit in such court houses and on such days as he specified. The maximum number of metropolitan magistrates who might serve at any one time was fixed at sixty, and of provincials at 40. In both cases these figures might be increased by Order in Council subject to affirmative resolution by Parliament. This limitation on the Lord Chancellor's power to appoint magistrates was somewhat incongruous having regard to the responsibility placed upon him to ensure that stipendiaries served in every area where there was a need for them, but fears in some quarters, including the Home Secretary and many of the lay justices, that some future Lord Chancellor might flood the country with stipendiaries induced Parliament to impose a maximum figure.

The Lord Chancellor showed no inclination to make any substantial increase in the number of professional magistrates, and sixteen years after the passing of the Act the total number of metropolitan stipendiaries was 49 and of provincials 14. The Lord Chancellor adopted a policy of appointing professionals only where this was clearly necessary, which usually meant where the work of the courts was falling into serious arrears and the JPs were clearly unable to dispose of it. Even then, if the problem seemed to be temporary, the Chancellor often resorted to the appointment of a deputy or acting stipendiary for a limited period to remove the backlog. This device was also used to deal with cases of particular difficulty or ones which were expected to last for an unduly long time. For some time previously it had been possible for stipendiary magistrates to appoint deputies to sit in their absence. The Stipendiary Magistrates Act 1869, allowed a stipendiary with the approval of the Home Secretary to appoint a deputy to act for him for not more than six weeks in a year, or in the case of sickness or unavoidable absence for up to three months at a time. Under an Act of 1956[29] the Home Secretary was replaced by the Lord Chancellor who was authorized to appoint a deputy on behalf of a stipendiary if the latter appeared to be incapable of doing so. He could also direct what remuneration the deputy should receive;

28. The next stipendiary appointment was that of Miss Jean Graham Hall, who joined the metropolitan bench in 1965 and was made a Circuit Judge in 1976. Meanwhile, women had begun to be appointed to other judicial officers as shown in ch. VI, *post*, pp. 220-1.
29. Criminal Justice Administration Act 1956, s. 16 and sch. 2.

payment being made by the local authority in the case of a provincial and by the Lord Chancellor "out of moneys provided by Parliament" in the case of a metropolitan stipendiary. This still did not give the Lord Chancellor unlimited discretion to appoint deputies where and when he thought fit, especially with the object of dealing with long and difficult cases or disposing of arrears, and the 1973 Act again provided an opportunity to establish a system which was to prove invaluable in meeting these problems. It enabled the Lord Chancellor, whenever he thought it expedient so to do in order to avoid delays, to appoint an acting stipendiary magistrate in any commission area in which a whole-time stipendiary might be appointed. For this purpose he could appoint not only barristers and solicitors who were not already on the bench but could also arrange for serving metropolitan or provincial magistrates to transfer temporarily to the area where they were required. The period of appointment could not be for more than three months at a time. These provisions were found to be of great assistance in dealing with short-term problems. A notable example of their use was the appointment of acting stipendiaries (who were usually already stipendiaries for other areas) to deal with the numerous cases of disorder by pickets during the miners' strike in 1985. The system would probably have been used more extensively had the Chancellor not been restricted by a shortage of suitably experienced persons able to undertake the work. Even if an existing stipendiary were used for the purpose, the pressure of work on magistrates' courts in general usually, though not invariably, made it necessary to replace him with an acting stipendiary during his absence. Notwithstanding these limitations, however, the employment of acting stipendiaries was of significance in the survival of the JPs who were liable to be overwhelmed by the increase in the complexity and length of cases, as well as by the sheer volume of work, which occurred in the last half of the century. The JPs' chances of avoiding extinction were greatly enhanced by the presence of a stipendiary system capable of relieving pressure on them without usurping their position.

The possibility of the JPs being replaced by a nation-wide system of full-time stipendiary magistrates was considered by the Royal Commission of 1948. One of the Commission's members, in a minority report, said:

"I think it is merely a question of time before lay justices disappear. It is a question not of whether but when they should be replaced by professionals."[30]

It is interesting to note that the member who made this comment

30.   Royal Commission on Justices of the Peace 1946-48 (Cmd. 7463) p. 99. Report by Lord Merthyr, para. 21.

was Lord Merthyr who later became the most distinguished and longest serving chairman of the Magistrates Association - the representative body for the lay justices - and who did more than almost anyone else to preserve the JP system.

The remaining 14 members of the Commission stated emphatically in para. 213 of their Report:

"We are in complete agreement with the view expressed by the Lord Chancellor, that, both on principle and on grounds of practical convenience, the present system ought to be retained."

They gave several reasons for reaching this conclusion. First, they agreed with the Lord Chancellor, Lord Jowitt, that it would not be possible in any event to find a sufficient number of professional lawyers of the right quality to replace the lay justices. What Lord Jowitt had said in his evidence to the Commission was:

"If you ask me to find 500 men, and that is the sort of number that would be required, who are competent to act and who would do this work as well as the magistrates of today, then I tell you I cannot possibly do it and, therefore, the question is an academic one so far as I am concerned."[31]

Lord Jowitt went on to say:

"Frankly I would be sorry to do it if I could. I think it is an excellent thing that justice should be administered by the ordinary lay people.

Apart from the impossibility of finding sufficient candidates for appointment, the Commission also agreed with the Chancellor in commending the existing system because, "like that of trial by jury, it gives the citizen a part to play in the administration of the law ... Its continuance prevents the growth of a suspicion in the ordinary man's mind that the law is a mystery which must be left to the professional caste and has little in common with justice as the layman understands it."[32]

The Commission also pointed out that a stipendiary magistrate sat alone and commented, "even a Judge of the High Court is never asked to undertake the heavy responsibility of trying a criminal case except with the assistance of a jury of laymen, to whom alone is left the decision on the facts." A lay bench of at least two, and usually more,

---

31. Royal Commission on Justices of the Peace 1946-48 (Cmd. 7463). Minutes of Evidence, Second Day, October 30, 1946, Question 223.
32. *Ibid.,* para. 214.

justices was therefore preferable to a single stipendiary in deciding questions of fact.

The Commission were not opposed to the retention of stipendiary magistrates but they would have liked to eliminate as far as possible the "single adjudicator" tribunal which they regarded as unsound. They were prepared to accept a mixed bench which combined the expertise of the professional with the public appeal of the lay justice. They therefore proposed that joint sittings of stipendiaries and justices should be extended. A similar suggestion had been made by the Conservative Party in a pamphlet published in 1945, but neither then nor in 1949 was it adopted by the Government. Further proposals along similar lines continued to be advanced from time to time, especially by the legal profession which was suspected of being motivated by self-interest. In 1967 the Law Society published a memorandum proposing that cases likely to give rise to difficult questions of law or complicated issues of fact should be dealt with by a bench of two lay justices sitting with a legally qualified chairman. This received little support. About the same time the Bar Council, in their evidence to the Royal Commission on Assizes and Quarter Sessions of 1966-69, recommended that stipendiaries should be appointed on a circuit basis and should travel from bench to bench taking the chair in turn at each one. They claimed that stipendiaries were better able to handle cases involving difficult points of law than a bench of lay justices even when assisted by an experienced clerk. This proposal was dismissed, however, on the ground that the occasions upon which such cases arise are few and far between and that when they do occur this often happens unexpectedly. It would not be possible therefore to ensure that the stipendiary was available to take them.

By 1988 a clearly defined dual system of stipendiary magistrates and lay justices had been established which seemed set to continue in the same pattern for the foreseeable future. The employment of stipendiaries had declined after World War II with the increased efficiency of the lay JPs and the disillusionment with the independent borough stipendiary magistrates, but the picture changed with the integration of the metropolitan and provincial stipendiaries into a co-ordinated system under the Lord Chancellor and with the increasing pressure on the lay justices. The stipendiaries were coming to be regarded as an essential element in the whole magisterial framework who could be called upon to dispose of the mounting complexity and volume of work, especially at moments of crisis, and to eliminate arrears. It seemed probable that they would have to be employed in this role to an ever increasing extent. To achieve this it would be necessary to ensure that a stipendiary or deputy would be readily available to sit, at least in every major centre, to take long or complicated cases or to dispose of a backlog. This was bound to involve an increase in the number of professional magistrates, and the principal object in the way of this process was recruitment. In the 1970s and 80s increasing commitments had led to a need for substantial additions to all levels of the judiciary and this outran the supply of suitably qualified members of the profession. In spite of new opportunities for the appointment of solicitors to judicial office - beginning with stipendiary magistrates in 1949 and extended subsequently to other posts, especially to the Circuit bench through service as a recorder under the Courts Act 1971 - the Lord Chancellor had great difficulty in finding sufficient recruits of the right calibre in the 1980s, especially for Circuit Judgeships. Most applicants were not of the quality required. For a time a stipendiary appointment was regarded as a stepping stone to the Circuit bench and the number of applicants for magisterial posts was swollen by those with an eye to further advancement (though it is also true to say that some stipendiaries considered their work to be more satisfying and rewarding than that of a Circuit Judge). By the late 1980s, however, this trend was less noticeable.

There can be little doubt that the future existence of stipendiary magistrates in England is assured, but the degree of their participation in the judicial process depends upon the quality of the individuals and their numbers, and this in turn depends upon satisfactory recruitment. The Lord Chancellor and others hoped that the problem would be solved by the end of the century at the latest when the growing number of men and women joining the legal profession had acquired sufficient knowledge and experience to qualify them for judicial appointment and enable them to fill the increasing number of vacancies. The future of the stipendiary magistrates undoubtedly depends to a great extent upon the outcome.

CHAPTER V

THE AGE OF REFORM
1820-1888

New era begins after the Napoleonic wars - Demands for fundamental reforms in all spheres coincide with growing discontent with the Justices of the Peace - Political controversy - Reform of Parliament 1832; followed by gradual transfer of justices' functions to new authorities - Municipal Reform 1835 - End of county Quarter Sessions' administrative role, 1888

IN THE NINETEENTH CENTURY a climacteric was reached in the history of the magistracy. At the beginning of the century, in spite of growing criticism, the Justices of the Peace were secure in their dominant position. Imbued with self-satisfaction they continued to rule the countryside with confidence and without interference from the Government or elsewhere. They were an oligarchy composed of the leading men of their locality, most of them wealthy and all of them influential. We have seen that the opportunities to exercise their influence through the Commission of the Peace had become more apparent towards the close of the eighteenth century and consequently members of the aristocracy, who had previously served on the commissions as absentees, began to take an active part in the justices' affairs, some becoming chairmen of Quarter Sessions. It looked as if the justices' entrenched position could never be effectively challenged, but we have also seen that for some time there had been growing discontent with the justices and with the way in which they exercised their extensive powers. This movement had little impact during the wars with Napoleon, when the country rallied to its established institutions and when it seemed that any undermining of the justices' authority while the country faced the common enemy might shake the whole national structure.

The situation changed abruptly in 1815. A generation of war was followed by a long period of peace, and the country which had been largely united against the foreign foe turned itself enthusiastically to an examination of the defects in its domestic affairs. In the age which lay ahead it found a need for new methods of Government at both national and local level. The face of Britain was changing rapidly. There was an enormous increase in wealth based on new British inventions and industry, which far outstripped that of other contemporary countries and placed her in the position of the leading manufacturing nation of the world. She also became the world's greatest colonial power whose colonies, some as we shall see with their own Justices of the Peace, were to play a significant part in the expansion of British commerce. This new modern nation was still being governed by what remained of the decayed Tudor system whose salient feature - effective supervision by the central Government - had completely vanished. Public opinion demanded that both the law and the mode of Government should be radically reformed and adapted to the new social and economic conditions. During the first decade after Waterloo, however, the Government remained in the hands of Tory Ministers who, together with their supporters, the squires in the countryside and wealthy merchants in the towns, were still shocked by the French Revolution and were firmly opposed to any change. Although Robert Peel, who became Home Secretary in 1822, seems to have recognized the problem and secured some reforms, as mentioned elsewhere, the Government as a whole was unfitted for the task of reconstruction which faced it in the aftermath of the war and in the new climate of industrial expansion which created formidable social problems.

At the end of the war the landowners in Parliament enacted the Corn Law to prevent the importation of cheap grain, thus raising the price of bread and causing a reaction by most of the population against the landowning class which comprised the majority of the county magistracy. This coincided with the general unpopularity which surrounded the justices' other activities, as mentioned in the last chapter. The justices were also blamed for the vast financial burden which the country now faced. Much of this was due to foreign war, but the cost of local government administration had also risen enormously during the last quarter of the eighteenth and the first two decades of the nineteenth century. This was the result of, in particular, the great increase in the amount expended on the poor, on prisons and on bridges; but whatever may have been the cause, there was a universal outcry against the extravagance of the justices. The climate deteriorated further with the outbreaks of industrial unrest which were brought to a head at "Peterloo." The financial crisis, and the rise in prices which made the manual workers destitute, created a new situation in which the established authority of the justices was suddenly challenged.

There were some among the Tories who realized soon after the end of the war that reform was inevitable, at least in some areas and, although the Government was set on maintaining the established system, it was soon obliged to take account of the growing strength of the Radical reformers who had carried little weight during the war but now attracted support from many different quarters. We shall see that

Peel was responsible for introducing important innovations, especially in respect of the police and the administration of criminal justice, but in general fundamental reorganization had to await the reform of Parliament itself.

The justices, although mostly landowners and supporters of the Tory Government, were not altogether blind to what was taking place. For some time there had been an awakening of responsibility among the magistracy and, had the country continued to develop gradually along the existing path, they might have retained for a time most of their old functions, albeit in a modified form. As it was, the whole concept of the JP system was unacceptable to the modern world which dawned at the close of the war. The justices, like their associates in the Government, reacted to the increasing outbreaks of unrest with a harsh policy based on the defence of property, but whereas it had been possible to suppress radical agitation during the war, the progressive organizations which supported extensive and fundamental reform now emerged and began to exert an influence on all sections of the population and not only on the manual workers. The Radicals, however, were not members of the Opposition in Parliament, for the Whig as well as the Tory leaders were landed gentry and were equally frightened by revolutionary propaganda. It was obvious from an early stage that the Radicals would make no progress unless their philosophy was accepted by Parliament and that this was impossible so long as the existing archaic structure of Parliament remained. All efforts were therefore directed towards Parliamentary reform.

At first the success of the Radicals was spasmodic, reaching its highest point after Peterloo and during the feud between George IV and Queen Caroline, and then subsiding. In 1830, however, liberal forces became active on the Continent and were acclaimed in England. There was an indecisive Parliamentary election, following which the Tories under Wellington were defeated and the King asked the Whig leader, Earl Grey, to form a new Government. Grey became Prime Minister and, although a prominent landowner whose interests were largely in his estates, he was impressed by the movement across the Channel and was not convinced, like Wellington and the Tories, that it would be folly to allow anything of the kind to occur in his own country. The new Government was threatened with a breakdown in law and order, particularly in the South-East counties, where rioting broke out after the justices had ordered more than 400 farm workers to be transported. The Whigs were at last convinced that the only way to save the situation was to reform Parliament.

Accordingly Lord John Russell introduced the first Reform Bill in March 1831. This provided for the abolition of the "rotten" and "pocket" boroughs and their replacement with new constituencies in the London area and in the industrialized parts of the Midlands and the North. It aroused the strongest opposition from the Tories who foresaw the end of the existing constitution based, *inter alia,* upon Government of the country through the landowning JPs. The Whigs, on the other hand, were encouraged by the enthusiasm for the new measures which was shown by the country at large and was voiced in innumerable journals and news-letters. The Tories succeeded in defeating the Bill, Parliament was dissolved and the elections which followed were fought entirely on the issue of reform. The result was an overwhelming victory for the Whigs, endorsing their policy and proving that even the limited electorate of those days was convinced that a reforming programme was essential. The Government's proposals for reform were, however, defeated in the House of Lords in October, and rioting broke out in many areas. The situation was menacing when the third Reform Bill was introduced in December, but although it passed the Commons with a large majority it was rejected again by the Lords in May 1832. There followed some bitter infighting in the course of which Grey resigned, Wellington was unable to form a Government, and Grey returned with the agreement of the King to create enough new peers to carry the Bill in the Lords if this should be necessary. The Bill became law on June 7, 1832. It added about 250,000 voters to the electorate which now numbered about 700,000.[1]

When the Whigs succeeded in securing the passage of the Reform Bill the gates seemed to be opened to a root-and-branch revolution in national and local government. The first extension of the Parliamentary franchise by the Act of 1832 laid open the way towards the more effective expression of the views of large numbers of citizens who had previously had no voice in the framing of legislation. All of them were people who had been excluded from the select ranks of the Justices of the Peace and who were not likely to support the oligarchal system however paternalistic it claimed to be. The Poor Law legislation of 1834 and the municipal reforms of the following year showed clearly how the wind was blowing. Thereafter the trend continued, yet with surprisingly less vigour than might have been expected. Important reforms continued to be made in most aspects of local government, all of which affected the justices to a greater or lesser extent, but for a further 50 years Quarter Sessions were to remain the local government authorities in the counties and also in those towns which were not included among the new municipal corporations. As we have seen, the new borough councils became responsible for all administration after 1835, but even there, instead of the justices being abolished and replaced with professional

---

1.   The total number of adult males was slightly over four million. It would be nearly 90 years before women were given the vote.

magistrates, the lay justice system was extended and the borough courts of summary jurisdiction were staffed exclusively by JPs appointed by the Lord Chancellor under a Commission of the Peace exactly as they were elsewhere.

During the years following the Reform Act the justices in the counties continued to dominate the local scene, and even to command respect, which seemed to increase after they had been divested of some of their more unpopular functions. The explanation of this resilience is to be found to a large extent in the fact that the propertied class to which the justices belonged remained the dominant power in the land. There can be no doubt that the justices still owed much to their close affinity with those who sat in both Houses of Parliament. New radical movements were unable to displace the hegemony of the landowning gentry even under Whig, and later Liberal Governments, but this was not solely because of the inherent strength of the aristocracy and other leading landowners. It was due even more to their ability to adapt to the changing scene as the Justices of the Peace had done in previous centuries. They took an active interest in all that was taking place and, far from ignoring the social and industrial revolution, many of them moved with it and succeeded in directing it towards their own ends. In so doing they managed to gain the trust and even the affection of the rest of the community. A notable example of the phenomenon occurred when the last vestige of administrative power was finally taken from the justices in 1888 and transferred to the newly created county councils, whose members were elected on a fairly wide franchise. These new elective bodies were composed to a large extent of the same people who also served on the Commissions of the Peace, and the councils looked much like the unrepresentative Quarter Sessions under a different name. In some instances the same magnate who had served as chairman of Quarter Sessions became chairman of the county council, as for example, the Marquess of Bath in Wiltshire. The aristocracy and leading gentry continued to dominate English local Government into the early part of the twentieth century, and the majority of the principal figures on the new councils were men who had been prominent as justices before 1889. Although in most counties the former chairmen of Quarter Sessions did not become chairmen of the council, as happened in Wiltshire, most of the new council chairmen were drawn from the principal landowners, many of them being members of the aristocracy.[2]

2. For example, in East Sussex the chairman of Quarter Sessions in 1888 was the Earl of Chichester who had already held that office since 1846. The first chairman of the new County Council was Lord Monk Bretton, also a JP, who held the chairmanship for two years when he was succeeded by Lord Chichester for three years, during which time Lord Chichester also remained chairman of Quarter Sessions. In Oxfordshire the first chairman of the County Council was the Earl of Jersey who, although not chairman of Quarter Sessions, was *Custos Rotulorum* of the county. He was succeeded shortly afterwards by the 11th Viscount Valentia, who was already an Oxfordshire JP and who retained the council chairmanship for a quarter of a century.

In spite of the continuing dominance of their class, however, the Justices of the Peace themselves had at last reached the end of the road in so far as part of their authority was concerned, yet it transpired that this was but a turning point in their long history. As individuals they had become in 1888 the new constitutional rulers but they no longer exercised these functions as justices. After 500 years Quarter Sessions ceased to be the governing authority of the county, and from then onwards its function was purely judicial. Similarly, the justices out of Quarter Sessions were concerned with exercising summary jurisdiction at Petty Sessions and with issuing warrants, attesting documents and performing certain other ancillary duties, but their only administrative function was the granting of liquor licences. There were some, like Maitland, who doubted whether anyone would wish to serve as a justice when the office had been divested of the whole of its governmental role. We shall see in the following chapters that these fears proved to be unfounded.

Commissions of the Peace

After 1835 the appointment of county justices continued to rest with the Lords Lieutenant, whereas in the boroughs the Lord Chancellor made the appointments at his discretion on the advice of anyone he chose to consult, who, as previously, was often the Member of Parliament for the constituency. In doing so he had no need to consider the property qualification because this did not apply to borough justices although it was still £100 for anyone placed on a county commission. In the counties the Lords Lieutenant, whose nominations were normally accepted without question by the Lord Chancellor, were themselves appointed by the Sovereign on the advice of the Prime Minister, who looked for eminent members of his own party in the House of Lords to fill the post. The result was that the local gentry who were placed on the county commissions were also mainly supporters of the party in office, though sometimes both the Lord Lieutenant and the magistrates changed their allegiance. A striking instance of this occurred during the Irish Home Rule crisis in 1886 when at least 14 Liberal Lords Lieutenant who had supported Gladstone became Unionists and were followed by their county justices. In most counties the Lord Lieutenant refused to nominate anyone who was not clearly within the limited social group and was not acceptable to those already on the commission. This close co-optive nature of appointment was shown by the lengths to which the existing justices were prepared to go to preserve the exclusiveness of their office. As mentioned earlier the only recorded strike of justices occurred in 1833 when those in the county of Merioneth refused to serve with a man who, although a wealthy landowner, had previously kept a retail grocer's shop and "still belonged to the Methodists." It seems that his principal fault was that his origins, education and occupation were not conducive to his associating with gentlemen, notwithstanding the fact that he was now a landowner like them. The attitude of the Merioneth justices was applauded in a number of quarters, and it was said to illustrate the fact that "the spirit of aristocracy in the county magistracy is the salt which alone saves the whole mass from inevitable corruption."[3] No one therefore could hope to be appointed to a county commission unless he was socially acceptable, and mere ownership of land was not sufficient for this purpose. In 1827 the Lord Lieutenant of Monmouthshire wrote to the Lord Chancellor explaining that, even though there was a serious shortage of justices in the mining districts of his county, he would oppose the appointment of the younger son of an ironmaster in spite of the fact that he had become a landowner in the area and was otherwise suitable.[4]

The position in the boroughs was quite different. A new spirit of democracy prevailed in the urban areas which was fostered by the councils and was reflected in the appointments made by the Lord Chancellor to the borough commissions. The borough benches, although composed of the most prominent citizens, were drawn from a different class from those in the counties and were more representative of the population as a whole.

There were no notable changes in the form of the commissions until the Crown Office Act 1877, which empowered the Queen in Council to prescribe the form in which documents were to be worded, including Commissions of the Peace. A new form was then issued which remained in use until 1973. The long list of names of Privy Councillors which appeared at the beginning of all commissions until 1878 was omitted from then onwards and was replaced with the collective form "Members of our Privy Council." The Lord Chancellor, the Judges and certain others still appeared at the head of the commission, though not by name (see Appendix I). The names of new justices were added at the foot of the commission on the authority of the Lord Chancellor's fiat (or that of the Chancellor of the Duchy in Lancaster). Similarly, names were deleted on the order of a fiat. It became rare for a new commission to be sealed except where a new area became entitled to its own commission.

---

3. *Report on Certain Boroughs* (Municipal Corporations Inquiry Commission), drawn by Thomas Jefferson Hogg, House of Commons, No. 686 (1838), p. 5.
4. PRO, Home Office Archives, November 1827.

Oaths of Office

Although named in the commission a justice was still precluded from acting until he had taken the prescribed oaths. The oaths laid down by the Acts of 1617 and 1661 were attached to the commission and had to be taken on appointment, in addition to the oaths which were administered to all officials. They had to be taken afresh on the demise of the Crown and on the issue of a new commission, but by the Act 7 Geo. III, c. 9, a justice who had once qualified did not have to take the oaths again on such occasions. By the Promissory Oaths Act, 1868[5] (ss. 2,4) the modern forms of oath were introduced and, by the explanatory Act of 1871,[6] the sections of the 1617 and 1661 Acts were repealed. The oaths required thereafter from a justice on qualification were the Oath of Allegiance and the Judicial Oath as prescribed by the Act of 1868 (s. 4).

Pay

The justices were still entitled to be paid four shillings a day when attending Quarter Sessions, under the statute of 1388, but this had fallen into disuse long before the nineteenth century, and by the 1820s they had begun to be referred to by their supporters as the "Great Unpaid." The first known use of this expression was in the *Edinburgh Review* in 1826. The right to receive a wage was finally removed in 1855 by the Act 18 & 19 Vict., c. 126.

Judicial Functions

Throughout the nineteenth century county justices continued to sit at Quarter Sessions, whereas in the boroughs, as we have seen, Quarter Sessions were held by the recorder alone after 1835.[7] The most notable feature of the justices' judicial work both in counties and boroughs was the massive extension of their summary jurisdiction but, before turning to the transformation of Petty Sessions, it will be convenient to note the significant changes in sentencing policy and the treatment of offenders which applied to all the courts.

---

5.   31 & 32 Vict., c. 72.
6.   34 & 35 Vict., c. 48.
7.   The Interpretation Act 1889 (52 & 53 Vict. c. 63, s. 13(14)) defined the expression 'Court of Quarter Sessions' as being "the justices of any county, riding, parts, division, or liberty of a county, or of any county of a city, or county of a town, in general or quarter sessions assembled, and shall include the court of the recorder of a municipal borough having a separate court of Quarter Sessions."

Sentencing

In 1842 the justices' power to try capital crimes was finally removed by statute though, as we have seen, for many years previously all such cases had been reserved for trial at Assizes. The 1842 Act was, however, an important landmark because it also removed the death penalty from most of the offences concerned and consequently they could again be tried at Quarter Sessions. In 1810 Sir Samuel Romilly, who had campaigned in Parliament for a reduction in the harshness of the law, commented that there was probably no other country in the world in which so many offences attracted capital punishment. At that time over 200 crimes involved the death penalty.

A House of Commons committee on capital punishment was appointed in 1819 but their recommendations were defeated. When Peel became Home Secretary in 1822 he initiated a number of reforms in the criminal law. An Act of 1822 introduced an improved procedure for the justices' courts and in 1827 he obtained the passage of an Act which repealed a large number of enactments dating from the sixteenth century and earlier, including many involving capital punishment.[8] Some authorities have argued that the majority of these statutes were passed during the eighteenth century and, in particular, reference is often made to the "Black Act" of 1723. In fact, that Act was passed quickly to resolve a local problem which was that some people were blacking their faces and stealing deer from Windsor Great Park, hence the title "Black Act," which was not a later cognomen for the evil nature of the legislation itself. The majority of the statutes carrying the death penalty which were consolidated by Peel's reforming legislation were passed before the Act of 1723 and many dated from medieval times. In any event the effect of Peel's reforms should not be exaggerated. What he actually promulgated were consolidating Acts which drew into a single piece of legislation the definitions of crimes carrying the death penalty but did not in the main relieve many crimes of this punishment, save insofar as the value of goods to be stolen was raised from a shilling to £5. Some might regard this more as an attempt to keep up with inflation than as a deliberate act of reform. The statutes which relieved many crimes of the death penalty were in fact passed in the following decade.

The first of the capital offences to go was the sending of threatening letters and the destroying of silk and cloth in a loom, and it was also abolished for pickpocketing, which had accounted for the largest number of death sentences in the past. In 1832 it was abolished for sheep and cattle stealing and for house-breaking without violence. It remained for arson of a dwellinghouse and robbery with violence, but

8.   3 Geo. IV, c. 23; 7 & 8 Geo. IV, c. 27.

in 1861, following the passage of the Offences against the Person Act, only four offences remained which involved the death penalty - treason, murder, piracy on the high seas and setting fire to HM dockyards and arsenals - and so it remained until the 1960s.

In place of capital punishment, transportation, which had remained within the capacity of Quarter Sessions, was invoked on a still wider scale than before and was imposed on juveniles as well as adults. It was inflicted even for trivial offences, some examples of which were given in the last chapter. The justices' readiness to use this option was one of the least creditable aspects of their record during the first part of the century. Transportation was a sentence which had a special appeal to the justices whose self-interest was often involved. We have seen that it was less costly to the county than some other penalties. There were further attractions. In the first part of the nineteenth century prisoners were often chosen for transportation on the ground that they would provide a suitable supply of unpaid labour. An example of this occurred at Gloucestershire Quarter Sessions in 1830 when 24 labourers were sentenced to transportation for their part in riots. The chairman of Quarter Sessions, Joseph Cripps, who represented the county in Parliament, was also a director of the Van Diemen's Land Company. He wrote to the chairman of the company saying that the prisoners were "all excellent workmen, strong and useful men" and he recommended that they be included in a batch which he and his fellow directors hoped could be sent by special ship to a place conveniently close to the company's estates where they should be put to work.[9] In fact the scheme misfired owing to the opposition of the Lieutenant Governor of the colony. There was, however, another side to the justices' behaviour, which is demonstrated by George Rudé in *Criminal and Victim*. He shows that they were not unduly harsh in dealing with many of the offenders who came before them. As mentioned in the last chapter he gives examples in the nineteenth as well as the eighteenth century of cases in which the maximum penalty was not imposed, and it is clear from the depositions sworn in evidence at the time of committal that the magistrates took into consideration the circumstances in which the crime was committed when deciding upon their sentence.

Apart from the sentences imposed by the justices many cases were dismissed before trial by the Grand Jury which continued to consider all those committed to Quarter Sessions. The Grand Jury often dismissed a case because they considered that there was insufficient evidence even when the charge was supported by witnesses. A typical example was to be seen at Gloucestershire Quarter Sessions on March

9.   Quoted by George Rudé, *Criminal and Victim*, pp. 120-121.

2, 1836 when 59 cases were brought, of which eight were discharged by the Grand Jury. The Grand Jury system which still obtains in America was not abolished in England and Wales until 1933, since when accused persons have been sent for trial direct from the preliminary inquiry by the justices.

In the face of increasing hostility from Australia, transportation was finally abolished in 1857. Fines and imprisonment became the usual form of sentence at both Quarter and Petty Sessions. The justices still had power to commit a convicted offender to the stocks, but by the 1860s this was no longer in favour, and in many places the stocks were allowed to fall into disrepair. The pillory had been abolished long before, in 1816, and public whippings ended shortly afterwards.

Offences tried at Quarter Sessions
Those charged before the courts were overwhelmingly from the lower classes. It was extremely rare for the justices to have to try anyone from their own level of society. During most of the nineteenth century larceny in all its forms still far exceeded all other types of crime and amounted to 75 per cent to 80 per cent of all cases tried at Quarter Sessions. Crimes of violence by individuals accounted for only a small proportion of the total coming before Quarter Sessions as indictments for such crimes tended to be taken at Assizes, though the sessions did receive a rising number of assaults on constables and other persons involved in keeping order. The most common offences were thefts from dwellinghouses, shops and the person. In the towns pickpocketing was conducted on a vast scale, especially in London where the art was immortalized by Dickens in the Artful Dodger and his band. It was punished with great severity. Burglary did not account for much of the time at Quarter Sessions until the middle of the century, when it increased rapidly, especially in the towns, and became responsible for at least a quarter of all cases at most sessions.

Although crimes of violence were comparatively few, there were exceptions in times of rioting which occurred fairly frequently, particularly in the industrial areas. These events could lead to a substantial temporary increase in the justices' work, both in and out of court. Sometimes the outbreaks occurred over a wide area, as in 1830 when a revolt, largely of rural labourers who complained of low wages, caused arson and destruction in 34 counties and added a total of some 2,000 for trial at their Quarter Sessions. About 1,200 of these were convicted, more than a half were sentenced to imprisonment and about 40 per cent to transportation.

It may be of interest to note here that benefit of clergy was finally abolished by one of the Bills introduced by Peel in the 1820s. It became the Act 7 & 8 Geo. IV, c. 28.

Summary Jurisdiction

From the point of view of the justices' judicial functions the most important legislation during the nineteenth century was contained in a number of statutes which extended their powers of summary jurisdiction and laid the foundations on which the modern law relating to JPs is based. We have seen that Petty Sessions had become established, though not in name, by the 1670s. An Act of 1828[10] gave Quarter Sessions power to make boundary changes in divisions and to increase their number provided that there were at least five resident justices in each. In 1847 came the first Act to use the term "Petty Sessions." It empowered justices in these sessions to try cases of petty larceny committed by persons under the age of 14. The most incisive development was to come in 1848 when four Bills relating to the work of justices were presented to the House of Commons.

In introducing the Bills the Attorney General drew attention to the difficulty faced by magistrates in trying to interpret the complicated mass of authorities which governed their work. He also commented on the divided opinions as to whether the amateur justices should be entrusted with extensive powers, but he concluded that, so long as they were required to exercise these powers, it was the duty of the legislature to give them all possible assistance. This was a reflection of the doubts which were being expressed at the time as to the viability of the whole JP system, but curiously it was almost from that moment that misgivings regarding the justices' judicial capability seem to have begun to recede. The Bills were referred to a Select Committee and, following its report which made some amendments to the original drafts, three were passed by Parliament before the end of 1848 while the one which dealt with the holding of special and Petty Sessions received Royal assent the following year. The object of the four Acts was to provide a complete code of practice for the guidance of magistrates.

The Indictable Offences Act 1848 aimed at facilitating the performance of the justices' duties with respect to persons charged with indictable offences. It dealt with the justices' preliminary examination of all persons accused of such offences and replaced the earlier haphazard proceedings with a judicial form of procedure. All sworn testimony of witnesses for the prosecution had to be taken down in writing and the accused was permitted to question them. The justices decided whether a *prima facie* case had been made out and whether the accused should be committed for trial at Quarter Sessions or Assizes. The proceedings did not, however, have to be in public and the accused was not allowed to give evidence on his own behalf until

---

10.   9 Geo. IV, c. 43.

1898.11 The Act was of the greatest significance to the future history of the justices because it made them responsible for the summary trial of large numbers of offences which, for a long time before 1848, had been committed for trial before a jury. During that time the main judicial duty of the justices out of sessions, when faced with either felonies or misdemeanours, had been to order the accused to be held in custody or bailed to appear at either Assizes or Quarter Sessions. Minor crimes, including those against property, such as destroying trees or fences, were now dealt with entirely by the justices at Petty Sessions, whose sentencing powers were less than those of the higher courts. It may seem that these reforms must have been inspired by the humanitarian movement, but there is reason to think that many of those who supported the measures did so more with a view to making the law more effective and inexpensive than from any other motive.

The Summary Jurisdiction Act was also passed in 1848.12 This was a lengthy enactment covering the judicial work of justices out of sessions. Although there has been much subsequent legislation on the subject, this Act is still the basis of the justices' summary jurisdiction and of their civil as well as criminal procedure. It paved the way for the huge expansion of the justices' judicial work in Petty Sessions during the nineteenth and twentieth centuries which resulted in their disposal of nearly 98 per cent of all prosecutions in England and Wales. It laid down for the first time a code of procedure which the justices were to follow and it was on this basis that almost all criminal cases came before them in the first instance. Until then the justices issued warrants for arrest, examined the accused (as a *juge d'instruction* in France still does today) and decided whether to commit him for trial or to discharge him. Now the preliminary hearing of criminal charges was regulated by statute. All aspects of the justices' jurisdiction was covered by the Act, including pre-trial procedure, and it therefore set out the action which a justice was to take on receiving a complaint (which related to a civil suit) or an information concerning an alleged breach of the criminal law. It prescribed the procedure for the issue and service of summonses and of warrants of arrest, which could now be issued on Sundays, and it defined the cases in which justices could and could not admit to bail. They were empowered to summon witnesses and to bind them and the prosecutor over to appear at the trial, and they could remand the accused. Justices in the county in which a person was arrested could examine the accused even though the offence was alleged to have been committed in another county. The Act also confirmed that an accused person could be represented

11. Criminal Evidence Act 1898, 61 & 62 Vict., c. 36, s. 1.
12. Commonly known as Jervis's Act as it, and the Indictable Offences Act, were largely the work of Sir John Jervis who was the Attorney General and later became Chief Justice of the Common Pleas.

before the justices by counsel. In respect of those cases which were triable in a higher court s.25 of the Act contained a clear direction that if, on hearing the evidence for the prosecution, the justices did not think that a *prima facie* case had been made out, they were to discharge the accused; but if they thought the evidence sufficient to put him on trial they must commit him. Section 12 provided that "The room or place in which the justices shall sit to hear any complaint or information shall be deemed an open and public place to which the public generally may have access." No longer would the justices try offenders in their private parlours from which the public were excluded. So long as they sat in public the Act did not prohibit them from sitting anywhere otherwise than in a prescribed courthouse, but they gradually acquired the use, at public expense, of suitable buildings as courts, and so the use of inns, where they had sat for generations, was eliminated. In the course of the debate in the Commons it was pointed out that the holding of judicial proceedings in a public-house was particularly unsatisfactory as it made it easy to interfere with witnesses.

The position of the justices was becoming increasingly precarious by reason of the number of occasions on which proceedings were taken against them for acts done in the course of their duty. The third Act which was passed in 1848 was therefore the Justices' Protection Act. This provided protection by giving them qualified immunity. It stated that no action should lie against them for anything done within their jurisdiction unless malice could be proved.

The last of the four Acts was the Petty Sessions Act, passed in 1849. It finally gave recognition to Petty Sessions and regulated the holding of the courts.

The justices' powers of summary jurisdiction were extended further in the 1850s. In 1853 an Act[13] empowered them to try cases of assault on females and on males under the age of 14, and another of 1855 extended their jurisdiction to all cases of simple larceny.[14] The Summary Jurisdiction Act 1857 provided for appeals to the High Court on points of law and enabled magistrates to obtain the guidance of the Higher Courts by means of "case stated."

The Summary Jurisdiction Act 1879 provided that when an accused person was liable, on summary conviction, to imprisonment for more than three months, he could demand trial by jury. It also provided for children to be tried summarily for indictable offences, as explained below. Other provisions of the Act required the sessions to keep specified types of register. Convictions, depositions and certificates had to be filed with the Clerk of the Peace. Until then the keeping of

13.   16 & 17 Vict., c. 30.
14.   18 & 19 Vict., c. 126.

any form of register by Petty Sessions had been casual, apart from the lists of those found guilty and of the sentences imposed which had to be reported to Quarter Sessions, but thereafter the business transacted at Petty Sessions was fairly fully recorded and can be studied in detail today in the county archive offices. These records provide an illuminating picture of the everyday life of the community at the time. In addition to numerous cases of minor crime they contain many references to administrative matters - highways, licensing, appeals against poor rates, settlement examinations, appointment of parish officers and many other items. Further adjustments to the 1848 Act were made by the Summary Jurisdiction Act 1881.

This development of Petty Sessions finally brought to an end the secluded administration of justice out of Quarter Sessions by magistrates sitting wherever and whenever it suited their personal convenience. Instead, they rode to the neighbouring market town for sessions which took place at regular intervals, and anyone who made application to them in their homes was usually referred to the clerk in his attorney's office, from which he also carried on his private practice. (As yet there was no justices' clerk's office provided at public expense). There were sometimes complaints that the justices had become far less accessible,[15] but on the other hand the public at large benefited from knowing the time and place of sittings well in advance and from being able to contact the clerk at his office at all reasonable times. As we have seen, each county was divided into a number of Petty Sessional divisions and in each of these courts were now held in one or more specified places. In those boroughs which had their own commissions there was a single division.

Although most of the justices' work was now performed in Petty Sessions, and to a lesser degree in Quarter Sessions, there were a few occasions when they might be required to act judicially in a different tribunal. The principal example of this arose under the Merchant Shipping Act, 1834, which empowered the Board of Trade to refer to the arbitration of two justices a claim for salvage when the amount claimed did not exceed £200.

Juveniles

As mentioned earlier, in Saxon times the age of criminal responsibility was 12 and a child below that age was held to be *doli incapax*. The Normans lowered the age of immunity to seven, where it remained for 900 years. Until the middle of the nineteenth century there were no special provisions for the treatment of children by the courts. They were tried in the same way as adults, either before a jury at Assizes or Quarter Sessions or by the justices at Petty Sessions, depending upon

15.   PRO. Home Office, Domestic State Papers, No. 4, March, 1830.

whether the offence was indictable or summary. The punishments which the courts could impose upon them were also the same and many received harsh sentences. It was common for youthful pranks to be followed by lengthy terms of imprisonment in the company of hardened criminals. There are recorded cases during the early part of the nineteenth century of children under the age of fourteen being sentenced to be hanged, and of eight or nine year olds to transportation. In 1820 a boy of nine was sentenced to death at the Old Bailey for stealing six handkerchiefs worth £1 from a shop, and as late as 1831 another boy aged nine was executed in Chelmsford for setting fire to a house, and in the same year yet another was hanged in Maidstone for theft. Although offences involving the death penalty were no longer tried at Quarter Sessions, the justices still dealt with many that led to their sending children to transportation until this ended with the departure of the last convict ship in 1857.

It was not likely that this state of affairs would be overlooked by the penal reformers, and a more humane approach had been gathering momentum for some time especially under the leadership of Elizabeth Fry. A few local schemes were introduced to deal with young offenders before anything was done on a national scale. For instance a farm colony was opened at Stretton-on-Dunsmore in Warwickshire in 1818 to receive boys from neighbouring gaols who were put to work on the land. The first Parliamentary measure was the Juvenile Offenders Act 1847[16] under which children not over the age of 14 charged with larceny could be tried summarily and convicted by two justices. This was extended by the Summary Jurisdiction Act 1879 to many offences committed by young persons under sixteen provided that the accused consented, and the Act also provided that a child below the age of 12 who was charged with any indictable offence other than homicide could be tried summarily by two justices with the consent of a parent or guardian. All this, however, amounted to little more than a simplification of procedure. The only step taken to rehabilitate young offenders before the end of the century was the establishment of reformatory schools under an Act of 1854. This Act, "for the better care and reformation of youthful offenders in Great Britain" provided for juveniles under the age of 16 to be sent to such schools for a period of not less than two nor more than five years, but this was to be ordered only on the expiration of a sentence of imprisonment of not less than 14 days. Three reformatories had already been opened on local initiative during the five years prior to the Act and a number were founded on a charitable basis after 1854. It was not until after the end of the century that the principle was clearly established that young

16.   10 & 11 Vict., c. 82.

offenders should be treated quite differently from adults, and in the meantime harsh adult sentences continued to be imposed on juveniles. In 1880 the Home Secretary, Sir William Harcourt, drew attention to numerous cases of children who had committed only trifling offences, such as playing pitch-and-toss or bathing in a canal, but who were sentenced to imprisonment. Harcourt sought to obtain remission for some of these children but he met opposition from Queen Victoria, who thought that he was unduly lenient. It was not until 1908 that the law was changed and in the meantime Britain lagged behind some other countries in the treatment of juveniles, notably the United States, where the first juvenile court was established in Chicago in 1881; though the basic function of the American courts was guardianship and they were not primarily criminal courts, as were the juvenile courts which became established in England at the beginning of the following century.

Domestic Jurisdiction
It is generally assumed that the beginning of the justices' jurisdiction in family cases dates from the latter part of the nineteenth century because authority to grant orders for separation and maintenance was conferred on them by the Matrimonial Causes Act 1878. In fact, the origins are much older because the liability of a man to maintain his wife and children dates from the Tudor Poor Law legislation under which, if he failed to do so, they would have to be maintained by the parish. As the justices were required to administer the Poor Law, it was part of their duty to ensure that as far as possible a man supported his family. From the reign of Elizabeth therefore, justices had power to make an order against a putative father. It is true to say, however, that the matrimonial jurisdiction of the justices does date from the 1878 Act. This empowered justices to make orders of non-cohabitation, maintenance and custody of children, where the husband had been convicted of an aggravated assault on his wife. Their jurisdiction was extended by the Married Women (Maintenance in the case of Desertion) Act 1886. Both this and the 1878 Act were repealed by the Summary Jurisdiction (Married Women) Act 1895, which consolidated the law. Another Act of 1886, the Guardianship of Infants Act, empowered justices to give consent to young persons to marry. We shall see in the following chapters how the justices' domestic jurisdiction increased in the twentieth century but also came to be criticized.

The extension of the justices' function in domestic matters was part of a movement which reflected a change of attitude towards matrimonial affairs. These had long been dealt with by the Church and, as late as the 1850s, a divorce could only be obtained by those rich enough to pay for a private Act of Parliament. In 1857, in spite of fierce opposition from Gladstone and the Opposition, divorce became obtainable in the courts. This was limited, however, to the High Court and, although it was extended in the twentieth century, the justices were never empowered to grant more than separation and maintenance orders.

Clerks to the Courts

The Clerk of the Peace

As the work of the justices out of Quarter Sessions increased some of the matters previously dealt with by the Clerk of the Peace were transferred to the Clerk to the Justices, but the office of Clerk of the Peace remained one of prime importance, and in fact the volume of work in which he was involved actually increased to such an extent that many clerks became full-time officers, whereas at the beginning of the century most clerks had continued to practise privately as lawyers. Until 1888 Clerks of the Peace continued to enjoy security of tenure and were still appointed by the *Custos Rotulorum*, though under the Clerks of the Peace Removal Act 1864 they could be removed by Quarter Sessions for misconduct otherwise than in the execution of their office. This Act was repealed by the Statute Law Revision (No. 2) Act 1893, except as to any clerk appointed before the Local Government Act 1888. The two shillings a day payable under the Statute of Cambridge 1388 continued until repealed by the Act of 1855,[17] but the clerk depended largely upon fees which were demanded of almost everyone who came to the clerk's office, with the occasional exception of paupers. These fees, like those of the clerks to Petty Sessions, became extortionate in many counties, but Quarter Sessions had no control over them until 1817, when an Act[18] gave them power to fix a table of fees subject to confirmation by the Judges of Assize. After 1848 the scale of fees was confirmed by the Principal Secretary of State.[19] In 1819 the West Riding Quarter Sessions arranged to pay their clerk a salary of £400 per annum in lieu of fees, but this was abandoned in 1828 when its legality was questioned. In 1834 the House of Commons Committee on County Rates recommended that Quarter Sessions should have a discretionary power to pay a salary to their clerk in lieu of those fees which were paid out of county funds, leaving the clerk in receipt of fees payable by individuals. This recommendation was not implemented by Parliament until 1851, but in

17. 18 & 19 Vict., c. 126, s. 21.
18. 57 Geo. III, c. 91.
19. 11 & 12 Vict., c. 43, s. 30.

the meantime many counties began substituting salaries for fees from 1835 onwards. Between 1841 and 1845 the average receipt of Clerks of the Peace throughout England and Wales was about £1,000 a year, ranging from about £180 in Anglesey to £4,500 in Lancashire.[20] Deputy clerks and other staff had to be paid by the Clerk of the Peace out of these sums. In 1851 an Act finally authorized Quarter Sessions to pay Clerks of the Peace by salary instead of fees at rates to be approved by the Secretary of State.[21] By 1861 four-fifths of the clerks received salaries and by 1894 all counties paid salaries.[22]

There was no statutory qualification for Clerks of the Peace, but in the nineteenth century almost all were lawyers, mostly solicitors.

Many of the Acts passed during the nineteenth century gave additional duties to the clerks, particularly regarding the custody of documents. The Summary Jurisdiction Act, as we have seen, required convictions, depositions and certificates to be filed with him. The Turnpike Roads Act 1822[23] directed clerks and treasurers of turnpike trusts to send copies of their accounts annually to the Clerk of the Peace, and proceedings for the amalgamation of trusts were also to be registered with him under an Act of 1849.[24] Extra work was created by the need for the clerk to act as a channel for returns to departments of state and also to the Houses of Parliament. One also finds numerous letters among the clerks' records dealing with such diverse matters as the appointment of high constables, traffic regulations, police, militia and the use of county buildings for the courts. The great interest taken in improved methods of transportation throughout the counties is shown in the numerous plans and schemes for public works which were prepared and deposited with Parliament, records being kept in the Quarter Sessions archives. The most numerous were for railways, but there were others for canals, docks, tramways and ferries. These records also included notes of compensation awarded for property acquired in the course of the work, which sometimes also involved street improvement in towns.

The Local Government Act 1888, in transferring the administrative functions of Quarter Sessions to the new County Councils, divided the responsibility of the Clerks of the Peace, but the individual who had held this office before 1888 became responsible for handling the work of the new bodies as well as remaining Clerk to the County Quarter Sessions. The Act expressly provided that the Clerk of the Peace should also be Clerk to the County Council. His appointment was removed from the *Custos* to the Standing Joint Committee of Quarter

20. House of Commons, Accounts and Papers 1845, vol. XXXVI, p. 265.
21. 14 & 15 Vict., c. 59, s. 9.
22. House of Commons, *ibid.,* 1861, vol. 51, pp. 459-474; 1894, vol. 71, pp. 5-13.
23. 3 Geo. IV, c. 126.
24. 12 & 13 Vict., c. 46.

Sessions and the County Council. Most of the clerks also held a number of other offices in the county, notably clerk to the Lieutenancy, under sheriff and, after 1910, secretary to the Lord Chancellor's Advisory Committee on the appointment of Justices of the Peace. This had the effect of enhancing the importance of his office still further because he was able to influence county affairs to a greater extent than almost anyone else, especially where the chairman of Quarter Sessions was not the same person as the chairman of the County Council. The fact that he was appointed on a permanent basis meant that in the course of time he acquired unrivalled knowledge and experience of county affairs and his advice was constantly sought by the Lord Lieutenant, members of the council, Justices of the Peace and all other persons of importance in the county. It is not surprising that many Clerks of the Peace tended to become arrogant and autocratic and sometimes abused their authority, but generally they performed their duties sensibly and efficiently. The concentration of so much authority in a single individual was obviously open to criticism, and in the twentieth century there were moves in some counties to restrict the number of offices the clerk might hold. There were, however, circumstances in which plurality of office was beneficial as it enabled the clerk to bridge gaps which might otherwise cause serious difficulties between different groups. Examples of this occurred when differences arose between county magistrates and the County Council as we shall see later.

The Clerk to the Justices

In the eighteenth century the clerks who assisted the justices out of Quarter Sessions were still mostly the personal servants of individual magistrates as they had been since Tudor times, though in some cases their services were shared by several justices. By the beginning of the nineteenth century, Petty Sessional benches were adopting the practice of placing a clerk, usually a local solicitor, in charge of their collective business, and when the justices' summary jurisdiction expanded from 1848 onwards the importance of the office of clerk advanced rapidly. A new era began for the summary courts and, as the volume of work at Petty Sessions exceeded that at Quarter Sessions, the justices came to rely more upon the Petty Sessional clerk than the Clerk of the Peace.

The clerk's salary, which previously had been paid by the individual justices who employed him, came to be derived from fees which had to be paid by complainants and parties to proceedings. In many instances these were statutory fees payable to the justices, who then assigned them to their clerk. Fees were charged on every conceivable occasion, including the taking of oaths by constables, surveyors, overseers and others who were obliged to take up public offices whether or not they themselves were entitled to remuneration. By the earlier part of the nineteenth century clerks were making many excessive and quite unjustified claims. In 1832 the Lord Chancellor, Lord Brougham, received a letter complaining that clerks made out long bills "totally disregarding all allowed tables of fees" which no suitor dared to dispute. In some cases the clerk had summonses and warrants ready signed which he then sold, a blank being left for the name and the cause of complaint.[25] In 1851 a Justices' Clerks Salaries Act made it permissible for clerks to be paid salaries out of public funds, and the Justices' Clerks Act 1877 required that they should all be salaried. This Act also recognized the importance of the clerks as legal advisers to their justices by providing that they should be either lawyers or men who had worked as assistants to a justices' clerk. The precise requirements of the 1877 Act (s. 7) were that the person appointed clerk (who might hold office on either a whole-time or part-time basis) must be either:

(a) a barrister of not less than 14 years standing,
(b) a solicitor of the Supreme Court of Judicature, or
(c) have served for not less than seven years as clerk to a police or stipendiary magistrate or to a metropolitan police court or to one of the police courts of the City of London but, where in the opinion of the justices there were special circumstances rendering such an appointment desirable, a person who had for not less than 14 years acted as, or as assistant to, a justices' clerk was also eligible for appointment.

The clerk was appointed by the justices for his division and he held office at their pleasure. This was confirmed by the Local Government Act 1888, s. 84. The clerks to borough justices were appointed in the same way under s. 159 of the Municipal Corporations Act 1882. In those boroughs which had a stipendiary magistrate he was served by the same Clerk as the Justices, but in districts which were not boroughs the stipendiary appointed his own clerk.[26] As the work increased it became necessary for clerks to appoint assistants, but they were obliged to pay them, together with all expenses, out of their own salaries.

The clerks began to see their office in a new light and in the 1830s they had already found a need for collective action, especially in support of claims for higher remuneration. Proposals for the formation of a Justices' Clerks' Society were made in 1837 in the *Justice of the*

25. Webb, *ELG, The Parish and the County,* p. 417.
26. Special provisions were applied to certain localities by a number of local Acts. See *Report of Departmental Committee on Justices Clerks* (Cmd. 6507), para. 18.

Peace journal, and resolutions for the foundation of such an association were passed at a meeting at the Law Institute in Chancery Lane, London, on January 31, 1839. The original founders of the Society seem to have been Charles Augustin Smith and John Drake Finch, who were both clerks to the justices at Greenwich.[27] The Society was incorporated in 1903. It was largely at the instigation of the Society that the Clerk's Salaries Bill was introduced in 1877. At first the Society was confined to justices' clerks in counties, but they were soon joined by members of another body, comprising clerks to borough benches, which had been formed in 1837. Even so, the membership of the combined Society amounted to only a small proportion of the clerks throughout the country. By 1870 there were about 200 members out of a total of some 800 clerks. The proportion increased thereafter and a point was reached in the mid-twentieth century when, for a time, every clerk, both whole-time and part-time, was a member.

The clerks to the metropolitan courts in London formed their own society, which also survives to the present day. This body, which is called the London Magistrates' Clerks' Association, was established in 1889.

Administrative Functions

Whereas local government of the boroughs had been transferred to the borough councils which were established in 1835, the county Justices of the Peace in Quarter Sessions and Petty Sessions remained responsible for the administration of their counties until 1888, but the extent of their authority was curtailed, or at least substantially altered, in a number of ways, mainly in the sphere of the police, prisons, lunatic asylums, poor law, wages, licensing, highways and in the raising of revenue.

Police
As in previous times peace-keeping in the early nineteenth century normally depended upon the high constables of hundreds, the petty constables of parishes and the night watchmen in the towns, all under the general supervision of the JPs. On occasions of serious disturbance the justices, if present, could call upon the military. A serious defect in the system was the incompetence of the constables and watchmen and the total absence of justices in the newly populated industrial areas, where most of the unrest occurred. This was usually due, as already mentioned, to the refusal of the Lords Lieutenant to nominate anyone who was not of the social status of the traditional county justice. They

27.   See James Whiteside, *The Justices' Clerks' Society* (1964) pp. 1-9.

were right to eliminate anyone whose financial circumstances might lay them open to corruption, but there were many who could have filled the office with credit, but who were discarded because they were not in the same social class as the landed gentry. There were therefore no resident justices in many areas where they were most needed, and there was no one to call upon the military at short notice to quell a riot. Much time was wasted seeking a justice in another area and persuading him to ride 20 miles or more to the scene of the trouble. The absence of magistrates also laid the way open to tyranny by constables and other parish officers whose arbitrary conduct was subject to no scrutiny or restraint.

England was probably the worst policed country in the civilized world. The situation in the towns has been described by many writers, including Dickens who, in *Barnaby Rudge*, refers to the "worst conceivable police." Of the watchmen he says "being selected for the office on account of excessive age and extraordinary infirmity, [they] had a custom of shutting themselves up tight in their boxes on the first symptoms of disturbance, and remaining there until they disappeared." The only improvements in the system since Tudor times had been those we have already seen in the London area - the Bow Street Runners and patrols and the Thames River Police who were introduced in the latter part of the eighteenth century.

We have also seen that in 1829 Peel established the Metropolitan Police which was the first effective police force in the country. It was extended in the metropolitan area during the next few years and became the pattern for other forces throughout the rest of the country. As was the case with other institutions, the extension began with permissive Acts for establishing municipal and county forces and these were followed by compulsory legislation. In addition to schemes modelled on the Metropolitan Police, some counties experimented in improving the established system. In 1829 Cheshire introduced a scheme whereby salaried, full-time constables were appointed to serve under the JPs in addition to the parish constables. This, of course, perpetuated the long established position of the individual justice as police officer, prosecutor and Judge. In 1839 Peel secured the passage of an Act[28] which provided that county forces should be under the control of Quarter Sessions, which were to fix the strength of the force and appoint and dismiss the constables.[29] The sessions could apply to

28. 2 & 3 Vict., c. 93; amended and extended by 3 & 4 Vict., c. 88, which gave the justices additional powers of management and enabled them to levy a police rate.
29. There was some uncertainty as to the extent of Quarter Sessions' authority over the chief constables. There is a reference to this in correspondence which appeared in the *Justice of the Peace* in 1863 (p. 717), where it seems to be confirmed that Quarter Sessions cannot dictate to a chief constable where he is to have his residence, even if he chooses to live in an inaccessible place.

the Home Secretary for authority to appoint additional constables to a division or to the county as a whole. The Home Secretary made rules as to pay and uniforms, but the whole cost of the police forces were to be borne by the county rates. This Act was permissive only and was adopted by just over half the counties. Others were deterred by the cost, the principal concern of Quarter Sessions being that, as the police forces were to be organized on a county basis, the rural ratepayers would be charged an excessive amount in order to provide police in the urban areas where they would be mostly employed. County records contain many petitions from this period in which parishes object to a paid rural police force on the ground that it was an unnecessary burden on the ratepayer.

Under the Municipal Corporations Act 1835 borough police forces were established under the control of watch committees which were composed of persons appointed by the council. The borough justices were not included *ex officio*.

It was not until 1856 that an Act (19 & 20 Vict., c. 69) made it compulsory for every county to have a police force on the lines of the 1839 Act. This Act also provided for the appointment of inspectors who reported to the Home Secretary. If he certified that a force was efficient, one fourth of its costs was to be paid by the state. Although responsibility for county police forces remained with the justices, supervision of this side of their work by the Home Secretary had been increasing since the Act of 1829, and it was one of the earliest illustrations of the growing demand for greater government control over local affairs.

With the establishment of County Councils in 1888, responsibility for the county police forces was removed from Quarter Sessions and vested in Standing Joint Committees composed of an equal number of members of the County Council and of county justices appointed by Quarter Sessions. This was to remain the position until 1964 when a uniform pattern of police authority was introduced for both counties and boroughs in the form of a committee which included justices, as we shall see in chapter IX.

As Keepers of the Peace it had been the duty of the justices to direct constables and to ensure that malefactors were apprehended and prosecuted, but after the establishment of regular police forces they no longer had any involvement in these tasks save through their membership of the joint committees with the local authorities.

Prisons

In 1815 the justices were still fully responsible for the prisons in their respective counties. We have seen that from the latter part of the eighteenth century they had taken greater interest in this side of their work than their predecessors. The correspondence and diaries of the early nineteenth century justices show that they had a decidely better knowledge of prison conditions than was the case in earlier generations and that many felt deep concern for the welfare of the prisoners; yet most were deterred from introducing appreciable improvements by considerations of expense. In some counties the justices visited their prisons fairly regularly and reported their findings to Quarter Sessions, though this did not always result in appropriate action being taken. At first the visits were carried out only by those justices who had been expressly appointed prison visitors, but the Prison Discipline Act 1824 enabled any justice, whether or not a visitor, to enter any prison and to report abuses to the next general or Quarter Sessions. We have seen that the justices' views on how prisons should be run differed considerably from one county to another, with the result that conditions varied enormously. Lack of uniformity was certainly an outstanding characteristic of prison management throughout the whole of the time that the justices were in control. In some counties the prisoners were reasonably well fed and housed and were subjected to a tolerable routine of work and discipline; in others they lived in squalor and were subjected to cruel punishment at the whim of sadistic, mercenary gaolers.

Until 1822 the central Government took no interest in what went on in the prisons and seems to have been uncaring of the scandalous conditions which persisted in many of them, not-withstanding the crescendo of criticism which had begun with John Howard in the 1770s. It was left largely to the justices themselves to initiate long overdue improvements insofar as they were prepared to do so. Reference has been made to Sir George O. Paul in Gloucestershire and to other eighteenth century reformers. Another justice and substantial landowner who was instrumental in achieving a degree of prison reform was James Nield, who followed in Howard's footsteps and took a special interest in the imprisonment of poor debtors.

The innovations which were introduced in some counties were not sufficient to satisfy the reformers outside the magistracy, and in the 1820s agitation grew for the introduction of a system of supervision, especially with a view to securing uniformity. A House of Commons Select Committee had urged the introduction of reforms in 1820,[30] but the first piece of legislation was largely the work of Robert Peel when he became Home Secretary. Peel was anxious to reform the criminal law in general and he began with the Gaol Acts. His Act of 1823[31] was the beginning of a series of reforming measures which followed over a

30.   Report of House of Commons Committee on the State of the Gaols, 1820.
31.   4 Geo. IV, c. 64. Another Act of the same year (*ibid.* c. 63) enabled justices to borrow money from the Exchequer for the building and repairing of gaols.

period of more than 50 years. It applied to both prisons and houses of correction and it introduced a number of innovations. Justices were required to organize their prisons according to a set plan and they had to report quarterly to the Home Secretary. They were to provide accommodation which was sanitary as well as secure. Gaols were no longer to be places which were run by the gaoler or master for profit. He was to become a salaried officer employed by Quarter Sessions or by the municipal authority. No prisoner was to be put in chains or irons or subjected to severe punishment without the visiting justices being informed. Female prisoners were to be under the control of officers of their own sex. This entirely novel arrangement was introduced largely at the instigation of the reformer Elizabeth Fry, who was also instrumental in introducing a provision in the Act for the education of prisoners, in particular that they should be taught to read and write. All prisoners were to be subject to reformatory treatment. The gaoler, chaplain and surgeon were required to visit every cell at specified intervals and were to present records of their work to Quarter Sessions.

The 1823 Act applied only to the prisons administered by county justices (numbering about 130) and to those of the cities of London and Westminster and 17 other towns (a few smaller towns contracted with the adjoining county for their prisoners to be kept in the county gaol). A more serious defect was that it did not make any provision for inspection by the central Government to ensure that the local authorities were doing their duty. There was therefore little supervision by the Home Office and, apart from spasmodic correspondence on specific issues, little effort was made to see that the Act was enforced. For ten years the Act's provisions were applied haphazardly and unevenly. The justices were now clearly responsible for the administration of all prisons to which the Act applied but they differed widely in their views as to how the system should be worked. In particular, there were divergent ideas on solitary confinement, prisoners' diet and the work they were required to perform.

Some further improvements were made in 1824 by the Act 5 Geo. IV, c. 85 under which prisoners could be placed in a number of classes (five for men and three for women) at the discretion of the visiting justices, except for prisoners for debt who were in a class of their own. The Act also provided that prisoners were not to be put to the treadmill before conviction, and that those committed for trial should be supplied with food but not obliged to work. It also provided that travelling allowances should be paid to discharged prisoners. Like the Act of the previous year, however, this enactment did not apply to all prisons and it was ineffective because of the inability of the Government to provide adequate supervision.

In 1832 the new Whig Government and the reformed House of Commons were struck by the dramatic difference between those prisons in which the inmates were made to undertake punitive labour on a minimum diet in unhealthy conditions and others where they lived in comparative comfort with ample food and profitable employment. It was obvious that steps had to be taken to secure uniformity and that these could be effective only if the Government intervened actively and consistently. Acts of Parliament were valueless unless the Government enforced them. Parliament concluded that although the justices in some areas had conscientiously carried out inspections and taken steps to remedy defects, they should not be relied upon to perform these duties in every county and borough and therefore a national inspectorate was essential. This view was taken by a House of Commons Committee in 1833, but it was not until two years later, after a House of Lords Committee had carried out a comprehensive inquiry into the prisons throughout England and Wales, that an Act[32] was passed implementing this policy.

The Prisons Act 1835, while leaving detailed administration to the local authorities, subjected them to supervision and control by a central authority. It introduced a number of improvements - some of them anticipated by Paul - and for the first time it took steps to ensure that they were implemented. Inspectors were appointed on a national basis and they were required to report to the Home Secretary on their periodical visits to the prisons. This was undoubtedly an important step forward. The Webbs commented:[33]

"By this revolutionary statute the immemorial autonomy of the two hundred local authorties in England and Wales which still maintained prisons, was, at one blow destroyed. For the next 40 years county and borough justices go on administering their gaols, and paying for them out of local funds, but subject always to ever increasing regulations made by the Home Office on every detail of prison life; incessantly watched and criticized by a staff of salaried inspectors reporting to the Secretary of State and to the public; and obliged, from time to time, to introduce whatever changes in regimen were dictated by prison reformers in Parliament."

The Webbs' description gives the impression that from then onwards the justices were tied hand and foot and could do nothing which did not meet with the full approval of the inspectors and the Home Secretary, but this was not entirely the case. Control of the prisons remained with the governors under the supervision of the

32.   5 & 6 William IV, c. 38.
33.   *English Prisons under Local Government (1922)*, p. 112.

justices who continued to make the rules, and, although the rules required the Home Secretary's sanction, there was nothing that he could do to force the justices to meet the inspectors' criticisms except to issue a reprimand which was often ignored. The result was that there were still great variations in the régime, the diets and the condition of prisoners in different parts of the country. In some prisons the inmates were either given no work at all or it consisted of the treadmill, the crank (a smaller but equally exhausting device which was used by the prisoner in his cell) or oakum picking, while in others they were taught trades. Some prisons were highly organized factories, whose object was either to benefit the prisoners on a permanent basis or to relieve the rates by making a profit from their work. The justices were particularly averse to introducing improvements which increased the county rates, and many fell far short of what the Home Secretary demanded.

The justices' shortcomings were made apparent in what the Webbs described as "the greatest scandal of English prison history of the nineteenth century,"[34] which took place at Birmingham prison between 1849 and 1854. A new gaol had been built at Birmingham, and the justices appointed as its first governor one Alexander Maconochie, who had published a well-known book on prison reform. It was the justices' intention that he should be given an opportunity to put his theories into practice. In the event, Maconochie spent so much time theorising and ventilating his views to committees and inquiries that he had little time to spend on supervising the actual administration of the prison. The justices therefore appointed a deputy governor, a Lieutenant Austin, who ran the prison with great severity. Becoming aware of this Maconochie asked the justices to dismiss Austin, but instead they called upon Maconochie himself to relinquish his post and he resigned. After his departure, Austin proceeded to inflict grossly cruel punishments which were illegal according to the existing law. This state of affairs did not come to the attention of the Home Office until one of the prisoners committed suicide and Austin's conduct came to light in the course of the inquest. The matter was then investigated by a committee of visiting justices who gave a favourable report to the Secretary of State exonerating Austin and other officers. There was suspicion of the justices' report and a Royal Commission was appointed to examine the situation further. The Commission's report revealed a horrific picture of conditions in the prison. They found that Austin had disregarded most of the regulations by which he was supposed to be bound and that the prisoner who died "had been punished illegally and cruelly, and was driven thereby to the

34.   *Ibid.* p. 170.

commission of suicide."[35] The commission were scathing in their comments on the visting justices:

"We are compelled to say that they seem from their absolute confidence in Lieut. Austin's administrative capacity, to have suffered the performance of their duty almost to degenerate into a mere routine form. In truth, no real supervision was exercised by them. They met once a week at their board room in the gaol; they had read to them the formal reports of the events and the statistics of the prison, but they never examined either the journals of the officers, or the books in which the discipline and its effects were or ought to have been recorded and from which, imperfect as they were, they would have learned, or at least must have suspected the existence of much illegal punishment and much deplorable suffering."[36]

The commission concluded that the senior officers of the prison had habitually neglected the rules without interference by the justices, and largely without their knowledge.

Another inquiry found similar cruelties at Leicester Prison, and in this instance they attached more blame to the justices than to the governor and his officers. In this case the justices themselves had introduced a new punishment, which involved stopping meals, without informing the inspectors or the Home Secretary that they had done so.

Before the inquiries at Birmingham and Leicester had made their disquieting revelations the Government had decided to experiment in new forms of custodial treatment. These needed to be carried out in purpose-built institutions and, as the Government had no power to compel the justices or the municipal authorities to alter existing prisons or to erect new ones, it was necessary for new construction to be carried out on the direct orders of the Home Secretary. The Government therefore embarked upon a programme of centralized prison building in the 1840s. In 1842 the first such prison was built at Pentonville, and others followed; in 1848 at Portland and in 1850 at Dartmoor (in a reconstructed building formerly used to confine French prisoners of war). In 1853 Brixton prison was taken over from the Surrey justices and converted for women convicts. In 1856 another prison was built for male prisoners at Chatham. Following 10 years of experiment in these institutions the conclusions reached were embodied in the Penal Servitude Acts of 1853 and 1857[37] which

35. Parliamentary Papers, 1854, XXXI.
36. *Ibid.,* p. 37.
37. Amended by Acts of 1864, 1871 and 1891.

established a new form of sentence to replace transportation. The Acts defined penal servitude, which was to begin with a period (at first of 12 months) of close cellular isolation, with a plank bed, restricted diet and no intercourse with other prisoners at any time. During this period the prisoner was forced to work in total isolation, but afterwards he was transferred to work in the open air in company with other prisoners but with whom he was forbidden to communicate. An important new provision was that the harshness of the treatment might be alleviated by remission which prisoners could earn for good conduct.

It was not until 30 years after the Act of 1835 that a point was reached where Parliament was ready to enact a new comprehensive Prisons Act. In 1863 a Select Committee of the House of Lords severely criticized the justices' administration of the prisons and drew attention to the lack of uniformity to which it led. Their recommendations were implemented in the Prisons Act 1865. This finally removed, at least in theory, the justices' autonomy by introducing provisions to ensure their compliance with Government policy and led to consequential uniformity in all areas. In every prison separate cells had to be provided for all prisoners, diets had to be approved by the Home Secretary,[38] and the prison authorities were obliged to comply with these and other directions. If they failed to do so, the Home Secretary was given a power of sanction whereby he could withhold at his discretion a Home Office grant in aid of expenditure. Certain powers were also conferred upon the visiting justices, who could order that a prisoner be flogged or confined in a punishment cell for a period of a month. The Act also provided for "hard labour" which it divided into two categories; (1) The treadmill (or treadwheel as it was more often called), crank, shot-drill, stone-breaking and similar demoralizing occupations, (2) Any hard bodily exercise that might be provided by the justices, who were given a considerable amount of discretion. The Act had the effect of persuading many of the smaller town and franchise authorities to transfer their gaols to the county justices.

In 1869 imprisonment for debt was abolished, though thereafter a debtor could be committed to prison for contempt if he failed to observe the terms of an order of court.

In spite of the 1865 Act, the justices continued to run the county prisons with a considerable degree of independence, and the extent to which they complied with the Home Secretary's directions was limited by a determination to avoid what they regarded as unnecessary expense. It looked as if no further progress could be made in forcing them to carry out all the reforms which the Government deemed

---

38.　　Government diet sheets of 1843 and 1864 are set out by the Webbs in *English Prisons under Local Government*, pp. 135 and 145.

necessary, especially when, in 1874 a new Government took office pledged to relieve the burden on the local rates. It was obvious that there could be no question of compelling the justices to build new gaols. Having regard to the Government's assurance that they would not only avoid any increase in the rates but would actually reduce them, there was just one way in which this could be achieved without interfering with the building of new gaols and that was by the Government taking over the entire responsibility of the local authority. A Bill to this effect was therefore introduced in 1879. The justices, mindful of the unrivalled opportunity to achieve a substantial reduction in the rates and to avoid heavy increase in expenditure on future building, made little effort to oppose it, even though it sought to deprive them of the whole of their remaining prison authority. It became law as the Prison Act 1877.[39] The Act, at a stroke, transferred the entire prison system from the JPs and the municipal authorities to the Home Secretary, in whom the ownership of all prisons was vested. The prison commissioners, in whose hands the administration of the new system was placed, were appointed by and responsible to him. Visiting justices retained the right to visit and inspect prisons, but they were under an obvious disadvantage compared with their predecessors. It was far more difficult for part-time amateurs to offer effective criticism of a professionally staffed Government institution than it was for the earlier justices to scrutinize prison administration for which they alone were responsible.

So ended a century of experiment. The justices deserve some credit for adopting an enlightened approach in many parts of the country, but unfortunately the opposite was the case in other areas. In some instances the justices had been eclectic and had tried to base their solutions on what they thought to be the best of the different philosophies which were expounded at the time. Their failure to reach a permanent solution was due to the refusal of many of their colleagues to show the same enlightened dedication. Even in the more progressive counties there was no consistent effort to enforce the new doctrines, while in others no serious attempt was made to do so at any time. This, coupled with an absence of any effective centralized control, made it inevitable that the old system under the management of the justices should be abolished; but why was responsibility not transferred to new local Government bodies under the overall supervision of a central ministry in accordance with the pattern applied to all the rest of the justices' administrative functions? The answer lay in contemporary politics. The Government recognized that in the current climate there could be no possibility of persuading

39.   40 & 41 Vict., c. 21.

Parliament to pass legislation which added to the burden of local finance; on the other hand they saw a golden opportunity to please the rate-paying electorate by transferring the cost of their most expensive liabilities to the Exchequer. A similar situation did not arise in respect of any of the justices' other administrative duties, all of which were transferred at various times to other forms of local authority.

Lunatic Asylums

One area in which the justices' administrative commitment was extended in the first half of the nineteenth century was the custody of the insane. Although private lunatic asylums had existed for some time and had been licensed by the justices, it was not until 1808 that an Act provided for the erection and maintenance of such establishments by public authorities. An Act of 1800[40] enabled the courts to commit to custody insane persons indicted of crimes, but it made no arrangements regarding the places where they were to be detained, and they were usually held in houses of correction, in poorhouses or in gaols, and often contracts were made for them to be kept in private asylums. In 1806 Sir George Paul, the Gloucestershire prison reformer, submitted a memorial to the Government which led to the passing of an Act two years later. This empowered Quarter Sessions to provide lunatic asylums for the housing of both pauper and criminal lunatics and to make orders for their maintenance. For this purpose they could combine with the sessions of adjoining counties. Any lunatic detained under the 1800 Act and any found wandering abroad could be committed by the justices to one of the new asylums. Visiting justices were to be appointed to inspect and supervise them. The 1808 Act[41] was amended in 1811 and 1815 and a further Act of 1819[42] provided that a pauper was not to be removed to an asylum without an order by two justices assisted by a medical practitioner. There was a further amending Act in 1824,[43] but this and the other statutes were repealed in 1828, when a new Act[44] was passed "for the erection and regulation of county lunatic asylums, and more effectually to provide for the care and maintenance of pauper and criminal lunatics." The justices were again empowered to erect and also enlarge asylums and to unite with subscribers to those existing asylums which were maintained by voluntary contributions. They could also appoint committees to manage the asylums, acquire land and buildings and levy a county rate to cover the cost. They might also borrow money to pay for building.

40.   39 & 40 Geo. III, c. 94.
41.   48 Geo. III, c. 94, amended by 51 Geo. III, c. 79; 55 Geo. III, c. 46.
42.   59 Geo. III, c. 127.
43.   5 Geo. IV, c. 71.
44.   9 Geo. IV, c. 40.

They made rules for the management of the institutions and appointed officers and visitors. Annual reports were made to the Secretary of State, who had power to order inspections himself. A separate Act of 1828[45] dealt with private asylums. Those in London were brought under the direct control of the Government through a board of 15 commissioners appointed by the Home Secretary, of whom at least five had to be physicians, but elsewhere supervision was entrusted to the justices, who exercised it both directly and through visitors whom they appointed and who were required to make regular inspections. Licences to keep asylums were issued by the justices, but no person could be confined in one without a certificate signed by two medical practitioners. The 1828 Act was amended in the following year and both Acts were repealed and the law consolidated in 1832.[46] Under the 1832 Act Quarter Sessions were obliged to appoint three or more justices and one or more physicians to be visitors, and a justice could order an asylum to accept a pauper lunatic while Quarter Sessions could order his release. Under an Act of 1845[47] the release could be ordered by two justices.

In 1853 responsibilty for providing asylums for criminal lunatics was transferred to the central Government.[48]

The Poor Law
The Poor Law, whose implementation during the previous two centuries had occupied a larger proportion of the justices' time than any other administrative function, was another sphere of their activity which met with general approval down to the end of the eighteenth century but suddenly aroused indignation among the reformers in the post Napoleonic war years. We have seen that the confidence of Parliament was confirmed by Acts of 1782, 1795 and 1796 which enlarged the justices' powers to order relief, and at the same time they were generally acclaimed as the guardians of the poor, but from the 1820s they were accused of gross, unjustified interference in all aspects of relief and of undermining the authority of the parish officers whose duty it was to administer the system from day to day. In 1820 Sydney Smith, in an article in the *Edinburgh Review,* said: "A poor man now comes to a magistrate any day in the week, and any hour of the day, to complain of the Overseers," and it was alleged that, in dealing with these complaints, the justices ordered payments to be made to those who were most vociferous but were least deserving, while they overlooked others who did not press their just claims. It was not

45.   9 Geo. IV, c. 41.
46.   10 Geo. IV, c. 18; 2 & 3 William IV, c. 107.
47.   8 & 9 Vict., c. 100.
48.   16 & 17 Vict., c. 97.

suggested that the justices acted from improper motives, or that they failed to act through laziness. Circumstantial evidence supports the view that they were moved by a desire to do what was best for all concerned, though they did not always act wisely. Their good intentions, however, were ignored and they were universally vilified. The Poor Law in the early nineteenth century left much to be desired and reform was undoubtedly overdue, but this was another example of the system becoming outdated and inadequate, rather than of those who sought to implement it being personally incompetent or corrupt or attempting to exceed the powers conferred upon them by Parliament. It is true that the justices were perpetually interfering, not only as a body but also as individuals (a single justice had discretion to order an overseer to pay a pauper whatever he thought fit) and the results left much to be desired. It could also be argued that in practice they exceeded the powers which Parliament had intended to confer upon them in that they presumed to dictate the solution to each individual case, whereas they were supposed to exercise a purely supervisory role and to stop abuses by parish officers. Whether or not this was so is not entirely clear, but in any event their motives in doing what they did were usually laudable. In so far as the system itself was concerned there were ample grounds for severe criticism. The overseers were often guilty of excesses, there was great inequality between parishes and there was a vast waste of money, none of which served to lighten the hardships of the poor. The Radicals, who were in the ascendant in the 1820s, chose to overlook these facts and, in launching their attack, made no distinction between the system and those who administered it. The justices had become universal scapegoats and provided a useful butt for attack when anything needed to be demolished. As the Webbs commented:

"Whether the justices interfered with the parish officers or let them alone, whether they adopted the newest economic philosophy or acted on the humanitarian principles in which they had been educated, it was, in 1828-1835, equally imputed to them as a crime."[49]

It may be argued that the justices were at fault in adopting fallacious policies, especially the Speenhamland system of supplementing wages from the rates to meet the cost of bread instead of directing employers to raise wages, but by the time the Speenhamland experiment was introduced in 1795 it is difficult to see what other course they could

49.   *ELG, The Parish and the County*, p. 594.

have taken to save the poor from starvation.[50] It was indicative of the attitude of their critics that, when the justices tried to reverse the Speenhamland system in 1815, they were subjected to as vehement denunciation as they had been before.

In spite of the mounting outcry, no steps to change the law were taken until 1832 but, in the same year that the new Government secured the passage of the Reform Bill, it also appointed a Royal Commission under the chairmanship of the Bishop of London "to inquire into the practical operation of the laws for the relief of the poor." Three of the nine commissioners were keen advocates of reform, especially Edwin Chadwick, and their enthusiasm carried their colleagues into adopting a long and far-reaching report based on detailed, on the spot, investigation in every part of the country. In their report, issued in February 1834, they showed the ineffectiveness of the existing system which they condemned, their criticism being directed more towards the system itself than the individuals who had to operate it. Of the justices they spoke in a somewhat condescending manner:

"Our appendix contains many complaints of the conduct of magistrates. It is to be observed that much of this is *ex parte* evidence, which the persons complained of had no opportunity of contradicting or explaining, and that the overseers from whom it was principally derived, may be supposed to have been anxious that the blame for maladministration should rest on any person but themselves. It must be acknowledged, however, that in so large a body as the magistracy, invested with powers so extensive and uncontrolled, cases of misconduct must from time to time arise. Admitting as we are anxious to admit, the general integrity and intelligence of the magistracy, and the importance of their services in the administration of justice, we yet cannot doubt that there are to be found among more than two thousand persons some exceptions to the general character. But we believe such exceptions to be rare and that in the great majority of instances - so great as to form the general rule - the magistrates have exercised the powers delegated to them by the Poor Law, not wisely indeed or beneficially, but still with benevolent and honest intentions, and that the mischief which they have done was not the result of self-interest or partiality, but was in part the necessary consequence of their social position and of the jurisdiction which was confided to them,

50. Malthus wrote in 1800: "The poor complained to the justices that their wages would not enable them to supply their families in the single article of bread. The justices, very humanely, and I am far from saying improperly, listened to their complaints, inquired what was the smallest sum on which they could support their families at the then price of wheat, and gave an order of relief on the parish accordingly ... To say the truth, I hardly see what else could have been done."

and in part arose from the errors respecting the nature of pauperism and relief which prevailed among all classes at the time when the allowance system and the scale was first introduced and still appear to prevail among the majority."

These somewhat patronising references to the magistrates probably represent a compromise between the differing views of the individual commissioners, but they are supported by circumstantial evidence which has become available more recently and which certainly shows a benevolent approach by the justices. The commission recommended the total abolition of the established system and its replacement by a national bureaucracy which was to be under the control of a Board of Commissioners. The commissioners were not to be permitted to become Members of Parliament and were to be independent of direct ministerial control, though they had to submit annual reports to the Secretary of State. Parishes were to be grouped into Poor Law Unions controlled by Boards of Guardians who included all the resident justices *ex officio* and also a number of persons elected by the ratepayers (there was to be plural voting according to the rate paid). The Royal Commission produced a draft Bill, embodying their recommendations, which was adopted by the Government and received Royal Assent on August 14, only four months after the Report was presented. It is interesting to note that the numerous JPs who were members of both Houses of Parliament did not seek to oppose the Bill which took away their rights, and some even spoke in support. They seem to have been just as ready in the 1830s to relinquish their Poor Law responsibilities as they were 30 years later to give up prison administration. It appears from their private correspondence that they were convinced that the existing system had to be replaced, and some also implied that they were glad to be rid of it. Their comments suggest that they agreed with public opinion that the established system was both inefficient and incompatible with modern trends, but it is probable that the considerations which were uppermost in their minds were, first, the intolerable and seemingly unrewarding amount of time that they had to devote to the problems of the poor and, second, the heavy and ever increasing cost which they and their associates were obliged to bear as ratepayers. As we have seen, the latter had long been a cause of complaint among the landed gentry who had to bear a share of the poor relief in the towns where it was far higher than in the rural parts of the counties.

The Poor Law Act 1834 did not entirely divest the Justices of the Peace of all responsibility for administering the Poor Law, though it went a long way in that direction. As already mentioned, all justices resident in a union area were to serve as guardians. In addition there were a few matters, such as the granting of emergency assistance, where the justices retained responsibility, and they also continued to approve the poor rates. Disputed cases of settlement were still dealt with at Quarter Sessions, but few such cases arose under the new statute. In providing for the inclusion of elected representatives of the community among the guardians in addition to the justices the Act was not introducing any novel provision, because the previous Poor Law bodies incorporated under local Acts had done the same. In some cases the incorporated guardians of the eighteenth century had been nominated by the vestry and in others they were elected by the inhabitants. Again, the bureaucratic element was not entirely new in 1834, as the earlier statutory bodies had operated through permanent, salaried officials. The most important innovation under the 1834 Act was the establishment of central control in the form of the Board of Commissioners to which the paid officials were responsible. The previous statutory bodies had been entirely free of any outside supervision both in the audit of their accounts and in the manner in which they performed their duties. The essence of the new system was that it was administered by officials responsible to Whitehall and acting under a code of regulations enforced through an inspectorate.

In view of the atmosphere in which the legislation of 1834 was introduced, one might have expected the new régime to have met with general approval but, although it was accepted in the south of the country where it was first applied and where the commissioners succeeded in organizing most of the counties into unions by 1837, it met fierce opposition in the Midlands and north. Dissatisfaction, which was enhanced by the economic crisis, was largely based on the fear of interference by the central Government. Most of the population still thought in terms of local self-government and, although strongly in favour of social reform and of representative institutions, were deeply apprehensive of anything which might lead to greater centralization. Those who attacked the new régime sometimes referred with approval and even nostalgia to the former rule of the justices through the overseers. Nevertheless, the Government, far from yielding to demands to repeal the 1834 Act, introduced new measures which were based on it. Thus in 1836, the areas of the Poor Law unions became the registration districts under the Births, Deaths and Marriages Act 1836, and in 1840 the guardians had to provide the newly introduced free vaccination service under the Vaccination Act.

Although the justices' involvement in the relief of the poor was minimal after 1834, it was not until the 1880s that it ceased entirely, at the same time as they relinquished almost all their other remaining administrative duties.

Although not within the Poor Law it may be convenient here to mention Friendly Societies which became popular in the eighteenth century. In accordance with the usual practice of placing everything under the responsibility of the justices, the societies were brought under their supervision. An Act of 1793 (33 Geo. III, c. 54) provided that their rules should be confirmed at Quarter Sessions and a duplicate kept by the Clerk of the Peace. Under an Act of 1819 (59 Geo. III, c. 128) the justices were empowered to publish rules for the formation of the societies. In 1829 a further Act (10 Geo. IV, c. 56, s. 34) provided that tables of sickness and mortality should be transmitted to the Clerk of the Peace at five-yearly intervals and forwarded to the Secretary of State. The provisions of the Acts regarding confirmation and enrolment were extended to Loan Societies in 1835 (5 & 6 William IV, c. 23) and to Benefit Building Societies in 1836 (6 & 7 William IV, c. 32). All these functions were transferred to the Registrar of Friendly Societies at various times between 1846 and 1896.

Control of Wages and Trade

The duty of the justices to fix wages was withdrawn by an Act[51] of 1813, but this did not affect the special Acts which gave the justices power to fix wages in particular trades. The justices continued to perform a useful function in this area, but the fixing of wages was unacceptable to the reformers and therefore all the Acts were repealed in 1824.[52] In spite of this, control of certain trades remained necessary, and during the early part of the nineteenth century a number of Acts were passed for this purpose, which placed responsibility for enforcement on the justices. There were also some further enactments which involved the justices in industrial relations. For example, the Employers and Workmen Act 1875, gave magistrates certain powers to compensate workmen who had been wrongfully dismissed; a duty which placed upon them the double task of adjudicating upon the circumstances of the dismissal and also of deciding who fell within the definition of a "workman". These duties however, came to be performed as part of the justices' criminal jurisdiction and they were no longer involved in an administrative capacity.

Licensing

We have seen that the policy followed by the justices in the granting of liquor licences became the subject of intense criticism notwithstanding the genuine efforts which they made to raise moral standards in the late eighteenth century. In accordance with the Royal Proclamation of 1787 they had tried to discover means of suppressing the drunkenness

---

51.   53 Geo. III, c. 40. An Act of 1814 (54 Geo. III, c. 96) repealed the Elizabethan apprenticeship statutes.
52.   5 Geo. IV, c. 66.

and disorder which was prevalent. The country soon forgot, or deliberately ignored, the measures which the justices had taken in the public interest to apply a uniform licensing policy, under which the number of alehouses was limited strictly to the needs of the locality and which subjected them to rigid rules as to hours of opening and behaviour of patrons.

As mentioned earlier, following the end of the Napoleonic war, there began a public outcry against the justices' licensing policy, the criticism being based on two assertions. First, that the limitation on the number of public houses gave a highly profitable monopoly to the already wealthy brewers, who established a tied-house system which raised the cost of beer. Second, it was claimed that many respectable persons were prevented from acquiring a licence and were so deprived of their livelihood. The idea of interfering with a man's freedom to follow whatever lawful occupation he favoured and to invest his money as he thought fit was anathema to the Radicals and also to the Whig politicians. It was said that, if beer were sold on the open market without restriction, the right number of alehouses would be opened in each area according to the principles of supply and demand. The Tories, who constituted the majority of the justices, favoured the retention of the justices' licensing powers, but the Tory Government did not wish to risk unpopularity by taking a course which would seem to curtail the pleasures of the people. Moreover, they shared with the Opposition the conviction that there should be no restriction on the way in which an individual invested his money or engaged in trade. If any thought were given to the crime and disorder which was likely to arise from the increased drunkenness, the Government assumed that this would be taken care of by the new police forces which it was their policy to introduce. Meanwhile the reputation of the justices throughout the whole country also suffered from the derogatory reports published by commissions of inquiry into the magisterial system in Middlesex.

Parliament, and especially the Commons Committees, seem to have been totally ignorant of the careful way in which the justices performed their duties from 1786 and the beneficial result which this had on the community. There were indeed instances where the justices themselves, well aware of the disadvantages of tied-houses, took active steps to curb the brewers' control of licensed premises.[53] In the teeth of clear evidence to the contrary, Parliament assumed that it would be in the general interest to deprive the justices of all their licensing powers, apart from seeing that an applicant for a licence should be a person of good character. This included not only the power to grant a

53. Examples are given by the Webbs in *The History of Liquor Licensing in England Principally from 1700 to 1830*, pp. 89-90.

licence at their discretion but also to impose conditions and to withdraw a licence if the licensee did not conduct his premises properly.

It seems curious that the justices themselves did not go to any length to refute the allegations. They seem to have assumed that the tide of opinion was so strong that resistance would be useless and that the loss of their licensing role was inevitable. They may also have been overawed by the weight of evidence of gross ineptitude and corruption which was accumulated in Middlesex. In addition to this, many justices, as landowners and farmers, saw advantages in a rise in beer consumption with its accompanying increase in the production of hops and barley. Little effort was therefore made to challenge the wild claims made against the existing system, and the only effect of the criticism was to deter the justices from continuing to pursue their previous policy.

The clamour for freedom of trade in all alcoholic drinks increased throughout the 1820s. The justices were accused of refusing any licences in the neighbourhood of their estates because alehouses spoiled the amenities and were the haunts of poachers. In 1823 and 1824 Acts[54] were passed relaxing the restrictions on the sale of beer and reducing the cost of spirit licences, the latter leading to a large increase in the number of alehouses selling spirits. In 1830 the momentous step was taken by Parliament of allowing any ratepayer to open a shop for the sale of beer on payment of a fee of two guineas. The Act,[55] which was passed by a majority of 245 to 91, deprived the justices of almost all their licensing powers, though they remained involved to a small degree. It prescribed hours during which sale was allowed, and breaches of the regulations were dealt with by the justices in the same way as other infringements of the law, but none of their administrative duties remained except the power to order a house to be closed in case of riot and for no other reason. Apart from this, there was virtually no control by the justices over the sale of beer, though it still applied to other alcoholic drinks as mentioned below.

The result was an enormous surge in drunkenness and crime and a rapid deterioration in the standard of the premises in which liquor was consumed. The Whig Government, however, disregarded the ensuing outcry, much of which came from the Church and the justices, and they even ignored the report of a House of Commons Committee on Drunkenness of 1834, which drew attention to the deplorable situation. Nothing therefore was done to alter the position apart from a few

---

54.   4 Geo. IV, c. 51; 5 Geo. IV, c. 54. In 1822 an Act (3 Geo. IV, c. 77) had defined the recognizances to be entered into by licensees and the certificates of good conduct which they had to produce. In 1828 there was a codifying Act which set out the law on justices' powers to grant licences to inns, alehouses and vitualling houses (9 Geo. IV, c. 61).

55.   11 Geo. IV & 1 William IV, c. 64.

minor enactments. One of these, in 1834, required applicants for excise licences to provide testimonials of character, and the justices were empowered to regulate opening and closing hours.[56] Six years later,[57] the rateable value of premises in which beer could be sold was raised, and in 1842 the justices were empowered to regulate the transfer of licences.[58] Meanwhile, the Act of 1828 remained in force so far as alcoholic liquors other than beer were concerned, and therefore any premises on which such drinks were sold were still under the control of the justices. The Webbs pointed out that, in view of this, the justices recognized from 1830 that the best policy was to press the beershop keeper to accept a spirit licence in order that his premises might come under some control.

It was not until 1869 that Parliament at last passed an amending Act which restored most of the justices' control over all licensed premises.[59] This Act provided that in future all licences for the sale of beer, cider or wine should be granted by the justices under the Act of 1828. From then onwards therefore no one could obtain an excise licence unless they were first granted a justices' licence, and in granting such a licence they had complete discretion,[60] except that they could only refuse an off-licence on four grounds: absence of evidence of good character, that the person who occupied the house was disorderly, that he had forfeited his licence for misconduct or that he was not qualified to hold a licence.

The 1869 Act was continued and amended by an Act of the following year, and a further Act of 1872 required the grant by the justices of a new licence to be confirmed by a standing committee of Quarter Sessions to be called the County Licensing Committee.[61] This Act also disqualified a justice, who was a brewer in the district where he acted, from adjudicating on licensing matters except where charges were brought against individuals for crimes committed in breach of the Act. The hours of closing of licensed premises were further regulated by an Act of 1874, which also provided for exceptions to the regulations to be made, particularly in favour of *bona fide* travellers and persons living in the house.

It had taken some 40 years for the disastrous provisions of the 1830 Act to be reversed, but by the 1870s the justices had regained the whole of their control over the sale of alcoholic drinks and were virtually restored to the position they had enjoyed previously and which they would retain to the present day.

56.   4 & 5 William IV, c. 85.
57.   3 & 4 Vict., c. 61.
58.   5 & 6 Vict., c. 44.
59.   32 & 33 Vict., c. 27.
60.   That the Act gave the justices complete discretion was confirmed by the House of Lords in *Sharp v. Wakefield* (1891), AC 173.
61.   33 & 34 Vict., c. 29; 35 & 36 Vict., c. 94.

Highways and Bridges

We have seen that one of the principal causes of the justices' unpopularity at the end of the eighteenth century was the frequency with which they stopped-up highways and footpaths, apparently in their own interest. This could be done by any two justices under Acts of 1773 and 1815. After the end of the war the justices' responsibility for the maintenance of highways continued for a time on the same basis as it had done before, with the local inhabitants being obliged to perform their common law obligation without payment, though salaried surveyors came to be employed to an increasing extent. During the following seventy years the responsibility was gradually transferred to a new type of local authority which operated through salaried officers. At the end of the period the highway functions of the county justices had all been placed under the new elected local authorities. In the boroughs they had already been placed under the new municipal authorities created in 1835.

Under the General Highways Act 1773 justices in general highways sessions had been empowered, at the request of two-thirds of the parishioners assembled in the vestry, to appoint a salaried surveyor for the parish to be paid out of the local rate, but little, if any, use had been made of this until early in the nineteenth century, when justices in several counties made various experiments. Recognizing the desirability of having the work done by persons with knowledge and experience of what they were doing, they introduced schemes under which the magistrates in each division were directly concerned in seeing that the work was carried out properly. The Webbs describe the experiment of the justices in the Southwell division of Nottinghamshire in 1830, where they appointed a permanent overseer to survey the roads, recommend improvements, instruct all the parochial overseers and report to the justices. The work was carried out as piece-work by paid workers.[62]

As in the case of other local Government reforms, there was a significant move under the Whig Government and the reformed House of Commons in the 1830s. After several abortive Bills, Parliament passed the General Highways Act in 1835,[63] which repealed and replaced most of the existing statutes. It enabled the vestry to appoint a surveyor, who might be paid a salary, with power to raise funds through a rate. The surveyor, however, was usually some local person who had other commitments and, being an amateur, had little knowledge of the work he was required to supervise. The justices lost their power to present and punish the inhabitants of the parish but they could fine the surveyors. Parishes with more than 5,000

62.   *ELG: The Story of the King's Highway*, pp. 196-7.
63.   5 & 6 William IV, c. 50.

inhabitants could elect a representative board of management. Responsibility for highway maintenance remained with the parish, and the administration areas were therefore far too small for efficiency. Although the Act authorized the county justices to unite parishes into highway districts, little use was made of this power.

During the next 25 years attempts were made in Parliament to provide a more unified system, but these were invariably defeated because of the unpopularity of the justices and Quarter Sessions who were the most obvious solution. There were several reasons why here, as in other sections of local government, Quarter Sessions, although providing a centralized county authority, were considered unacceptable. They were a non-elective body, they were blamed for the great increase which had occurred in the rates and, as the justices were predominantly Tory, the Whig Government were averse to extending their powers. For the next 30 years therefore, highway maintenance was mainly conducted on a parish basis, and the justices' only control was an ill-defined supervision of the surveyors. There might still be an indictment before Quarter Sessions for misfeasance but this was rarely used. The only other involvement of Quarter Sessions was where parishes applied to them to be combined in a highway district, but a spirit of independence and mistrust of their neighbours deterred parishes from taking this course.

Nothing was achieved until 1862, when a new Highways Act[64] enabled Quarter Sessions to make compulsory orders dividing counties into highway districts as they thought fit. Each district was controlled by a board composed of local justices *ex officio* and a number of way wardens elected by the constituent parishes. As the Act was only permissive, a number of counties took no action and by 1894 there still remained about 5,000 highway parishes in England maintaining their own roads. Those which did implement the Act adopted a variety of different areas for the purpose. Some of these were coterminous with petty sessional divisions, some with Poor Law unions, while others did not accord with any existing area.

The Home Office had been the government department in charge of highway affairs, but in 1872 the Public Health Act transferred the Home Secretary's responsibility for highways and turnpikes to the newly created Local Government Board, which was placed in charge of public health and Poor Law administration. After 1875 the functions of the highway boards were gradually taken over by the rural sanitary authorities - and in the boroughs and urban districts by the urban sanitary authorities - which were created by the Public Health Act of that year.

---

64.   25 & 26 Vict., c. 61.

As regards the turnpike roads, we have already seen that these were being abolished by the 1870s because road traffic was declining with the building of railways, which began with the construction of the Stockton to Darlington line in 1825. The Trusts were unable to compete and were wound up. Turnpikes had depended for a large part of their revenue on the stage coaches, but these could not compete with railways either in cost or speed and, when the stage coach was driven out of business, so too were the turnpikes. The London to Birmingham coaches were withdrawn as early as 1839. In 1841 the Government sought to give some relief to the turnpikes by empowering the justices in special sessions to order a contribution to be made from the highway rates towards the repair of turnpike roads when the toll revenue was insufficient.[65] From 1876 a Government grant in aid was made towards the cost. In 1878 the Highways and Locomotives Act required Quarter Sessions to contribute from county funds half the annual cost of maintaining roads disturnpiked after 1870. This Act also provided that all such roads should be styled "main roads" and that the justices in Quarter Sessions might declare other important roads to be main roads.

All main roads became the responsibility of the new County Councils under the Local Government Act 1888, while other roads were made the responsibility of the District Councils after the Local Government Act 1894. The County Councils might contribute to the District Councils' expenses at their discretion.

Bridges had become the clear responsibility of Quarter Sessions by the beginning of the century, although, if they were erected after June 24, 1803 by private persons, they were not county bridges unless built to the satisfaction or under the supervision of the county surveyor.[66] In 1841 an Act (4 & 5 Vict., c. 49) gave county justices power to borrow money for the repair of county bridges. In 1888 all main road bridges, like the main roads themselves, became the responsibility of the county councils, who had to carry out their repair.

Military
The militia had become a body of paid volunteers trained for home defence, but the importance of their role diminished in the early nineteenth century with the growth of the yeomanry regiments, which were the force most often used to quell riots. The justices still had responsibilities relating to the raising and maintenance of the militia, but otherwise their only military involvement was in reading the proclamation under the Riot Act and ordering the troops (regular, yeomanry or militia) to quell disturbances. Although the Act remained

65.   4 & 5 Vict., c. 59; extended in 1863 by 26 & 27 Vict., c. 94.
66.   43 Geo. III, c. 59.

in force throughout the century the occasions when justices needed to operate it became rare with the establishment of the county and borough police forces. The Militia Acts were consolidated by the Militia Act of 1882.

Until 1871 responsibility for the efficiency of the militia remained with the Lord Lieutenant, who was the overall commander and appointed the other officers, but the Army Regulation Act of that year and subsequent legislation brought to an end the Lieutenant's position as a military chief. Thereafter, apart from ceremonial, his principal concern lay with the county magistrates. This arose from his responsibility for nominating appointees to the commission, which was derived from the fact that he also held the office of *Custos Rotulorum*, but as Lord Lieutenant he was also a justice *ex officio* in his own right and as such he headed the list of such justices in the commission.

Rates

As previously, the cost of local county government until 1888 had to be met from rates levied by the justices in Quarter Sessions on the owners of property in the county. As we have seen there had been vast increases in expenditure from the latter part of the nineteenth century, especially on gaols, bridges and lunatic asylums, and this had greatly added to the justices' unpopularity even though the mounting cost of some items such as prisons was inevitable. Obviously the subject of rates could not escape Parliament's attention in the new atmosphere of progress and reform. Small changes in the method of assessing and collecting rates had been made in Middlesex by an Act of 1797 and this was extended to other counties by another Act of 1815,[67] and a number of Acts were passed from the 1830s onwards with the object of relieving the burden on the ratepayer. They therefore met with at least partial support from the justices who were among the largest ratepayers, though they now also had to pay income tax, which was first introduced during the Napoleonic wars and had subsequently become permanent. Not all the justices were in favour of some of the new legislation which was to transfer responsibility away from Quarter Sessions.

An Act of 1836[68] clarified the liability to rates by defining the term "net annual value" on which it was based, and this was extended by an Act of 1874.[69] A distinction was made between the valuation of

---

67.   37 Geo. III, c. 65; 55 Geo. III, c. 51. The latter statute was amended by a further Act in 1816 which empowered the justices to fix the boundaries of counties and of parts of counties for rating purposes.
68.   6 & 7 William IV, c. 96.
69.   37 & 38 Vict., c. 54.

agricultural land and that of other property in the Lighting and Watching Act 1833 and in the Public Health Acts 1848 and 1875, under which the rates levied for the purpose of the Acts were in certain cases substantially higher on houses and buildings. The 1836 Act also required the justices to hold four special Petty Sessions a year to hear appeals against assessment. The question of assessment was taken further by an Act of 1852,[70] under which Quarter Sessions were required to appoint committees to prepare a basis for rate assessment. After hearing objections, the committees had to obtain confirmation from Quarter Sessions of their assessments, and the sessions might hear appeals against rates that had been confirmed. Under an Act of 1862[71] boards of guardians also had to appoint assessment committees to hear objections against valuations made by the overseers. Appeals against the committees' decisions lay to Quarter Sessions.

As we have already seen, it was the practice of Quarter Sessions to deal with administrative matters in private sessions, but the 1852 Act directed that all rating business should be conducted in open court and that county treasurers should publish annual abstracts of their accounts in a form settled by the Secretary of State.

There was an important development in 1834, when a House of Commons Committee recommended that a portion of the cost of administering the criminal law should be borne by the state. Accordingly in 1835 the Exchequer accepted responsibility for the whole of the cost of the removal of prisoners to convict prisons and half the cost of prosecutions at Assizes and Quarter Sessions. This was extended in 1846 to cover the whole of the cost of prosecutions and of some other local government expenditure. As we have already seen, the Prisons Act 1877 transferred to the state the cost of maintaining prisons, and an Act of 1856 provided for the state to defray a quarter of the cost of county and borough police forces, provided that the Home Secretary certified them to be proficient, and this was raised later to a half.

In spite of these alleviations, the rates continued to be substantial in consequence of additional demands on local funds. Reference has already been made in this chapter to some of these, such as increased highway maintenance following the disappearance of the Turnpike Trusts. A substantial addition was incurred after 1870 under the Education Act.

In the boroughs the new municipal authorities had been responsible for levying and collecting rates from 1835, but in the counties Quarter Sessions continued to undertake these duties until they were taken

---

70.   15 & 16 Vict., c. 81.
71.   25 & 26 Vict., c. 103. Other Acts which related to the method of collecting rates and determining who was liable were passed in 1844 (7 & 8 Vict., c. 33); 1849 (12 & 13 Vict., c. 65; and c. 82) and 1869 (32 & 33 Vict., c. 41).

over in 1889 by the county councils under the provisions of the Local Government Act.

Justices' Textbooks and Other Literature

Dr Burn's *The Justice of the Peace and Parish Officer* remained the principal textbook for justices in the first half of the nineteenth century, but there were also some new ventures as already mentioned in vol. I, ch. VIII. Stone's *Justices' Manual* was first published by Samuel Stone, Clerk to the Justices for Leicester, in 1842. It is still the principal work of reference for all magistrates' courts. Its annual editions are now far more voluminous than those of the mid-nineteenth century, even though the latter dealt with the justices' administrative duties as well as their judicial work which now occupies the whole of three volumes.

As already mentioned, the *Justice of the Peace* journal was first published on January 28, 1837. A perusal of the fortnightly editions provides an instructive picture of the numerous matters which occupied the larger part of the justices' time. They contain a summary of new legislation and other Parliamentary proceedings, and also editorial comment on the likely effect on the justices of proposed reforms. They also report court decisions, one of the earliest being a report of a dispute as to whether a threshing machine was exempt from paying toll on a turnpike road. It was held that it was exempt in itself but that if it were drawn by a steam-driven engine the engine must pay toll. There is also lengthy correspondence in which justices seek guidance and in reply are given much useful advice by the editor. Thus, a letter asking in what circumstances justices might commit for contempt received the reply:

> "Pollock, now Chief Baron, and Sir William Follett, when Law Officers of the Crown, advised that justices have no power to commit for contempt, and that the proper course is to indict the offender, a proceeding which, it is understood, would be originated by the Secretary of State, on the circumstances appearing to justify such a measure."

Although the publication was aimed primarily at the lay justices it included reported decisions of the stipendiary magistrates where these were of interest to the lay courts; an example being a decision of the Lambeth Police Office in 1862 on the fees to be paid to medical practitioners acting under coroners' warrants. The subjects which figure most frequently in the earlier editions are alehouses, game, highways, poor law, workhouses, rates and tithes (the church retained the right to levy a rate for ecclesiastical purposes from parishioners of all denominations until 1869).

Reference has been made earlier in this chapter to the foundation of the Justices' Clerks' Society following a suggestion in one of the early numbers of *Justice of the Peace* in 1837. There are many other references to the clerks, especially on the subject of their pay. The clerks themselves were prolific writers, though they seem to have devoted their time to subjects of general interest rather than to the keeping of minutes of proceedings, which were extremely sparse and sometimes non-existent. Some wrote textbooks; notably George C. Oke, Clerk to the Justices at Newmarket, who in 1850 published the first edition of *The Magisterial Formulist* which remained a leading work for magistrates in the twentieth century.

The End of the Era
The demise of almost all the justices' administrative functions during the six decades from the 1820s was inevitable, not only because popular opinion would not tolerate the continuance of an outdated, undemocratic institution, and not only because the system was incapable of meeting the challenge of higher standards of efficiency required in a modern world, but also because it would not have been able to cope for much longer with the sheer volume of work. One may speculate upon what would have been the fate of the Justices of the Peace if they had not lost their local government role before the end of the century. Those who predicted that the office would fade away because no one would be willing to serve once it had been bereft of its administrative importance were proved wrong, but what seems far more likely is that, had they been obliged to retain this growing burden, the justices could not have survived much longer, and certainly they could not have discharged the enhanced exercise of summary jurisdiction which they were to assume with success during the course of the twentieth century. The weight of their work was already the subject of bitter complaint by the end of the eighteenth century. Although they were divested of some of this during the half century following 1830, it was more than replaced by the ever increasing volume of business which built up during the same period. It seems obvious from the experience of the County and District Councils almost from their inception that the army of part-time amateurs, even if they had been doubled in number, could not possibly have continued for long to dispose of their administrative and executive work in addition to discharging important judicial duties. These reflections seem to have been in the minds of many of the justices themselves, and they appear to have accepted the prospect with some sense of relief. As we have seen, they made no noticeable effort to resist the removal of several of their principal administrative functions, notably those relating to the Poor Law and prisons. When, in 1888, the final curtain

fell on their performance as governors and administrators there were many justices who appeared to bemoan the event, but it is likely that in their hearts they recognized the inevitable and, as individuals, looked forward to continuing to rule their counties through the new system that had replaced the old.

There was therefore no plausible alternative to the removal of the Justices of the Peace from the centre of the local government scene. Their departure, however, was not wholly in the interests of the people. The justices were in close touch with local affairs and they understood the peculiar needs of their respective areas. Their presence in Parliament enabled them to ensure that local interests were not overlooked when framing legislation, and they were able to judge at first hand the effect that new measures had on the people in their own neighbourhood. The task of implementing as well as making the law rested with them and they were able to observe what went on "at grass roots." They were in a position to note that the provisions of a particular Act might be all very well in theory but that there were circumstances where they were wholly impracticable, and they had the ability to take remediable action. The reforms of the nineteenth century transferred power to the departments of central government, while Parliament itself came to consist of men who had far less experience than their predessors of local administration. The result was that those responsible for governing the country were no longer in close touch with the area communities and they tended to apply political policies that were not always practicable.

CHAPTER VI

1888 - 1945

FROM ADMINISTRATORS TO JUDGES

*New scope for exercise of judicial powers - Expansion of justices' work in
courts of summary jurisdiction - Novel matrimonial and juvenile work -
Probation - End of the property qualification - Royal Commission
1909; new system of selection and appointment - First women
magistrates - Renewed criticism of the JPs*

ON MARCH 24, 1888 THE *Justice of the Peace* journal published an
article on the Local Government Act 1888 and commented, "It will
certainly tend to diminish the prestige of the county justices," and it
was therefore to be regretted, but the article went on to say "but the
change was inevitable, and it must therefore be accepted." There were
mixed feelings among the justices themselves, some thinking that the
total demise of their office was imminent while others felt that a purely
judicial role could still have some attraction and were prepared to face
the future with equanimity. Those justices who were on borough
commissions were disinterested because they were unaffected by the
change.

The Act of 1888 laid the foundations of the modern system of local
government in England and Wales. In that year the patriarchal rule of
the county justices was replaced by the Government of the new,
elected County Councils, a process which was carried further a few
years later by the establishment of elective urban and Rural District
Councils to govern the subdivisions into which the counties were
divided. The Municipal Corporations Act of 1835 had applied to only a
limited number of towns and most remained under the authority of the
county justices. The 1888 Act introduced a uniform system for all
urban areas, the larger towns being boroughs or county boroughs and
the others urban districts each with its own District Council. In the
metropolitan area the territory outside the boundary of the old City
was placed under a newly created London County Council which
replaced a bewildering number of other authorities which had
previously been responsible for the affairs of the metropolis.

In future, the work conducted by both county and borough justices
would be the same, save that the county justices would continue to sit
at Quarter Sessions whereas in boroughs the recorder sat alone at
Quarter Sessions as had been the case since 1835. Under the Act the

county justices lost virtually all their administrative functions which they had discharged for centuries. We have seen that before 1888 they had already been divested of some of their administrative and executive duties, notably in relation to police and the poor, but a substantial number still remained at the beginning of the year, including the levying of rates, the maintenance of highways, bridges and rivers, the control of weights and measures, the appointment and pay of county officers and the control and management of many county institutions, such as lunatic asylums and reformatory schools, though the gaols which the justices were still required to visit were no longer in their possession. All of these duties and many others were transferred in a moment of time to the councils. All that remained with the justices of their former administrative functions was licensing, which was considered to be an unsuitable task for the new elective authorities. Apart from this nothing was left to the justices except their judicial duties which remained intact. The justices had become primarily Judges and their future lay solely in the administration of justice.

There were many at that time who bemoaned the change. Maitland wrote:

"The outlook is certainly gloomy. If the justices are deprived of their governmental work, will they care to be justices any longer? This is a momentous question; on the answer to it depends a great deal of the future history of England."[1]

Maitland's gloomy foreboding proved to be unfounded. The justices, having lost their administrative functions, turned themselves wholeheartedly to their judicial work which was expanded during the following hundred years to an extent which would have been quite impossible if they had not been relieved of their other duties. This was particularly noticeable in the extension of summary jurisdiction whereby a large number of cases which were previously triable only with a jury were brought within the jurisdiction of the justices at Petty Sessions. This expansion of the work of the lay justices did not extend to Quarter Sessions where, although the court's jurisdiction was to be extended during the twentieth century, it was brought more and more within the authority of the professional judiciary; a trend which culminated in the establishment of the Crown Court in 1972. The opposite was to happen in the Petty Sessions' courts where the lay justices took the place in the trial system of the lay jurymen who had previously tried many of the types of case now dealt with summarily,

1.   F.W. Maitland, *The Shallows and Silences of Real Life, Collected Papers* (1911) Cambridge UP, p. 472.

while points of law were dealt with, not by professional magistrates - a course which was often advocated - but by the justices' clerks whose advice to the justices was based on their legal experience.

For the first time in their history the justices' work developed on a systematic basis. The position they occupied in the judicial structure was analysed and further duties were allocated to them on a methodical basis as the need arose. In accordance with the new philosophy various steps were taken from the early twentieth century onwards and they soon began to play a prominent part in the remodelled arena. At the same time, although any moves to make the magistrates an elective body like the local authorities were firmly resisted, the composition of the benches became more representative of the community as a whole. Once again the Justices of the Peace survived because they adapted to a new revolutionary situation which they embraced with enthusiasm, even to the extent of taking the lead in such matters as a novel approach to the treatment of offenders both adult and juvenile.

The personnel of the commissions and the officers of the courts

We have seen that from 1835 appointments to borough commissions were made by the Lord Chancellor who exercised an unfettered discretion in the choice of candidates, though he usually consulted the municipal authorities and local Members of Parliament. This freedom of action did not always make his task an easy one for, although he might consult whomsoever he should choose, some Lord Chancellors were not happy with the advice they received. Lord Loreburn, in a speech in the House of Lords, said:

"There is no one to advise me or give assistance of any sort, kind, or description. There is no Lord Lieutenant in any borough ... Personal knowledge I can have none, nor can any Lord Chancellor have it, and through this open gap - open because there are no resources to obtain the proper and necessary information - party claims on both sides are thrust forward, constantly with clamour, and sometimes with menace."[2]

In the counties on the other hand, although appointments were also made by the Lord Chancellor on behalf of the Crown, in practice the candidates continued to be chosen by the Lord Lieutenant. Indeed there were many who maintained that the Lord Chancellor was obliged to accept without question the names put forward by the Lord Lieutenant.

2.   32 House of Lords Debates, 5s. col. 2724.

"By long established and inviolable usage he makes no inquiries into the recommendations of the Lords Lieutenant before acting upon them, unless there is something on the face of the recommendation pointing to an improper recommendation, or unless someone calls his attention to any specific disqualification attaching to any particular gentleman whom the Lord Lieutenant proposes. I do not think that the fact of a man being one of the small fry would without more induce any Lord Chancellor to interfere."[3]

One interesting aspect of the 1888 reforms which has already been mentioned was that they brought no immediate radical change in the personnel of the bodies who ran county affairs. Throughout the country as a whole rather more than a half of those who previously governed their counties through Quarter Sessions became members of the new County Councils and, as we have seen, the chairmen of the two bodies were sometimes the same individual. Considerable changes would occur during the following hundred years in the composition of both County Councils and county commissions, but nevertheless, until the middle of the twentieth century there continued to be a marked similarity between those who served on the two bodies, notwithstanding the fact that service on one was dependent upon democratic election and on the other upon appointment by the Crown. The reason for this was that there continued to be a number of persons among the upper sections of society who had both the desire and the time to take an active part in public affairs in the countryside and who were also capable of attracting support from the population because of their status. Their social background enabled them to gain appointment as justices through nomination by the Lord Lieutenant and it was also still an asset for candidates in local elections. However, similarity between benches and councils must not be exaggerated, and it became less noticeable as the importance of county society diminished while able persons whose public image did not depend upon their social background were able to make their mark. These people might still find it difficult to obtain appointment to the Commission of the Peace, especially if they were reputed to hold extreme political views, but an increasing number were elected to the local government authorities as the century progressed.

Reference has already been made to the Home Rule crisis of 1886 in which Gladstone and his Liberals lost the support of the landowning class. Only three English Lords Lieutenant remained loyal to Gladstone's party out of a total of 42, and there was a corresponding change among the county justices of whom barely 15 per cent

3. Letter from Sir Henry Hope to the Prime Minister's secretary, 1892. Salisbury papers, Christchurch Library.

supported Gladstone's ministry. Radical members of the Liberal party demanded a reform of the system which would either replace the lay justices with stipendiaries (a course which even the Unionist leader, Lord Salisbury, was prepared to accept) or would ensure that an appreciable proportion of justices were drawn from their own party supporters. Asquith, who was Home Secretary from 1982 to 1895 and was to become Prime Minister in 1908, suggested that magistrates should be nominated by the new County Councils. The Lord Chancellor, Lord Herschell, however, was not prepared to make any appointments except on merit, and he refused to be moved by the pressure that was put upon him by the whips and the party members. In May 1893 Sir Charles Dilke moved a resolution in the House of Commons which was carried by a small majority,

"That in the opinion of this House it is expedient that the appointment of county magistrates should no longer be made by the Lord Chancellors of Great Britain and Ireland for the time being only on the recommendation of the Lords Lieutenant."[4]

Following this Lord Herschell made a number of appointments to the county commissions from among Gladstonian Liberals and he largely ignored the views of the Lords Lieutenant, but when the Liberal Government fell in 1895 the new Lord Chancellor, Lord Halsbury, reverted to the old system.[5] This remained the position until the Liberals under Balfour were victorious at the general election of 1906, and one of the first measures to be passed by the new Parliament (the Justices of the Peace Act 1906) removed the property qualification for county justices, thus placing them in the same position as those in the boroughs. Henceforth it became possible for anyone regardless of his social position to become a magistrate.

Two other provisions of the 1906 Act need to be mentioned. One of these enabled a county justice to act as such even though he resided outside the county boundary provided that his residence was within seven miles of it. The other was of greater importance. Section 4 provided that "Any person who is a Justice of the Peace by virtue only of holding or having held any office may be excluded from the exercise of his function as such by the same authority by which other justices can be removed from the commission of the peace." This was directed mainly at those who became justices by virtue of being elected to a local Government office - as mayor or chairman of a council. There was a strong feeling, which seemed to be justified by the facts, that a

4. 12 Parliamentary Debates, 4s. col. 258.
5. When giving evidence to the Royal Commission on the Selection of Justices of the Peace of 1910, Lord Halsbury said that in 99 cases out of 100 he accepted the recommendations of the Lord Lieutenant as a matter of course.

number of people who became justices by this means were not suitable for the office and would not have been appointed had the selection rested with the Lord Chancellor or the Chancellor of the Duchy of Lancaster. These two ministers were therefore empowered to make exclusion orders preventing an individual from exercising any magisterial functions during such time as he remained a justice *ex officio*. Thereafter such orders were made from time to time, but the occasions were rare. This was partly because the power was usually exercised only when the person concerned had been convicted of some offence, and seldom on the ground that he was morally or intellectually unfit to administer justice. Another reason why successive Chancellors rarely exercised the power of exclusion was because there was no machinery for informing them of cases where their intervention was required. Even instances where a mayor or chairman had been convicted of a serious offence were often overlooked. The only way of ensuring that only those who were well qualified to serve became justices was to provide that no-one should attain the office except by appointment to a Commission of the Peace by the Chancellor. This step was finally taken 60 years later.

In 1906 the Liberal party supporters also pressed for the political balance of the benches to be adjusted by the appointment of large numbers of Liberal justices. The Lord Chancellor, Lord Loreburn, aroused indignation in the party by resolutely refusing to pack the benches with Liberals. Although he disregarded some of the Unionist candidates put forward by Lords Lieutenant and instead appointed a certain number of Liberals he fell far short of the drastic reconstruction which his party demanded. Between January 1906 and November 1909 he appointed a total of some 7,000 justices of whom only 3,197 were known to be Liberals.[6] Some dissatisfied Members of Parliament again pressed for the justices to be nominated by the local authorities. H.C.F. Luttrell, Member for Tavistock, having urged this course in 1906, introduced a Private Bill to the same effect in 1909, but without success.[7]

Loreburn's firm stance was a credit to the Lord Chancellor who recognized the vital constitutional principle which distinguished between the political and judicial sides of his ancient office, and in making judicial appointments he firmly refused to be influenced by party considerations. In consequence his relationship with his own party became seriously strained. His position was made more difficult by the fact that his Conservative predecessor, Lord Halsbury, had seldom appointed anyone other than a Conservative supporter, and

6.   32 House of Commons Debates, 5s. col. 2724.
7.   The same proposal was put forward in a Private Member's Bill introduced in the House of Commons in 1977 by Mr. Bruce Grocott, the Labour Member for Lichfield and Tamworth, but he too was unsuccessful.

undoubtedly the benches were heavily overweighted with Conservatives. The difficulties which Loreburn had to face, not least the pressure from his own party, and his highly creditable approach to his duties and to those of the justices are revealed in correspondence between him, the chief whip and the Prime Minister's secretary at the end of 1906.[8] A letter from Loreburn to Ponsonby, the Prime Minister's secretary, of November 22, 1906, contained the following comments:

"The duty of JP has very serious sides to it. They deal out justice to the poorest and with little appeal in practice. I should be a coward if I made what I think unsuitable appointments to appease the clamour of MPs; all who complain, and they are few, are new MPs. And from this little group I receive offensive letters and a scarcely concealed demand that I should act as their Registrar and put on whomsoever they nominate, which I will never do.

Now the work is largely judicial and I treat the appointments as in a great degree judicial appointments. I most firmly believe it is necessary to appoint Liberals, but the grumblers when they come privately to my office confine themselves to urging the claim of a few persons who are their supporters and to whom they have in some cases promised the appointments on their own responsibility. I have already appointed about three times as many justices as have been appointed on the annual average of ten years and I believe have appointed twice as many as have been appointed in any single year, with infinite labour and trouble, the vast majority being Liberals.

I venture to think that this should be considered from a wider point of view. It is impossible for me to give my reasons as to individuals or to render an account of my actions to individual members. No man can be more anxious to redress the balance than I am but those who complain make it difficult by sending my names, not of the best men, but of the snob and the hacks whom they wish to reward."

On December 3, the chief whip, George Whiteley wrote to the Prime Minister:

"May I say that it is impossible to exaggerate the mischief being done in the Country by the action of the Lord Chancellor in his magisterial appointments.

I *most* carefully and advisedly use the phrase that he is upsetting and most seriously damaging our Party.

8.   Add. MSS. 41222, ff.194, 196, 197. Quoted by R.F.V. Heuston in *Lives of the Lord Chancellors 1885-1940* (1964) Clarendon Press, pp. 154-6.

I do not know quite what is my duty in the matter. We have honestly tried to keep our people quiet. But they are indignant beyond restraint, and I do not wonder at it.

May I enclose you the third remonstrance by this morning's post, this from no less a Liberal than George Cadbury ... As I do not wish to go behind the Lord Chancellor's back in writing to you thus, I will send to him a copy of this letter and also Mr. Cadbury's. I know you are aware that our County Members are leaguing themselves to vote a reduction in the Chancellor's salary."

Whiteley sent a copy of this letter to Loreburn and asked him for a meeting. The Lord Chancellor replied on December 10:

"I have only just seen your letter to me about Justices of the Peace. I believe you wish to be friendly to me and I can only say that if the Liberal Party in the Ho. of Commons wants to see done what the complaining members privately asked me to do (*viz.* to job the Judicial Bench), I do not wish any longer to belong to that Party.

I will see you whenever you like, but all I can tell you is that this is an attempt to force upon me what I regard as a prostitution of my office and that I will resign the Great Seal sooner than do it.

Don't you think it might be worth your while to ascertain the facts before you take sides against me?"

Whitely replied the following day, hotly denying that he had taken sides against the Lord Chancellor and claiming that not a day had passed during the last two months when he had not spent some of his time defending him. He continued, not unreasonably expressing the point of view of a party manager:

"But, with respect - to say that the Party want you to 'job the judicial bench' is contrary to the facts. For 20 years the Tories have done so. The result is that the Bench in various localities is generally composed of from twenty to ten Tories and one Liberal. All that we ask from you is to bear this in mind. We are suffering now the most colossal injustice in these matters. We ask for some rectification of it, and we want *you* to make our magistrates, and not Tory Lords Lieutenant and local Tory Caucuses. We known we are safe with you, but we are galled by the others. I have the exact figures for Shropshire: Previous to this year, 214 Tories, 10 Liberals. Appointed by you, 8 Tories, 7 Liberals. The packed Bench there now consists of 222 Tories and 17 Liberals."

Loreburn stuck to his guns, though in some counties he appointed a rather larger proportion of Liberal justices than he had done before. Criticism of his policy continued, but for the next few years it was less vituperative. It was obvious that the system of choosing and appointing magistrates required thorough investigation and overhaul, if only to satisfy the vociferous critics, but it was not only pressure from outside that finally induced the Government to take action. Loreburn himself came to realize that some fundamental changes were necessary and he formulated ideas of his own as to what form these should take. Before introducing them, however, he wished to have the backing of an independent authority. These were the considerations which led the Government in November 1909 to set up the Royal Commission on the Selection of Justices of the Peace - the first Royal Commission to be concerned entirely with the appointment of magistrates.

The Royal Commission of 1909

The Royal Commission was appointed under the chairmanship of Lord James of Herefore, an old friend of Lord Loreburn and one time Chancellor of the Duchy of Lancaster. Its terms of reference were:

> To consider and report whether any and what steps should be taken to facilitate the selection of the most suitable persons to be Justices of the Peace irrespective of creed and political opinion.

The commission presented its Report[9] in July 1910 and it was accepted almost in full.

In his evidence to the commission Lord Loreburn said:

> My view is that no Lord Chancellor ought to admit any right in anyone to control his judgment. It would be intolerable if he were required to bear the whole responsibility for appointment which the law entrusts solely to him, but were constrained to act upon the opinion of someone else. My own practice has been to communicate freely with the Lords Lieutenant, and I have done so with every one of them whenever any difficulty has arisen, or any complaints from any county. With very few exceptions they have been quite willing to co-operate, and have taken a great deal of trouble. My endeavour has been, in the first instance, to procure an agreement in the county itself, so that if possible the Lord Lieutenant should communicate himself with representative people of all opinions in the county, and frame a list which would give general satisfaction. This has been done in something like 35 or 40 counties out of 98,

9.   Cd. 5250 Minutes of Evidence, Cd., 5358.

including sokes, liberties, ridings, and counties of cities. In a good many of them it already had been the practice of the Lord Lieutenant to gather opinion on the spot and make recommendations accordingly, and no substantial complaint had ever reached me in regard to those counties. Where, however, this has not been practicable, and trouble has arisen accordingly, I have interposed. The result has been that I have acted with the concurrence of the Lords Lieutenant in regard to almost all the appointments that I have made in my term of office. In the years 1906-7, 1908, and 1909, 5,531 Justices of the Peace were appointed in counties - that is including sokes, liberties, ridings, and so forth, and I should think 98 or 99 per cent have been appointed with the concurrence of the Lord Lieutenant. It is only in a very few cases that I have been obliged to appoint without his concurrence.[10]

Earlier in his evidence Lord Loreburn had remarked that "it is contrary to public interest that the authority of the Bench of justices should be weakened by any widespread suspicion that the members of it are not fairly selected." He went on to make the following observations which supported the tendency for benches to be overweighted in favour of the Conservatives:

"Social life in most counties among those who are well-to-do is mainly Conservative, and in a good many places political feeling is apt to run high. There is often a large field of selection, and it is natural that men should regard more favourably those who are of the same opinions as themselves. I think this largely accounts for the fact that there is a constant disposition to prefer Conservatives in the recommendations made to the Lords Lieutenant, apart from any intention of doing what is unfair. In a few counties, which I happen to know about, there has been a distinct and deliberate wish to exclude Liberals because they are Liberals, but I do not think that is usual, and in hardly any case is that the wish of the Lord Lieutenant. It is done, where it is done, by the political partisanship of those upon whom he relies for advice. I do, however, think that party and social predilection have the effect automatically of causing a great predominance of gentlemen of one set of opinions being brought before the Lord Lieutenant, though there may be no deisre to act unfairly."[11]

Commenting on these remarks by the Lord Chancellor the commission observed that the preponderance of Conservatives was no

10.   Loreburn, Q. 646, p. 36.
11.   Loreburn, Q. 243, pp. 11, 12.

doubt accentuated by the secession in 1886 from the Liberal party of those who were opposed to Gladstone's Home Rule policy; and that another cause was the property qualification which was not abolished until 1906. "This qualification automatically restricted the field of selection and no doubt excluded a large number of Liberals who were otherwise suitable for the position."

As the commission recognized, a Lord Lieutenant could not be acquainted personally with every possible candidate for the bench and he was therefore obliged to seek advice from others. The commission found that the persons most usually consulted were the chairman of Quarter Sessions, the chairmen of Petty Sessions, the Clerk of the Peace and Clerks to the Justices and also a number of the Lord Lieutenant's personal friends. The commission also found that, in addition to the recommendations made by the Lieutenant, the Lord Chancellor received a large number of recommendations from Members of Parliament, and even from political associations and agents and sometimes from trade unions. This was especially the case in the boroughs. The commission concluded that many of those making recommendations to the Lords Lieutenants, and to the Lord Chancellor in respect of the boroughs, were motivated by a desire to reward and encourage political support. One reason why a large majority of those appointed to the county commissions were Conservatives was probably that "the majority of persons with whom the Lord Lieutenant is personally acquainted and from whom he probably derives his information are Conservatives in politics."

Other defects in the existing system were, according to the commission, that no limit was placed on the number of justices in each area and that many of those appointed failed to do their share of the work.

In making their recommendations the commission pointed out that "appointments influenced by considerations of political opinion and services are highly detrimental to public interests, and tend to lower the authority of the magisterial benches in the country." They expressed the confident view that "political opinion or political services should not be regarded as in any way controlling or influencing the appointment of justices. The man most fitted to discharge the office should be appointed." On the other hand they were equally firmly of the opinion that no one should be excluded on account of his religious or political opinions. "For as we have said, the strength of these magisterial benches depends upon the respect in which their occupants are held ... To earn that respect and confidence it is well that the public should recognize that the benches are open to men of every shade of political opinion and of every religious faith."

The commission did not support the view expressed by Lords

Lieutenant and by Justices of the Peace in previous centuries that it was in the interest of the administration of justice that magistrates should all be drawn from the upper levels of society in order that they should enjoy the respect of the community. This was the first time that such a view received official recognition. The commission went on to state that men of every social grade should be admitted to the bench and that "it is in the public interest that working men with a first-hand knowledge of the conditions of life among their own class should be appointed to the county as well as to the borough benches." This recommendation was accepted at the time and continued to receive general approval for the next 50 years but, as we shall see later, it has never been implemented to the extent that was probably envisaged by the commission of 1909.

As to the authority which should appoint Justices of the Peace, the commission were strongly of the opinion that this should remain with the Crown and they firmly dismissed any idea of justices being elected. They commented that "the appointment of judicial officers of any kind by direct popular election is altogether opposed to English constitutional usage. Popular election would probably mean political election. The influence which we have so strongly condemned would thus be rendered all powerful." By inference they were also opposed to justices being nominated by local authorities, for they went on to say "neither can we accept a popular electorate as furnishing good judgment in the selection of men for magisterial office."

The commission also recommended that the Lord Chancellor should remain the minister responsible for advising the Crown on the appointment of justices (except in the Duchy of Lancaster where responsibility should remain with the Chancellor of the Duchy). He was the obvious choice because, (1) He was Keeper of the Great Seal under which the Commissions of the Peace were issued; (2) He was head of the judiciary and in that respect was responsible for advising the Crown on the appointment of all the Judges; and (3) He was a "Minister of the highest dignity and importance" and was unlikely to be subject to influence or political pressure.

Turning to the sources from which the Lord Chancellor should seek advice on the choice of candidates, the commission thought that recommendations in counties should continue to come through the Lord Lieutenant because, (1) He occupied a unique position in the county as the Crown's personal representative; (2) He had unrivalled opportunity to obtain trustworthy information; and (3) As *Custos Rotulorum* he was head of the magistracy in the county. The commission went on, however, to recommend the introduction of a new element in the selection procedure. They proposed that in every county the Lord Chancellor should appoint one or more committees to advise him on, (1) The number of justices taking an active share in the discharge of magisterial duties in each division, and the number required for the due discharge of such duties; (2) The necessity, if it existed, for appointing additional justices; and (3) The desirability of calling upon justices in certain cases to resign on account of non-attendance. The Lord Lieutenant should be a member of such a committee in his own county. The Lord Chancellor should have power to appoint similar committees in boroughs.

The concept of local advisory committees was not new. In 1893 Lord Herschell praised the example set by one petty sessional bench which had set up a committee to advise the county Lord Lieutenant, and Lord Loreburn had mentioned the advantage of advisory committees during a debate in the House of Lords in 1907. Later in that year he encouraged the Lord Lieutenant of Devon to form an advisory committee, which was the first to be established with the Lord Chancellor's approval. Lord Loreburn subsequently advanced proposals for an advisory committee system in his evidence to the Royal Commission, and their recommendations embodied the scheme which he had proposed.

Other recommendations contained in the commission's report were that unsolicitated recommendations should not be accepted from Members of Parliament or political agents, and that there should be justices resident in every part of every division of a county "so as to avoid any inconvenience in obtaining the issue of summonses, the taking of declarations, and the performance of other magisterial duties exercisable out of sessions." Some attempt was made initially to implement both of these recommendations but as time passed they were largely ignored. By the middle of the century, although there was no longer any question of Members of Parliament having a right to secure the appointment of their nominees, recommendations were usually accepted without question from both Members and agents, but those put forward often failed to be appointed because the Lord Chancellor considered that other candidates were more suitable. As to having justices resident in every area, it was generally felt at the time when the second Royal Commission was appointed in 1946 that the need had been exaggerated and that to appoint justices on this scale would make the benches unacceptably large.

The appointment of advisory committees, which was the most novel of the commissions recommendations, was implemented in full. Lord Loreburn, having advocated such a system in his own evidence to the commission, proceeded to put this and most of the commission's other proposals into effect without waiting for Parliamentary approval, though it was some years before advisory committees were established in all areas. By the beginning of 1912 committees had been set up in most counties and the others followed shortly afterwards. In the boroughs the process was slower for two reasons. First, in the counties the work of establishing the committees was expedited by the Lords Lieutenant who took an active part in the operation and particularly in selecting the committees' members. Secondly, in the boroughs the Lord Chancellor already had a variety of potential advisers, in spite of what Lord Loreburn had said to the contrary, and the need for committees was not considered to be as urgent as elsewhere.

Although the commission had suggested that there might be several committees in a single county only one was appointed for each commission area, however large it might be. There was therefore one committee only for every county unless it was divided into parts each with a separate commission, such as East and West Sussex. Likewise, there were still some liberties with their own commissions and each one was given its own committee.[12]

The commission assumed that the Lord Lieutenant would normally serve as chairman of the advisory committee in his county. This was based on the view which had been held for some time that it was in his capacity as Lord Lieutenant that he had in the past nominated candidates for the Commission of the Peace, but the validity of this assumption is questionable. When the office of Lord Lieutenant was first introduced the holder was not even included in the commission (it was much later that he became a county justice *ex officio*) whereas the *Custos Rotulorum* had been recognized as the head of the county magistracy since at least the fifteenth century and probably the fourteenth. This was clearly indicated in his terms of appointment. Later, as we have seen, when the Lieutenancy had become well established, confusion arose as to whether or not the *Custos* should be consulted on appointments, though there can be no doubt that in law it was his office and not that of the Lieutenant which was responsible for the magistrates. The Royal Commission of 1909 seem to have been oblivious of the distinction, but it was recognized by the next Royal Commission of 1946-48 who, when referring to the chairmanship of county advisory committees, made it clear that in their view the Lord Lieutenant acted as chairman only because he was also *Custos*. "It must be understood that we are only concerned with the Lord Lieutenant in his capacity as *Custos Rotulorum*."[13] Lord Loreburn himself seems to have been unaware of the importance of the distinction, but it was certainly recognized by his successors from the middle of the century onwards. A consideration which was of particular significance from the Lord Chancellor's point of view was that the Lord Lieutenant was appointed by the Sovereign on the recommendation of the Prime Minister whereas the *Custos* was appointed separately on the recommendation of the Lord Chancellor, and by the 1960s a practice

12.   These were: the Isle of Ely, the Cing Ports, Peterborough, Ripon and Haverfordwest.
13.   1948. Cmd. 7463, para. 65.

had become established whereby the Prime Minister's Appointments Secretary consulted the Lord Chancellor's Secretary of Commissions before the appointment of a Lieutenant was confirmed in order to make sure that the Lord Chancellor regarded the candidate as suitable to act also as *Custos* and chairman of the county advisory committee. No occasion arose in the twentieth century when different individuals were appointed to the two posts, but had they done so it seems probable that the Lord Chancellor would have appointed the *Custos* rather than the Lord Lieutenant to be chairman of the committee.

In 1911 Lord Loreburn adopted a general rule that the Lord Lieutenant should be chairman of each county committee, but at first there were some committees on which the Lord Lieutenant did not serve, although even in these cases the committee's recommendations were submitted to him before being forwarded to the Lord Chancellor. It was soon recognized, however, that there were clear advantages in the Lord Lieutenant presiding over his county committee, and this came to be the practice in almost every case. In boroughs the Chancellor chose at his discretion some suitable person, usually though not invariably a local magnate, to serve as chairman.

Members of advisory committees were mostly justices for the area covered by the commission and were drawn from both political parties, though there was a slight preponderance of Liberals on the early committees. Appointment was at first for life, but in 1927 Lord Chancellor Cave began to appoint members for six years, half of each committee having to retire every three years when they were usually replaced by new members; though there was a tendency around the middle of the century to reappoint the chairman for at least two consecutive terms. Lord Cave's practice as regards the retirement of members has been followed by his successors to the present day.

The introduction of advisory committees had a marked effect on the composition of the Commissions of the Peace, especially those for the counties. This would not have been possible to the same degree if the property qualification had not been removed in 1906, but this change finally broke the link between the magistracy and the landed gentry. Even before the Royal Commission the county benches had become less exclusive, and after 1911 they began to include numbers of individuals who were unconnected with landed property and who were also drawn more evenly from the two political parties. On the other hand there was little sign on county benches of the working-class men whom the Royal Commission wished to see appointed. This was not because of any deliberate policy on the part of the committees to exclude the working-class. It was due partly to a tendency of the committees to choose persons who occupied prominent positions in public life and whose capability could be judged by their performance in other fields, but the principal reason was that it proved to be far more difficult than had been expected to find numbers of working class men, and later women, who were both suitable for appointment and also able and willing to serve. More will be said on this subject when considering the state of the benches in the last half of the century.

During the first part of the twentieth century a new political party emerged to take its place in Parliament, and when the first Labour Government with a Parliamentary majority took office in 1929 they were faced, like the Liberal Government of 1906, with a noticeable absence of their supporters on the commission but although the proportion of Labour justices increased during the next few years no attempt was made to flood the benches. This was due partly to the comparatively short period during which Ramsey Macdonald headed the purely Labour Government before he was obliged to accept a coalition, but also to the reluctance of his Lord Chancellor, Lord Sankey, to contrive a drastic swing to the left. During his term of office on the Woolsack from 1929 to 1935 Sankey appointed more Conservative than Labour justices and he included a reasonable proportion of Liberals and Independents, the figures being:

England and Wales

Conservatives	1,401
Labour	1,166
Independents	650
Liberals	620

Scotland

Conservatives	643
Independents	453
Labour	378
Liberals	325

The Supplimental List

In 1925 public attention began to be directed towards cases where chairmen of benches and other justices had become inefficient by reason of age or infirmity, and attempts were made by the Lord Chancellor to persuade these persons to resign. This met with little success. In 1938 Lord Chancellor Hailsham issued a comprehensive letter to all Lords Lieutenant and chairmen of advisory committees dealing with the question of the retention on the Commissions of the Peace of those justices who, from whatever cause, found themselves unable regularly to discharge their duties. The letter pointed out that those who failed to attend without good cause were under a duty to resign, but it suggested that those who were aged or infirm should transfer to a Supplimental List. A justice who took this course would no longer be summoned to either Quarter Sessions or Petty Sessions, but would remain a justice and would not forego any of the rights and privileges of the office and could continue to take part on ceremonial occasions. In November 1940 Lord Chancellor Simon addressed another letter to Lords Lieutenants and chairmen, stating that the number of transfers to the Supplimental List had not come up to expectations and that in the case all future appointments the prospective justice would be required to give an undertaking to ask for his name to be transferred to the Supplimental List when he attained the age of 75. This arrangement received statutory authority in the following year in the Justices (Supplimental List) Act 1941, which was passed on July 2. Section 1(2) and (3) of the Act provided that:

"(2) A Justice of the Peace whose name is for the time being entered in the supplemental list kept in connexion with any Commission of the Peace shall not be qualified to sit as a member of any court of Quarter Sessions or court of summary jurisdiction or as a licensing justice or as a member of any confirming authority or compensation authority under the Licensing (Consolidation) Act, 1910:

Provided that a justice whose name is so entered shall not be disqualified from taking part in any business of a court of Quarter Sessions relating only to the appointment of committees or other like administrative matters, or from sitting as a member of such a court while such business is being transacted.

(3) If the Lord Chancellor is satisfied, with respect to any justice named in a Commission of the Peace, that it is, by reason of his age or infirmity or other like cause, expedient that he should cease to exercise judicial functions, the Lord Chancellor may direct that the name of that justice shall be entered in the supplemental list kept in connexion with that Commission of the Peace."

On September 16, 1941 Lord Chancellor Simon made Rules under the powers conferred on him by the Act (SR & O, 1941, No. 1446 L. 26). Further changes in the application of the Supplimental List were to take place after the war and will be described in ch. VII.

The idea of a Supplimental List originated in the Duchy of Lancaster. In 1912 the Chancellor of the Duchy introduced what was called the Retired List to which a county, but not a borough, justice might be transfered at his own request if he could show that he was no longer physically able to attend court or to hear properly. The effect of the transfer was to relieve him of responsibility to attend court and committee meetings. Sometimes the Chancellor received a report that a particular justice, who had not applied for a transfer, was no longer an asset to his bench, and in such a case the Chancellor would suggest that he should apply. In the rare cases where the justice declined to do so the Chancellor might remove him from the commission. The example set by the Chancellor of the Duchy was not followed immediately by the Lord Chancellor because Lord Loreburn, who occupied that office until June 1912, thought that the undertaking not to adjudicate which was given by a justice on the Retired List could not be enforced and amounted to an unconstitutional prohibition by a Minister of the exercise of powers conferred upon the justice by his commission. Loreburn's view was accepted by his successors for the next 25 years, though it may be noted that the undertaking given by all justices on appointment from 1912 onwards to resign if they failed to perform their share of the duties was little different from that of a justice joining the Retired List. In either case the only sanction was the removal of the justice's name from the commission. The Retired List in the Duchy was renamed the Supplimental List from January 1, 1969.

Women as magistrates

The social and political changes in the magistracy which have just been described were among the most important developments in the history of the Justices of the Peace, yet of even greater significance for the future was a totally new innovation - the apppointment from 1919 of women to the commissions.

It has generally been assumed that at common law women were ineligible for appointment as justices, yet there was no clear authority for this, and some have held that there was no bar to such an appointment. The fact that some earlier statutes refer only to 'men' is not conclusive. The enactment of 1327 (1 Edw. III, st. 2, c. XVI) which is sometimes quoted in this context, although it states that "in every county good men and lawful shall be assigned to keep the peace," is referring to the appointment of Keepers of the Peace and not to justices. Furthermore, some of the Norman French expressions which appear in the early statutes such as "gentz" or "persones" might be interpreted as including both sexes. Marowe, writing in 1503, clearly took this view and implied that women, whether or not they were married, could be appointed Justices of the Peace, and he even discussed the legal effect of the marriage of a woman justice.[14] Some others shared Marowe's view. Edmund Dudley in his readings in Gray's Inn in 1496 claimed that the King could appoint women to be Justices in Eyre, but it is possible that he and Marowe were influenced by a desire to please the court, especially the Countess of Richmond, mother of the King, Henry VII. Subsequent writers including Lambard

14.   Lecture IV.

and Crompton make no mention whatever of the possibility of women becoming justices.

So far no convincing evidence has been found of any woman having been appointed as a Justice of the Peace before 1919,[15] though it is quite possible that some did act in that capacity without being strictly entitled to do so in law. Queen Eleanor, the wife of Henry III was appointed Keeper of the Great Seal, apparently because the King felt that she was the most suitable person to be trusted with the Seal during his absence in France, but as far as is known she was not named in any commission for keeping the peace. There are several instances after 1361 of women being alleged to have held the office of justice, but none of these provide conclusive evidence. The Countess of Richmond mentioned above, was said to have sat judicially as a Justice of the Peace, and the King's Attorney claimed that he had seen many "arbitraments" made by her but he had been unable to find her commission though he had searched the records.[16] A possible explanation which has been suggested for this is that her husband the Earl was on the commissions of all the northern counties in connexion with the Council of the North and her commission may have been identical with his and was not enrolled.[17] Of all the cases that have been revealed so far, that of the Countess of Richmond is the most likely instance of a woman having acted as a Justice of the Peace before 1919, though there may have been others. Lady Bartlet of Gloucestershire was said to have sat regularly as a justice on the county bench in the sixteenth century. It was alleged that she had been appointed to the commission by Queen Mary after complaining to the Queen that she had suffered grave injustice at the hands of some persons in Gloucestershire and wanted to be in a position to secure redress. The Queen was said to have granted the request and made Lady Bartlet a justice.[18] Another example which is sometimes quoted is that of a woman in Suffolk named Rowse. There is no doubt that someone of that name served on the commission but it is not completely clear that the individual in question was a woman.

The possibility that one or two women held office as Justices of the Peace during the first three or four centuries after the office was established cannot therefore be ruled out, but their disqualification seems to have become well established as a principle by the seventeenth century. From then onwards women were not considered

---

15. Such evidence might be obtained from a thorough examination of all relevant documents, especially the Patent Rolls. The author's attempts to carry out such a work have necessarily been limited; and in some instances it has been impossible to reach a firm conclusion because there are certain names appearing in the lists which could refer to either a man or a woman.
16. Harlian MS., 980, f. 81.
17. R.R. Reid, *The King's Council in the North,* p. 88.
18. Harlean MS., *ibid.*

to be eligible for most public appointments, and this view was upheld by the courts. For instance, a decision by the Dorset justices that they could not appoint a woman as overseer of the poor at Chardstock was upheld by the courts on *mandamus*. Curiously it was not until 1907, shortly before the principle was abolished, that it finally received statutory recognition. The Qualification of Women (County and Borough Councils) Act 1907, which enabled women to serve on county and borough councils expressly provided (s. 1) that if they became chairman of a council or mayor of a borough they might not also become a JP, notwithstanding the fact that a man who held one of these posts became a justice *ex officio* during his term of office (and for one year afterwards in the case of a mayor). This attitude was bound to succumb to the campaign for the emancipation of women which dominated the early twentieth century and led to their gaining the Parliamentary franchise. The Justices of the Peace (Qualification of Women) Bill which was introduced in 1919 became on December 23 of that year the Sex Disqualification (Removal) Act. It enabled women to be appointed to the Commissions of the Peace and to various other public offices. It also repealed s. 1 of the Qualification of Women Act 1907, so as to enable women mayors and chairmen of councils to become justices *ex officio*, with the result that any woman holding one of these offices on December 23, 1919 immediately became a justice. There was only one such person, Mrs Ada Summers the mayor of Stalybridge in Cheshire, who is therefore the first woman who is known for certain to have become a justice, for there had been no time by then for the Lord Chancellor to select and appoint any women to the commissions. Mrs Summers sat on a number of occasions and exercised her right to preside when present.

The Lord Chancellor, Lord Birkenhead, was not slow in creating women justices in all parts of the country, and immediately after the Act was passed he set up a committee whose remit was to recommend suitable women candidates for appointment to the benches throughout England and Wales. The chairman was the Marchioness of Crewe and the other members were Beatrice Webb (co-author with her husband Sydney of the many great works which have been cited earlier), Margaret Lloyd George (wife of the Prime Minister), the Marchioness of Londonderry, Gertrude Tuckwell, and Mary Ward. As soon as they were appointed Lord Birkenhead also appointed those of them who were willing to serve to be justices in their respective counties.

Lady Crewe's committee worked quickly and by July had compiled a list of 212 women drawn from every county in England, Scotland and Wales which they submitted to the Lord Chancellor. Lord Birkenhead accepted all the recommendations and they were appointed under a fiat dated July 14, save for twelve who declined appointment.

Appointments were made to both county and borough commissions. Details are given in Appendix V. When submitting names the committee said that they had tried to make it representative of various public activities and different types of experience throughout the country, including some women who had achieved general distinction in medicine, education and letters. The committee also explained that they had recommended a greater number of candidates for appointment in certain areas to meet the wishes of the Home Secretary who wanted to be able to appoint women to the visiting committees of the prisons at Holloway, Durham, Leeds and Birmingham. As regards Scotland, the committee said that they had put forward more names for appointment in Lanarkshire, Stirling and Fife in view of the fact that there was more scope for the administration of justice by women in these counties.

In Lancashire appointments were made by the Chancellor of the Duchy and women appeared on the bench earlier than in the rest of the country as it took less time to compile the lists. The Chancellor signed the first fiat on March 11. The names, which are far more numerous than for any other county are also given in Appendix V.

Although women became eligible under the 1919 Act to serve as stipendiary magistrates and Judges of the higher courts it would be many years before any woman attained a judicial office other than that of a Justice of the Peace. The principal reason for this was that neither women nor men could serve in any professional judicial capacity unless they were practising members of the Bar.[19] The first call to the Bar of a woman was by the Inner Temple in 1922, and the number of women barristers remained fairly small for some time. In the 1920s and 1930s there were no women barristers who were considered to be of sufficient standing to be acceptable for judicial office. The first woman to be given any professional judicial appointment was Miss Sybil Campbell, as we saw in ch. IV, who became a metropolitan stipendiary magistrate in 1945. She was also one of the first women barristers, having been called in 1922. No other women were appointed stipendiaries nor given any other judicial appointment for a further 20 years when Miss Jean Graham Hall (a barrister and a former probation officer) was appointed to the metropolitan bench in 1965. Miss Hall became a Deputy Chairman of Inner London Quarter Sessions in 1971, and in 1972 she was among the first people to become a Circuit Judge. The first woman recorder was appointed in 1956 and the first woman County Court Judge in 1962, and she (Dame Elizabeth Lane) was also the first to become a High Court Judge, in 1965. As late as 1983 only four women held office as stipendiary

19. As mentioned in ch. IV, solicitors became eligible for appointment as stipendiary magistrates under the Justices of the Peace Act 1949.

magistrates (out of a total of 46 in London and 12 in the rest of the country), 22 were recorders (out of a total of 453), 10 were Circuit Judges (out of 342) and three were High Court Judges (out of 77). The picture presented by the lay justices was very different. In January of the year 1983, to which the above figures refer, there were as many as 10,328 women Justices of the Peace out of a total of 25,934 justices in England and Wales, including the Duchy of Lancaster. This reflected the policy adopted by successive Lord Chancellors from 1920 of increasing the proportion of women on the benches with a view especially to ensuring that there were sufficient women magistrates to staff all the juvenile and domestic courts. This had not been as successful as was hoped, and by 1947 there were still only 3,700 women in a total of 16,800 justices, and in that year the pressure on advisory committees to increase the proportion of women was intensified. It was not until 1954, however, as explained later, that there were deemed to be sufficient women magistrates to justify an amendment to the Juvenile Courts Constitution Rules so as to make it obligatory for every juvenile court to comprise at least one woman. In 1983 it looked as if it would not be long before the number of women justices equalled that of the men, but this prospect failed to materialize as will be shown in the next chapter.[20]

Invidious comparisons have been made when comparing women and men in the manner in which they performed their magisterial duties. No attempt will be made here to enter the arena beyond mentioning two characteristics which were frequently the subject of comment in reports to the Lord Chancellor from his advisory committees. First, it became clear from figures of attendances that women were on the whole better attenders than men and more assiduous in the performance of their duties. This may have been due at least partly to the fact that men were more heavily engaged in other work and found it more difficult than did the women to give time to court duties. This interpretation is supported by the fact that, as we shall see, the attendances of women magistrates approximated more closely to those of the men in the second half of the twentieth century when more women had jobs of their own. The second point noted by the committees was that women found it more difficult than their male colleagues to differentiate between judicial and welfare functions and therefore tended to become more emotionally involved in cases coming before the bench.

The Magistrates' Association

The need to meet the challenge of the magistrates' new judicial role

20.   The number on the commissions in this period is shown in Appendix II.

and to adapt to the changing social climate led a number of forward thinking justices to form associations in several parts of the country, and in October 1920 a meeting of some 200 justices in the Guildhall of the City of London resolved to found a national Association which was to become the Magistrates' Association of England and Wales. This was formally established on October 21, 1921 and the inaugural meeting was held in the Central Hall, Westminster on October 28 of that year, when the Lord Chancellor, Lord Haldane, was elected the first President. From then onwards each Lord Chancellor has become President (until 1962 by election and thereafter *ex officio* under the Association's charter). In 1923 the Scottish justices founded the Scottish Justices' and Magistrates' Association under the Presidency of Lord Ashmore, a Senator of the College of Justice.

The principal object of the Association at that time was the education of its members in their magisterial duties or, as Lord Haldane said at the inaugural meeting, "the primary purpose of the Association is to collect and bring together that common body of knowledge and to diffuse it amongst the magistrates everywhere." The Association was governed by a council composed of members elected by branches throughout the country. The council's first meeting at which 29 members were present was held in the Home Office on November 25, 1921 and it elected an executive committee which since then has been responsible for running the Association. The first chairman of the council and of the executive committee was Sir Collingwood Hope CBE, KC, chairman of Essex Quarter Sessions. In the course of time other committees were formed to deal with various subjects.[21]

The Association's journal, *The Magistrate*, was first published in May 1922, and its first editor was J. St. Loe Strachey the editor of *The Spectator*, who was himself a justice.

In its early years the Association's membership was fairly small and accounted for only a fraction of the total number of justices in the country. It was not regarded very seriously by the Government or by other institutions. It was a club for those justices who regarded themselves as the élite of the magistracy, most of whom were drawn from the upper levels of society in the counties and cities. They were, however, genuinely interested in their work and they included some remarkably able people who ensured that the Association did not stagnate. The chairmen of the council were all eminent members of the legal profession and there were some outstanding members who would not accept the complacency which characterized the majority of their fellow magistrates. The most notable of these was Margery Fry,

---

21. In 1989, in addition to the executive committee there was a legal committee and six others: domestic courts, juvenile courts, overseas, road traffic, sentencing of offenders and training.

who was one of the first women to be appointed a justice in 1921 and was one of the new breed of magistrates far removed from the Tory landed gentry. She was organizer of the Howard League for Penal Reform and was the first education adviser to Holloway prison in 1922. Among her later posts was that of Principal of Somerville College, Oxford and Governor of the British Broadcasting Corporation.[22] Margery Fry was a driving force in the Association and was a member of its council and of several of its committees until 1944, taking a special interest in sentencing of offenders, juvenile courts and relations with overseas countries. The first office of the Association was in her own house. In the 1930s the Association began to widen the scope of its activities, but it was still regarded as being of no great significance and its views had little impact on the country as a whole until after the war when, as we shall see, it entered an entirely new phase.

The Clerk of the Peace

We have seen that under the 1888 Act the duties of the Clerk of the Peace as such were confined to his service as clerk to Quarter Sessions, but the Act provided expressly that the Clerk of the Peace should also act as clerk to the council. Consequently the same individual held both posts and continued to be responsible for the former administrative functions of Quarter Sessions which had now been transferred to the councils. The clerk's salary for both branches of his work was paid by the council. The power to appoint the clerk was transferred from the *Custos* to a Standing Joint Committee of Quarter Sessions and the council.

The clerk's tenure of office remained the same as it had been since the reign of Elizabeth, and many clerks served for life. Even in the twentieth century there were some who held this important office for very long periods. H.P. Markham who had been appointed Clerk of the Peace of Northamptonshire in 1846 served for 58 years until 1904. Sir Thomas Franklen of Glamorgan held office for 50 years from 1878 to 1928.[23] As we have seen, the Great Seal Act 1689 (1 William & Mary, c. 21) provided that a Clerk of the Peace might hold office for so long as he should well demean himself, and this was confirmed by the Court of Appeal and the House of Lords in the case of *Thorneley* v. *Leconfield* in 1924. Thorneley, the Clerk of the Peace of West Sussex, brought an action against Lord Leconfield, the Lord Lieutenant and

22. Margery Fry was a member of the Labour party from 1918 until 1939 and was deeply involved in the campaign for the abolition of capital punishment. She was author of several important books relating to the courts: *A Notebook for the Children's Court* (1942), *The Future Treatment of the Adult Offender* (1944) and *Arms and The Law* (1951).
23. W.J. Freer of Leicestershire and Sir Hubert Thornley of the North Riding both served for forty-four years, the former from 1888 to 1932 and the latter from 1916 until 1960.

Custos of the county in his capacity as chairman of the Standing Joint Committee. The Court of Appeal reversed the decision of the trial Judge and gave Thorneley a declaration that the tenure of office of both Clerk of the Peace and of the council was as stated in the 1689 Act, and this was affirmed by the Lords. Shortly afterwards a Royal Commission on Local Government was appointed to consider among other matters the position of the clerks. Their recommendations on this issue were implemented in the Local Government (Clerks) Act 1931, which provided that all clerks of County Councils appointed thereafter should hold office during good behaviour and should retire on reaching the age of 65, and that the same should apply to Clerks of the Peace if they also held office as clerk to the council. If, however, a Clerk of the Peace was not also clerk of the council he was not affected by the age limit and might continue in office until he became incapable through permanent ill-health or had been guilty of misconduct. This somewhat confusing Act also provided that in future Quarter Sessions should appoint their Clerk of the Peace and the County Council their clerk. The procedure to be followed when a vacancy occurred was that the County Council, before filling a vacancy, should inquire of anyone whom it wished to appoint whether he was willing to serve also as Clerk of the Peace and to notify Quarter Sessions accordingly. Quarter Sessions might then accept the new clerk to the council as Clerk of the Peace or within a specified period might appoint someone else.[24] The Act of 1931 was partly replaced by the Local Government Act 1933. This enabled Quarter Sessions to appoint virtually anyone they pleased as Clerk of the Peace. In fact the same individual continued to hold the two offices in most counties until Clerks of the Peace were abolished at the end of 1971.[25] There was still no statutory qualification for appointment, but in practice every clerk was a member of the legal profession. In contrast to the Justices of the Peace themselves and to clerks in petty sessional divisions the office of Clerk of the Peace remained an exclusively male preserve and there were no women clerks to the end of their history. The salary of the Clerk of the Peace was fixed by Quarter Sessions under the 1888 Act, subject to an appeal to the Home Secretary either by the council or by the clerk himself. As already mentioned, the salary was paid by the council. All fees payable

24. On these occasions Quarter Sessions were obliged to make the appointment through a committee composed of their chairman and of those justices who had been appointed by the sessions to be members of the Standing Joint Committee (ss. 2 & 12).
25. Under the 1933 Act, whenever a vacancy occurred in the office of clerk to a council the latter were still obliged to inquire of the candidate whether he would also be willing to serve a Clerk of the Peace, and they then had to consult with the chairman of Quarter Sessions, but it was open to the sessions to appoint whomever they chose. When the office of Clerk of the Peace became vacant, the County Council had to inform Quarter Sessions whether the Clerk of the Council was willing to serve also as Clerk of the Peace. If so, he was deemed to have been appointed unless within six months of the vacancy occurring, or such further term as the Home Secretary might allow, Quarter Sessions appointed someone else.

to the clerk had to be paid to the county fund.

In 1888 the Clerk of the Peace was still a part-time officer but within the next half century the pressure of work made it necessary to convert the post into a full-time appointment. Some of the tasks assumed by the clerks were not necessarily tied to the work of Quarter Sessions nor to that of the licensing committee, but in every case they were regarded as being of importance in county affairs and were arrogated by the clerks as being in keeping with his county status. Principal among them were the offices of clerk to the Lieutenancy, under sheriff, secretary of the county advisory committee on Justices of the Peace and, after 1949, clerk to the magistrates' courts committee. It was not possible, of course, for the clerks to attend to all these matters personally and many of the duties were performed by deputies. The Clerks of the Peace had long exercised an enormous amount of influence in their counties. In the twentieth century their impact on county affairs was greater than ever.

The history of the Clerks of the Peace was to continue for only some 25 years beyond the end of the second World War. The time would then come when the part-time courts of Quarter Sessions had to be replaced by a full-time modernized courts' system and, as we shall see in ch. VIII, with the demise of Quarter Sessions the office of Clerk of the Peace vanished also.

The Clerk to the Justices

The great expansion in the justices' work at Petty Sessions would have been impossible had the magistrates not had the advice and assistance of their justices' clerks who were the linchpin of the system whereby justice was administered by part-time laymen. In consequence of the developments which took place from the late nineteenth century onwards changes also had to be made in the office of justices' clerk itself. Like the position of the Justices of the Peace that of the clerk had been the outcome of historical developments which depended in their earlier stages more upon accident than design, but from the end of the nineteenth century further advances were made on a systematic basis.

Until the middle of the twentieth century the principal Act relating to the office of the clerks remained that of 1877, though additional duties were placed upon them by later statutes. In addition to being clerks of Petty Sessions and special sessions, which involved attending the courts and often questioning parties and witnesses, the clerk had long been responsible for a number of out of court duties, and during the early part of the century he became clerk or secretary to a number of new bodies through which the justices operated. In particular, he became secretary to the probation committee for his division, which was established under the Probation of Offenders Act of 1907, and clerk to the confirming authority which was introduced by the Licensing Act of 1910. The office work, involving the keeping of records, registers and accounts, the enforcement of orders, the organizing of meetings and arrangement of business and much correspondence, increased with the growth of the justices' duties and involved considerable managerial skills.

All acts done and decisions taken by the justices continued to be at their discretion and they were not obliged in law to follow the advice of their clerk. This applied both to proceedings in court and to acts done out of court. A justice could therefore receive an information or issue a summons in the absence of his clerk. The clerk remained, however, adviser to his justices on points of law and procedure, and although they might disregard his advice they did so at their peril.

The appointment of justices' clerks rested, as it had always done, with the justices in their respective divisions who could also dismiss them,[26] but under the Criminal Justice Act 1914, the Home Secretary's confirmation was required before an appointment could become effective. From the late nineteenth century a clerk had to have certain statutory qualifications. On appointment he had to be either

(a) a barrister of not less than 14 years standing; or
(b) a solicitor; or
(c) he must have served for not less then seven years as clerk to a police stipendiary magistrate or to a metropolitan police court or to one of the police courts of the City of London; or
(d) (where the justices thought such an appointment desirable) he must have served for not less than 14 years as assistant to a clerk of a Petty Sessional division or a clerk to the justices of a borough.[27]

It was a long time before the importance of the key position occupied by the clerks and of the duties they performed was appreciated. It may be for this reason that there was no comprehensive inquiry into the work and conditions of service of clerks until 1938 when the Home Secretary appointed a Departmental Committee on Justices' Clerks under the chairmanship of Lord Roche, a Lord of Appeal, "to inquire into the conditions of service of clerks to justices and their assistants, including qualifications, appointment, remuneration and duties." The committee's report,[28] presented to

26. This was confirmed in the case of counties by the Justices' Clerks Act 1877 (s. 5) and in boroughs by the Municipal Corporations Act 1882 (s. 59(1)).
27. Justices' Clerks Act 1877, s. 5; Municipal Corporations Act 1882, (s. 59(1)).
28. Cmd. 6507.

Parliament in March 1944, contained a comprehensive account of the clerk's functions followed by a considerable number of recommendations for the improvement of the existing system. As the publication of the report took place when the country was engaged in fighting the war its implementation was postponed for five years when, as we shall see, its recommendations were combined with those of the subsequent Royal Commission on Justices of the Peace in the Justices of the Peace Act 1949.

The committee were opposed to the existing preponderance of part-time clerks. They accepted that the part-time system had been sufficient in the past when the work of the courts had been far lighter, and they recognized that part-time clerks who were solicitors in good general practice were "amongst the most highly qualified and wisest advisers for a lay bench", but they had no doubt that where the work was sufficient to justify the appointment of a full-time clerk such an appointment should be made if a suitable candidate could be found. A change of this kind was opposed by many who gave evidence before the committee on the ground that an extension of the whole-time system could only take place if the clerk served a wider area, and this would militate against the accessibility of the clerk to magistrates, police and members of the public, which was an essential element of the system. The committee, basing its findings partly on the example of the County Courts where there had been a considerable extension of the appointment of whole-time registrars, concluded that the weight of evidence indicated that the time was right for an extension of the whole-time system to more courts, but that it was not possible at once to make such a system universal. They also concluded that a considerable extension of the whole-time system might be accomplished by grouping divisions and that the smaller boroughs might be brought into such grouping schemes. In this context they also recommended that the existing divisions should be reviewed and, with a view to reducing the number of small divisions, that all Commissions of the Peace for boroughs with populations of less than 25,000 should be abolished unless there were special circumstances which made this undesirable. As regards the larger boroughs which retained their separate commissions, it was recommended that those with populations of over 75,000 should not be liable to be grouped into combined areas, while those with smaller populations should be within the schemes for combined areas.

As to the qualifications of clerks, the committee recommended that every clerk should be legally qualified and that persons without legal qualification should no longer be eligible for appointment by virtue of their service as assistants to clerks. Part-time clerks who were solicitors in private practice should be restricted as to the classes of work they might undertake and the public appointments they might hold. No clerk should be appointed below the age of 30 nor over the age of 50, and the retiring age for all clerks should be 72.

The committee interpreted its terms of reference as being wide enough to enable them to make recommendations improving the magistrates' courts system in general. One of their most important proposals was for the establishment of what were to be called magistrates' courts committees to administer the courts. This included the appointment and pay of lcerks and court staff and the grouping of divisions. In the case of each administrative county the committee was to be composed of county justices together with justices from each borough within the county having a separate commission and a population of under 75,000. In boroughs of over 75,000 population the justices should have the powers of a Magistrates' Courts Committee.

After the 1888 Act county funds as well as those for the boroughs continued to be responsible for meeting the costs of the magistrates' courts. The expenses arose largely from the upkeep of court buildings and the salaries of staff. Fines and fees were paid into these local funds unless a statute directed otherwise.[29] In the past the fines and fees had exceeded the cost, but by the time the Roche Committee was appointed the position had been reversed as a result of the increasing cost and the diversion of all road traffic fines to the Exchequer. Consequently local authorities were obliged to make good the loss out of the rates. The committee therefore recommended that all fines and fees should be paid to the Exchequer which should pay to the authorities the amount it had received in fines and fees and that any additional sum required to meet the cost should be shared between the Exchequer and the authority.

Another important recommendation of the committee was that a rule committee should be established to advise the Lord Chancellor on the making of rules of procedure in courts of summary jurisdiction. They also proposed that the courts themselves should be known as "magistrates' courts" instead of "police courts," so as to make it clear that the police did not enjoy any special privilege in these courts. These and the committee's other recommendations were implemented 15 years later in the Justices of the Peace Act 1949.

Unlike the Clerks of the Peace, the Clerks to the Justices came to be infiltrated by a female element. Women began to be employed in the clerks' offices in the first half of the century, and the first to be appointed to the post of justices' clerk itself was Miss L.M. Hollowell of Stowmarket in 1944, though she held office only on a part-time

---

29. Fines for customs and excise offences were paid to HM Customs and Excise, and after 1920 fines for road traffic offences, which soon amounted to far more than any others, were paid to the Exchequer.

basis. The first whole-time lady clerk was Miss Joan Adair of Kingston-upon-Thames who was appointed in 1947. From then onwards the numbers increased but lady clerks were always far outnumbered by the men. In January 1989 15 women were clerks (all full-time) in a total of 285 clerkships.

A major criticism which has often been levelled against the justices' clerks is that they dominate the court. This is obviously undesirable and it undermines the confidence of the public in their magistrates. The fault was very real at the end of the nineteenth century and in the first part of the twentieth, and there were some notorious examples in the 1940s when this defect in the system was condemned by the Roche committee in their report (para. 64). It was to become far less prevalent in the second half of the century in consequence of changes in the personnel of the justices and of the clerks themselves. As a result of more effective selection of candidates for the bench and of steps to ensure that those appointed performed their functions competently, coupled with the introduction of training and of an age limit, all justices became far more capable of conducting their affairs and were not obliged to leave matters to their clerk to the same extent as before. This change coincided with the appointment of a new type of whole-time clerk in most divisions who was more dedicated to his work and far less prone to dominate the proceedings than the solicitors in private practice who formed the bulk of the earlier clerks.

Extension and diversification of jurisdiction

Although in 1888 the justices lost most of their administrative functions the volume of the work which they had to do increased steadily in consequence, as already mentioned, of a formidable extension of their judicial duties. Many offences which were previously triable only at Assizes were brought within the scope of Quarter Sessions while large numbers of cases which had been triable only before a jury became triable summarily at Petty Sessions.

While this process was taking place the justices continued to be engrossed in much work of the kind that had occupied their time in the past. This included one of their earliest tasks, namely that of taking surety to be of good behaviour. The extent of the power conferred on justices for this purpose in 1361 was challenged in the courts in 1913 in the case of *Lansbury* v. *Riley.* Mr. George Lansbury the Labour politician was charged with inciting the suffragettes who were campaigning for women's rights to commit breaches of the peace. A stipendiary magistrate ordered Lansbury to enter into recognizances in the sum of £1,000 and also to find two sureties for good behaviour in the sum of £500 each. In default he was to serve three months imprisonment. Lansbury appealed by way of case stated (a procedure explained later) to the Divisional Court who were required to interpret the statute of 1361. It was argued on Lansbury's behalf that the 1361 Act, which refered to "pillors and robbers", was intended to apply only to habitual criminals like the Plantagenet soldiers who returned from France and roamed the country committing offences. It did not therefore apply to law-abiding citizens like Lansbury. The appeal was dismissed, and it was established that it was open to magistrates to order accused persons to enter into recognizances for good behaviour whether or not they were, in the words of the statute, "of good fame." The court also ruled that an order might be made even in the absence of evidence that the defendant had caused anyone to go in bodily fear.

As the century progressed there was also a vast change in the types of cases that were brought before the magistrates. In 1900 the great majority of these were still minor breaches of the peace, petty thefts (especially pickpocketing) and drunkenness, with a fair number of poachers in the rural areas. Virtually none of the offenders came from the upper classes of society. This scene had changed little with the passage of time; certainly not since the days when the justices were also faced with appreciable numbers of religious offences and charges of dereliction of public duties. Revolutionary changes were to take place during the twentieth century as a result of two unprecedented developments: the motor car and sophisticated crime on a vast scale.

Road traffic cases in the magistrates' courts increased from none at the turn of the century to a point where they accounted for well over half the total. The number of persons charged before the magistrates with motoring offences reached a million in 1977. This accounted for 59 per cent of all cases that they had to try and about 75 per cent of non-indictable offences. This was accompanied by a change in the type of person who appeared in the dock. The majority of those charged with motoring offences were respectable, law-abiding citizens who resented being classed as criminals. This resentment on the part of a large and articulate part of the population caused the justices' courts to lose much of the public respect which they had previously enjoyed among most classes. The time spent by the courts in dealing with these offenders was also abnormally great because the culprits tended to ignore summonses more often than in any other type of case. The traffic laws, especially the Road Traffic Act 1930, also added to the volume and complexity of the cases coming before the courts by creating a variety of new offences of differing degrees of seriousness, from illegal parking and obstruction, through exceeding the speed limit, driving without due care or when under the influence of alcohol, to driving dangerously and manslaughter. The 1930 Act also stated (s. 113(1)), "Save as otherwise expressly provided, all offences under this Act shall be prosecuted under the Summary Jurisdiction Acts."

When it came to sentencing, traffic offences presented an extra dimension in that they might involve disqualification in addition to the more orthodox penalties. We shall see later that in the latter part of the century various devices were introduced with a view to relieving the pressure on the courts, yet the total amount of time spent on dealing with this side of the justices' work continues to increase.

Although a more reputable defendant appeared in response to motoring summonses the courts were also faced from the earlier part of the twentieth century onwards with the opposite extreme - an increasing number of skilled criminals who readily engaged in violence and were often organized in gangs. Many were involved in new phenomena such as traffic in drugs or complicated frauds involving lengthy trials. Among other new problems was the fact that, although picking pockets declined, it was replaced by an increase in shoplifting which posed peculiar psychological questions and, with the courts' more liberal approach to delinquency, involved them in distinguishing between greed, exhibitionism, mental depression and inadvertance.

Quarter Sessions

In the latter half of the century it became necessary, as explained later, to replace the existing judicial system of the higher courts with a new form of whole-time tribunal, but before then some steps were taken to increase the contribution of Quarter Sessions to the disposal of business. We have seen that in the first part of the nineteenth century there was a convention whereby Quarter Sessions did not deal with any cases which carried the death penalty. This meant that at that time a very wide range of cases were tried only at Assizes. During the century, however, the number of capital offences was reduced substantially and at the same time a list was drawn up of indictable offences which could be tried at either Assizes or Quarter Sessions. The list was extended as pressure on Assizes increased and finally in 1938 Parliament passed the Administration of Justice (Miscellaneous Provisions) Act which was designed to relieve Assizes by increasing the jurisdiction of Quarter Sessions when they were constituted in a special manner by having a legally qualified chairman or deputy chairman who complied with the requirements of the Act. Until then every chairman or deputy chairman had been elected by the sessions (though Lancashire, Middlesex and Hertfordshire had obtained special powers in local Acts to appoint salaried chairmen and deputy chairmen[30]). Under the 1938 Act any county Quarter Sessions might apply to the Lord Chancellor for the appointment as chairman or

---

30.   The 1938 Act superseded the provisions of the local Acts relating to Hertfordshire and Middlesex but the Lancashire Acts remained unaffected.

deputy chairman of a person who was a barrister or solicitor of not less than ten years standing "having such legal experience as to qualify him in the opinion of the Lord Chancellor to act as chairman or deputy chairman." The appointment might then be made by the King on the Lord Chancellor's recommendation.[31] Quarter Sessions were then empowered when presided over by a person appointed in this way, or by certain other members of the judiciary[32] to try a number of offences which were not otherwise within their jurisdiction. These additional offences were set out in the First Schedule to the Act and included several relating to malicious damage, forgery and offences against the person.

In the case of boroughs which had separate courts of Quarter Sessions the 1938 Act empowered the recorder to exercise the same extended jurisdiction as a chairman appointed under the Act provided that the borough had a population of not less than 50,000.

The initiative lay with the justices in each county to obtain the appointment of a chairman who was qualified under the Act to exercise extended jurisdiction, but the Lord Chancellor and his staff encouraged all counties to take this step in order to reduce the burden on Assizes. Most complied, but by 1947 there were still three counties[33] with neither a qualified chairman nor a deputy chairman. By 1951 all had qualified chairmen and only seven were without a qualified deputy. In every case except London and Lancashire they were appointed for a period of three years under a Royal warrant which stipulated that the Lord Chancellor might terminate the appointment prematurely if he thought this desirable for any reason. These appointments therefore constituted a complete negation of the principle of judicial independence. Chairmen virtually held office at the pleasure of the Lord Chancellor. He could terminate an appointment at his discretion and he could decline to renew it without

31. Before submitting a recommendation the Lord Chancellor was required to consider any representations made to him by Quarter Sessions and also take account of the desirability of having a chairman or deputy chairman who was resident in the county or otherwise connected with it and in the case of Monmouth and the Welsh counties that he should be able to speak the Welsh language.

32. These were the holders, past or present, of the following offices: members of the Judicial Committee of the Privy Council, Judges of the Supreme Court, Official Referees, Railway and Canal Commissioners, the Attorney-General, Solicitor-General and the Director of Public Prosecutions. In each case the individual must have been elected by the court as chairman or deputy chairman. Those appointed under the Act served for such period as was specified in their appointment. They might be paid a salary by the County Council at such rate as was agreed between the council and Quarter Sessions and agreed by the Lord Chancellor. If not already a Justice of the Peace for the county the chairman of deputy became a justice *virtute officii* but he might not act as chairman or as a justice in the county until he had taken the oaths required of a JP. In 1947 the salaries paid in the 10 counties which had chairmen at that time ranged for £2,500 for the whole-time chairman of London sessions to £31 for the part-time chairman of Shropshire sessions who sat on only six days a year. At that time the salary of a High Court judge was £5,000 and that of a Permanent Secretary in the Civil Service £3,500.

33. Brecon, Denbigh and Huntingdon.

showing cause. The reason behind the assumption of these omnipotent powers was that they were desirable as being a subtle way of eliminating dead wood, which had been found on occasions to be an impediment to the efficient administration of justice. In fact, the Lord Chancellor seldom found it necessary to make use of these powers. Between 1938 and the end of Quarter Sessions in 1971 no chairman and only one deputy chairman was removed before his time had expired and about six were not reappointed because of some inadequacy which in several cases amounted to an inability to maintain a good relationship with their justices.

Many counties took the opportunity to comply with the Act by electing as their chairman someone who held or had held high judicial office, and the status of Quarter Sessions was enhanced by the large numbers of Judges, many of them among the most senior in the land, who held office as chairman or deputy chairman. They included several Lords of Appeal and one former Lord Chancellor.[34]

Another step that was taken in the 1938 Act to reduce the load on Assizes was the repeal (in s. 6) of part of the Assizes Relief Act 1889, which empowered justices to direct that a person charged with an indictable offence triable at Quarter Sessions should be tried at Assizes. Under the 1938 Act they could no longer do this unless satisfied that the case was an unusually grave or difficult one or that serious delay or inconvenience would be occasioned by committal to Quarter Sessions.

At the end of World War II the work of Quarter Sessions consisted mainly of trying indictable offences, hearing appeals against conviction or sentence by magistrates in Petty Sessions and hearing rating and licensing appeals. Their work was increasing, partly in consequence of the Act of 1938 which was successful for a time in relieving pressure on Assizes, but Quarter Sessions remained essentially a part-time body which was totally unfitted to cope with the great surge of work which occurred after the war. As we shall see in ch. VIII, after some tentative steps to establish a few full-time courts it was found necessary to replace all Quarter Sessions with the new whole-time Crown Court.[35]

---

34.   Lord Dilhorne was deputy chairman of Quarter Sessions in Northamptonshire after he left the Woolsack.
35.   In 1945 there were 62 county Quarter Sessions (49 in England and 13 in Wales) most of which still sat only four times a year, and 38 of them did not average more than three days at a time. In 1947, 22 sat for 10 days or less and the total number of sitting days for all Quarter Sessions in England and Wales other than London was 1,134. London, Lancashire and Middlesex had what were termed whole-time courts but they were not in constant session. In 1945 Lancashire sessions sat on only 55 days and Middlesex on 62, while even London sat on only 168 days.

Petty Sessions

As already mentioned, Petty Sessions were finally recognized as courts by the Petty Sessions Act 1849, and the remarkable expansion of the justices' summary jurisdiction had begun with the Summary Jurisdiction Act of the previous year which, subject to subsequent amendments, governed the procedure at Petty Sessions for more than a hundred years. In 1889 Petty Sessions were statutorily defined as "A court of summary jurisdiction consisting of two or more justices sitting in a petty sessional courthouse."

From the beginning of the twentieth century it was clear that any doubts as to the survival of the lay justice system had been dispelled and that the justices were set for a promising future as judicial officers, at least in the sphere of summary jurisdiction. We have seen that a number of Acts had already increased their summary powers. Some had even given them jurisdiction over certain indictable offences; and in the early twentieth century further legislation followed as the justices became recognized as the obvious authority to dispense justice among the people. One of the Acts passed during this period was the Criminal Justice Administration Act 1914, which extended the powers conferred on justices by the Summary Jurisdiction Acts of 1879 and 1890. These were mostly in respect of monetary penalties which might be awarded and of bail and remand. The dramatic extension of the justices' powers of summary jurisdiction really culminated, however, in the Criminal Justice Act 1925, under which a large number of offences which were previously triable only with a judge and jury were brought within the jurisdiction of the justices. The lay Justices of the Peace had been vindicated and their transition from an essentially administrative function to one which was purely judicial was complete. Under the Act the accused had a right to elect trial by jury if he wished, but he could not choose to be tried summarily without the consent of the justices who had a complete discretion. If they decided not to allow summary trial they committed the accused to the higher court if they were satisfied that there was a *prima facie* case to answer. Since the Act was passed the great majority of accused have chosen to be tried summarily, their motives for doing so being partly to have the matter disposed of rapidly but mainly because the justices' powers of punishment (amounting initially to six months' imprisonment or a fine of £100 in most cases) fell well short of what could be imposed on trial by indictment. From 1925 there was an impressive increase in the number of cases tried at Petty Sessions until some 98 per cent of all criminal charges were being disposed of by these courts. The Act achieved its object of lowering the pressure on the higher courts, at least for the time being, and it confirmed the confidence of Parliament and the public in the justices' judicial role.

In addition to the justices' criminal work the twentieth century saw an increase in their civil jurisdiction and even to some extent in their administrative duties. This embraced matrimonial proceedings, guardianship, licensing and the treatment of children and young persons.

Matrimonial and affiliation proceedings

We have seen that a man's responsibility for maintaining his wife and family was a matter which engaged the attention of the justices when administering the Poor Law from Tudor times.[36] During this period, however, they were concerned solely with the problem of relieving the ratepayers of the cost of maintaining paupers, and the law was not interested in the personal plight of the wife. In 1878 the Matrimonial Causes Act gave a wife relief if her husband was found guilty by the magistrates of aggravated assault upon her. This was the beginning of a new era of domestic and matrimonial jurisdiction which came to occupy a considerable amount of the justices' time. In 1895 the Summary Jurisdiction (Married Women) Act empowered magistrates to make a non-cohabitation order and to award maintenance, costs and custody of the children in favour of a wife who could prove desertion, aggravated assault, persistent cruelty or wilful neglect. These provisions, which were the equivalent of judicial separation, were the foundation of the justices' matrimonial jurisdiction.

There were obvious disadvantages in leaving the consideration of intimate matrimonial problems to the magistrates' courts which were still called "police courts" and were concerned principally with the trial of criminal offences. Any chance of eliciting the full facts from the embarrassed parties and of achieving reconciliation in such cases was remote. This was recognized by the Royal Commission on Divorce and Matrimonial Causes of 1912[37] which commented: "The evidence satisfies us that the general administration of the Acts is not satisfactory where these cases are dealt with by the lay magistrates." Nevertheless from the beginning of the twentieth century a number of further Acts extended the justices' powers. In 1902 the Licensing Act enabled them to give redress where the husband was a habitual drunkard, and five further Acts followed during the 1920s and 1930s.[38]

---

36.   As already mentioned, the mother as well as the father of an illegitimate child could be subjected to harsh punishment. In 1844 the mother of such a child was herself able to get an order for maintenance against the putative father.
37.   Cd. 6476.
38.   These were the Married Women (Maintenance) Act 1920, the Maintenance Order (Facilities for Enforcement) Act 1920, the Summary Jurisdiction (Separation and Maintenance) Act 1925, the Summary Procedure (Domestic Proceedings) Act 1937 and the Matrimonial Causes Act 1937, which was replaced by the Matrimonial Causes Act 1950.

These various statutes conferred upon the justices, either in ordinary Petty Sessions or in special domestic proceedings courts, extensive powers which were equal to those of the High Court apart from the ability to grant a divorce and dissolve a marriage.[39] There was also overlapping jurisdiction with the County Courts as well as with the High Court which led to some confusion for there was no coherent principle. Matters arising out of the guardianship of infants for example might come before the High Court, County Court or a magistrates' court. More will be said about this when describing developments in the last half of the twentieth century, but before then the magistrates' family jurisdiction came to include separation, maintenance, affiliation, guardianship and custody of children, and consent to marriage.

A Departmental Committee on Social Services in Courts of Summary Jurisdiction was appointed in 1936 to consider the practical working of the justices' matrimonial jurisdiction, and its recommendations[40] were implemented in the Summary Procedure (Domestic Proceedings) Act 1937. An important innovation was that instead of cross-examination which was the universal method of examining parties and witnesses, the parties were allowed to tell their story in their own words and, after hearing the statements, the court was to put to each witness on behalf of either party any question that they might consider necessary. It had long been urged that the number of justices hearing matrimonial cases should be limited so as to avoid the intimidating atmosphere of a large bench, and from 1937 the court when hearing such cases had to consist of not more than three justices who had to include, where practicable, a man and a woman. For the same reasons the Act decreed that matrimonial hearings should take place separately from other proceedings and that the public should be excluded. Newspaper reports were limited to the names of the parties, the grounds for the application, legal submissions and statements by the court.

Family jurisdiction became among the most important of the justices' functions and it was also among the most time consuming. The volume of work increased formidably in consequence of the vast rise in the number of disputes between husbands and wives which came before the courts. Moreover, an individual case might occupy more time than any other type of business because it could last indefinitely if the order had to be varied from time to time. The amount of money involved could also be considerable, for although the maximum

---

39. Divorce jurisdiction was first given to the higher courts by the Matrimonial Causes Act 1857. County court judges began hearing undefended divorce cases following the recommendations of a committee under the chairmanship of Lord Denning in 1946, but at first they sat as commissioners of the High Court.
40. Cmd. 5122.

maintenance that the magistrates could award until 1949 was £2 a week for a wife and 10 shillings for a child, the total amount payable under an order over the years could far exceed the maximum fines that the justices could impose for most of the criminal cases coming before them.

Before 1949 it was to the magistrates' courts that the less wealthy members of society invariably took their matrimonial problems mainly because they could not afford the cost of the High Court. Proceedings before the magistrates were far cheaper, and were conducted more expeditiously, than before the higher courts, and it was not until 1949 that the Legal Aid and Advice Act provided a scheme of legal aid which enabled parties to pursue cases in the High Court with financial assistance on a graduated scale.

Licensing

The only administrative function remaining to the justices after 1888 was the licensing of the sale of intoxicating liquor. This was, of course, quite distinct from the judicial work of the justices when they dealt with breaches of the criminal law on licensed premises. We have seen that there was considerable fluctuation in the duties placed on the justices by Acts passed in the nineteenth century relating to the sale of beer, spirits and wine, some of which extended their powers while others removed their control of some branches of the trade almost entirely. The Alehouse Act 1823, remained in force until 1910 when the Licensing (Consolidation) Act repealed thirteen earlier Acts in whole or in part and consolidated the justices' licensing powers. Although there were further Acts passed in the second half of the century, the work of the justices in licensing matters from 1910 was basically the same as it is today. It was work which was of considerable importance to the community, its object being the protection of the public.

Throughout most of the present century the magistrates have had power to grant licences for the sale of liquor consumed on the premises and also, quite separately, for consumption elsewhere. They could grant or refuse new licences and agree to the renewal or transfer of existing ones. They could also authorize or require structural alterations to licensed premises and authorize removals.

Procedure was much the same as it had been in the previous century. The general annual licensing meeting, or Brewster Sessions, was held in the first fortnight in February and dealt with grants of licences. The adjourned meeting was held after Brewster Sessions to consider any outstanding business. Transfer sessions were held between four and eight times a year at which an existing licence might be transferred from one holder to another. Occasional licences might be granted at any time to authorize holders of existing licences to sell alcoholic drinks elsewhere than on licensed premises on special occasions, such as sporting and social events.

The 1910 Act set out the grounds on which the justices might refuse to renew licences which amounted to either the unsuitable character of the applicant or the fact that the premises were disorderly or were frequented by persons of bad character. The justices were required to give their reasons in writing for refusing to renew an "on licence."

The justices who were authorized to perform licensing duties varied according to the kind of area in which they served. In counties all justices in each Petty Sessional division could act. In county boroughs the powers were restricted to a licensing committee composed of not less than seven justices. In other boroughs which had ten or more justices there was a licensing committee of three members who dealt with new licences and ordinary renewals, while for other purposes all the borough justices could act. In boroughs with less than ten justices all the justices were empowered to perform all the duties. Justices who had any beneficial interest in the liquor trade or in the premises concerned could not act as licensing justices, and if they did so they were liable to a penalty not exceeding £100 for each offence.[41]

There was also a confirming authority and a compensation authority. The former whose duty it was to confirm or refuse new licences granted by the licensing justices was composed of all justices sitting at Quarter Sessions in the case of counties and all the borough justices in boroughs, except where the borough had less than 10 justices in which case the confirming authority was composed of a joint committee of three boroughs and three county justices. The compensation authority compensated licence holders and owners of licensed premises for licences extinguished on the ground of redundancy.

Anyone aggrieved by a refusal of licensing justices to renew or to agree to the transfer of a licence might appeal to the county Quarter Sessions, even where the premises were situated within a borough having separate Quarter Sessions. The appeal was heard as a rehearing and the decision was final.

There can be little doubt that a large proportion of the justices, including many who attended licensing meetings, did not fully appreciate the basic difference between their licensing functions and those they performed in their criminal courts. Lord Halsbury, when Lord Chancellor at the beginning of the century, pointed out that

41. The 1910 Act which imposed this penalty disqualified anyone who was in partnership with, or held any share in any company which was a common brewer, distiller or maker or retailer of intoxicating liquor in the district or neighbouring districts.

justices at licensing meetings were not a court and did not occupy the position of Judges. They were merely exercising a discretionary jurisdiction as to how many public houses they should permit in a district and which persons should be allowed to conduct them. It followed from this that it was open to the licensing justices to base their decisions on their own personal knowledge rather than upon that of witnesses to a greater extent than when they sat as Judges in their courts. Moreover, a licensing justice needed to be well acquainted with his own district and to have a personal knowledge of its requirements. In practice, the justices seem generally to have acted on this principle, but on the other hand they tended to attach considerable weight to the maintenance of law and order which was rightly part of the content of their criminal judicial function but not that of the grant of licences.

A notable defect in the system as it operated throughout the first half of the century was that there was no limit on the number of justices who could appear at the meetings to grant new licences, and a vast throng of magistrates often appeared on the bench, many of whom were not well qualified to deal with the work. We shall see later that steps were taken to improve the situation soon after the second World War.

Juvenile courts

Probably the most outstanding development of all in the history of the justices' during the twentieth century was the establishment and development of special courts to deal with the problems of children and young persons. As we have seen, this trend began in the nineteenth century as part of a powerful movement for penal reform in general. It culminated in the creation of special bodies of justices who were responsible for matters of general welfare of children in addition to and quite distinct from the process of dealing with those who committed offences.

In the last chapter we saw that until 1847 children charged with indictable offences were tried at Assizes and Quarter Sessions in the same way as adults. The first sign of special consideration being given to the treatment of young offenders appeared in the provision of separate institutions for those who received custodial sentences. Probably the earliest of these was the farm colony established in 1818 at Stretton-on-Dunsmore in Warwickshire to which boys were sent from neighbouring gaols and put to work on the land. The feeling of revulsion against the established penal system which was growing in momentum from the end of the eighteenth century began to have a new emphasis when directed towards the treatment of youthful delinquents and there were many, including a number of justices, who were convinced that an entirely new approach was required to the subject. It was in response to this that in 1836 a Royal Commission was appointed to consider "whether there ought to be any distinction in the method of trial between adult and juvenile offenders." In their report the commission made the significant comment, which was to have a profound influence on the future of the courts, that such a distinction would not be desirable unless it was brought about by way of increasing the summary jurisdiction of magistrates. For some time after this pronouncement, however, progress was made more in the direction of improving the institutions to which delinquents were sent than in changing the jurisdiction and constitution of the courts. In 1854 an Act, which has been mentioned earlier, "for the better care and reformation of youthful offenders" provided for juveniles under the age of sixteen to be sent to a reformatory school for a period of not less than two years nor more than five, but only on the expiration of a sentence of 14 days' imprisonment. This Act was inspired by three reformatory schools which had already been established during the previous five years - at Redhill, Birmingham and Kingswood in Gloucestershire - and by 1858 there was at least one such school in 33 out of the 42 English counties. Some of these were run by the county magistrates and others by charitable institutions, but in 1860 they were all placed under the Home Secretary.

In 1879 the Summary Jurisdiction Act provided that where a child under the age of 12 was charged with any indictable offence other than homicide the justices might, with the consent of the parent or guardian, deal with the case summarily and impose penalties limited to one month's imprisonment, a fine of 40 shillings and six strokes of the birch. The Act also applied the same provisions to certain offences of larceny, embezzlement and receiving committed by young persons between the ages of 12 and 16, provided that the accused consented to summary trial. In such cases the sentence was imprisonment for not more than three months, a fine of £10 and twelve strokes of the birch for a male child under the age of 14.

In spite of these changes and of the general climate of reform which had long pervaded the country, Great Britain lagged behind some other countries in introducing special courts for its juvenile offenders. The United States in particular was well ahead in this field, and as mentioned earlier the first American juvenile court was established in Chicago in 1881. From the beginning of the twentieth century, however, Britain began to make up the lost ground and became one of the leaders in the development of special courts for the young. This was another example of reforms being initiated, at least partly, by the justices themselves, and at first courts began to be formed unofficially by those magistrates who were particularly interested in the subject. One of these, which met with notable success, was established by the

Birmingham justices in April 1905. The courts were introduced on a national basis by the Children Act 1908 which finally established the principle that young offenders should be treated differently from adults. Those under 16 were to be tried in special juvenile courts which were courts of summary jurisdiction sitting in different places or at different times from the ordinary magistrates' courts. No child under the age of fourteen might be sent to prison and those under sixteen might be sent there only if the court certified that they were unruly. Pending a decision by the court the offender was to be detained in a new form of institution called a remand home. Imprisonment for those over 17 was aimed at reforming the offender rather than at punishment. Informality was to be the essence of the trial and, as in matrimonial cases, the public were excluded from the court.

The juvenile court was soon firmly established as an outstanding feature of the magisterial system, and it inspired enthusiastic admiration throughout Britain and also overseas. The Act of 1908 was followed by others in 1910, 1913, 1930, 1932 (following the report of a Committee on the Treatment of Young Offenders in 1927[42]) and finally a major piece of legislation in 1933. The Children and Young Persons Act 1933, although amended by subsequent Acts, remains to this day the principal piece of legislation governing the juvenile courts. Its essence was the welfare of the child and it contained the provision (s. 44(1)) which was to guide all courts in the future:

"Every court in dealing with a child or young person who is brought before it, either as being in need of care or protection or as an offender or otherwise, shall have regard to the welfare of the child or young person and shall in a proper case take steps for removing him from undesirable surroundings and for securing that proper provision is made for his education and training."

The Act also provided that "any local authority, constable or authorized person having reasonable grounds for believing that a child or young person is in need of care or protection may bring him before a juvenile court." Being in need of care or protection was interpreted fairly widely and included cases where parents were thought to be unfit to look after their children. Parents themselves were enabled to bring their own child before the court on the ground that he or she was beyond control. The court might then make a "care order" committing the child or young person to the care of the local authority, or it might send him to an approved school (being a school which had been approved by the Home Secretary as suitable for the education and training of those sent to it by the juvenile courts (s. 79)).

42.   Cmd. 2831.

The jurisdiction of the court was therefore twofold. Part was criminal, involving the trial of offenders for breaches of the criminal law, and part was civil designed to cater for the care and protection of the young. As regards criminal offences, the Act increased the age of criminal responsibility from seven to eight.[43] Some of the most difficult problems facing justices in any branch of their work were those in which they had to decide what was in the best interest of the child or young person.

The constitution of the juvenile courts is still governed by rules made by the Lord Chancellor under the 1933 Act. Each court must consist of either a single stipendiary magistrate or three justices drawn from a panel elected by the justices in their division. Until 1954 each court had to include at least one man and "as far as practicable" one woman. The reason for this sex discrimination was simply that before that date there were not thought to be sufficient women on all the commissions to staff every juvenile court, but by 1954 the numbers had increased sufficiently to enable the rules to be amended so as to place men and women on an equal footing.[44] The rules also provided for the appointment of regular chairmen of juvenile courts.

Mention has already been made of the fact that in London juvenile courts were composed solely of stipendiary magistrates from their inception in 1908 until 1933 when stipendiaries began sitting with lay justices. After 1945 the stipendiaries gave up this work, but resumed again on a smaller scale in 1950.[45] Another difference between London and the rest of the country was that the chairmen and members of the London courts were appointed specifically for the work by the Home Secretary and did not serve in any other magistrates' courts. The appointments were transferred to the Lord Chancellor in 1964 as explained in the ch. VIII.

Guardianship

An expansion of the justices' civil jurisdiction also occurred in their ability to deal with cases of guardianship which were previously within the exclusive jurisdiction of the Chancery Division of the High Court. Under the Guardianship of Infants Act 1886, which was extended by

43. Under the Act a child meant anyone under the age of fourteen and "young person" those between the ages of fourteen and seventeen. A child under the age of eight was considered to be *doli incapax* or incapable of forming the intent to commit a crime, but this presumption could be rebutted by proof that the child knew that what he was doing was morally wrong. *R.* v. *Owen* (1830), 4 C & P, 236. This is still the case though the age of criminal responsibility has been raised to ten.
44. Juvenile Courts (Constitution) Rules S.I. 1954, No. 1711/L. 21. The Rules provided that a juvenile court should comprise both a man and a woman, but that if at any time no man or no woman was available the court might proceed with only men or women present.
45. Some of the stipendiaries were highly successful in this work and played a prominent part in the development of the system, notably Sir William Clarke Hall, in commemoration of whose pioneering work the Clarke Hall Fellowship was founded.

an Act of the same name of 1925, there was a concurrent jurisdiction of the High Court and Petty Sessions for the custody and maintenance of children. The effect of this legislation and of the Administration of Justice Act of 1928 was that application might be made to the court by either the mother or father of a child whose custody or upbringing was in dispute. Where custody was awarded to the mother the court had power to make an order for the maintenance of the child by the father.

Adoption

Adoption was unknown to English law although it had been a feature of Roman law, and until 1926 it was not possible to adopt a person of any age in England. This was changed in 1926 by the Adoption of Children Act, which was extended by a further Act of 1939 and replaced by the Adoption Act 1950. The magistrates' courts (concurrently with the High Court and the County Courts) were enabled to make adoptions orders authorizing an applicant to adopt a infant. Such an order transferred all the rights and duties of the natural parents to the adopter. This jurisdiction was, and still is, exercised by those justices who are on the juvenile panel, and although they have to give careful attention to the facts of each case this work usually proceeds without difficulty as all concerned are anxious to ensure the welfare of the infant and are working towards the same end.

Consent to Marriage

Mention has already been made of the justices' power to grant a juvenile permission to marry against the wishes of its parents. This was introduced by the Guardianship of Infants Act 1886 and was re-enacted in the Marriage Act 1949 which remains in operation. The court which gives consent must be the one in which the parent refusing it resides.

Like many good things the juvenile courts had their defects, but these were not the subject of serious criticism until the second half of the twentieth century. In ch. IX we shall see that these courts were subject to a considerable amount of critical scrutiny, sometimes influenced by political theory, which led to a number of amendments to the existing law. The system would succeed, however, in surviving concerted attempts to replace it.

Appeals

At the beginning of the twentieth century there were no methods of challenging the decisions of the courts apart from those mentioned earlier. A small step forward was taken in 1848 in respect of Quarter

Sessions and Assizes when the Court of Crown Cases Reserved was set up, but no case could come before it unless a Judge or chairman of sessions decided to reserve the case for the court's consideration. The Judicature Acts 1873-75 established the Court of Appeal, but this heard appeals only from County Courts and the civil side of the High Court and was not concerned with appeals from the decisions of magistrates. The lack of any effective means of disputing the convictions and sentences of the criminal courts could not long survive when faced with the spirit of fair treatment for individuals at all social levels which was the ethos of the new era. Even so it was not until 1907 that Parliament was moved to legislate following a serious miscarriage of justice in the case of Adolf Beck who was kept in prison for years although innocent. The Criminal Appeal Act 1907 created the Court of Criminal Appeal to hear appeals from Quarter Sessions and Assizes. The court was composed of the Lord Chief Justice and the Judges of the King's Bench Division of the High Court to whom appeals lay from decisions of Quarter Sessions and Assizes.

Appeals from Petty Sessions and from the decision of the licensing justices continued to lie to Quarter Sessions where they amounted to about a third of the total number of cases dealt with. This procedure was extended in the twentieth century and was regulated by the Criminal Justice Act 1925. In general an appeal lay to Quarter Sessions on both law and fact and against both conviction and sentence. A defendant could appeal against conviction if he had not pleaded guilty at first instance. He could appeal against sentence whether he had pleaded guilty or not. Also, under the Probation of Offenders Act 1907, where magistrates found a charge proved without proceeding to conviction the defendant could appeal against the determination. These appeals were heard in counties by the Appeal Committee of Quarter Sessions and in boroughs with their own Quarter Sessions by the recorder who sat alone except to hear appeals from juvenile courts when he sat with two justices (who had to be members of the juvenile court panel). Quarter Sessions could confirm, reverse or vary the decision of the justices. They might therefore increase the sentence - a risk which deterred many from lodging an appeal.

Until 1933 defendants were also deterred from appealing to Quarter Sessions by the necessity to give security for cost or to find others who would stand surety. Following the recommendation of a committee in 1933[46] the Summary Jurisdiction (Appeals) Act 1933 (re-enacted by the Criminal Justice Act 1948) was passed which abolished security for costs and made provision for free legal aid.

Appeals to Quarter Sessions took the form of a complete retrial but

46.   Cmd. 4296.

without a jury, and it was open to both prosecution and defence to adduce fresh evidence which had not been presented at the hearing in Petty Sessions. The evidence coming before Quarter Sessions on appeals might therefore differ substantially from that presented in the magistrates' court.

Appeals in matrimonial and guardianship proceedings went straight to the High Court except that in affiliation cases an appeal by either the father or the mother lay to Quarter Sessions.

On a point of law an appeal lay also to the High Court from Petty Sessions by a process known as "case stated." This enabled an aggrieved party to ask the magistrates to give a written statement of the facts of the case and of the legal point at issue for consideration by the High Court. To hear these appeals the High Court was usually composed, as it still is, of three Judges and was known as a Divisional Court. This procedure has usually been followed whenever some statute or regulation required interpretation, and for this reason appeals by way of case stated have been made more often by prosecutors than by defendants. The prosecutor, who is usually the police or some local authority, wishes to have an authoritative ruling for future guidance and is more ready than a defendant to incur the substantial High Court costs which are involved.

None of the changes mentioned above affected the right to proceed by prerogative writ. Proceedings in magistrates' courts could still be scrutinized and corrected in the High Court by this means and it was not uncommon for applications to continue to be made for *mandamus* and *certiori.*

Appeals against the decisions of magistrates' courts have always been few in comparison with the total number of cases coming before them. By the 1940s only about one convicted offender in every 750 appealed to Quarter Sessions and a much smaller proportion appealed to the High Court by way of case stated. This was widely cited as an indication of public satisfaction with the way in which the magistrates did their work. There is some justification for this view, but there are several other cogent reasons why a convicted person often decided not to pursue the matter further. Foremost among these was a desire not to prolong the period of uncertainty and also a fear that an appeal might involve him in much time and expense and that his sentence might be increased.

Treatment of offenders

A new approach towards the treatment of offenders had begun to appear in the eighteenth century and we have seen that some of the justices were prominent among those who strove to ameliorate the rigid harshness of the penal laws. This trend, which had continued throughout the nineteenth century, achieved impressive levels in the twentieth.

Reference has already been made to the changes which took place during the nineteenth century in the types of sentence imposed by the courts. Imprisonment became the principal penalty apart from corporal punishment and fines. Transportation had been abolished, and the death penalty, which could no longer be imposed by Quarter Sessions, had also disappeared except for treason, murder, piracy on the high seas and arson of certain Crown property. As the twentieth century progressed the emphasis of custodial sentences switched from punishment and deterrence to reform and rehabilitation of the criminal. The new era had begun in 1895 when the Gladstone Committee proposed that imprisonment should be aimed at reforming the offender, but it was some time before any significant progress was made in this direction except in the treatment of young offenders. We have seen that this was one of the underlying principles of the juvenile courts established in 1908. It was also the basis of a new form of institution known as a Borstal to which Quarter Sessions but not Petty Sessions could sentence young people who were thought to be in danger of becoming professional criminals and who were between the ages of 15 and 21. The first of these institutions was opened at Borstal in Kent in 1902. The sentence lasted for a period of not less than two nor more than three years, but a boy might be released on licence at any time after six months and a girl after three months. The inmates underwent strict training and instruction but were not subject to punitive treatment. Although a Borstal sentence could not be imposed at Petty Sessions the magistrates might commit an offender to prison pending the next Assize or Quarter Sessions with a view to a Borstal sentence. They could do this when they convicted a young person who qualified for such treatment of an offence for which a sentence of one month or more without the option of a fine could be imposed. Borstal treatment was much in favour during the first half of the century and by 1930 there were seven such institutions for boys and one for girls, but enthusiasm waned in the second half in a new atmosphere of penal philosophy and the system was replaced by other forms of treatment in 1982 as we shall see later.

We have seen that a fine was not a sentencing option that was open to the justices during the earlier period of their history, but at the beginning of the twentieth century fines had become the most common form of penalty imposed by courts of summary jurisdiction. By 1945 they were imposed far more frequently than any other sentence, much of the increase being due to the rapid growth in road traffic offences, and there was increasing criticism of the growing prison population which resulted from this. The subject was considered by the

Committee on Imprisonment by Courts of Summary Jurisdiction in Default of Payment of Fines and Other Sums of Money whose Report[47] was implemented by the Money Payments (Justices' Procedure) Act 1935. This Act, which applied only to the magistrates' courts, imposed restrictions on the use of the fine as an option and was followed immediately by a considerable drop in the number of committals to prison. After the war, however, the numbers again increased steadily, leading to further action as described in ch. VIII.

Probation

The roots of the system of placing an offender on probation lie in the distant past. It developed from the practice of requiring a person to give an undertaking to keep the peace which, as we have seen in earlier chapters, was one of the first duties of the Keepers of the Peace who were the precursors of the justices. Since then "binding over" has been one of the most important and valuable functions performed by the justices during the intervening centuries.

It was a shortcoming of the original system that there was no authority expressly charged with the duty of supervising those who were bound over so as to ensure that they complied with their undertaking. It was not until the nineteenth century that some experiments were made in placing offenders on probation. As far as is known the first of these was introduced by Warwickshire magistrates in 1820. According to a Home Office Committee on the Treatment of Young Offenders which reported in 1927,[48] these justices passed a sentence of imprisonment of one day on a youthful offender on condition that he returned to the care of his parent or master who was to supervise him with greater care in the future. The committee's report added that this practice was followed and carried further by the recorder of Birmingham, Matthew Davenport Hill, who in 1834 "instituted a register of the forerunners of probation officers, and caused inquiry as to the young offender's conduct to be made by the police from time to time."

In the latter part of the nineteenth century some religious bodies began to appoint police court missionaries who presented the courts with the opportunity to place convicted prisoners in their care, and the London magistrates were the first to avail themselves of this. Progress was made with the assistance of Parliament which, in the Summary Jurisdiction Act 1879 and another Act of 1887, empowered the courts in certain cases to discharge a convicted person upon his giving security to keep the peace and to present himself for judgment. Many

47. Cmd. 4649.
48. Cmd. 2831.

magistrates in exercising these powers directed that the offender should be under the supervision of the police court missionary. This practice had become common by the beginning of the twentieth century but it was, of course, possible only in courts where there was a missionary or where the magistrates themselves had appointed probation officers. The first to take this course were the justices of Birmingham in 1906 - the same justices who had set up one of the earliest juvenile courts in the previous year.

In the meantime a system of probation had been developing in the United States which again led the way towards reform in the criminal justice system. In 1841 a cobbler in Boston, Massachusetts, named Augustus, offered to stand bail for a man charged with being a common drunkard. His offer was accepted by the court and when the offender returned for sentence three weeks later he gave indications of being a reformed character, apparently in consequence of Augustus's influence during his bail. The court, instead of sentencing the man to imprisonment, imposed a nominal fine of one cent, with costs. Subsequently Augustus stood bail for many more defendants and undertook to supervise them and to give them guidance pending their return to court for judgment. Statutory effect was given to this practice by a law of Massachusetts of 1878 which provided for the appointment by the mayor of Boston of a paid probation officer who should be some suitable person, either from among the police of the city or "from citizens at large." The officer so appointed was under the control of the chief of police of Boston and his duties included advising the courts on the suitability of probation, reporting periodically to the chief of police and visiting probationers to whom he was to give "such assistance and encouragement as will tend to prevent their again offending." This example was followed by six other states at the turn of the century.[49]

England was the first country to introduce a probation system on a national basis. The Act of 1879 had empowered a magistrates' court to discharge a person accused of a trifling offence without punishment, even though the court decided that the charge had been proved. It could then either dismiss the case or bind the accused over to appear for sentence or to be of good behaviour. In 1887 the Probation of First Offenders Act, which was the first British statute to refer specifically to probation, gave courts power to release an offender "on probation of good conduct" instead of imposing any punishment.

After some experience had been gained in applying the Acts of 1879 and 1887 a comprehensive probation system was introduced by the Probation of Offenders Act 1907. This enabled magistrates to adopt one of three courses: (1) To discharge the offender without imposing

49. Missouri (1897), Vermont (1898), Illinois, Minnesota, and Rhode Island in 1899 and New Jersey in 1900.

any punishment though he might be ordered to pay costs or compensation; (2) To bind him over to be of good behaviour for a specified period, usually 12 months. If during this period he committed any further offence he might be punished for the original offence in addition to receiving punishment for any new offence; (3) To place the offender on probation. The Act therefore allowed three options; discharge, binding over and probation.

The full wording of s. 1(1) of the 1907 Act was:

"Where any person is charged before a court of summary jurisdiction with an offence punishable by such court and the court thinks that the charge is proved but is of opinion that having regard to the character, antecedents, age, health, or mental condition of the person charged, or to the trivial nature of the offence, or to the extenuating circumstances under which the offence was committed, it is inexpedient to inflict any punishment, or that it is expedient to release the offender on probation, the court may, without proceeding to conviction, make an order either

(1) dismissing the information or charge; or
(2) discharging the offender conditionally on his entering into a recognizance with or without sureties to be of good behaviour and to appear for conviction and sentence when called on at any time during such period not exceeding three years as may be specified in the order."

Under s. 2 the recognizance might contain a condition that the offender should be under the supervision of such persons as might be named in the order. The Criminal Justice Administration Act 1914, provided (s. 8) that the recognizance might also contain such additional conditions in regard to residence, abstention from intoxicants and other matters as the court might think desirable.

Any of the three courses which magistrates might adopt under the 1907 Act could be taken "without proceeding to conviction." This was severely criticized by the Divisional Court in 1919 in *Oaten* v. *Auty*. Darling J., who presided pointed out that the wording of the Act was illogical in that it aimed at finding people not guilty when the court had concluded that they were guilty. The effect was unsatisfactory because in the minds of the public probation came to be synonymous with "letting-off." A Home Office Departmental Committee in 1936[50] also criticized the wording of the Act and suggested that when a person had been found guilty of a criminal offence the fact ought not to be concealed by the technicality that he had not been "convicted." To

---

50.　Report of Departmental Committee on Social Services in the Courts of Summary Jurisdiction (1936), Cmd. 5122.

maintain the existing practice would in their view be injurious to the probation system. Nevertheless it was not until 1948 that the wording was amended by the Criminal Justice Act, but in the meantime the use of probation increased considerably,[51] with generally satisfactory results.

The 1907 Act empowered the courts to appoint paid probation officers who were to be officers of the court, but it did not make the arrangement compulsory and a Home Office Committee in 1922[52] found that at that time 215 courts had not appointed any probation officers and that the conditions of service of the officers in many areas was unsatisfactory. Accordingly the Criminal Justice Act of 1925 made the appointment of probation officers compulsory in all magistrates' courts. It also required the justices to set up probation committees. The 1907 legislation partly retained the old missionary spirit by enabling voluntary societies to select and appoint probation officers and to pay them one third of their salaries and expenses, the remainder being defrayed from public funds. Numbers of officers were provided in this way, the principal source being the Church of England Police Court Mission. Many of the magistrates themselves, however, failed to appreciate the potential value of probation and appointed officers merely because they were obliged to do so. They therefore made the appointment on a part-time basis and at the lowest possible salary. As late as 1934 there were eighty-three officers with salaries of £5 a year or less and 213 with £20 a year or less.[53] The result was that although many of the officers were dedicated to their work much was left undone, and that which was carried out was not always done efficiently. This unsatisfactory state of affairs began to improve after 1938 when the voluntary societies shifted their attention to the provision of hostels and ceased to be concerned with the probation officers.

By the beginning of 1940 reform of the probation system was overdue, but in spite of mounting criticism no further action was taken because of the war, and it was not until 1948 that the lessons of the past 40 years were incorporated in the Criminal Justice Act, to which reference has already been made, which wholly repealed and replaced the Act of 1907. The new Act placed the probation officers on a more satisfactory basis and made considerable changes in the system. The existing practice of inserting conditions in a recognizance was replaced by one in which the court made an order requiring the person to be

---

51.   Between 1910 and 1933 the percentage of persons placed on probation by magistrates' courts following decisions that they had committed offences rose from 11 per cent to 19 per cent in the case of indictable offences, and in the case of those appearing before the juvenile courts it rose from 26 per cent to 54 per cent in the same period. *Ibid.*
52.   Cmd. 1601.
53.   Committee on Social Services in the Courts of Summary Jurisdiction. Cmd. 5122.

under supervision. The Act also provided that in all courts there must be a conviction before the probation procedure could operate. These changes will be described further in ch. VIII, but before leaving the Probation of Offenders Act 1907, it may be noted that it was cited with approval at the United Nations where it was pointed out that it had had a far-reaching influence on the development of probation in many parts of the world. "Although no longer in force in the United Kingdom, the Act retains its importance as the classic embodiment of the principles underlying the probation system in widespread parts of the world."[54]

Legal aid

The cost of proceedings has always placed a heavy burden on the parties in both criminal and civil courts. It was not until shortly after World War II that a comprehensive system of legal aid was introduced in Great Britain and still later that it embraced virtually all types of proceedings. These later developments will be described in chs. VIII and IX, but the process began in the criminal courts at the beginning of the century. Under the Poor Prisoners Defence Act 1903, which applied only to trials on indictment, the court could grant legal aid after considering the defence disclosed by the defendant. This meant that the accused had to disclose the whole of his defence earlier than he or his advisers might otherwise have thought desirable. In 1926 a committee,[55] which had been appointed in the previous year to inquire into legal aid, concluded that the existing system was satisfactory but that it might be improved. It recommended that legal aid should be extended to preliminary inquiries and to cases heard summarily in magistrates' courts. These recommendations were implemented in the Poor Prisoners Defence Act 1930. Under that Act, where a person appeared before a court of trial or at a preliminary hearing he might be granted a "legal aid certificate" which enabled him to have a solicitor to appear on his behalf. Before granting a certificate the justices did not have to consider the whole of the defence but they had to be satisfied that the defendant had insufficient means and that, because either of the gravity of the charge or of the exceptional circumstances, it was in the interests of justice that he should receive free legal aid to assist him in the preparation and conduct of his case. The Act also provided that where justices committed a person for trial for an indictable offence they might grant him a "defence certificate" which enabled him to have counsel and a solicitor for the preparation and conduct of the case at trial. Before granting the certificate the

54. *Probation and Related Measures,* United Nations Department of Social Affairs (1951).
55. Cmd. 2638.

justices had to be satisfied, as in the case of a legal aid certificate, that the defendant's means were insufficient and that in all the circumstances it was desirable that he should have aid. In cases of murder, however, the justices were obliged to grant a defence certificate if satisfied only as to the insufficiency of the defendant's means.

The 1930 Act did not operate very successfully, largely because magistrates were generally reluctant to grant certificates and also because some continued to assume that the defence still had to be disclosed before they could reach a decision. It was clear that the legal aid scheme needed thorough overhaul and expansion, and a Departmental Committee under the chairmanship of Lord Rushcliffe was appointed for this purpose by the Lord Chancellor in 1944. Their recommendations were to be implemented by the Legal Aid and Advice Act 1949, as described below in ch. IX.

The war years

Wars have always added to the task of the Justices of the Peace. Additional burdens were naturally placed upon them when hostilities took place in their own land, but we have seen that they were also involved in dealing with problems arising from foreign wars, particularly in raising and maintaining military forces and in the defence of the coasts, as well as handling numerous related matters ranging from shortage of food to deserters. This was especially so during the Spanish wars in the sixteenth century and the war with Napoleon, in the nineteenth. During the two World Wars in the twentieth century the justices no longer had any role to play as magistrates in military affairs, but the fact that many of them served in the armed forces added to the burden of those who were left to carry on the work of the bench which was conducted largely by the more elderly and infirm and which increased substantially during the war years. This increase occurred during both World Wars in the twentieth century and was due partly to an escalation in criminal activity which is the inevitable concomitant of all wars and partly to the large number of temporary regulations which had to be enforced. This was most noticeable during the war of 1939-45 owing to the widespread destruction of urban areas and the prolonged application of rationing and many other regulations which continued in force long after the end of hostilities. This was one of the many occasions in their history when the justices were obliged to undertake duties which made them unpopular with the community. Although the public generally accepted the restrictions as being essential to the conduct of the war there were instances where magistrates were thought to have applied them unfairly.

There were also situations where the justices themselves disapproved of a regulation and were reluctant to impose it. The leading case of this kind occurred in 1947, but although this was just after the end of the war fuel rationing was still in force. One of the many people who disapproved of the regulations governing the use of concessionary petrol for motor vehicles was the chairman of the Carmarthen Justices, Colonel Delmer Davies-Evans, who emphasized his disapproval by imposing only a nominal fine of one shilling on a convicted motorist. When the Lord Chancellor pointed out to him that it was the duty of every magistrate to apply the law however distasteful this might be, he claimed that he and his colleagues had fulfilled their duty by convicting the defendant and that they were entitled to express their disapproval by imposing a derisory penalty. The Lord Chancellor, Lord Jowitt, removed the Colonel from the bench on the ground that he had failed to comply with the terms of his commission. There was an outburst of protest at the dismissal and the Member of Parliament for Carmarthen moved a motion on the adjournment in the House of Commons. This provided an opportunity for the Attorney General, Sir Hartley Shawcross, to explain the constitutional principles governing the removal of magistrates. He stated that the Lord Chancellor would never dismiss a justice for some isolated criticism of an Act of Parliament but that he would be obliged to do so where the justice had allowed his dislike of an Act to influence his judicial administration of the law.

The system of lay Justices of the Peace negotiated the transition from local governors to judges of the inferior courts with success, and it also went a long way towards absorbing the new tasks arising within the redefined parameters of the treatment of offenders and expanded summary jurisdiction. At the same time considerable progress was made during the first part of the century in widening the area from which the justices were drawn, and the hubristic image which had attached to the magistracy in the eighteenth century was finally expunged in the twentieth, though benches still fell far short of being the microcosm of the local community which many wished to see. In view of this and of the commendable conduct of the justices during the war the country might have been expected to feel indebted to those who held the fort on the home front during the absence of their colleagues on active service and who discharged their onerous duties with dedication. There was, however, a change of feeling towards the magistracy which was due to a more demanding attitude towards all those who held public office and also to dissatisfaction with a number of isolated incidents which tended to bring the system into disrepute. In the new social and political climate and the increasingly entrepreneurial environment which developed at the end of the war, when all established institutions were subjected to critical scrutiny, the justices failed to meet the criteria that were demanded. Once again it was a question of the existing institutions either adapting to fundamental changes or being abolished. The far-reaching reforms which were to be introduced immediately after the war would enable the Justices of the Peace to survive yet another climacteric.

CHAPTER VII

1945 - 1989 A NEW CHALLENGE
PART I - THE JUSTICES OF THE PEACE
IN THE POST-WAR ERA

The lay magistracy faces a new world in the post-war period - Quality of the Justices of the Peace raised by radical reforms in recruitment, retention, conditions of service and training

THE THIRTY YEARS which followed the Second World War were among the most interesting in the history of the Justices of the Peace. This was a period in which the magistracy had to adjust to steady national decline, during which their country lost its pre-eminent position as one of the world's greatest powers and the centre of a vast empire, and this was accompanied by profound changes in the social, economic and political structure of British society. When the period began, the established order was still held in respect and the Justices of the Peace, as an integral part of that order, suffered more acutely than almost any other group in the community from the subsequent shock of national decline which coincided with deterioration in national standards and erosion of law and order. All this imposed a severe strain on the magistrates' responsibility for administering justice, but in addition to this it was an era which saw a revolt against established authority, which was accompanied by a denigration of the spirit of voluntary public service and a general condemnation of the old order with which the justices were identified. Public opinion became more critical and, in spite of the fact that the magistrates had borne a heavy burden during the war and had performed their duties reasonably well, their conduct was the subject of greater condemnation than had been seen for a hundred years.

The lay Justices of the Peace were the kind of historical legacy that one would have expected to be the first to founder in the revolutionary flood of the post-war years. That they survived this crucial period was due to the ability of the system to adapt once more to a new situation, as it had done on many occasions in the past. It could not have survived had it not undergone extensive changes which rendered it acceptable to successive Governments and to the public at large.

Substantial criticism of the magistrates had begun even before the war. This was probably due largely to the fact that many members of the articulate upper classes were finding themselves in the magistrates' courts for the first time, particularly on charges of motoring offences, as we saw in the last chapter, and this phenomenon was extended by an increase in the number of fines imposed for forgetfulness, resulting in such offences as failing to pay for a wireless licence or dog licence. In addition to this, there were instances of miscarriages of justices and of incompetence by the justices which received publicity on a scale which had not been known in the past. Three such cases occurred in 1945 and 1946, and each was the subject of an inquiry at the direction jointly of the Lord Chancellor and the Home Secretary. This procedure had been extremely rare until then, and its adoption was an illustration of the more critical attitude which the Government itself was beginning to assume.

In the first of these cases, in 1945, a priest was charged before the Stoke magistrates with indecent assault on a boy. The Clerk to the Justices, who had been approached by a mutual friend on behalf of the accused, arranged for the case to be heard by two of his junior justices an hour before the normal sitting of the court. The prosecution were not informed of the arrangements and were not represented at the hearing. The accused elected summary trial and pleaded guilty, and the two justices, neither of whom had had much experience of court work, bound him over for 12 months. In fact, they had no power to hear the case at all without first taking account of any representation by the prosecution that it was fit for summary trial, but they seem to have been unaware of this and the point was not brought to their attention by the clerk. Lord Goddard (who became Lord Chief Justice in the following year) was appointed to hold an inquiry, and his report (not a command paper) castigated the two justices, and above all the clerk. All three were dismissed - the justices by the Lord Chancellor and the clerk by the Stoke magistrates. *The Times* commented:

"If they [the justices] had not the authority and strength of character to stand up to their clerk when he oversteps his proper sphere, they may be acquitted of conscious transgression, but they certainly ought not to be on the bench."

In the second case, which also occurred in 1945, the chairman of the Gillingham bench in Yorkshire wished to evict his groom, whom he had dismissed, from one of his cottages. He took proceedings for recovery of possession in a specially convened court composed of two of his colleagues, who issued a warrant of ejectment. The chairman had good grounds for dismissing the groom, who knew nothing about horses and had obtained the post by false pretences, but the chairman could have sought an ejectment order in the County Court. He chose to proceed at a special sitting of his own court because he was in a hurry to get another groom to look after his hunters. It was a classic example of justice being done but not manifestly being seen to be done. An inquiry was held by Lord Justice Tucker, following which the chairman was dismissed from the commission. In his report (Cmd. 6783) Tucker commented:

"In my view a magistrate, so far from using his position to further his own private convenience, should be prepared to put up with a greater degree of inconvenience than an ordinary litigant if there is any danger of conflict between his rights as an ordinary citizen and his position as a Justice of the Peace."

The last of these three cases occurred in 1946. It involved the Aberayron bench in Cardiganshire whose clerk was prosecuted on behalf of the Minister of Food in that, without authority under the Defence Regulations, "he did cause to be slaughtered livestock for human consumption, to wit one pig," and that he had made a false statement regarding the ownership of the said pig. He was tried by seven of his own justices who dismissed both charges without calling upon the defence. Lord Justice Tucker was again appointed to hold an inquiry. He found that the justices, in reaching what was clearly a bad decision, had not acted dishonestly or with conscious bias, but that they had obviously acted wrongly. He commented that:

"They obviously needed some guidance as to what were the real issues to which they should address their minds. Such guidance was not forthcoming from their chairman, who is well advanced in years and was, I think, lost without the assistance which he was accustomed to receive from his clerk. They seemed to me to have been in the position of a jury retiring to consider their verdict without having heard any summing up!"[1]

The ageing chairman was removed from the commission.

For some time there had been a growing awareness that reform of the magistrates' courts was necessary, but no action had been taken by the Government. The new Labour Government, however, which took office in July 1945, was moved to immediate action, partly by the public outcry which followed these three cases, but largely by the resentment of their party at the paucity of their supporters on the Commissions of the Peace. The situation was similar to that facing the Liberal Government when they decided to set up a Royal Commission

---

1. Proceedings at the hearing of two informations before Justices of the Aberayron Division of the County of Cardigan on April 24, 1946, Cmd. 7061, para. 23.

on Justices of the Peace in 1909. The Labour Government considered that a further inquiry into the magisterial system was long overdue and, in 1946, they decided to appoint another Royal Commission which was to study in depth all aspects of the magistracy. The precise form of the study was the result of a compromise between conflicting views of the then Lord Chancellor, Lord Jowitt, and the Home Secretary, Mr. Chuter Ede. Ede wanted the inquiry to be limited in scope. He feared that root and branch investigation would take an intolerable time and might in the end prove fruitless. Jowitt, on the other hand, felt that no worthwhile result would emerge from a narrow inquiry and that in any event the time had come for a thorough reappraisal of the administration of summary jurisdiction. A compromise solution was agreed in cabinet and the Royal Commission's terms of reference embraced the appointment and removal of justices and their conditions of service, but it was to be assumed that the existing system of lay justices was to be maintained.

The Commission's terms of reference were much wider than those of the previous Royal Commission of 1910. They were required to review the arrangements for the selection and removal of Justices of the Peace in Great Britain, the qualifications and disqualifications for appointment and the tenure of office of justices. They were also to report on justices *ex officio,* chairmen of benches, juvenile courts, the expenses of justices, stipendiary magistrates and on the allocation of work between stipendiaries and lay justices. In their Report, published in July 1948,[2] the commission made a large number of far-reaching recommendations, virtually all of which were implemented either by administrative action or by statute. Most were covered by the Justices of the Peace At 1949, which also implemented the proposals of the Roche Committee on Justices' Clerks which was mentioned in the last chapter. The implementation of the commission's proposals brought about important changes in every aspect of the Justice of the Peace system - in the administration of the courts, in their procedure and in the quality of those who held the office of justice. These various reforms will be described below under each of the separate topics to which they relate.

The Commissions of the Peace

In 1945 there were 381 separate Commissions of the Peace in Great Britain. In England and Wales these were composed of 63 county commissions (including Lancashire, Haverfordwest, the Cinq Ports and the Liberties of Peterborough and Ripon) and 281 boroughs.[3] In

2.   Cmd. 7463.
3.   See Appendix II. The 281 boroughs included 31 in the Duchy of Lancaster.

Scotland, which is the subject of vol. III, ch. III, there were 37 commissions.4 The fact that a borough had a separate commission did not necessarily exclude the county justices from acting in matters arising within the borough, the position depending upon the terms of the borough's charter, but it was unusual for such intervention to occur. The form of the commission was the same as it had been since the Crown Office Act of 1877, and the wording was virtually the same as it had been since 1590.5 As in previolus centuries it was issued under the Great Seal which was affixed in the Crown Office (situated in the House of Lords) to the bottom of the parchment scroll on which the commission was written. The names of the justices appeared in a schedule attached to the end of the commission. New names were added and existing ones removed by the Crown Office on the authority of a fiat signed by the Lord Chancellor. If a justice was still on a commission at the time of his or her death the name was allowed to remain undisturbed, a practice which added considerably to the task of ascertaining the number of justices serving at any one time.

Custody of the commission lay usually with the Clerk of the Peace in a county or the town clerk in a borough, and whenever names had to be added or removed it was sent by post to the Crown Office and later returned when the insertion or deletion had been made. This procedure was clearly inconvenient, but no attempt was made to change it until a general reappraisal of all commissions became necessary in consequence of local Government reform in 1972. The Local Government Act 1972 established a new pattern of local Government. It replaced all the old administrative counties and municipal boroughs with metropolitan and non-metropolitan counties divided into districts. Until then there had been a separate Commission of the Peace for each administrative county and liberty and for certain boroughs, but when these local government areas were abolished their Commissons of the Peace also became defunct. To meet the new situation the Administration of Justice Act 1973 provided that in future a separate Commission of the Peace should be issued for every metropolitan and non-metropolitan county and for no other area except the five commission areas of Greater London and for the City of London. At the same time the opportunity was taken to replace the otiose verbage of the old commissions with a shorter, modernized version. In fact this new commission, although tidier and more intelligible to the modern reader than its predecessors, made little practical difference to the power of the justices. The commission was the justice's authority to perform his duties, but what those duties

4. In Scotland there were separate commissions for the 33 counties and for the four Royal Burghs of Edinburgh, Glasgow, Aberdeen and Dundee.
5. For the wording of commissions see Appendix I.

were and how he was to execute them was, as previously, to be found mainly in the many Acts of Parliament which applied to magistrates.

The 1973 Act also brought about a change in the method of appointment of justices. It formally recognized what had been the practice for centuries, namely, that the Lord Chancellor (and the Chancellor of the Duchy of Lancaster) appointed justices on behalf of the Sovereign. It therefore provided expressly that justices should be appointed "on behalf and in the name of Her Majesty by instrument under the hand of the Lord Chancellor," and that "a justice so appointed may be removed from office in like manner."[6] The former fiats were therefore superseded by documents signed by the Lord Chancellor, of which the originals were kept in the Lord Chancellor's Office while copies were sent to the Kepper of the Rolls in the county. The old title *Custos Rotulorum* was now formally changed to Keeper of the Rolls by the Act, which also altered the method of appointment to that office by providing that "in any commission area other than the City of London such one of the justices as may be designated by the Lord Chancellor shall be keeper of the rolls." There was no longer a schedule of justices at the foot of each commissions and the latter was kept permanently in the area to which it applied.

Ever since the appointment and removal of justices had been effected by fiat in the eighteenth century the Lord Chancellor had always signed every fiat personally. By 1970 this fairly simple task had become a burden by reason of the frequency by which changes to the commission had to be made. In particular, the number of insertions and deletions had increased considerably since a new practice was introduced by Lord Chancellor Gardiner whereby any justice who moved from one commission area to another and who had served for at least five years could apply to be transferred immediately and automatically from his old commission to the one for the new area in which he now resided.[7] Each of these involved the signing of two fiats (of removal and reappointment) and they became ever more frequent as a result of the rise in the number of justices and of the greater propensity of the population in general to move about. In 1971 Lord Chancellor Hailsham decided that these routine transfers should not be allowed to disrupt his time and he therefore delegated the signing of the fiats (and after 1973 of the new instruments) to the Secretary of Commissions and his deputy. Responsibilty for issuing Commissions of the Peace and for actually inserting and removing names still rested with the Clerk of the Crown, who by that time was invariably the same

6.   Section 1(2).
7.   In order that this arrangement should not cause some benches to become overstaffed with justices, anyone who was transferred in this way was placed on the Supplemental List until such time as the advisory committee for his new area asked for him to be placed on the Active List.

individual as the Permanent Secretary to the Lord Chancellor, but the clerk could act only on directions contained in a fiat signed by the Lord Chancellor, or henceforth by the Secretary of Commissions or his deputy. This was the first recorded instance for more than two centuries of anyone other than the Lord Chancellor himself being authorized to appoint or remove a justice. Lord Hailsham concluded that he had power to delegate in these circumstances even though the Secretary of Commissions had to exercise his discretion in determining whether each set of circumstances fell within his remit. The legality of the practice was open to doubt until 1982 when it was regularized by the Administration of Justice Act which removed the previous statutory requirement that appointments must be under the hand of the Lord Chancellor.

Composition of the benches

(1) Qualification and disqualification

After the abolition of the property qualification in 1906 the only statutory requirement for appointment as a Justice of the Peace was residental. Under the Justices of the Peace Act 1906 (s. 2) a county justice had to reside in or within seven miles of the county boundary at the time of his appointment, but apparently he could move beyond this area subsequently without becoming disqualified. Under the Municipal Corporations Act 1882 (s. 157(3)) a borough justice was obliged to reside in the borough or within seven miles of it, or occupy a house, warehouse or other property in the borough. All these provisions were repealed by the Justices of the Peace Act 1949 which extended the qualifying area to 15 miles from the commission boundary (s. 1(1)), but the Lord Chancellor was empowered (s. 1(2)) to exclude anyone from disqualification if he considered it to be in the public interest that the individual should act as a justice. Considerable importance was attached to the principle that a justice should be available to perform his duties and that therefore he must live in the area for which he was responsible. The provisions of the 1949 Act were therefore re-enacted in the Justices of the Peace Act 1979 (s. 7) and they remain the only statutory qualification to the present day. There have also been a few statutory disqualifications,[8] to which Lord Chancellors added a

---

8.   Bankruptcy under the Bankruptcy Acts 1883 and 1890; conviction under the Corrupt and Illegal Practices Prevention Act 1883, the Municipal Elections (Corrupt and Illegal Practices) Act 1884, the Representation of the People Act 1918, the Forfeiture Act 1870 and the Criminal Justice Act 1948; serving as a sheriff under the Sheriffs Act 1887. A solicitor and his partners were not permitted to act in connexion with proceedings before any justices who were attached to the same Petty Sessional Division as himself (Solicitors Act 1932; Justices of the Peace Act 1949; Administration of Justice Act 1973).

number of administrative grounds upon which they would refuse to make an appointment. These bars became fewer in the second half of the twentieth century and by the end of 1989 the only persons who would not be accepted for appointment were:

A person over 60 years of age or under 21.

A person convicted of certain offences, or subject to certain court orders.

An undischarged bankrupt.

A person whose sight or hearing was impaired, or who by reason of infirmity could not carry out all the duties of a justice.

A serving member of Her Majesty's forces; a serving police officer or member of the Special Constabulary or a traffic warden.

A close relative of a person who was already a justice on the same bench.

Someone whose occupation was incompatible, for example a probation officer or a member of the staff of a penal institution.

(2) Number of justices

The Royal Commission estimated[9] that in 1948 the number of names on the Active List were about 16,800 (13,100 men and 3,700 women), the remainder being on the Supplemental List. There were also about 2,500 justices *ex officio*. The Commission pointed out that many benches were overstaffed, and the Lord Chancellor accordingly adopted a policy of drastic pruning which he achieved both by reducing the number of new appointments and by persuading many of those who were ineffective to transfer to the Supplement List. The numbers on the Active List were also reduced by some 1,900 when a compulsory age limit of 75 was imposed by the Justices of the Peace Act 1949 (s. 4(4)(a)), as explained below. The result was that by the beginning of 1951 the numbers on the Active List had been reduced to 14,100. Thereafter there was a slow increase to meet the growing work-load and by 1969 the total on the Active List returned to 16,000. In 1970 the rate of growth was accelerated to meet new demands and particularly to anticipate the likely requirements of the Crown Court when it was established in January 1972 - a prospect which failed to materialize - and by 1977 the numbers had risen to 23,483. By January 1983 there had been a further rise of 10 per cent bringing the Active List to 25,933, and by January 1989 the total in England and Wales, including the Duchy of Lancaster was 28,211 (24,112 men and 4,099 women). During the 40 years from 1949 the Lord Chancellor's Office had monitored the requirements of each bench and the performance of its

---

9.   Cmd. 7463, paras. 21, 22.

serving justices in order to ensure that there were enough but not more than enough magistrates in each area. The continued increase in numbers was therefore a genuine reflection of the growth in the volume of business.[10]

Since 1945 the total number of justices throughout the country has been governed to some extent by limits which have been imposed on the size of each bench. These have applied both to the numbers serving in each petty sessional division and to those who were allowed to sit at a time in each court for various purposes, both at Quarter Sessions and at Petty Sessions. In 1945 Lord Jowitt introduced a system of limits on the number of justices in each division which was governed by the frequency with which courts were held. This system, which is still in operation, was based on the principle that not more than five justices at the most should sit at any one time, and this was combined with the requirement that, in order to comply with his undertaking to do a fair share of the work, every justice should attend court not less than 26 times a year.[11] If therefore five justices were present on each occasion a bench with a fortnightly court would be allowed a maximum of five justices. Allowance was made, however, for absence through ill-health or other acceptable reason and the rule imposed by the Lord Chancellor was that a court which sat once a fortnight or less frequently should be allowed seven justices. The numbers increased, but at a reduced rate, where the number of sittings was more frequent.[12]

As regards the number of justices who could sit at any one time, the Lord Chancellor made rules for the adult courts under the Justices of the Peace Act 1949 (s. 13) whereby the most who could sit in a court of

10. County advisory committees were inclined to press for rather more appointments than were really necessary, whereas some borough committees, who liked to restrict their benches to a select few, tended to ask for less new justices than were actually required.
11. Where a bench sat less frequently than once a fortnight the justices were expected to attend on at least three-quarters of the occasions on which they were summoned. Sittings for domestic, juvenile and licensing work were regarded as attendances satisfying the requirement. Until 1973, attendance of a justice throughout a whole day constituted only one attendance, but thereafter, if a justice sat in the morning and also in the afternoon on the same day this counted as two attendances, provided that the afternoon sitting was of at least one hour's duration.
12. The rules laid down by the Lord Chancellor as to the number of justices permitted in a petty sessional division were:

Number of Regular Adult Courts per week	Maximum Number of Justices
1	14
2	20
3	25
4	30
5	35
6	40
7	45
8	50
9	55
10	60

Quarter Sessions was eight in addition to the chairman (as recommended by the Royal Commission) and the maximum for adult courts sitting at Petty Sessions was seven.[13] In a separate announcement of November 30, 1950, however, the Lord Chancellor expressed the view that the best number of justices to try a case at Petty Sessions was three and that, save in exceptional circumstances, there should be no more than five. When the Crown Court was established in 1972 the number of justices who might sit in that court both at first instance and to hear appeals was limited by the Courts Act (s. 5) and rules made thereunder.[14]

As already mentioned, separate limits were imposed on the number of justices sitting for special purposes, such as juvenile courts. These will be dealt with at greater length below. There were still a few types of cases on which a single justice could adjudicate alone, for instance to deal with drunks or vagrants, but his powers were very limited.

(3) Attendances
In 1945 many justices never attended their courts at all, notwithstanding the undertakings they had given since the Royal Commission's Report of 1910 to do their fair share of the work, and notwithstanding attempts made by the Lord Chancellor from 1935 onwards to secure the resignation of those who were ineffective, as mentioned in the last chapter. This unsatisfactory state of affairs was confirmed by an inquiry carried out by the Royal Commission of 1946 who found that in counties 12.6 per cent of the male justices and 7.2 per cent of the female justices attended no sittings during a period of 12 months. In boroughs the figures were 8.7 per cent and 4.2 per cent respectively.[15] It was also found that among those who did attend, women justices did so more regularly than men. Apart from those justices who did not attend their courts at all, the inquiry showed that there were many who sat less often than once a month. This was particularly so in the counties, where more than half the male justices were either permanent absentees or appeared less often than monthly. In boroughs the attendances were more frequent, but this could be accounted for partly by the fact that many magistrates' courts in counties did not sit more often than once a month whereas those in the boroughs were held more frequently, in some instances there being more than one court every day.

The last chapter described the steps which were taken by the Lord Chancellor before 1945 to eliminate ineffective justices and in

---

13.   Justices of the Peace (Size and Chairmanship of Bench) Rules 1950.
14.   See below p. 329.
15.   Cmd. 7463, para. 25. This also gives a table showing the percentage of justices attending their courts from one to more than a hundred occasions in a period of 12 months.

particular to persuade the aged and infirm to transfer to the Supplemental List. On March 1, 1946 Lord Chancellor Jowitt issued a letter to the chairmen of all county and borough advisory committees referring to Lord Chancellor Hailsham's circular of January 1, 1938, drawing attention to the Supplemental List Act of 1941 and explaining what action would be taken to give effect to it.[16] In fact, by the time that the Royal Commission reported in 1948, the Lord Chancellor had found it necessary to resort to his compulsory powers of transfer in only a very few cases. In all others the justice concerned had accepted, sometimes after prolonged pressure, the suggestion that he should transfer voluntarily.

After 1948 the Lord Chancellor's Office took more positive steps to ensure that all justices complied with the undertaking which they gave at the time of their appointment to do a fair share of the work. Advisory committees were required to submit annual reports on the state of their benches, which included a statement of the number of attendances of each justice during the previous 12 months. Where a justice consistently failed to attend without good cause the Lord Chancellor exercised his power to remove him from the commission, but although the Chancellor was entitled, at least in theory, to dismiss a justice without showing cause, his Office invariably gave the reason in such cases as failure by the justice to perform his duties. In 1988 advisory committees were given a discretion to give up to six months leave of absence without referring to the Lord Chancellor.

On a number of occasions from 1950 onwards successive Governments were urged to introduce legislation which would oblige employers to allow employees who were magistrates time off from work to perform their duties. For some time no action was taken for fear that such a law would prejudice the employee's chances of promotion within his firm or that it would make it more difficult for him to find a job if he were unemployed. In 1968, however, such a law was passed under the Labour Government. Under the Employment Protection Act employers were obliged to allow their magistrate employees, and certain others, sufficient time away from their work, but the amount, the occasions and the conditions applied had to be reasonable having regard to a number of factors, including the circumstances of the employer's business and the effect of the absence on the running of the business. The Labour Government secured the passage of this Act thinking that it would make it easier for working people to serve on the commissions. In fact there were many who found the opposite to be the case. When an employee wished to change his job he often found that a new employer was reluctant to

---

16. The letter is set out in full in Appendiz 1, p. 62, to the minutes of evidence taken before the Royal Commission on October 23 and 30, 1946.

accept him because of the statutory obligation to allow him time away from his work.

Where absence was due to chronic ill-health the justice was transferred to the Supplemental List. As we have seen, the Supplemental List was designed primarily as a means of enabling justices, who through age or ill-health were incapable of continuing to perform their duties, to be relieved of the requirement to attend court while remaining on the Commissions of the Peace. This raised the question of the age at which justices should retire from active duty which is discussed in the following paragraphs.

(4) Age of justices
In 1945 many very elderly justices were still on the Active List. In 1947 the Royal Commission found that 65 per cent of all male justices were over the age of 60 and 28 per cent were over 70. At that time no less than 14 Active List justices were 90 years of age or more, one being over 95. The Royal Commission concluded that, on balance, a retiring age of 75 was desirable, and they recommended that it should be made statutory. They recognized (para. 110), however, that the sudden application of a compulsory retiring age for all justices would leave some benches inadequately staffed, and they therefore recommended further that during a transitional period, not exceeding five years from the enactment, the Lord Chancellor should have discretion to continue a justice beyond 75.

We have seen that justices appointed after November 1940 were required to undertake to transfer to the Supplementary List on attaining the age of 75, and that statutory authority was given to the arrangement by the Supplemental List Act 1941. A defect in this Act was that any justice could transfer to the list without the Lord Chancellor's authority merely by instructing the Clerk of the Peace or town clerk, who had custody of the commission, to place his name on the list. A number of justices took this opportunity to avoid their magisterial obligations while retaining the social advantages of the office. This was remedied when the Justices of the Peace Act 1949 implemented the Commission's recommendations. The Act provided (s. 4(5)) that no one might transfer to the Supplemental List on his own application, except with the Lord Chancellor's approval, and also (s. 4(4)(a)) that every justice must transfer to the list on reaching the age of 75 unless he held or had held high judicial office within the meaning of the Appellate Jurisdiction Act 1876.[17] The Commissions's further recommendation that, in order to have enough experienced justices, the Lord Chancellor should have a discretion to retain

17.   In the five years following the 1949 Act some 4,300 justices were placed on the Supplemental List on reaching the age limit.

individuals beyond the retiring age during a five-year period, was also implemented (s. 4(6)). The task of choosing which justices should be reprieved proved to be highly invidious. It exacerbated the feeling of grievance among those who were obliged to retire immediately and it convinced the Lord Chancellor and his staff that the practice should never again be adopted.

There had been a number of people, both in and out of Parliament, who had thought that the age of 75 was too high and that no justices should serve beyond the age of 70 or even lower,[18] but after 1949 no attempt was made to reduce the age until 1968 when Lord Chancellor Gardiner's reforming mind came to the conclusion that judicial office at most levels ought to end at the age of 70. The first opportunity to achieve this reform was a Justices of the Peace Bill which applied only to lay justices and stipendiaries. This Bill, which became the Justices of the Peace Act 1968, accordingly provided (s. 2) that the retiring age for lay justices should be reduced to 70[19] and that a stipendiary magistrate appointed after the passing of the Act should vacate his office at the end of the completed year of service in the course of which he attained the age of 70. As mentioned in ch. IV, it was Lord Gardiner's intention to apply the same limit to Judges - at least to those below Supreme Court level - but the opportunity to do so did not arise before he left office. As we have seen, the discrepancy between stipendiaries and Judges was a source of considerable grievance to the former, and was only partially relieved in 1973 by the Administration of Justice Act which enabled stipendiaries to be extended in office to 72 at the Lord Chancellor's discretion.

It will be noted that, unlike the Act of 1949, that of 1968 did not provide for a transitional period during which the Lord Chancellor might extend justices beyond the statutory retiring age. Instead, in order to avoid a sudden, substantial loss of experienced magistrates, it included arrangements for reducing the limit from 75 to 70 by five annual instalments. The number of justices who were over the age limit at this time was, however, very small when compared with that of 1949, and during the five years following the 1968 Act the additional transfers to the Supplemental List resulting from the reduction of the age limit numbered only 460. Proposals for a further reduction in the retiring age of lay justices in the adult courts continued to be advanced

18. The 1949 Act followed the Royal Commission's recommendation in fixing the age limit at seventy-five, but while the Bill was before Parliament some Members, including several Ministers, thought that it should be lower, and it was agreed that the Bill should be amended in Committee so as to reduce it to seventy. On the day that the amendment was to be moved in the Commons, however, Winston Churchill reached his 75th birthday and no one on either side of the House was prepared to move.
19. If a justice was chairman of his bench when he reached 75 he could remain on the active list until the end of his current year of chairmanship.

from time to time, but they were always defeated on the grounds that a large proportion of the most experienced justices were over the age of 60 and that they had more time to devote to their magisterial duties than younger people.

After 1949 successive Lord Chancellors attempted to reduce the average age of benches by making more appointments from the lower age groups than had been done previously. They were less successful than they hoped because, in the new era, business and the professions allowed little time for citizens to undertake public work, especially in the early stages of a career, and the same applied to young mothers with families. Nevertheless, there was an appreciable increase in the proportion of justices in the younger age groups during the 30 years following the report of the Royal Commission. In 1947 only 12 per cent of justices on the active list were under 50 and 1.3 per cent under 40; in 1977 43.2 per cent were under 50 and 8.9 per cent under 40.

Although there was no statutory limit for first appointments, 21 had long been regarded as the lowest age at which anyone could be placed on a commission. We have seen that in past centuries it was not uncommon for sons of the nobility and of other existing justices to be appointed at or soon after reaching that age. From the end of the Hitler war, the Lord Chancellor was often urged to appoint candidates in their early twenties, but he declined to do so on the ground that they lacked sufficient experience and were not likely to have the confidence of the public. Only in exceptional circumstances were appointments made below the age of 30. During the three decades following the 1949 Act only 24 such appointments were made of whom the youngest was 23.

The Royal Commission made special proposals regarding the ages of justices serving in the juvenile courts. "We regard the question of the appropriate ages of justices sitting in the juvenile courts as one of great importance" (para. 184). They were particularly concerned at the impression that the age of justices might have on the juvenile who came before the courts and also on their parents, and they thought that the ages of juvenile court justices in most parts of the country at that time were too high, though in the metropolitan area it was nearer to what they thought was ideal. The Commission was of the opinion that "the most suitable age for appointment is between 30 and 40 and we recommend that no one, save in exceptional circumstances, should be appointed for the first time to a juvenile court panel when over 50. We further recommend that justices should in every case be required to retire from the panel on attaining the age of 65" (para. 185). The Lord Chancellor agreed with these views and he would have liked to impose a maximum limit of 50 for first appointment to a juvenile panel, as he was empowered to do by rules which are explained below, but he did not take this course for fear that there might not be sufficient justices below that age who were prepared to serve on a panel. He did, however, implement the last of the Royal Commission's recommendations and, under the powers conferred on him by the 1949 Act (s. 14(1)), he imposed a compulsory retiring age of 65 on all juvenile court justices.

Although the Lord Chancellor did not lay down a maximum age for first appointment to the juvenile court panels, he accepted the need to do so for all appointments to the Commissions of the Peace. Here again he would have liked to have placed the limit at fifty, but the increasing difficulty experienced in finding suitably qualified candidates in the lower age groups who were able and willing to give the appreciable amount of time that was required, obliged him to adopt a higher level. In deciding where to set the limit the Lord Chancellor was also faced with another factor, namely the need for justices to be able to serve for a reasonable period before reaching superannuation. New justices needed several years in which to learn their duties, first under the newly established training schemes and later in practical experience in court, before they could be regarded as wholly effective members of the bench. If, at the end of this period, they were close to retiring age the time would have been wasted. In the light of these considerations the Lord Chancellor gave directions to his advisory committees that no candidates submitted to him for appointment should be over 60[20] and that so far as possible those recommended should be well below that age. Very occasionally exceptions were made to this rule, usually in favour of persons who were legally qualified and who had already had experience of the courts.

(5) Occupation and social level

An inquiry carried out by the Royal Commission of 1946-48 indicated that little progress seemed to have been made in implementing the recommendations of the earlier Commission of 1910 that benches should include men of all social classes and of all shades of political opinion, and particularly that "working men with a first-hand knowledge of the conditions of life among their own class should be appointed to the county as well as the borough benches." In 1948 the proportion of serving male justices who were not engaged in earning their income was 30.5 per cent in counties and 24 per cent in boroughs, while those who were paid wages represented 13.9 per cent of the county justices and 17.5 per cent of those in the boroughs. Those who were employers of 10 or more people, or were directors or higher managers in business or industry, formed the largest group accounting

20. Until 1975 the Chancellor was prepared to consider candidates between 60 and 63 if they were exceptionally well qualified.

for 29.6 per cent of county and 31.4 per cent of borough justices. As regards women justices, most were without gainful employment, as would have been expected, but a substantial number were in the professional group.

It was the declared policy of all Lord Chancellors from Lord Jowitt onwards to secure a reasonable social spread (as well as a political balance as mentioned later) and to make each bench a microcosm of the community it was required to serve. This proved to be a far more difficult task than had been expected. Many wage-earners were unwilling to accept appointment and those that did often moved up the social scale and ceased to be remunerated on a wage-earning basis. The problem was particularly acute in rural areas where it was found, to Lord Jowitt's surprise, that very few agricultural workers were willing to accept appointment. The result was that, in spite of efforts made to widen the representation, the justices on the county benches continued to be drawn from the squires and landed gentry with a small component of doctors, teachers and the occasional transport employee. There was also a difficulty experienced in all areas in defining "wage-earner". The Royal Commission took it to mean persons who were paid on a weekly basis, but the proportion of the population who were weekly wage-earners declined steadily from then onwards and large numbers of those who might have been regarded as representative of this class became salaried workers. It was therefore open to some observers to claim that the composition of the benches deteriorated after 1948 in that the proportion of justices drawn from the lowest social class diminished, but this was not the true picture.[21]

The approximate figures compiled in the Lord Chancellor's Office showed that by the end of 1977 the proportion of manual workers on the commissions was 8.2 per cent of the total, but some of these were not paid by the week. Those employed in clerical work accounted for 5.7 per cent, but again some were salary earners and were not paid weekly. At that time, the largest section of the magistracy was composed of the "professional" class of whom the most substantial element, amounting to 12.5 per cent of the total, was drawn from the teaching profession in universities, technical colleges and schools. The medical profession accounted for 10 per cent while lawyers formed only 1.4 per cent and former members of the armed forces 1.1 per cent (serving members of the armed forces and of the police were disqualified from serving).[22] Teachers made a substantial contribution

---

21.   This point is discussed in more detail in *The Changing Image of the Magistracy*, 2nd ed. (1983) pp. 61-64.
22.   Trade union officials were also included in the "professional" class. Figures are not available for these officials who were on the benches in 1947, but in 1952 whole-time trade union officers amounted to 1.2 per cent of the total number of justices and by 1977 this had risen to 2.7 per cent.

to the work of the magistracy and their numbers on the benches would probably have been even greater had it not been for the difficulty which many experienced in being allowed sufficient time by their employers, and also for the fact that, as local authority employees, many were disqualified from hearing cases in which the authority was involved.

The same disqualification also applied to councillors who served as members of local authorities. The Royal Commission had drawn attention to the fact that, when they reported, 37 per cent of the justices in the counties and 33 per cent in the boroughs were members of local authorities, and it was pointed out that such large numbers were undesirable because an authority was frequently a party to proceedings before the court. Accordingly the 1949 Act (s. 13) expressly excluded member of local authorities from acting as members of a court of Quarter Sessions or of a magistrates' court in any proceedings brought by or against the authority or any of its committees or officers. Following this legislation, the Lord Chancellor issued a direction to his advisory committees that no more than one-quarter of the justices in any petty sessional division should be members of any one local authority (excluding parish councils). This led to a substantial reduction in the proportion of councillor justices on benches throughout the country; yet the numbers always remained fairly high. Those who served on local authorities were usually persons who were both interested in public work and who played a prominent part in many local affairs. It was natural therefore that they should attract the attention of the advisory committees when candidates were being chosen.

(6) Political influences
Earlier chapters have shown that party politics played a prominent part in the appointment of Justices of the Peace from the end of the seventeenth century. In spite of the strong views expressed by the Royal Commission of 1910, many appointments continued to be made on political grounds. The advisory committees, which were introduced in accordance with the commission's recommendations, were intended primarily to curb political influence on the appointment of justices, but during the period from 1910 to the appointment of the next Royal Commission in 1946 they clearly failed to achieve this object. This was largely because the committees themselves were overwhelmingly political. Recommendations were often the outcome of party bargaining on the committee, and it was common practice for members to fill vacancies in agreed proportion, each accepting the nominees of the others. The worst example of this was in the county of London where appointments were invariably the result of a political carve-up.

Three member of the 1948 Royal Commission expressed the view, in a dissenting memorandum, that so long as justices were drawn from every social class no regard should be had to political affiliations in the composition of either advisory committees or of benches. The majority of the Royal Commission, however, did not seek to eliminate the consideration of political views when choosing candidates for the bench, but they emphasized the importance of not giving an unfair preponderance to any particular party and of including persons with no known political persuasions.

Almost from the first moment when the Labour Government took office in 1945 the Lord Chancellor, Lord Jowitt, came under pressure from his party, including his Government colleagues, to counteract the preponderance of Conservatives on the commissions by flooding the benches with Labour supporters. Like Lord Loreburn in 1908 he resisted the onslaught, though not quite as dogmatically as his predecessor. As with Loreburn, Jowitt was among the strongest advocates for the appointment of a Royal Commission and, when one was set up in 1946, he looked to it to strengthen his hand. As soon as their Report had been presented he set about proclaiming his policy, and this was explained in a letter to advisory committees which stated:

"The Lord Chancellor cannot emphasize too often or too emphatically that the first and much the most important consideration in the selection and appointment of justices is that the candidates should be personally suitable in point of character, integrity and understanding and should be generally recognized as such by those among whom they live and work. ... Subject to this overriding consideration Lord Jowitt is of opinion that it is impracticable to disregard political affiliations in making appointments. Once an adequate number of suitable persons is available it is of the very greatest importance (a) that they should be drawn from all sections of the community so as to represent a microcosm or cross-section of all shades of opinion and (b) that there should be no overweighting in favour of any one section ... In carrying out the duty entrusted to him by the Crown the Lord Chancellor finds that political affiliations are a convenient guide to follow but this does not imply that he will only appoint persons who are known to be adherents of a particular party. Persons of no known political affiliations or those who are known to be independent of any party will also be appointed."

It was not the policy of Lord Jowitt nor of any of his successors to seek proportional representation any more than it was their aim to achive a precise numerical balance between representatives of each social group. This would have been impossible because the composition of the benches could not have been kept up to date with fluctuations in the electorate. The committees were required therefore to avoid a political imbalance rather than to secure an exact balance, and to ensure that benches did not become overweighted in favour of any one section of the community whether it be political, social or occupational. Each bench was treated as a separate entity and efforts were made to see that in every area the magistracy reflected the social structure of the local population. Even this proved to be more difficult to achieve than had been anticipated. This was due partly to the reluctance of many suitable candidates, especially among the wage-earners as already mentioned, to serve on the commissions; the insistence upon all magistrates performing their full share of the work proved to be a real deterrent. It was also due to the difficulty experienced by advisory committees in finding suitable candidates from some sectors in contrast to the large numbers submitted to them from other quarters. It was routine practice for committees to approach the principal local organizations and inquire whehter they wished to suggest candidates.23 Although most of these bodies were non-political, a very large proportion of the persons they recommended tended to be Conservatives, and it was only the trade unions and the local party headquarters who consistently put forward Labour supporters. The result was that most committees had far more Conservative candidates than they required but a paucity of Labour and practically none from the Liberals. In such circumstances a committee would take the simple course of submitting a predominantly Conservative list, but no Lord Chancellor, whether Labour or Conservative, accepted such a list from a committee without

---

23. The Lord Chancellor's instructions to his advisory committees contained the following direction.

It is the duty of Advisory Committees and subcommittees to find suitable candidates from all sections of the community in their area. Committees should use their own methods of approach, such as inspired articles in the press or press announcements, and they and their members should approach local employers and organizations and invite them to recommend candidates. The following organizations, among others, may be found useful for this purpose:

Athletic Clubs	Medical Practitioners
Clergy and Religious Organizations	Political Parties
Chambers of Trade or Commerce	Professional Organizations
Co-operative Societies	Teachers Organizations
Councils of Social Service	Trade and Labour Councils
Employers Organizations	Trade Union Branches and Organizations
Ex-Service Organizations	Women's Organizations
Friendly Societies	Working Men's Clubs
Industrial and Commercial Firms	

It must be emphasized however that no organization has any right of representation on a Bench.

question, and it was not uncommon for him to refer the list back to the committee with instructions to achieve a better political balance. Even so the Chancellor was often obliged in the end to accept a list which was unduly overweighted in favour of the Conservatives. On other occasions, his insistence upon a wider political spread had the effect of debasing the quality of the bench. Advisory committees who had already devoted much time to preparing their lists, and who received no reward for their services, would take the easy way out and put forward some Labour candidates to satisfy the Chancellor, even though they might not consider them to be entirely suitable; and the opposite sometimes occurred in industrial boroughs where the population was preponderantly Labour.

When new political parties emerged, advisory committees were asked to bear them in mind when submitting candidates. The first Plaid Cymru justices were appointed in Wales in 1972 and the first Social Democrats in 1981.

The result of these practices was that even under Labour Governments there was always a preponderance of Conservative justices on the benches. The only noteworthy difference in practice between Labour and Conservative Chancellors was that the former were more insistent than their Conservative counterparts that committees should find more Labour justices, with the result that the proportion of Labour magistrates was larger in times of Labour administrations. Thus, in 1977, when a Labour Government had held office for three years, the proportions were: Conservatives 34 per cent, Labour 31 per cent, Liberals 14 per cent and "Independent and Not Known" 21 per cent. Six years later, when the Conservatives had been in office for three years, the proportions were: Conservatives 41 per cent, Labour 28; per cent, Liberals 11 per cent, SDP 1 per cent, Plaid Cymru 0.3 per cent, "Independent and Not Known" 18.7 per cent.[24]

Members of Parliament and Political Agents: The predominant position which the Justices of the Peace had held in the Parliaments of earlier centuries was no longer to be found in the twentieth, and Parliamentary matters had ceased to be discussed in Quarter Sessions since 1888. Indeed, the view that politics must be clearly divorced from the administration of justice was emphasized in a rule adopted by the Lord Chancellors from 1946 onwards that Members of the House of Commons, prospective candidates for Parliament, party-political agents and the spouses of any such persons might not serve as justices

---

24.	These figures, for both 1977 and 1983, are taken from the Lord Chancellor's Office records which were based on statements made by justices at the time of their appointment.

in any part of their respective constituency areas.[25] However, a significant number of justices continued to be Members of both Houses. In 1977, seventy-four Members of the House of Commons and 121 Peers in the Lords were Justices of the Peace.

(7) Clergy

We have seen that at the end of the eighteenth century a large proportion of the parish clergy were on the Commissions of the Peace. This era came to an end early in the following century and by the twentieth it was rare for clergymen to be justices. The Lord Chancellor adopted a policy of deliberately excluding a beneficed clergyman, or the minister of any denomination in charge of a church, on the ground that his duty to his flock might conflict with his obligation to the administration of justice. It therefore became the rule that no such person should be appointed unless no other suitable candidate could be found in the locality. This was the position in 1945, but the Royal Commission, when it reported in 1948, commented (para. 138):

"There may be reasons personal to himself, which make a clergyman or other minister particularly suitable for the bench, and if such a man is able and willing to undertake the duties of a magistrate, we think that it would be wrong to treat him as disqualified for appointment by reason of his office."

Soon after the publication of the Report the Lord Chancellor modified his policy and from then onwards the directions issued to advisory committes contained the words:

"Priests and ministers of religion may find that their pastoral duties conflict with the functions of a local magistrate in that their parishoners may appear before the Bench and they may also hear a great deal about cases before they come to the court. Priests and ministers are often fully occupied in their spiritual duties and may well exercise even greater and more valuable influence in the community in which they work if they are not closely associated with the investigation and punishment of crime. If however, a priest or minister appears particularly suitable for the Bench, and if he is able and willing to undertake the duties of a magistrate, he should not be regarded as disqualified from appointment by reason of his office."

25. The Lord Chancellor's directions to advisory committees stated that disqualification applied to "a Member of Parliament, a candidate for election to Parliament who has been formally adopted as a prospective candidate, the secretary of a party constituency organization, a party political agent (whether part-time or whole-time, paid or unpaid, and the spouse of any of these persons, if the area of the Petty Sessional Division for which the candidate is proposed covers any part of the constituency area."

This had no significant effect upon the number of clergy appointed to the commissions, and only a few became justices during the ensuing 40 years.

(8) Ethnic groups

In the course of time the policy of adjusting the composition of benches so as to mirror the social structure of their respective areas gave rise logically to a need to include a proportion of black and coloured justices drawn from the immigrant populations which began to arrive in large numbers after the war. By the 1960s many immigrants were established as permanent residents in certain parts of the country, bringing with them many novel and formidable problems. The Lord Chancellor of the day, Lord Kilmuir, accepted the proposal of his advisers that advisory committees in these localities should be asked to consider the appointment of some of these persons to the bench and, in April 1962, the first immigrant to be appointed a justice was placed on the Nottingham bench.[26] During the following 15 years 78 non-white immigrants, mostly from the West Indies, India and Pakistan, had been appointed to the commissions in many parts of the country. Some were distinguished individuals such as Lord Pitt, who began his life in Grenada, and Sir Roy Marshall, Vice-Chancellor of Hull University, who was born in Barbados. Most of them, however, were faced with problems with which the indigenous white population did not have to deal, and some were unable to withstand the pressures to which they were subjected. They were links between their own communities and the administration of the law, and sometimes found themselves in conflict with their own people. Also, as magistrates, they were obliged to deal with all classes of persons who came before the court, including members of other ethnic groups different from their own, and their knowledge and understanding of these sections of the population was often limited. It was not surprising therefore that in the early years of the new experiment a number found the stress too great and abandoned the office.

By the 1980s the ethnic populations included numbers of adults who had been born in the United Kingdom and were brought up to understand the way of life of the indigenous population, even though they preserved many of the distinctive characteristics of their race and of the countries of their ancestors. Some of these were appointed to the commissions, bringing the total of non-white justices to 455 in

26.   He was Mr E.G. Irons, a West Indian engaged in welfare work.

1986.[27] After 1987 the Lord Chancellor's Department did not monitor the total numbers but they took steps to ensure that in all areas where there were substantial ethnic minorities they were reasonably represented on the local benches. Since then recruitment of justices from these minorities has run ahead (in the equivalent age groups) of the relevant proportion of magistrates.

27. In 1986 a committee established by the National Association for the Care and Resettlement of Offenders (NACRO) issued a report entitled "Black People and the Criminal Justice System" which was critical of the progress made in appointing black persons (meaning Africans, West Indians and Asians) to the bench. Lord Chancellor Hailsham then decided that a national survey should be conducted into the ethnic composition of the magistracy. This was carried out by the Lord Chancellor's Department in consultation with the Office of Population Censuses and Surveys. The results of the survey are shown in the following tables:

Table 1
Black Magistrates serving on January 1, 1987

Age of Appointment	West Indian Guyanese African		Indian Pakistani Bangladeshi		Others		Totals	
	M	F	M	F	M	F	M	F
34 and under	10	10	22	8	1	-	33	18
35 to 44	45	26	85	26	1	1	131	53
45 to 54	63	22	84	22	4	-	151	44
55 and over	10	1	13	1	-	-	23	2
Totals	128	59	204	57	6	1	338	117

Table 2
Period of appointment of black magistrates serving on January 1, 1987

Period	M	F	Total
1962-70	13	2	15
1971-79	86	29	115
1980-86	239	86	325
Total	338	117	455

Table 3
Appointments since 1980

Year	Total Number of Appointments	Number of black magistrates appointed in the year serving on 1.1.87			Black magistrates serving on 1.1.87 shown as % of the total appointed in the year
		M	F	Total	
1980	1298	18	t	23	1.77
1981	1552	25	5	30	1.93
1982	1410	24	11	35	2.48
1983	1576	37	11	48	3.05
1984	1691	41	23	64	3.78
1985	1524	49	13	62	4.07
1986	1379	45	18	63	4.57

(9) Foreign subjects

There is no recorded instance of a foreign national being appointed a Justice of the Peace in England or Wales. The only occasion when the question was considered by the Lord Chancellor was in 1962 when Princess Chula-Chakrabongse of Thailand was recommended by the Cornwall advisory committee for appointment to their county commission. She was an English woman and resided in Cornwall, but she had renounced British nationality and had become a foreign subject on marrying a Thai prince. The Lord Chancellor, Lord Kilmuir, came to the conclusion that an alien was not disqualified from appointment, but he decided nevertheless that as a matter of policy the subject of another country ought not to become a justice because he or she must be assumed to owe allegiance to a foreign power rather than to the United Kingdom. The appearance of such a person on the bench might therefore give rise to a misapprehension in the minds of those who appeared before the court and consequently justice might not manifestly be seen to be done.28

(10) Justices ex officio

In 1945 there were some 2,550 persons who were justices by reason of holding some other office. In the case of counties these were made up of three groups, the first two of which derived their authority from the

---

28. In considering this case the Lord Chancellor and his advisers decided that the law on the matter was as follows. At common law there is no bar on the appointment of aliens as justices. If such a person were to become a justice there seemed to be no reason why he should not take the oath of allegiance so as to enable him to act, though of course this might cause him personal embarrassment in the country of which he was a national. The problem which then arose was how to interpret the Act of Settlement of 1701 and subsequent legislation. The Act of Settlement provided that no person born outside what is now the United Kingdom or HM Dominions, unless born of English parents, should be capable of enjoying any office of trust, whether civil or military. The relevant passage was repealed by the Fourth Schedule to the British Nationality Act 1948, in so far as it was applicable to British subjects, including subjects by naturalization. It followed that the Act of 1700 still applied to a foreign-born alien whose parents were also foreigners. There was nothing in the Act of 1948 which would preserve the position of such an alien who had once been a British subject by naturalization but subsequently renounced British nationality. Appointment to a Commission of the Peace was undoubtedly a civil office of trust. In *R.* v. *de Mierre,* 5 Burrows' Reports, 2989, 98 ER 463, it was held that the office of constable was an office of civil trust. *A fortiori,* the office of magistrate must be such. The consequence was therefore that a foreign-born person who was not for the time being a British subject could not hold a Commission of the Peace. This, however, had no relevance to the case of a British subject by birth, notwithstanding that he or she subsequently acquired another nationality and renounced British citizenship. There was nothing therefore to prevent the appointment of Princess Chula as a justice, notwithstanding that by virtue of her renunciation she had lost her status as a natural-born British subject and became an alien. In reaching their decision the Lord Chancellor and his advisers were aware that Halsbury (3rd ed. vol. 1, p. 506) stated categorically that aliens could not hold office of profit and cited the Act of Settlement. There was no qualification of this statement, however, to cover natural born British subjects who renounced their nationality. It was noted that Davies in *Law Relating to Aliens,* p. 79, suggested that there was no common law bar on aliens and that the Act of Settlement was caused by a wave of anti-Dutch feeling. If this was right, in cases where the Act of Settlement did not bite, an alien was not disqualified, and Halsbury was therefore *pro tanto* inaccurate.

fact that the Commissions of the Peace were directed to them, and the third from various statutes. These three groups were: (1) national figures who included the Lord Chancellor, Privy Counsellors and Judges of the Supreme Court; (2) certain local dignitaries, including the Keeper of the Rolls of the county who was also invariably the Lord Lieutenant; (3) a large number of persons who derived their position from various statutes.[29]

The position in boroughs has been described in vol. I, ch. X, where it was shown that the commission was addressed only to the mayor and to the County Court Judge, but the mayor was also a justice by statute and so too was the immediate past mayor. The precise position varied between different kinds of borough. In county boroughs the mayor was a justice for the borough during his term of office and for 12 months thereafter. In a non-county borough with a separate Commission of the Peace the mayor was both a borough justice and a county justice,[30] while the ex-mayor was a borough justice only. In a non-county borough without a separate commission the same provisions applied but, as the Royal Commission pointed out, the position of the ex-mayor was obscure because he had no authority to try county cases. In practice it was usual for the work in such areas to be divided and for the ex-mayor to sit only to deal with cases arising within the borough.

The Royal Commission was critical of the local government group of justices on the ground that they served for very limited periods and had little chance of gaining much experience. The commission quoted with approval the convincing statement made to them by the County Councils Association that "if any approach is to be made to the ideal that only the most suitable persons are appointed to the Commission of the Peace, then chairmen of county, borough, urban and rural district councils should cease to qualify for admission to the list merely by their assumption of these offices. The qualities which enabled a chairman of a local authority to perform his duties with success are not

---

29.   The Statutory justices *ex officio* numbered nearly 2,000. They were of three kinds, by far the largest group being members of local authorities:

    1. The Archbishop of York and his Chancellor, the Bishop of Durham and his Chancellor, the Bishop of Ely and his Steward (by 27 Henry VIII c. 24, s. 22), the Chancellor, Vice Chancellor and Deputy Vice Chancelor of the University of Oxford (by Charter of Henry VIII and Oxford University (Justices) Act 1886) and the Vice Chancellor of the University of Cambridge (by Municipal Corporations Act 1882, s. 249).
    2. The chairman and deputy chairman of the County of London Sessions, chairmen and deputy chairmen of Quarter Sessions appointed under the Administration of Justice (Miscellaneous Provisions) Act 1938, s. 1(1), recorders of boroughs, stipendiary magistrates, and Metropolitan Police Magistrates. These numbered about 170.
    3. Mayors, ex-mayors, and chairmen of county councils, urban district councils and rural district councils. They numbered about 1,800, but the numbers varied from year to year according to the number of ex-mayors who had been mayor in the previous year.

30.   Local Government Act 1933, ss. 7 & 8.

of necessity those requisite for the office of Justice of the Peace, added to which there is the point that in many areas the office of chairman is a matter of rotation rather than of distinctive merit. In any event, if a chairman of a local authority is suitable for appointment as a Justice of the Peace, the ordinary procedure should suffice to ensure his consideration for that office."

The Royal Commission thought, however, that special considerations applied to the mayor because "a borough commission of the peace is addressed to the mayor" and "mayors have had for centuries the special responsibility for keeping of the peace in the boroughs; that responsibility is ultimately dependent on his position as a justice" (para. 158). The commission therefore recommended that only the chairmen of County Councils and of urban and rural district councils and ex-mayors of boroughs should cease to be justices *ex officio*. The Government were prepared to accept this recommendation but, although it was supported by the County Councils Association, the Association of Municipal Corporations and the rest of the local Government lobby which was strongly represented in the Commons firmly opposed any change, and the Justices of the Peace Act 1949 did no more than remove the ex-mayors from the bench and, as we shall see later, deprived the mayors of the right to take the chair. An amendment to the Bill which would have abolished all local Government *ex officio* justices was moved in the Lords by Lord Merthyr, who had been a member of the Royal Commission, but it was heavily defeated.

It looked as if this would remain the position for all time in spite of the obvious disadvantages of the sytem which had become more apparent in recent years. There were instances of magistrates who were far from being of impeccable character. Lord Merthyr, in his minority Report for the Royal Commission, recalled a mayor who had been convicted 79 times before he became mayor and twice more while he was serving as mayor. In a case such as this the Lord Chancellor could exercise his powers under the Justices of the Peace Act 1906 to disqualify the mayor from sitting, but usually he did not become aware of his shortcomings until it was too late. Even the law-abiding citizens who assumed municipal office were often unable to adopt a judicial approach and treated the court like a council meeting. Notwithstanding these defects the municipal lobby succeeded for twenty years in stifling all attempts to remove them. In 1968, however, Lord Chancellor Gardiner's progressive mind was not deterred by the previous failures. He concluded that all Justices of the Peace *ex officio* were objectionable and he set about securing their extinction. His hand was strengthened by the scheme of compulsory training for newly appointed justices which had been introduced in 1966, as explained below. It was not practicable to apply any form of training to justices *ex officio* because most of them did not serve for sufficiently long periods, and consequently their competence fell still further behind that of justices appointed by name whose training became progressively more effective. Lord Gardiner sought to persuade the Government to introduce legislation abolishing all justices *ex officio,* (including the higher judiciary, and even the Lord Chancellor himself), but at first he was unable to convince his colleagues of the desirability of such a course which they assumed would be unpopular politically. Gardiner was able to show, however, that contrary to general belief, the justices *ex officio* included far more Conservatives than Labour. Not only did those appointed at the head of each commission come within this category but out of a total of 1,470 local authorities, only 364 were Labour-controlled. This enabled him to secure approval of a Bill based on the premise that personal suitability for the office of magistrate should be the sole criterion for appointment to the commissions and that only those who had been personally selected with this object in mind should serve on the bench.

The Justices of the Peace Act 1968[31] provided that, with very few exceptions, no one might become a justice unless appointed to a commission by name. The sole exceptions to this universal rule were recorders, chairmen and deputy chairmen of Quarter Sessions, stipendiary magistrates, the Lord Mayor and aldermen of the City of London and the Commissioner and Assistant Commissioner of Police for the Metropolis.[32] The first four of these groups needed to be justices in order to perform their judicial duties. The other two categories require separate explanation.

We have already seen that the City of London had been in a unique position from early times by virtue of its charters. Even when it was provided in 1848 that courts of summary jurisdiction must consist of not less than two lay justices (save in a few circumstances) or one stipendiary, an exception was made in favour of the Lord Mayor and aldermen of the City, and in 1968 the Lord Mayor and each of the 26 aldermen still sat alone. When Lord Gardiner's Bill was introduced in Parliament its provision for the extinction of justices *ex officio* extended to the City but, as already mentioned, the Corporation and its supporters secured an amendment which preserved the *status quo,* save that s. 1(4) provided for additional justices to be appointed under a commission which might be issued to the City, and under the Second Schedule the powers and jurisdiction of the Lord Mayor and aldermen

---

31.   The provisions of the Act relating to justices *ex officio* were brought into operation on February 1, 1969 by the Justices of the Peace Act 1968 (Commencement No. 1) Order 1968. SI 1968, no. 2035 (c. 31).
32.   All the exceptions apart from those of the Lord Mayor and aldermen of the City of London were set out in sch. 1 to the Act. The position in the City was governed by s. 1(2) and sch. 2.

as justices were assimilated in all respects to those of persons appointed by the commission.

As regards the Commissioners of Police for the Metropolis, although it had long been established that a serving member of a police force must not be a magistrate, the Commissioner and his deputy continued to be exceptions to the rule. This anachronism had survived from the establishment of the first regular police force in London in 1829 when, as we have seen, its control was vested in two justices who were specially appointed for the purpose. These two officers later became Commissioners of Police, but they continued to derive their authority from their appointment as magistrates. In 1968 there was insufficient time to draft the fairly complex legislation required to remove this anomaly, and it was not until the Administration of Justice Act 1973 that the Commissioner and Assistant Commissioner finally ceased to hold magisterial office. It could be said therefore with some justification that the ancient police functions which had been exercised by the Justices of the Peace and by their predecessors, the keepers, from the twelfth century, were preserved in these two officers until the year 1973.

Chairmen of county Quarter Sessions and old-style recorders remained Justices of the Peace *ex officio* until both these offices were abolished under the Courts Act 1971. From then onwards no one except the Lord Mayor and aldermen of the City of London could become justices unless they were appointed to a commission by name or became stipendiary magistrates.

The effect of s. 1 of the 1968 Act was to abolish not only the statutory justices *ex officio* but also those, like the Lord Chancellor himself, to whom the Commissions of the Peace were addressed. Among those who ceased to be justices were Judges of the Supreme Court who, like the magistrates, habitually bound people over to be of good behaviour and to keep the peace. It was generally assumed that this power was derived from their being themselves Justices of the Peace *ex officio* and that when this was abrogated they would cease to be able to perform this useful function. The Act therefore provided (s. 1(7)) that:

"Any court of record having a criminal jurisdiction has, as ancillary to that jurisdiction, the power to bind over to keep the peace, and power to bind over to be of good behaviour, a person who or whose case is before the court, by requiring him to enter into his own recognizances or to find sureties or both, and committing him to prison if he does not comply."

(11) Women as justices
The last chapter showed how women became eligible for judicial

appointment and that the proportion of women to men justices increased during the 60 years after 1920. This continued for a time after 1945 when strenuous efforts were made to increase the number of women on each bench to ensure that there should be at least one present in every juvenile and domestic court, and by 1983 the proportion of women to men had risen to 1 to 1.5. From the mid-1980s, however, the proportion tended to drop slightly. This was not due to any change in policy, although the pressure to find more women justices which was placed on advisory committees by the Lord Chancellor was relaxed when it was thought that ample numbers of women were available to staff all the courts. The drop in relative numbers was the result largely of the fact that the names of far fewer women were submitted to the advisory committees. One of the reasons for this was that in the era following World War II women became involved in careers of their own and in numerous activities outside the home, and in the field of public work there was plenty of scope apart from sitting on the bench - a commitment which became far more exacting than it had been before. Although women were no less interested than previously in magisterial work, a smaller proportion were inclined to seek appointment, and many of those who did so were considered by the advisory committees (all of which included women members) to be less well qualified than some of the male candidates. In spite of this, women played a prominent part in all aspects of magisterial work throughout the period. A great many were chairmen of their benches and a large number played a leading part on departmental committees and in the Magistrates Association.[33]

System of appointment

In 1945 there were still two ways in which a person might become a Justice of the Peace, through appointment to a commission by the Lord Chancellor (or the Chancellor of the Duchy of Lancaster) or by virtue of holding some other office. As we have just seen, the latter method had been eliminated by 1973. The Royal Commission expressed the view that the Lord Chancellor and the Chancellor of the Duchy respectively should remain the Ministers responsible for the appointment of all justices. This remains the position to the present day.[34] As an indication of the importance attached by the Royal

---

33. Lady Ralphs was Deputy Chairman of the Council of the Association from 1979 to 1981 and Chairman from 1981 to 1983. Mrs C.M. Romanes, Mrs J.D.H. Rose and Mrs R.E.R. Thomson all served as Deputy Chairmen of the Council, Mrs Rose becoming chairman in 1990. Many lady members were Chairmen of committees.

34. The Chancellor of the Duchy of Lancaster makes appointments within the counties of Greater Manchester, Merseyside and Lancashire; elsewhere in England and Wales they are made by the Lord Chancellor. As explained in vol. III, ch. III, appointments in Scotland have been made since 1955 by the Secretary of State for Scotland instead of the Lord Chancellor. In Northern Ireland, on the other hand, the Lord Chancellor replaced the Governor as the appointing authority in 1974 (see vol. III, ch. II).

Commission to the appointment of JP's they also recommended that the Lord Chancellor's staff should be increased significantly, and they cited the office of the Director of Public Prosecutions as an indication of what they thought should appertain to that of the Secretary of Commissions. This recommendation was only partially implemented.[35]

The system of appointment by the Lord Chancellor has occasionally been challenged by those who claimed that it was inappropriate in a democratic society. Only once in recent years, however, have proposals to revolutionize the method of appointment been laid before Parliament. In June 1977 Mr Bruce Grocott, Labour Member for Lichfield and Tamworth, was given leave to introduce a Bill in the Commons which provided that District Councils should nominate all those who were to be appointed to the commissions. The councils were to vote openly on the issue so that everyone should know who had been recommended and why certain people had been rejected. Mr Grocott claimed that this would dispel the atmosphere of secrecy in which appointments were then shrouded. For procedural reasons, and because of pressure of time, the introduction of the Bill was not opposed, but it got not further. The viewpoint which it represented had little support, principally because it was thought on both sides of the House that magisterial appointments should be totally divorced from party politics which would inevitably influence local government voting. This continued to be the prevailing view.

Advisory Committees

We have seen that from 1910 the basis of the appointment system had been the advisory committees which were responsible for finding suitable candidates and submitting their names to the Lord Chancellor when vacancies occurred. As the Royal Commission of 1948 pointed out, however, the recommendation of the 1910 Commission that those appointed should represent different views and currents of opinion had been interpreted by successive Lord Chancellors as requiring representation of the main political parties, with the result that the attempt to carry out the 1910 proposals had resulted in advisory committees becoming overwhelmingly political.[36] Those concerned with the appointment of justices had lost sight of the fact that the advisory committee system was supposed to have been introduced for

---

35.　In 1949 the senior staff in the Secretary of Commissions office consisted only of the secretary himself and one Assistant Secretary of Commissions. By 1961 there were three Assistant Secretaries (one of whom was training officer) and also a Deputy Ssecretary of Commissions. In 1989 the post of Secretary of Commissions was combined with that of Deputy Secretary to the Lord Chancellor.

36.　Cmd. 7463 para. 18. The Royal Commission reported that in 1946 the Lord Chancellor's Office had classified the membership of the committees in England and Wales as: Conservatives 35.5 per cent, Labour 30 per cent, Liberal 23.5 per cent and Independent 11 per cent.

the purpose of curbing political influence on the appointment of magistrates. Instead, the committees themselves, which were constituted on a political basis, became purely centres for party bargaining. It became common practice for vacancies on the bench to be filled in an agreed proportion, each party accepting the nominees of the other without questioning their qualifications. Consequently, very few persons who were not active in party politics were even considered, and many of those appointed were not wholly suitable. The committees therefore exacerbated the evil they were supposed to cure.

The 1948 Royal Commission considered the advisory committee system in some detail and took account of various proposals that had been put to them, including the suggestion that committees should be constituted of persons nominated by local bodies which they rejected emphatically. The Commission recommended that the committees should continue to be appointed by the Lord Chancellor and that their membership should remain confidential. They also recommended that, as was then the case, the chairman of a county committee should normally be the Lord Lieutenant (in his capacity as *Custos Rotulorum*) and that in a borough the Lord Chancellor should appoint some suitable person at his discretion.[37] Each committee should have a secretary whose name should be published with a view to publicizing the work of the committee and its accessibility to members of the public who wished to recommend candidates.[38] The Commission had a good deal to say about the composition of advisory committees, which

---

37. The Royal Commission envisaged the possibility of the Lord Chancellor appointing someone other than the Lord Lieutenant as chairman, though there were some who regarded the Lieutenancy as carrying with it the chairmanship *ex officio*. To remove any doubt on the latter point an arrangement was introduced in 1955 whereby each new Lord Lieutenant ws invited by the Lord Chancellor to become chairmen and if he accepted he was formally appointed as such. There were only two instances of Lords Lieutenant not being chairmen of their county committees. The first was in Essex in 1950 where Lord Chancellor Jowitt appointed a justice on his own knowledge of the candidate without consulting the advisory committee, and the Lord Lieutenant, Sir Francis Whitmore, resigned in protest. The other instance was in the county of London where appointments had become dominated by political intrigue, especially since the chairmanship of the Marquess of Crewe. Subsequent Lords Lieutenants had endeavoured to break this influence but without success. Lord Chancellor Gardiner decided to overcome the problem by moving the committee's venue from County Hall to Inner London Sessions and bringing it under the control of members of the higher judiciary. He took the opportunity, when Field Marshall Sir Gerald Templer succeeded Lord Alexander of Tunis as Lord Lieutenant in 1967, of appointing Lord Denning, the Master of the Rolls as chairman - to the considerable annoyance of Sir Gerald.
     In the case of liberties, the chairman of the advisory committee was the Lord Lieutenant of the adjoining county. The Cinque Ports, however, were in a unique position as the office of Lieutenant was exercised by their Lord Warden. It was therefore the Lord Warden who was appointed chairman of the committee. Winston Churchill was chairman while he was Lord Warden after the war.
38. Before this time the secretarial work, such as it was, was often handled by the chairman or by one of the members. In the counties it was done by the Clerk of the Peace, who was usually also Clerk to the Lieutenancy. By the early 1950s every borough also had a secretary who was usually the Clerk to the Justices.

they thought should be small, and about the directions which they should receive in carrying out their duties. It may be convenient to quote in full the summary of those recommendations as set in their Report (para. 348), because these were accepted by the Lord Chancellor and were the basis on which the committees operated thereafter, though as we shall see the good intentions were not entirely fulfilled.

"The first aim should be to appoint as members of such committees judicially-minded people who will recognize that the selection of men and women to sit in judgment on others is a high responsibility, that their duty as members of an advisory committee is to find the men and women who are best qualified for this office, and that in making recommendations to the Lord Chancellor they must subordinate to this all other considerations. Secondly, members of advisory committees should be drawn from different sections of the community, so that as far as possible the advisory committee will represent a cross-section of society - the members being people who have such local knowledge and associations that they can provide or obtain the information which the committee requires to enable it to select from persons in various walks of life those men and women who are best fitted to be justices. Thirdly, the proportion of members of the committee who are appointed because of their affiliation with political parties should be restricted, so that their influence shall not be predominant and that room may be found for other members whose interests and associations lie in other fields than political work. Fourthly, if in any area it is found practicable without including persons chosen because of their affiliation with political parties to constitute an effective committee which will have the requisite local knowledge and the requisite impartiality and freedom from political bias, the Lord Chancellor should feel free to appoint such a committee.

Advisory committees should be given general directions on the carrying out of their duties. These should include the following:

(*a*) No member of the committee should regard himself as the representative of any politcial party, and that it is the duty of each and every member of the committee to be vigilant to prevent the recommendation of any person for appointment or the exclusion of any person from appointment as a justice, on the sole ground that he is a member of a particular party.

(*b*) In appointing justices the paramount consideration is the person's fitness for the discharge of judicial duties.

(*c*) Care must be taken to see that there are persons in the commission representative of various sections of the community.

(*d*) If, after a preliminary selection has been made, it is found that a considerable majority of the proposed new justices are of one political faith, the list should be revised with a view to seeing whether equally good, or better, nominations can be made from among members of other political parties. If the answer is that they cannot, then the original list should stand."

The Royal Commission commented upon the Lord Chancellor's current practice before appointing a political member to a committee of ascertaining from the headquarters of the party concerned whether he was in fact known to be a member of that party. The Commission concluded that the objections to such inquiries outweighed any advantages they might have and recommended that they should cease. This, however, was one of their proposals which the Lord Chancellor did not accept. If it were agreed that there should be members of each committee who were supporters of each of the leading political parties, the Lord Chancellor's Office found from experience that the only way to be sure of achieving this object was to consult party headquarters. If this were not done it was quite common for the person appointed to be subsequently disowned by the party and its supporters. Furthermore, one of the commonest complaints received by the Lord Chancellor regarding the appointment of justices had come from party organizations who claimed that they were being overlooked when appointments were made in a particular area. The Lord Chancellor therefore introduced the rule that he would not accept any recommendation unless it had the support of every member of the committee. Consequently, no party could complain if they had previously confirmed that the committee in question contained one or more of their own members.

The ideal of having a reasonable proportion of "independent" members on each committee proved to be unexpectedly difficult to achieve. This was largely due to the fact that most members of the population, even if they do not tend to share the views of one of the political parties, are assumed to do so by their fellow citizens. The Lord Chancellor found that his well-intentioned efforts to implement the Royal Commission's proposals were thwarted by the attitude of the political members of the committees who claimed that the independent members were in fact supporters of a party opposed to their own and that therefore the committee was overweighted against them. To meet this the Lord Chancellor appointed a number of County Court Judges, and later Circuit Judges, to the borough committees, some of whom became chairmen, but after a time he abandoned his attempts to increase the non-political element on the committees and the proportion of independents remained fairly low. Because of this, although the standard of person appointed to the benches were distinctly higher during the 40 years following the Royal Commission's Report than it had been before, too much emphasis was laid on political considerations and candidates were still drawn from a narrower field than was either necessary or desirable.

Members of advisory committees were appointed on the basis of their involvement in and their knowledge of the local community. Most were JPs; only about 8 per cent had never served as such.

In recommending that all advisory committees should be small, the Royal Commission seem to have regarded six or seven members as sufficient in most cases. At the time when they reported most committees were slightly larger than this but not greatly so.[39]

Membership of advisory committees was regarded as confidential, the object being to protect members from being lobbied. There were instances of members whose identity had become disclosed being subjected to such undue influence and persistent importuning that they felt obliged to resign. Experience also showed that disclosure of the composition of the committee led to dissatisfaction among sections of the local population. It was not practicable to include members of every section of the community, but if this were not done those who were not represented complained. There was, however, no general rule of secrecy imposed by the Lord Chancellor who left the matter to the discretion of each individual committee. The Inner London committee made its membership public from 1970 but few others followed and in the face of growing public criticism Lord Chancellor Mackay took the decision in 1989 that all advisory committees must disclose the names of their members by the end of 1992; the reason for the delay being to give members a chance to opt out. By the end of 1989 the majority of committees had already complied. On the other hand, the Lord Chancellor continued to apply a strict rule that the proceedings of advisory committees were confidential, the principal reason for this being that personal matters which might be embarrassing to a candidate were often disclosed. In support of this confidentiality it was

---

39.   The County of London was exceptional in that its committee had 40 members (37 men and three women) but it was divided into seven sub-committees. Next among the counties came Middlesex with 15 members (13 men and two women), Monmouth with 12 (10 men and two women) and Durham and Oxfordshire with 11 each. Of the boroughs Birmingham was exceptional with 12 members (11 men and one woman) plus the lord mayor and deputy lord mayor *ex officio*. Otherwise no borough committee had more than seven members. In all there were 66 county and 279 borough advisory committees in England and Wales including the Duchy of Lancster.

established in the courts that proceedings of committees were privileged.[40]

In addition to choosing suitable candidates for appointment, advisory committees were also involved in constant scrutiny of the effectiveness of the justices after they had been appointed. They were required to review the magisterial position in their respective areas and to draw the Lord Chancellor's attention to any need for additional appointments when these were required. Each committee submitted an annual report to the Lord Chancellor's office on the state of its benches and on the performance of the justices, including a list of individual attendances.

Until 1972 there was one advisory committee for each area having a separate commission of the peace and for nowhere else. When many commmission areas became larger in consequence of the local government reorganization the advisory committee structure was also altered to bring each commmittee into closer contact with the locality for which it was responsible. Some large urban areas, although they no longer had their own commissions, were given separate advisory committees, and in the non-metropolitan counties a number of sub-committees or area panels were established with the principal duty of discovering and interviewing candidates and submitting their findings to the main committee. In 1989 there were 255 committees and sub-committees in England and Wales, including the Duchy of Lancaster, with a total membership of just over 2,000.

Before the 1960s committees did not interview candidates, partly because it was feared that this would disclose the identity of the members who would become open to lobbying. The result was that on a few occasions a person whose credentials seemed excellent on paper proved to be wholly unsatisfactory when he appeared on the bench. In

---

40.   The first occasion on which a claim of privilege in respect of the proceedings of an advisory committee was considered by the courts was in 1949 in a libel action brought by a Mrs Esther Iwi, a justice on the Hendon bench in Middlesex, against her fellow magistrates (the case and its background are described in *The Changing Image of the Magistracy* 2nd ed., pp. 164-166). The Attorney General, Sir Reginald Manningham-Buller (later Lord Chancellor Dilhorne) appeared on behalf of the Lord Chancellor to claim Crown Privilege for all communications passing between the Lord Chancellor, the Secretary of Commissions, advisory committees and chairmen of benches. He asserted that, in the public interest and to ensure proper administration of justice in magistrates' courts, the contents of such documents ought not to be disclosed and that complete security and immunity should be assured for all persons who volunteered information, or who were asked to give information, to the Lord Chancellor or an advisory committee or to any person acting on his or their behalf. The court upheld the Lord Chancellor's claim and Mrs Iwi was therefore unable to obtain discovery of a number of documents which she considered material to her case. Although the law relating to privilege has been modified since 1949 it is still assumed that all communications between the Lord Chancellor and his advisory committees are protected. This was accepted by the parties in several cases in the 1960s, particularly in view of the decision in another case which was heard in 1958. In *Doubleday* v. *Graham,* between the Clerk to the Justices and the Town Clerk of Hull, which was tried at Leeds Assizes, Paull J., upheld the Lord Chancellor's claim for privilege in similar circumstances.

the late 1960s some committees began, with the Lord Chancellor's approval, to interview those candidates who seemed from their written credentials to be suitable, but before a final decision was reached. The Chancellor made this arrangement compulsory for all committees in 1972. In February 1988 a comprehensive set of notes on interviewing was sent to all advisory committees. It was pointed out that interviewing gave some assurance to the public and to the candidates that all candidates received equal consideration before names were recommended to the Lord Chancellor. The primary purpose of the interview, however, was said to be to assess the candidate's suitability for appointment, which in essence meant establishing whether or not he possessed or had the potential to acquire in sufficient degree the qualities[41] expected of a magistrate. So far as possible every candidate who was not disqualified was to be interviewed, even if he was known personally to one or more members of the committee. The notes contained very detailed advice on how and where the interviews should be conducted, and they also encouraged the introduction of a two-stage interview process. The main purpose of the first interview, which was carried out by two or three members of the committee, was to assess the personal qualities of the candidate, and in particular to determine his intelligence, integrity and motivation. It also provided an opportunity to explain the appointments process and to make sure that the candidate fully understood the commitment required of a magistrate and that he would be able to meet it. Unless it appeared from the first interview that the candidate was unsuitable, he was invited to attend a second interview which was intended to be a test of judicial potential and involved the candidate in being asked to discuss certain set cases which had been sent to him to read in advance of the interview. The interviewing panel for the second interview was rather larger than the first and at least one of those present at the first was required to attend the second. All this placed a substantial, additional

---

41.   The qualities listed in the Lord Chancellor's notes were:

Good reputation.
Personal integrity.
Appearance and manner which on and off the bench will give confidence to all.
Ability to identify and comprehend relevant facts reasonably quickly.
Ability to think logically.
Reasonable powers of expression.
Ability to advance views firmly but tactfully and a readiness to listen and comprehend others' views and modify his own views where it is proper to do so;
Ability to work with others.
Recognition of his own prejudices and a readiness to make due allowance.
Ability to reach a decision reasonably quickly but not prematurely, ie, not before having weighed all relevant evidence and arguments based on it.
Some experience, understanding or knowledge of and sympathy for life outside his own immediate circle of family and work.
Appreciation of the need for the rule of law in society.

burden on those justices who served on the advisory committees. Some small relief was given by bringing in other justices to assist with the interviewing, but the task of the committees by the end of 1989 was formidable, and the great care which they took to discharge this duty was an impressive indication of their dedication to the office of magistrate.

The introduction of the advisory committee system did not curtail the Lord Chancellor's freedom of choice in selection and appointing justices. The committees were not statutory bodies and the Lord Chancellor appointed them at his discretion. They existed merely to assist him in finding suitable candidates and in keeping him informed of the state of each bench. He was under no obligation to accept their recommendations, and it was not uncommon for him to decline to do so.[42] He and he alone was responsible to the Crown and to Parliament for the effectiveness of the system and he therefore retained complete freedom to act as he thought fit.

Removal

We have seen that the circumstances under which justices were removed from the commissions and the frequency with which this occurred varied greatly from one era to another during the earlier history of the office. In the twentieth century there was no question of a justice being dismissed for his political views or because he did not find favour with the Government, but he was far more likely than ever before to be removed for inability to fulfil his obligations or for misconduct.

It has also been mentioned, when considering the age of justices, that in 1949 transfer to the Supplemental List at 75 became compulsory under the Justices of the Peace Act, and that this was reduced to seventy in 1968. The steps taken to remove justices who failed to perform their share of the work have also been noted under the heading *Attendances,* when it was explained that anyone who, without good cause, failed to attend his court at least twenty-six times a year was required to resign. About one per cent of all justices on the Active List were obliged to relinquish their office each year because they were unable to complete the minimum number of attendances, and a further one per cent became residentially disqualified.

There were, however, other circumstances in which a justice's continued presence on the bench was thought to be undesirable. The principles applied by the Lord Chancellor to such cases in the twentieth century have been summarized as follows:

"The Lord Chancellor's approach to all these cases is based on the

42.   This was usually on the ground that the bench was already sufficiently staffed or that the proposed addition would upset the balance. It was extremely rare for him to refuse to appoint a candidate because he did not consider him to be suitable.

hypothesis that the independence of the magistracy must be maintained and that no justice should be removed, suspended or reprimanded except for substantially indisputable cause. Independence requires some tolerance of magisterial behaviour, and conduct which would exclude a person from appointment does not necessarily justify removal if it occurs after he has become a magistrate. The retention on the bench of a few unsatisfactory or ineffective justices is, in the words of the Royal Commission of 1948, 'the price that has to be paid for the principle of security of tenure.' It is in the public interest that judicial independence be preserved and therefore no judge or magistrate is removed from office unless this course is unavoidable in the public interest. When, however, such a situation does arise the reputation of the bench takes precedence over the reputation of the individual justice; the overriding consideration being that public confidence in the administration of justice must be preserved. The test of public confidence has often been the yardstick by which judicial misconduct has been measured during debates in both Houses of Parliament. This means that, although an ineffective justice may be allowed to remain a magistrate if he can be carried by his colleagues without unduly inflaming public opinion, conduct which clearly tends to undermine confidence in the bench will result in disciplinary action."[43]

This policy sometimes seemed to operate harshly on justices who found themselves, through no fault of their own, in a position which was open to criticism, whereas at other times it allowed a justice to remain on the bench in spite of a general feeling that he ought no longer to be there. Even the conviction of a justice for some offence did not always entail his dismissal. In the case of minor breaches of the law, such as exceeding the speed limit when driving a motor car, justices would receive only a reprimand from the Lord Chancellor, although they would be removed if they repeated the offence on several occasions (on the ground that this showed an inclination to break the law). An example has also been given in the last chapter of the removal of a magistrate for failing to apply the law,[44] and in vol. III, ch. I we shall find references to cases where justices in Wales were liable to dismissal for failing to apply the law in cases involving the use of the Welsh language.

The policy adopted in the twentieth century of extending the Commissions of the Peace to include persons from all sections of the

---

43. *The Changing Image of the Magistracy,* 2nd. ed. p. 154. Only the Lord Chancellor (or Chancellor of the Duchy) has power to take disciplinary action against a magistrate. He may reprimand, suspend from sitting for a period or remove a magistrate from the commission, but in every case he will only act for indisputably good cause.
44. Above p. 264.

community, led to a new phenomenon in the creation of a substantial group of magistrates who were in sympathy with those who broke the law in support of what they regarded as a worthy cause. Sympathy for the less fortunate members of the population had been exhibited by justices in previous generations, but they were not prepared to take militant action on behalf of the oppressed. On the contrary, the earlier justices regarded it as their duty to adopt whatever harsh measures might be deemed necessary to quell disturbances and, as we have seen, it was quite common for them to call out the militia or, in earlier times, to appear sword in hand at the head of their own retainers to suppress a riot. By the 1920s, the presence on the commissions of large numbers of trade unionists and wage-earners and of others who were closely associated with them, led to justices becoming actively involved in industrial disputes, including strikes. During the general strike of 1926, several justices who were involved with the strikers in clashes with the police were arrested. They were treated leniently by the Lord Chancellor and, after the strike collapsed, most were allowed to remain on the bench.

By the end of the 1960s these incidents were becoming more numerous. Some justices with socialist views considered it to be their duty to join picket lines, and some were actively involved in organizing demonstrations. Altough those were lawful pursuits they could, and sometimes did, lead to violence. When such cases which did not result in a breach of the law were reported to the Lord Chancellor his usual practice was to point out to the justice concerned the undesirability of the course he had taken and to remind him that if he accepted the office of magistrates he must also accept certain inhibitions on his behaviour. In every such instance the justice either desisted from further action or resigned. It was a different matter if the justice's behaviour led to a breach of the peace. In such cases it was normal for the Lord Chancellor to remove the justice from the bench, although there were occasions when he or she was allowed to remain after giving an undertaking not to participate in such avtivities in future.[45]

45. An example of this occurred in 1969. Mrs Betty Bell, a Hampshire Justice, participated in a demonstration protesting against a proposed increase in the admission fee to a public park in Havant. The police made complaint to the Petersfield justices under the Justices of the Peace Act 1361, asking that Mrs Bell, her husband and four other persons principally involved should be bound over. Complaint was made to the Petersfield bench because Mrs Bell was attached to the Havant bench. The court granted an adjournment for three weeks to all the defendants, but in view of the evidence which had been adduced of a breach of the peace on the previous Sunday, and the probability of similar breaches on the following Sunday, they ordered all the defendants to enter into recognizances (without sureties) to be of good behaviour and to keep the peace until the final hearing of the complaint. Mrs Bell refused to be bound over although she said that she realised the alternative. She and the other defendants were then committed to prison. On appeal the order was revoked on a technical point, but Mrs Bell was suspended by the Lord Chancellor until the matter had been resolved. She subsequently gave the Lord Chancellor an undertaking not to take part in further activities of this kind and she was allowed to remain a magistrate. *The Changing Image of the Magistracy*, p. 159.

The position was less clear where a justice had not been convicted of an offence nor been involved in any reprehensible incident, but was alleged to be unsuitable to hold the office. This might arise from mental or physical incapacity, from his being temperamentally or intellectually unfit to adjudicate or from his gaining a reputation for scandalous conduct. As mentioned above, the removal of a justice in any of these circumstances was always subject to the principle of maintaining the independence of the judiciary. The new advisory committee arrangements and the reforms which were introduced after 1949, combined with a far greater public scrutiny and criticism of all courts of law during this period, ensured that, on the one hand, few if any deficiencies among the magistrates were not brought to the Lord Chancellor's attention, but on the other that the quality of the magistrates themselves and of the justice they administered was greatly improved and that there was a steady reduction in the number of occasions when the Lord Chancellor found himself obliged to take action after inquiry into the conduct of an individual justice or of a bench. As regards the latter, it was not found necessary to hold any further public inquiries after the one at Aberayron in 1946. As to individual justices whose conduct was considered by the Chancellor to be so reprehensible as to warrant dismissal, there were only slightly more than 50 such instances during the 40 years between 1949 and 1989. Those who resigned at the Lord Chancellor's request were more numerous, but even they did not amount to more than one per cent of the total serving at any one time. When considering these figures it should also be borne in mind that it was an easier and more simple matter to remove a lay justice than it was to terminate the appointment of a member of the higher judiciary. The lay justices and provincial stipendiary magistrates still held office at pleasure, whereas the others were governed by strictly worded statutes, and the Judges of the Supreme Court could be removed only by the Sovereign on an address from both Houses of Parliament.[46] It has been noted that some members of the higher judiciary were convicted of driving while under the influence of alcohol but retained their offices, whereas lay justices who committed the same offence were usually dismissed. The very small proportion of lay justices who were removed during the four decades beginning in 1950 is a clear indication that the time when lay benches were encumbered with dead wood, incompetence and improper behaviour was at an end.

The Lord Chancellor's power to remove justices is discussed in Appendix VI.

---

46. For examples of individual cases and for further consideration of this topic see *Ibid.,* pp. 161-165.

Personal liability

We have seen that some attempt was made in the nineteenth century to protect justices against legal action brought against them for acts done in good faith in the course of their duties, but the position remained obscure. The Justices of the Peace Act 1949 (ss. 25 and 26) enabled a magistrates' courts committee to authorize the payment out of local funds of costs and damages awarded against a justice in respect of acts done out of Quarter Sessions, while acts done in Quarter Sessions were covered, at the discretion of the standing joint committee, by the Local Government Act 1888. There were no provisions for dealing with actions against clerks of the peace and justices' clerks. An Inter-Departmental Working Party under the chairmanship of the author was appointed by the Lord Chancellor and the Home Secretary in 1961 to inquire into the arrangements for meeting out of public funds the expenses incurred by justices, Clerks of the Peace and justices' clerks in connexion with legal proceedings brought against them in respect of acts done or words spoken in the execution of their duties, and the costs awarded against them in such circumstances. The question of the legal liability of justices and their clerks was, however, not within the terms of reference. The Working Party recommended that justices and clerks should be entitled to indemnification for acts done in good faith in the execution or intended execution of their duties, that no distinction should be made between judicial and administrative functions and that this protection should extend to stipendiary magistrates, recorders and chairmen and deputy chairmen of Quarter Sessions. The decision whether payment should be made to a justice or clerk was to rest with the magistrates' courts committee, subject to appeal to an authority appointed by the Lord Chancellor. These recommendations were implemented in the Administration of Justice Act 1964 (s. 27). This did not apply, however, to prerogative writs nor to acts done in Quarter Sessions. In such cases the Lord Chancellor was given a discretionary power to defray costs and damages out of public funds (s. 28). The provisions of the 1964 Act were invoked, on average, less than once a year. This was done more often on behalf of a justice than of a clerk, and the outcome was not always in favour of the justice.[47]

In 1974 the justices were much encouraged by the decision of the

---

47. In 1969 the accused in a case which had come before the Welwyn bench applied successfully to the Divisional Court for prerogative orders on the ground that he had not had a fair hearing because of constant interruption and comments by the chairman, Lord Lindgren. The Divisional Court severely criticized the justices and ordered them to pay the costs of the application. The justices asked the Lord Chancellor to exercise his powers under the Acts and to pay the costs amounting to £599. He did so in the case of the other two justices because they were not in a position to restrain their chairman, but he ruled that Lord Lindgren's share should be paid out of his own pocket and not from public funds.

Court of Appeal in *Sirros* v. *Moore* which appeared to place JPs on the same footing as Judges in other courts in so far as personal liability was concerned. The court (Denning M.R., Buckley L.J. and Ormrod L.J.) ruled that all members of the judiciary were protected from actions brought against them in respect of judicial acts, whether within or without their jurisdiction, provided that they honestly believed that they were acting within their jurisdiction. The court was concerned, however, only with an action against a Circuit Judge and therefore their comments, which embraced the lower as well as the higher judiciary, amounted only to obiter dicta in so far as magistrates were concerned. The position of the justices seemed to be strengthened by ss. 44, 45 and 52 of the Justices of the Peace Act 1979, but their feeling of relief was shaken in 1985 when the House of Lords in the case of *In Re McCann*[48] held that members of a juvenile court who made a training school order without first informing the respondent of his right to legal aid had acted without jurisdiction and were therefore subject to civil action. In 1988 the Court of Appeal held the Manchester City justices liable to a rates defaulter for damages at large following his committal to prison on the ground that the justices made insufficient inquiry.[49] The matter was brought to a head in 1989 when a single justice in Worthing was ordered by a Divisional Court to bear the costs, amounting to £3,211.00, because she had failed to give a respondent in a domestic case an opportunity to make representations as to the venue of the hearing.[50] The justice had acted entirely in good

48. 1985 AC 528. The court considered the implications of ss. 44 and 45 of the Justices of the Peace Act 1979 and concluded that although justices might have conducted the trial impeccably, they might nevertheless be liable in damages on the ground of acting in excess of jurisdiction.

49. *R.* v. *Manchester City Justices, ex parte Davies. The Independent*, August 5, 1988. The order of committal to prison had been quashed by Webster, J., on September 22, 1987 on the grounds that the justices had not considered, in accordance with s. 103 of the General Rate Act 1967, whether the ratepayer's failure to pay was due to his culpable neglect. On the issue of damages the Court of Appeal considered whether costs and damages against the justices were limited to one penny under s. 52 of the Justices of the Peace Act 1979 and decided that they were not. O'Connor L.J., confirmed that s. 44 of the 1979 Act protected justices for acts done within their jurisdiction, but that protection was withdrawn by s. 45 for acts done in excess of jurisdiction.

50. *R.* v. *Wareham Justices, ex parte Seldon*. [1988] 1 All E.R. 746, 1 W.L.R. 825. In this case the Wareham justices ordered a husband to pay weekly maintenance for his wife and two children of his marriage. He fell into arrears and enforcement proceedings were instituted. The husband was unemployed and was dependent upon social security, and he therefore applied for a variation order. He was then living in Godstone whereas the wife was still living in Wareham. The arrears enforcement proceedings were alread;y before the Godstone court, and the justice, Mrs A. Scott, before whom the question of the venue of the hearing was placed decided that the variation application should also be heard at Godalming. The procedure was prescribed in r. 41 of the Magistrates' Courts Rules 1981 under which the magistrate had to determine at which magistrates' court "the complaint could more conveniently be dealt with". There was no requirement in the rules that the magistrates should first consult the person who would be defendant to the proceedings. The Divisional Court Judge, McCullough J., held, however, that fairness required that the opportunity should be given to make representations, regardless of the silence of the 1981 rules. He therefore ordered that the question as to where the application should be heard should be reconsidered and that the costs of the proceedings thus far should be borne by the magistrate, Mrs Scott.

faith and in accordance with procedure prescribed by the statutory regulations. She had accepted the legal advice offered by her clerk and had given a decision based on what appeared to be the most convenient solution. The Divisional Court appeared to be oblivious of the previous practice of that court not to make orders against justices unless they had acted reprehensibly. This case aroused considerable misgiving, and Lord Chancellor MacKay, in his presidential address to the Magistrates' Association in October 1989, announced that a Bill would be introduced in the following session which would give protection to justices in such circumstances in future. In the meantime the Worthing justice was indemnified by her magistrates' courts committee.

Allowances for justices

Although the liability of justices for legal costs had not been entirely resolved in their favour by 1989, they were able by then to recoup almost all other expenses which they incurred in the course of their work. This was the outcome of an entirely new approach towards the office of Justice of the Peace which was ancillary to the involvement of a far wider proportion of the population in public work. Previously this work had been done almost exclusively by the more wealthy members of society who could easily afford to defray the cost themselves. The new era of popular participation in all branches of government and administration involved a large number of peole who had formerly been excluded from such activities and who did not have the means to pay out of their own pockets the expenses that were involved. The trend, especially from the end of World War II onwards, was for all those who served as members of county, district and borough councils and on other local government bodies to be granted more and more allowances until virtually all their expenses were defrayed from public funds. In the case of the Justice of the Peace the tradition of unpaid public service did not yield easily to the pressure of the new environment, but in the course of time the justices too were absorbed into the general pattern. As mentioned earlier, pay for justices, which had been introduced in 1388, was formally abolished in 1854, but it had fallen into disuse long before. For a century, the idea of any form of payment, even of allowances, to lay justices was repugnant to the public and to the magistrates alike. Within a few years of the end of the last World War opinions began to change. In 1947 a Local Government Act[51] provided for the payment of expenses to members of local authorities, and in 1948 the Royal Commission on Justices of

51. This implemented the Report of the Committee on Expenses of Members of Local Authorities (1947). Cmd. 7126.

the Peace recommended that justices should be able to recover their expenses incurred in attending courts, but they were firmly opposed to any payment to them for subsistence or for loss of remunerative time. It is interesting that whereas the evidence submitted to the Royal Commission by local authority organizations urged that all the allowances payable under the Local Government Act should be extended to justices, the Magistrates' Association, while in favour of the payment of travelling expenses, thought that it would not be desirable to include payments for loss of remunerative time. The Commission considered the question at some length. They examined the possibility that the lack of remuneration might deprive the public of the services of a considerable number of able and suitable persons, but they concluded that this was not the case. On the other hand, they feared that if justices were to be compensated for loss of time "the prestige of the bench would be diminished", because at least some of the persons so remunerated would become virtually a new class of lay stipendiary magistrate and that "these justices would, we think, be regarded by the public as particularly open to criticism". They therefore recommended that justices should be entitled to travelling expenses and lodging allowances for absence from home overnight, which should include those incurred when attending meetings and training functions, but not for subsistence or loss of remunerative time. The recommendations were implemented in full by the Justices of the Peace Act 1949 (s. 8).

In para. 206 of their Report, the Royal Commission expounded what was still the general accepted view of the office of Justice of the Peace upon which they based their conclusion:

"The Justice of the Peace occupies an unique position. He is not chosen by popular election, but is selected by a Minister of the Crown. His most important duty is to sit in judgment on his fellow-citizens. That duty can never be satisfactorily fulfilled if justices are not respected by the community. The evidence, and our own knowledge and experience, satisfy us that, as a general rule, to which no doubt there have been at times unhappy exceptions, our lay justices have succeeded in retaining the respect of the public and in upholding that dignity which is so indispensable a part of the equipment of any court of law. Their impartiality and independence (again, as a general rule) are taken for granted. We have no doubt that this fortunate result is due in part to the fact that it is generally recognized that the work of the justice involves some self-sacrifice and loss (if only the loss of leisure) and no possibility of gain".

The first four sentences in this paragraph remain true, of course, to the present day, but the attitude of the public, the Government and the justices themselves changed radically during the next forty years in so far as financial assistance was concerned. An amendment which had been moved in 1949 to the Justices of the Peace Bill while it was before the House of Commons and which would have entitled justices to compensation for loss of earnings, received only six votes, but by 1968 there was a *volte-face*. This was due to a number of factors, of which the principal were the feeling in the Labour party that more of their supporters would be willing to serve as magistrates if they were to qualify for a loss-of-earnings allowance and the fact that more and more persons who were engaged in voluntary public work became eligible for reimbursement for financial loss. It was also realized that the Royal Commission's comment that public respect for the justices was due in part to the realization that they performed their duties at some loss to themselves and no possibility of gain was no longer apt, because the vast majority of the public were totally unaware that justices served without pay. The trade unions and the Labour party organizations were particularly vehement in urging an extension of the scope of allowances, and in 1968 the Labour Government included a provision in what became the Justices of the Peace of that year which amended the 1949 Act by providing (s. 4) that justices should also be entitled to a financial loss and loss of earnings allowance.[52] This was interpreted fairly liberally and was taken to include payment for a "babysitter" and a person to look after a shop while the justice was attending court.

In the years that followed there was no evidence to show that these amendments had any effect on the recruitment of justices from the wage-earning section of the community, as the trade unionists had hoped. The latter began therefore to press for the payment of an attendance allowance in addition to other expenses. This was resisted, even by Labour Governments who were convinced that it was unnecessary. Had the proposal been implemented it might have been the end of the lay justice system and led to its replacement by stipendiary magistrates though, as mentioned later, it is unlikely that a sufficient number of lawyers could have been found for a very long time to man all these posts.

Training

It is generally assumed that until the mid-twentieth century Justices of the Peace, like other members of the judiciary, received no training of any kind in the important work which they were required to perform.

---

52. Small changes to meet the growing feeling had been made in 1964 when the Administration of Justice Act (s. 31) amended the 1949 Act by substituting "subsistence" for "lodging" and "accommodation for the night."

Although this had been trued during the previous two hundred years, it was not an altogether accurate description of earlier times. We have seen that for a considerable period many of the gentry who became Justices of the Peace had studied at one of the Inns of Court where they received a good deal of education in the working of the courts, even though most of them did not become legal practitioners. Those who did qualify as lawyers were regarded as a special assset to the bench and were made members of the *Quorum,* whereby their presence enabled the courts to exercise extended jurisdiction. We have also seen that it was customary until the eighteenth century for Assize Judges to disseminate information to the county justices on changes in the law and to advise them on any matters which were causing them difficulty. It is true to say, however, that until the mid-twentieth century there was no systematic training of justices to fit them to perform their duties. There was no suggestion that either a lawyer or a layman needed to be trained in the discipline of being a Judge, and it was generally assumed that no one who was appointed to judicial office required any special instruction or even guidance in his duties. They were deemed to be endowed by nature with the ability to dispense justice.

Although this attitude persisted in respect of the Judges and stipendiary magistrates until the 1960s, a need for lay justices to have some guidance in the performance of their duties began to be recognized 40 years earlier. The first step towards systematic training were taken by the Magistrates' Association when it was founded in 1920. The Association encouraged its members to undertake basic training immediately after appointment, and thereafter to keep up to date with changes in law and procedure. It provided facilities in the form of lectures, conferences and literature. When the Association was granted a Royal Charter in 1962 one of its objects was stated to be to "educate and instruct magistrates in the law, the administration of justice, the treatment of offenders and the best methods of preventing crime." The Association received no assistance from the Government until 1970 when an annual contribution to its training expenses began to be made in a grant from the Lord Chancellor's Department.[53]

For some time the response to the Association's efforts were disappointing and by 1949 the great majority of justices had had no

53.   The grant for the year 1970 was £2,000. In 1977 it was £10,500, which was slightly under one-third of the Association's estimate of the cost of the training services which it provided. In 1982 the grant was £47,860 which was about half the estimated training cost. By 1989 this had risen to £141,506 of which £33,000 was designated to fund the three national training conferences organized by the Association. The rest of the grant was intended to assist the Association's work generally. A significant portion of this went to funding the Association's journal *The Magistrate,* but steps were taken from 1988 onwards to make it self-supporting. The Association claimed consistently that the amount of the grant was not sufficient to enable them to improve their services in the training of the magistracy.

training of any kind, but the Royal Commission drew attention to the importance of the subject, especially in the new era which they expected to develop in the second half of the century. Until then the need for training had certainly not been as great as it later became. The law and procedure which magistrates were required to administer was fairly simple and easy to understand. In the twentieth century, however, and even earlier, successive statutes began to make the magistrates' duties more complex. A wider range of sentencing options with restrictive provisions for their adoption, and entirely new procedures in matrimonial, juvenile and other spheres made it necessary for the justices to receive some instruction before they could be expected to operate effectively. The Royal Commission foresaw that this process would continue and probably accelerate in the years which lay ahead, but quite apart from this they commented that "judicial conduct is not ensured by intellectual ability or even by the possession of a suitable temperament; it is a specialized discipline or technique that has to be learned". They recommended (paras. 88-94) that justices should receive some instruction, particularly in evidence, procedure and on the various courses that were open to them, and that new justices should be given a short manual on their duties. They also recommended that every justice on appointment should give an undertaking to follow a course of instruction and not to adjudicate until he had done so.

Most of the Commission's recommendations regarding training were implemented in the Justices of the Peace Act 1949, which provided that the magistrates' courts committees set up under the Act should make and administer schemes of instruction in accordance with arrangements made by the Lord Chancellor. These provisions were not brought into operation until April 1953, because it was necessary at first to set up the committees and let them settle. Ministerial responsibility for the training of justices was placed by the 1949 Act on the Lord Chancellor alone for the whole of England and Wales, including the Duchy of Lancaster (but not Scotland to which the Act did not apply). This remains the position. The Royal Commission's recommendation that justices should give an undertaking at the time of their appointment to follow a course of instruction was not implemented at that time because it was thought that some well-qualified persons might be deterred from accepting appointment if they were not certain that they would be able to honour the undertaking. It was also thought to be unnecessary, on the ground that if the system of selection operated effectively it should be assumed that those appointed were the kind of people who would do all they could, without additional incentive, to fit themselves for the work. This assumption proved to be correct in so far as most justices were concerned, but exceptions were sufficiently numerous to induce the

Lord Chancellor to introduce a system of undertakings in 1966, as mentioned later.

Before 1953 the Lord Chancellor's Office issued a model scheme to assist magistrates' courts committees in framing their plans for training, and by 1954 almost all committees had either adopted the model scheme or evolved one of their own based closely upon it. The results were varied. While most committees discharged their duties conscientiously and effectively there were some who made little effort to comply with their obligations. At the same time, there were many individual justices who did not avail themselves of the schemes, not so much because they did not wish to do so but because they were unable to attend at the times and places arranged. There was little that the Lord Chancellor could do to improve the situation because there were no sanctions by which the committees could be compelled to operate schemes or individual justices forced to attend them. In any event, it was some time before the Lord Chancellor became apprised of the shortcomings of the arrangements because he had no inspectorate or means of monitoring the schemes and assessing their effectiveness. Soon after the schemes came into operation, however, the Magistrates' Association, in co-operation with the Lord Chancellor's Office, produced a postal course which was designed particularly for those justices who found it difficult to attend courses, and between 1955 and 1965 about 3,000 justices took this course at their own expense. In 1953 the Lord Chancellor's Office also prepared a booklet called *Notes for New Magistrates* based on one previously published by the Magistrates' Association, which was sent to all newly appointed justices. It was fairly elementary, but was intended to initiate the new justices into the ways of the bench. Arrangements were also made from 1953 onwards for justices to visit prisons as part of a training exercise and for them to engage in sentencing conferences.

By 1960 there was good reason to believe that an appreciable number of justices had benefited from the schemes and that the standard of work in the magistrates' courts had risen in consequence of this. It was equally clear that the standard needed to be raised further and that this could not be achieved unless the system of training was also radically improved.

In 1960 there were still many who held the view that no form of training was required - among some this view persists to the present day. This was the opinion held by most of the professional Judges; on the other hand, increasing numbers of the justices themselves were taking a different view. In 1961 some members of the Magistrates' Association began to canvass the proposition that all new justices should be subject to obligatory training. At the Annual General Meeting of the Association in 1962 a resolution was passed by a majority of 4:1 urging "amending legislation to provide a basic form of obligatory training to be completed by newly appointed justices before taking up magisterial duties." This was not accepted by the Lord Chancellor, Lord Kilmuir, and when he left the Woolsack in 1963, Lord Dilhorne who succeeded him was even more convinced that training could serve no useful purpose. The Lord Chancellor's staff, however, had no doubt that arrangements for training needed to be extended on an obligatory basis and that they must be under the direct control of the Chancellor. Lord Dilhorne was gradually persuaded to accept the opinion of his office, and in 1964 he agreed to several novel and productive reforms, all of which were introduced by administrative action.

A National Advisory Council on the Training of Magistrates was appointed under the chairmanship of Sir Carl Aarvold, the Recorder of London, to study all aspects of the training of magistrates and to advise the Lord Chancellor on the preparation of an improved system and on planning for the future. A new post of training officer[54] was established in the office of the Secretary of Commissions and the same individual was appointed secretary to the council. Lord Dilhorne was gratified to find that these arrangements were well received by Parliament and the public.

This was the beginning of a period of development and expansion of systematic training for lay magistrates which was followed consistently thereafter. The needs of the justices in each of their areas of responsibility were studied carefully and a fairly sophisticated system was gradually introduced, but the process had to be governed by the amount of time that the justices were able to give to their work and by the consideration that those suitable for appointment to the bench might be deterred from accepting office by fear that they would not be able to comply with the training requirement.

The National Advisory Council carried out exhaustive inquiries into the working of the existing system and found that newly appointed justices were almost unanimously of the opinion that they needed some form of basic training and many thought that it should be compulsory. The council then prepared a syllabus for the basic training of new justices and also of those newly appointed to juvenile court panels. In both cases instruction was to be carried out in two stages, the first to be completed before the justice adjudicated in court, or served on the panel, and the second within a year of appointment to the bench or the panel. The Government indicated their intention to

54. The first training officer was A.M.F. Webb CMG, QC, a member of the English Bar who had formerly been Attorney-General of Kenya immediately before that country's independence. His three successors have all been justices' clerks. E.R. Horsman OBE (who was later editor of *The Magistrate*) was followed by B.J. Reason, who in turn was followed by Geoffrey Norman (who was by then a JP and had formerly been secretary of the Magistrates' Association).

implement these recommendations in a White Paper published in 1965, and therefore the decision was at last taken to accept the principle of obligatory training, at least for newly appointed justices and those serving in the juvenile courts. (It was subsequently extended to members of domestic court panels). It was decided to recognize the voluntary nature of a justice's service by not imposing compulsory training by statute. Instead, every justice approved for appointment from January 1, 1966 was required to give an undertaking that, if appointed, he would complete a prescribed course within a year and would tender his resignation if, for any reason, he failed to do so. No person who was asked to give this undertaking objected to obligatory training.

The National Advisory Council also produced a comprehensive *Handbook* for new justices which was sent by the Lord Chancellor's Office to every justice on appointment from 1974. This superseded *Notes for New Magistrates.* The *Handbook* was not, however, comprehensive and it contained no guidance on the treatment of offenders. This was remedied by the publication by the Home Office of *The Sentence of the Court,* which was issued by the Lord Chancellor's Office to every newly appointed justice and to Judges and stipendiary magistrates. It had already been published by the Home Office for a number of years following a recommendation by the Streatfeild Committee[55] that there should be a booklet of general information for all sentencers. Whereas the *Handbook* was amended from time to time and kept reasonable up to date, *The Sentence of the Court* was allowed to become outdated, and this constituted a serious defect in the training system.

Training remained localized in accordance with the 1949 Act and responsibility for operating the schemes still rested with the magistrates' courts committees, but each committee was required to appoint a training sub-committee and one or more training officers who conducted the work at ground level. These officers worked under the guidance of manuals and notes prepared by the National Advisory Council and circulated by the Lord Chancellor's Office. Most of the officers were justices' clerks who were a natural choice for the job, and some had organized courses for new justices in their own divisions even before 1948; though employment of clerks in this role was sometimes criticized on the grounds that it left them insufficient time to attend to their traditional duties. There were also some who thought it wrong in principle for a clerk to train his own justices as this might induce them to rely on him implicitly when they were later acting

---

55.   Committee on the Business of the Criminal Courts. Cmnd. 1289 (1961).

judicially.[56] In 1979 a Standing Conference of Training Officers was established to promote, co-ordinate and improve consultation and co-operation between officers.

The work of the National Advisory Council was fruitful, but by 1973 it was considered to have completed the task for which it was appointed and it was disbanded. It was recognized, however, that a body to adivise on training generally and to initiate schemes of instruction was essential, and in 1974 the Council was replaced by a new body with wider terms of reference. This was the National Advisory Committee on the Training of Magistrates whose chairman was Mr Justices Boreham of the Queen's Bench Division of the High Court. The author was appointed vice-chairman and the members included representatives of the Magistrates' Association, magistrates' courts committees, justices' clerks, the Home Office, practising lawyers and teachers. The Committee, which presented an annual report to the Lord Chancellor, formulated policy and produced handbooks for both basic and specialist training, and also manuals for the guidance of those responsible for administering the schemes. A good deal of attention was paid to sentencing and, in 1977, on the committee's advice, the Lord Chancellor informed all magistrates' courts committees that he wished every justice, whatever his length of service might be, to participate in a sentencing exercise at least every two years and preferably every year. The object of this was not only to help justices to acquire sentencing expertise and an understanding of penology, but by bringing together magistrates from a wide area to minimize disparity in the level of sentences imposed by different justices and different benches.

The committee's terms of reference covered both the training of newly appointed justices and also the provision of refresher training for experienced magistrates. Some members of the committee saw objection to any form of obligatory refresher training. They feared that justices would resent any compulsion beyond the stage of basic training and that this would deter still more from accepting appointment. There was the further fear that the magistrates' courts committees and training officers would not be able to undertake the additional burden of monitoring the system. Again, there was the question what should be done with senior justices who were unable to follow the training but whose removal would leave their benches denuded of some of their most experienced members. The Lord Chancellor and his staff shared these doubts about the validity of obligatory refresher training and for some time they were convinced that the difficulties outweighed the

---

56. By 1966 universities and other centres of higher education came to play an increasing role in magisterial training. Some organized courses of their own for justices and some provided the venue for conferences and exercises run by the national training authorities.

advantages, but they were persuaded to change their minds by two bodies who would be most closely affected by the introduction of such a scheme. Both the central council of magistrates' courts committees which represented the training authorities and the Magistrates' Association, which spoke on behalf of most of those justices who would be affected, urged the National Advisory Committee to advise the Lord Chancellor to introduce obligatory courses for all magistrates at regular intervals throughout their service on the bench. The Justices' Clerks Society, upon whose members the administration of the proposed courses would mainly fall, remained sceptical for a time, but by the end of 1977 they had come to accept what seemed inevitable, provided that they received better remuneration for their services. After consulting all other interested bodies, the Advisory Committee recommended to the Lord Chancellor that every justice appointed after January 1, 1979 should be required, in addition to basic training, to undertake to attend approved training totalling not less than 12 hours every three years. It was not suggested therefore that those who were already serving on the commissions should suddenly be subjected to a new obligation, but that the scheme should apply only to those who could see what was likely to face them before they agreed to accept appointment. In spite of this, the Lord Chancellor was at first reluctant to accept the recommendation for fear that it would lead to the loss of many potentially good candidates. He was persuaded to agree by the discovery that the great majority of justices already underwent as much voluntary refresher training as could reasonably be expected of them, and therefore the introduction of compulsory further training would not add to their burden; while, on the other hand, about twenty per cent of all justices never attended anything beyond their court sittings once they had completed their basic training. Clearly, the only people who might find compulsory further training particularly irksome were the more ineffective justices. The Lord Chancellor therefore directed that obligatory refresher training as proposed by the Advisory Committee should be introduced for all justices on or after January 1, 1980.

The provisions of the 1949 Act were re-enacted in the Justices of the Peace Act 1979,[57] but latent defects in the system were already apparent. It was based on localization, on the ground that local conditions varied so greatly that centralized administration would be impossible, and also that it was wrong in principle for the executive in the form of the Lord Chancellor or the Home Secretary to be

---

57.   This also enabled the Home Secretary to provide courses of instruction for justices' clerks and their staffs. Justices in the Inner London area were governed by the Administration of Justice Act 1964, s. 16(2).

concerned in directing those holding judicial office.[58] It was for this reason that the statutes placed responsibility for training on the magistrates' courts committees, financed by the local authorities, and gave the Lord Chancellor only a supervisory role which did not enable him to compel the committees or the local authorities to fulfil their duties. In 1973 the Administration of Justice Act (s .3(2)) provided that where a magistrates' courts committee did not administer courses of instruction to the Lord Chancellor's satisfaction he might intervene to make good the default and to provide additional training himself out of public funds. He might recover the cost from the committee.

A highly significant development which occurred in the 1970s and which had considerable relevance to the future of magisterial training, was a total change of perspective regarding the training of professional Judges. In a short space of time the abhorrence which all concerned had previously shown to such a concept was abandoned and, although the expression "training" remained unacceptable on the ground that the independence of the judiciary would be undermined if they were told what they should do, it was agreed that some degree of judicial education was desirable.[59]

In 1975 the Lord Chancellor, jointly with the Lord Chief Justice and the Home Secretary, appointed a Working Party under the chairmanship of Lord Justice Bridge[60] to study the need for training and information among those engaged in sentencing offenders. The Working Party concluded that the existing facilities were too restricted in scale and availability, and in April 1976 they issued a consultative paper embodying provisional proposals which included a three to four week initial training course which all new Judges were to be required to attend on their appointment As was to be expected, these proposals met with strong opposition, especially from the judiciary, and the Working Party revised their proposals in a final report which they published in April 1978. This included the recommendation that all newly appointed full-time Judges and stipendiary magistrates should be required to attend an initial study programme which, for those with previous judicial experience, was to last for one week and for the

---

58. The second of these notions was mistaken because it contemplated the Lord Chancellor solely in his executive capacity and ignored the fact he was also head of the judiciary and already exercised direct supervision over Judges and magistrates through his power of removal, a duty which he traditionally exercised in a judicial manner.

59. Among the earliest manifestation of the changing approach to judicial training was a controversial report entitled *The Judiciary* which was published in 1972 by a sub-committee of *Justice* (the British Section of the International Commission of Jurists). This report recommended that a Judge should receive training for a period of three to six months after appointment and should be required to visit a variety of penal institutions. The sub-committee also thought that there was "very considerable need for some sort of judicial staff college, training centre or judicial institute" where courses for Judges, magistrates and members of administrative tribunals could be held.

60. In 1980 be became Lord Bridge of Harwich, a Lord of Appeal in Ordinary.

others two weeks. They were also to be required to attend continuing study programmes of not more than one week's duration, initially after two years from appointment and thereafter every five years. The scheme was to be administered by a new body to be called the Judicial Studies Board. The title was the outcome of an exercise in semantics which was undertaken by the Working Party with a view to avoiding the objection that "training" provided the means of influencing or conditioning the mind of the trainee and could constitute a threat to judicial independence. The fact remained, however, that whatever view may be held on this subject, the proposed arrangements did amount to what most people would regard as training. Moreover, the expression training had been the term invariably used in statutes relating to Justices of the Peace.

The Studies Board was to have a salaried director and a secretariat provided by the Lord Chancellor's Department.[61] It was to have responsibility for all judicial studies and was to report to the Lord Chancellor, the Lord Chief Justice and the Home Secretary. The Working Party's recommendations were accepted and a Judicial Studies Board was appointed in 1979 with Mr Justice Watkins, V.C. (later Lord Justice Watkins) as its first chairman.

The significance of these developments for the Justices of the Peace was that much of what was contained in the Bridge Report was relevant also to the training of lay magistrates and that, shortly after the Judicial Studies Board was set up, the National Advisory Committee on the Training of Magistrates was disbanded and responsibility for the training of justices was transferred to the new body. In October 1985 a magisterial committee was added to the Judicial Studies Board and was charged with the general supervision of all magisterial training and also with formulating the principles on which this should be based. The committee was under the chairmanship of Judge Stuart-White and was composed of two Justices of the Peace (one of whom was an academic lawyer), three justices' clerks and representatives of the Lord Chancellor's Department and the Home Office.

It was left to the magistrates' courts committees to organize specific training programmes as required by the 1979 Act, but the magisterial committee had authority to devise and recommend additional training at national level if it thought fit. Since then there have been many notable advances. There has been further improvement in the programmes produced by the sub-committees of the magistrates' courts committees[62] and administered by the training officers, while

61.   For most purposes the term "Lord Chancellor's Department" replaced "Lord Chancellor's Office" after the Courts Act 1971.
62.   The central council of magistrates' courts committees set up a permanent Law, Procedure and Training Committee as a forum for discussion of training issues.

the Magistrates' Association has shown that it can continue to make a valuable contribution. Perhaps the most noticeable improvement has been an expansion in the range and content of the course included in the programmes, especially those on chairmanship, on ethnic minorities, on magistrates and the media and on the work of the training officers.[63]

For some time before the establishment of the Studies Board the importance of chairmanship in the magistrates' courts had been recognized and special courses had been arranged for them. The last policy decision taken by the National Advisory Committee was to support the introduction of training packs, particularly on chairmanship. Special short chairmanship courses began to be held in 1985 and by 1989 there had been 14 such courses which, in the latter year, were attended by 90 newly elected chairmen. A particularly successful bench chairmanship course was held at Madingley Hall in Cambridgeshire in November 1989.

An entirely novel development was the introduction of training for justices in ethnic minority cultures. This began with a seminar in June 1987 organized by the magisterial committee of the Judicial Studies Board, though courses on this subject had previously been arranged locally for the justices in certain areas. It was agreed that justices needed help in understanding and in dealing with Africans, Asians and Caribbeans who appeared in their courts. Emphasis was therefore placed on racial and human awareness training.

The magisterial committee also issued cards and guidance on verdict, sentencing, mode of trial, adjournment, remand and maintenance in domestic cases. It also inquired into and issued guidance on monitoring the effectiveness of schemes, particularly in terms of the competence of training officers and tutors. In 1986 the Lord Chancellor approved the magisterial committee's recommendation that members of juvenile and domestic court panels should receive twelve hours further training in each three-year period.

Sometimes the initiative was taken by the Magistrates' Association or the Justices' Clerks' Society. In 1989 both these bodies assisted the Lord Chancellor in preparing guidance to magistrates on their relationship with the media, which was disseminated in March. The *Handbook* which the Lord Chancellor's Office began to send to every justice on appointment from 1974, remained in use, but although it was subject to periodical revision it sometimes tended to get out of date.

An important decision was taken in 1986 when Lord Chancellor Hailsham directed that it was not appropriate for training or for any

---

63. The magisterial committee of the Studies Board was well aware of the importance of training those who were called upon to train the justices. From 1974 particular attention had been given to training the trainers and small groups of justices' clerks and other staff from the courts involved in training attended courses for this purpose at Homerton.

other purpose for magistrates to accompany police officers carrying out operational duties. Until then it had not been uncommon for justices to visit police stations or to accompany officers in squad cars or at football matches or when performing other duties, with a view to studying their work. The Lord Chancellor, however, took the view that the independence of the courts might well be undermined if it were known that magistrates went to the police for some form of instruction. He made the further point that magistrates might use what they observed on such occasions in substitution for or in addition to the evidence presented in actual cases before them. On the other hand, the Lord Chancellor considered it to be proper for police officers to be invited to demonstrate their equipment or to participate in discussion of topics on which they had special knowledge and experience.[64]

The objectives of training policy remained basically the same as they had been since 1949. No attempt was made to transform lay magistrates into lawyers. Law and procedure were matters for the clerk, though a general knowledge of the rules of procedure were considered essential for chairmen and a distinct advantage for other members of the court.

The great advances that were made in magisterial training in a space of 25 years were impressive, and the resulting improvement in all aspects of the justices' work was considerable. There had been a steady advance since 1964 in the ability of magistrates to perform their duties, but this was particularly noticeable during the 1980s. Training sub-committees of the magistrates' courts committees provided well-planned, balanced training programmes and training officers became far better organized and qualified for the work. The Lord Chancellor's training officer and his department applied an active and progressive policy, while the magisterial committee of the Judicial Studies Board, though concerned mainly with principles and general supervision, exercised a stimulating influence.[65] The prospect for the future appeared encouraging, though subject to the perpetual problem presented by the limited amount of time available to both trainees and trainers (who include many senior justices as well as clerks). The magisterial committee made it clear that it was not its intention that there should be any increase in numbers of hours of training, though it is not easy to see how the one can be achieved without the other. Efforts to do so in the late '80s were focused on an extension of "training on the job," so that as far as possible the time spent by a justice on training was also occupied in sitting on his bench. The Lord

64. LCD Circular MCC (86) 4. Confirmed in 1988 by LCD Circular MCC (88) 6.
65. The rapid changes and developments which occurred in the training of justices were recorded in the annual reports of the Lord Chancellor's training officer which were issued by the Department from 1986/87 onwards.

Chancellor himself indicated that he was sensitive to the fact that justices are volunteers, and that he would call a halt if he believed that the burden of training was becoming more than they could be expected to bear. The aim was not more training, but better training. The justices, for their part, showed a keen desire to improve their ability to meet the challenge of the new era, and most were prepared to devote a commendable amount of time to acquiring and maintaining the essential expertise.

Although the improvements which have been described in the selection of candidates for the bench, in the elimination of those who were ineffective and in the procedure and administration of the courts have all done much to enable the lay justice system to meet the challenge of the modern era, none has been of greater significance than the advanced system of training which now goes far beyond the merely informative stage and which assists the justices, in the course of discussion and practical exercises as well as lectures, to identify and to understand the innumerable facets of their work. Had it not been for this addition to the reforms of the post-war period, the survival of the Justices of the Peace as a serious institution would be far more uncertain than it is.

This chapter has been devoted to a description of the Justices of the Peace themselves and of the various influences to which they were subjected during the forty years from 1949. The next two chapters will describe their duties and the environment in which they performed them during the same period.

CHAPTER VIII

1945 - 1989 A NEW CHALLENGE
PART II - THE JUSTICES' CRIMINAL COURTS

Criminal jurisdiction - Quarter Sessions and the Crown Court - Petty Sessions - Practice and procedure - The treatment of offenders - Juvenile Courts

AFTER 1945 THE JUSTICES OF THE PEACE continued to exercise criminal and civil jurisdiction and to perform certain administrative functions as they had done before the war. The civil business, which consisted mostly of family matters, was conducted in special courts, and so too was that connected with juveniles. Criminal cases, which accounted for by far the largest part of their work, were dealt with at Petty Sessions and at Quarter Sessions, until the latter were superseded by the Crown Court in 1972. This chapter describes those of the justices' courts which exercised criminal jurisdiction. Chapter IX will cover the remainder of the justices' duties and the courts, committees and other surroundings in which they were carried out.

The Criminal Courts in 1945

In 1945 there were three levels of criminal courts of first instance, as there had been since the Middle Ages. At the highest level was the criminal side of Assizes; below that were Quarter Sessions, and at the lowest level were Petty Sessions where almost all criminal cases were started and where about 98 per cent of them were disposed of entirely. Of the few that remained, the less serious were normally committed to Quarter Sessions and the most serious to Assizes. Assizes and Quarter Sessions both sat with juries and the procedures were almost identical. There were no juries at Petty Sessions where the Justices of the Peace combined the roles of jury and Judge by deciding both verdict and sentence.

Quarter Sessions and the Crown Court

Committals from the magistrates' courts in England and Wales continued for a quarter of a century after World War II to lie either to Assizes or to county or borough Quarter Sessions. Quarter Sessions were still organized on a county and borough basis and, although they were obliged to sit at least four times a year as they had been since 1362, they were expected to sit as often and for as long as was necessary to deal with the business. In fact, most of the county sessions in 1945 still sat only four times a year and 38 of them did not average more than three days at a time.[1] Even the "whole-time" sessions in London sat on only 168 days. Quarter Sessions remained essentially part-time courts, and although steps were taken during this period to improve their performance, this was always subject to a policy of retaining the traditional pattern. Not until 1970 was a final decision taken to introduce an entirely new structure.

In 1945 the work of Quarter Sessions was basically the same as it had been during the first half of the century. It consisted mainly in trying indictable offences, hearing appeals against either conviction or sentence from the magistrates' courts and hearing rating, bastardy and licensing[2] appeals. An appeal to Quarter Sessions might be against conviction or sentence, and in the latter case an appeal lay even if the appellant had pleaded guilty or admitted the truth of the information. On an appeal from Petty Sessions, Quarter Sessions might confirm, reverse or vary the decision of the court below, or remit the matter with their opinion to the lower court. They might also award any punishment whether more or less severe than that awarded by the magistrates.[3] In a borough the recorder heard appeals alone (except for appeals from juvenile courts when two justices had to sit with the recorder as assessors under the Children and Young Persons Act 1963), while in counties the appellate work of Quarter Sessions was delegated to a standing committee appointed annually by the sessions, and each appeal was heard by not less than three nor more than 12 members of the committee.[4]

The extent of Quarter Sessions' jurisdiction at first instance depended upon whether or not the chairman was legally qualified in accordance with s. 1 of the Administration of Justice (Miscellaneous Provisions) Act 1938, as described earlier. Whereas in boroughs the recorder sat alone, there was no limit on the number of justices who could sit for trials at county Quarter Sessions, although two were sufficient to form a quorum. As there were more than 300 justices on

1. Twenty-two sat for 10 days or less, and the total number of sitting days for all Quarter Sessions in England and Wales was 1,302. This included the three "whole-time" sessions in London (168 days), Middlesex (62 days) and Lancashire (55 days).
2. Licensing (Consolidation) Act 1910, under which Quarter Sessions acted as compensation and confirming authority. County Quarter Sessions performed these functions through committees appointed under s. 6 of the Act.
3. Summary Jurisdiction (Appeals) Act 1933, s. 1(1)(vii) and (viii).
4. *Ibid.*, s. 7(3).

some county commissions[5] there was a potential risk of it becoming impossible to accommodate them all, but in practice only those who felt so inclined attended. Even so, it was not uncommon for as many as 40 to crowd on to the bench, presenting an undignified scene and causing considerable delay when decisions had to be taken. Delays were not, however, as great as might be assumed because the workload was not heavy and it was customary to commit to Assizes cases which were expected to last for more than a day. Nevertheless, the practice was clearly unsatisfactory and the Royal Commission of 1948 recommended that not more than nine justices, including the chairman, should adjudicate at Quarter Sessions. This was implemented in 1950 by rules made by the Lord Chancellor under the Justices of the Peace Act 1949 (s. 13(1)).[6] This had no noticeable effect on the number of justices attending Quarter Sessions even though they could not longer all adjudicate, the reason probably being that they wished to take part in the administrative meetings for which there was no limit, and they also enjoyed the social side of the sessions which were still a meeting place for the county élite who gathered convivially over lunch provided by the local authority.

The chairman of Quarter Sessions: Not until 1951 did all county Quarter Sessions have a legal chairman appointed under the 1938 Act,[7] and by then there were only seven without a legally qualified deputy chairman. As we have seen, the "legally-qualified" chairmen under the Act included not only persons appointed by the Crown but also those who held or had held high judicial office and were elected chairmen or deputy chairmen by Quarter Sessions. This latter course was followed frequently in counties which had an eminent member of the judiciary among their residents. The sessions found it gratifying to have a distinguished Judge as their chairman and they usually derived some benefit from the guidance he was able to give them. When the Royal Commission reported in 1948 there were 31 chairmen and 26 deputy chairmen who held office under the Act.[8] This practice remained the same up to the time when Quarter Sessions, and with them their chairmen, were abolished in 1971.

Apart from licensing, and a few insignificant tasks, Quarter Sessions had only a criminal jurisdiction. The lower level of civil court was the

---

5. For numbers on all commissions see Appenix II.
6. Justices of the Peace (Size and Chairmanship of Bench) Rules 1950.
7. As late as 1947 there were still three counties without legally qualified chairmen; Brecon, Denbigh and Huntingdon.
8. Five were High Court Judges, one an official referee, two were recorders and 18 County Court Judges. Later, some appointments were of even higher standing. As mentioned earlier, Lord Parker, when Lord Chief Justice, became chairman of Staffordshire Quarter Sessions and Lord Dilhorne, after ceasing to be Lord Chancellor in 1964, sat as deputy chairman of Northamptonshire sessions.

county court which, as mentioned earlier, was established in 1848. Those who adjudicated in the County Court had the title of judge, but until a short time before Quarter Sessions were abolished their chairmen enjoyed no such distinction. This was probably due to a large extent to the unique character of the office of chairman which was not thought to require further enhancement. It may also have been due to the part-time nature of the appointment; all County Court Judges served on a whole-time basis. The latter consideration came to the fore after whole-time chairmanships were established in London, Lancashire and Middlesex and were faced with a rising workload. Proposals that they should be given the same style as County Court Judges met with general support, especially as it was hoped that the enhanced status would encourage abler applicants to seek appointment. At that time, those who were sufficiently attracted by the posts to give up their legal practices were not considered to be of the standing required to staff the second tier criminal courts which, it was hoped, would in future relieve much of the pressure on Assizes. It was not, however, until 1969 that The Queen declared that every salaried, whole-time chairman and deputy chairman of Quarter Sessions should "be called, known and addressed by the style and title of "His Honour" prefixed to the word "Judge" before his name."[9]

Borough recorders: As in the counties, borough Quarter Sessions in the first half of the twentieth century operated on a part-time basis, except in the City of London which had a whole-time recorder who exercised the jurisdiction of a Commissioner of Assize. The latter arrangement was extended to Liverpool and Manchester by the Criminal Justice Administration Act 1956. Apart from London, the recorders of all other boroughs had been appointed by the Crown since the Municipal Corporations Act 1835. By custom this was done on the recommendation of the Home Secretary, but in 1949 the Justices of the Peace Act (s. 39) transferred this responsibility to the Lord Chancellor.[10] Recorders held office during good behaviour until the Criminal Justice Act 1956 (s. 13(2)) enabled the Lord Chancellor to dismiss a recorder for inability as well as misbehaviour, but this

9. Warrant under the Royal Sign Manual, dated July 31, 1969 and published in the *London Gazette* on August 1. On the same date the title was also conferred on the additional Judges of the Central Criminal Court.
10. Section 39(1) of the Justices of the Peace Act 1949 made the Lord Chancellor the authority for the appointment of a recorder under s. 163 of the Municipal Corporations Act 1882 and of a paid chairman or deputy chairman of the County of London Quarter Sessions under the Local Government Act 1988. Section 39(2) of the 1949 Act also transferred from the Home Secretary to the Lord Chancellor responsibility for approving the appointment of an assistant recorder under s. 168(6) of the Municipal Corporations Act 1882.

power was never exercised.[11]

The 1956 Act also provided (s. 13(1)) that a recorder should vacate his office at the end of the completed year of service in the course of which he attained the age of 72, but that the Lord Chancellor might extend this to 75 if he considered it to be in the public interest to do so.

Jurisdiction: Cases could be committed for trial at either the county or the borough Quarter Sessions in the area. In practice far more came before the county sessions because the recorders, who fixed the dates of their own sittings, usually arranged them shortly after those of the county when little work would be left. Apart from this there were some boroughs, mainly small ones, which attracted very little work and during the first part of the century there was a growing feeling that those Quarter Sessions which were unproductive should be abolished. As already mentioned, this objective was pursued in the Justices of the Peace Act 1949 which provided for the abolition of all recorderships serving a population of less than 20,000.

The volume of criminal business coming before the courts at all levels increased rapidly from the 1950s[12] and the old part-time system which still operated in most areas was proving to be inadequate in spite of the attempts which had been made to patch and rejuvenate it. As mentioned earlier, the Assize system had existed for 800 years from the reign of Henry II, and Quarter Sessions from the fourteenth century. The Lord Chancellor, Lord Gardiner, commented that it had continued to be fairly adequate in the days of the state coach but was wholly unacceptable in the twentieth century. In 1961 a Committee on the Business of the Criminal Courts under the chairmanship of Lord Streatfeild[13] expressed the view that the time between committal and trial should be not more than eight weeks, but a survey by a Home Office unit in the previous year had shown that, whereas courts which were in continuous session like the Crown Courts at Liverpool and Manchester, disposed of the bulk of cases within this time, Assizes and part-time Quarter Sessions took four months or more.

An attempt to relieve pressure on Assize was made in the Criminal

11. There were several occasions when a recorder's conduct did not meet with the Lord Chancellor's approval but where his behaviour was not considered to amount to inability or misbehaviour within the meaning of the Act. In most of these cases the recorder had imposed sentences which were thought to be too severe or too lenient. Although it was not open to the Lord Chancellor to direct recorders on the level of penalties they imposed, successive Chancellors considered it their duty to draw the matter to the recorder's attention and to advise them to change their policy. During the 20 years prior to 1972, four recorders who followed a consistent course of gross leniency were sent for by the Lord Chancellor and each responded, at least to some extent, to the advice he received.

12. The Royal Commission on Assizes and Quarter Sessions (1969) (Cmnd 4153, Appx. 5) found that between 1957 and 1967 the number of persons for trial on criminal charges at Quarter Sessions and Assizes rose by 32 per cent, the number sentenced by these courts after summary conviction by 258 per cent and the numbers appealing after summary conviction by 317 per cent.

13. Cmnd 1289.

Justice Administration Act 1962 which extended further the jurisdiction of Quarter Sessions. This increased the number of those sessions which sat on virtually a whole-time basis, but it would have led to serious difficulty in securing the presence of a sufficient number of justices throughout every trial. This problem was foreseen and was dealt with by a provision in the Act under which legally qualified chairman or deputy chairman might sit alone if justices were not available. These measures were not sufficient, however, to stem the rising tide of arrears which was accelerated by increasing civil work at Assizes. In 1966 a Royal Commission was appointed, under the chairmanship of Lord Beeching, to inquire into the arrangements for the administration of justice at Assizes and Quarter Sessions in England and Wales outside Greater London, and to report what reforms should be made for the more convenient, economic and efficient disposal of civil and criminal business. They were also to consider and report on the effect that their proposed reforms would have on the High Court, the Central Criminal Court, the Courts of Quarter Sessions in Greater London and the County Courts throughout England and Wales. This was the first time that any inquiry into the courts and the legal system had not been chaired by a lawyer. The decision to appoint Lord Beeching, Deputy Chairman of Imperial Chemical Industries and a former Chairman of British Railways, was taken largely at the suggestion of Lord Gardiner who thought that the situation demanded extensive knowledge and experience of administrative techniques rather than of the law. He was not disappointed.

The Commission in their Report[14] found that the circumstances for which the existing pattern of courts was devised no longer existed and had not done so for a long time, and that "attempts to overcome its shortcomings by patching rather than reforming have met with only temporary success and the defects resulting from a failure to change the system have been made more serious in recent years because of a sharp increase in civil and criminal business." They added that "many Quarter Sessions are attempting to dispose of a full-time load with part-time resources." They accepted that the dependence of Quarter Sessions on part-time Judges had some advantage in that it provided "a flexible source of capacity to meet fluctuating demands in a large number of places, making some high judicial potential available which it might be difficult to obtain in other ways, and gives experience to successful members of the Bar which both develops their talents and facilitates the Lord Chancellor's selection of new High Court Judges." On the other hand, it was pointed out that "dependence on part-time Judges, whose availability is subject to pressure from their other

14. Cmnd 4153 (1969).

occupations, leads to bunched sittings of the courts with resulting overloading of the Bar and others providing services to groups of courts. It also leads to cases being unnecessarily postponed or committed to Assizes as well as making it more difficult to achieve consistency of sentencing." The existence of independently administered borough and county sessions intensified the difficulties caused by overlapping, resulted in duplication and made it harder to provide suitable court accommodation on an economical basis. Referring to Quarter Sessions in London, the Commission criticized the distribution of work which resulted in two of them being seriously overloaded, while the full-time chairmen were "exposed to the dangers arising from the monotony of being engaged continuously on one type of work in the same place." On the other hand, the Commission regarded the Crown Courts at Liverpool and Manchester as being a success, their only serious defects being the limitation of the recorder's work to crime and to a single court location. The Commission were highly critical of court administration, especially the divided responsibility which led to a number of defects of which the most pernicious was poor court accommodation.

The Crown Court: The Commission's Report contained a clear prescription for the ills it described. Its recommendations were based on two propositions: first, that all criminal courts, including Quarter Sessions and Assizes, above the magistrates' courts, should be abolished and their jurisdiction merged in one new whole-time court to be known as the Crown Court, which would have jurisdiction throughout England and Wales; and, second, that a new unified court service should be created under the Lord Chancellor for all courts, both civil and criminal, except the magistrates' courts. In spite of the fact that these recommendations involved the most comprehensive reforms in judicial administration since the twelfth century, they were implemented in record time.[15]

Although the Royal Commission were not concerned with the structure and administration of magistrates' courts, their recommendations were bound to have an effect on the Justices of the Peace, and in fact the steps which were taken to introduce a new system following the Commission's Report were of greater significance to the justices than the Commission had intended. Their Report did

15.   The Report was published in September 1969, accepted immediately by the Government of the day as the basis for planning, and accepted again by the new Government in August 1970. Legislation was introduced in the autumn of that year and became the Courts Act 1971, which was brought into operation on January 1, 1972. At the same time administrative action had been under way since the autumn of 1969 to implement those recommendations which did not require legislation, and these multifarious activities led to dramatic changes in the Lord Chancellor's Office, which was transformed from a small group of personal advisers to the Chancellor into a Government department with a staff of about 10,000.

not recommend that Justices of the Peace should sit as full members of the new Crown Court for trials but only as assessors. This was a compromise reached after intense argument between those members of the Commission who wished to limit the JPs entirely to the petty sessional courts and others who felt that justices might still play a useful part in the higher courts as they had done at county Quarter Sessions. The majority of the Commission were prepared to have the justices associated with the work of the Crown Court as assessors, but only because they thought that this would provide the justices with useful training. This was illogical because if justices were to be present in the Crown Court only to enable them to learn their job they ought not to have been in a position to influence the proceedings even as assessors. The Magistrates' Association opposed the Commission's recommendations and urged that JPs should be full members of the Crown Court. Lord Chancellor Gardiner agreed to this, subject to the Association being able to satisfy him that the justices could give sufficient time to the work of the new court. This they did in a memorandum which they submitted to the Lord Chancellor in March 1970, and their proposals were then accepted by Lord Gardiner and later by Lord Hailsham[16] who succeeded him as Chancellor in June. They were included in the Courts Act 1971 which implemented the rest of the Royal Commission's proposals. Under the Act it was obligatory for justices to be present in the Crown Court to hear appeals and committals for sentence from the magistrates' courts, but it was merely permissible for them to participate in trials. Under s. 5, the Crown Court when hearing any appeal or proceedings on committal for sentence had to consist of a High Court or Circuit Judge or a recorder sitting with not less than two nor more than four JPs. For trials at first instance the court, which sat with a jury, might consist of a Judge or recorder sitting with not more than four justices, subject to certain limitations mentioned later. The cases or classes of cases which were to be allocated to a court comprising Justices of the Peace were to be determined in accordance with directions given by the Lord Chief Justice with the concurrence of the Lord Chancellor.

The Act of 1971 was based on the understanding that the justices themselves wished to play a prominent part in the new court system and that they were capable of discharging the additional functions which were involved. With a view to increasing the supply of experienced justices who could sit in the new Crown Court provision

16.　Lord Hailsham of St Marylebone was the son and heir of Viscount Hailsham who was Lord Chancellor in the Conservative Government from March 1928 to June 1929 and in the National Government from June 1935 to March 1938. The son succeeded to the Viscountcy on the death of his father in 1950 but renounced the peerage in 1963 in order to sit again in the House of Commons. He became Lord Chancellor, with the life title of Baron Hailsham of St Marylebone, in 1970. He remained Chancellor until 1974 and served again on the Woolsack from 1979 to 1987.

was made in the Administration of Justice Act 1973 for justices on the Supplemental List to serve in that court, if the Lord Chancellor approved, until they reached the age of 72.

The Judge or recorder did not have a casting vote and there was always the risk that he might be outvoted by the justices sitting with him, some or all of whom might be inexperienced. For this reason the Lord Chancellor and the Lord Chief Justice would have liked to disqualify all justices from sitting in the Crown Court until they had served in Petty Sessions for at least five years. A qualifying period would, however, have reduced still further the number of justices available to attend, and the furthest the Lord Chancellor felt able to go was to ask that no justice should be called on to ajudicate in the Crown Court unless he had completed both stages of his basic training and, in so far as it was practicable, had at least two years experience as a magistrate.[17]

The Act sought to eliminate the former localized approach to the administration of justice which had always dominated the JP system. Whereas the jurisdiction of Quarter Sessions had been limited to the area of the county or borough, the justices when sitting in the Crown Court could exercise jurisdiction over all parts of England and Wales.

The performance of the justices in the Crown Court during the 1970s and 1980s proved to be a disappointment to the many people who had thought that they would be just as useful and effective in the new tribunal as they had been at Quarter Sessions. As time passed it became clear that the Crown Court could never rely upon a supply of justices sufficient to staff every sitting, and on a great many occasions a Judge or recorder was obliged to sit alone, either because no justice was available or because those who did appear were unable to attend throughout the whole of the hearing.

It soon became apparent that there were several essential differences between the county Quarter Sessions and the Crown Court which militated against the presence of JPs in sufficient numbers to meet all requirements. Trials lasted longer in the Crown Court than they had done at Quarter Sessions because in the past most long cases had been committed to Assizes, even though Quarter Sessions were fit to try them, so that it was rare for a Quarter Sessions case to last for more than one, or at the most two days. Many Crown Court cases took much longer, and when they did so the justices who were sitting often found that their other commitments obliged them to leave before the end. Not only was this unsatisfactory from the point of view of the court, and distinctly disturbing to the accused, but the justices themselves felt that they had wasted their time because they were not

17.   Secretary of Commissions Circular, November 1971.

present at the moment when they should have exercised their paramount role of deciding sentence. The fact that many cases took longer to try in the Crown Court led to a further disincentive in that a justice might present himself in response to a request to attend on a stipulated date only to find that all cases had begun on previous days and were still being heard, and therefore there was no court in which he could sit.

Yet another disincentive was the attitude towards JPs which was adopted by many of the Crown Court Judges and by the staff. At Quarter Sessions the justices sat under the chairmanship of a member of the professional judiciary who was a prominent figure in their county, whom they knew personally, who had had considerable experience of sitting with lay justices and with whom they discussed their problems frankly and with confidence. In the Crown Court the justices usually found themselves sitting with a stranger who was often the holder of a part-time judicial office, sometimes with less experience of sentencing than themselves, and who often resented their presence. Justices seldom sat with members of the higher judiciary as they had done at Quarter Sessions because the senior judges were present only for the trial of the more serious offences which did not come within the justices' jurisdiction.[18] Similar differences arose with the Crown Court staff. Many of the staff were inclined to regard justices as an unnecessary nuisance and avoided summoning them to attend whenever possible. At Quarter Sessions the staff were part of the county and had a special loyalty to their justice, who knew tham all as individuals. The 1971 Act destroyed local loyalties and transferred control from the justices to a national court service. At the outset most of the Crown Court staff, like many of the Judges and recorders, had had no experience of working with justices and there was much misunderstanding, giving rise to resentment on both sides. Finally, the facilities provided for justices in the Crown Court often fell far short of those to which they had been accustomed at Quarter Sessions, where they met in a sociable atmosphere and where everything was done for their convenience. It was impossible to achieve the same standard in most Crown Court centres, and in some not even refreshments were available.

The Royal Commission foresaw the need to fill the gap created by the abolition of the office of chairman of Quarter Sessions, and they proposed that certain Circuit Judges should be allocated to groups of petty sessional divisions with a view to the justices turning to them for help and advice. This suggestion was accepted and an individual who was called a "Liaison Judge" was appointed in each area. During the first few years most of them were also appointed to the Commission of

18.   Very occasionally a senior Judge did sit with justices. The Lord Chief Justice, Lord Widgery, sat with justices in the Crown Court in London in 1974.

the Peace and were co-opted as members of the magistrates' courts committee for their respective areas. Their principal duties were to smooth the relationship between the justices and the Crown Court, to give the justices guidance and advice on the performance of their duties and to assist generally in their training, but attempts to define their role in a set of rules were defeated by the wide variations between the needs of different areas and the ability of individual Judges to meet the requirements. Although some Liaison Judges were ineffective, many were highly successful in assisting the justices to perform their duties both in the Crown Court and at Petty Sessions, but none of these Judges could replace entirely the chairman of Quarter Sessions who was the leader and the focal point of the old county magistracy. In the course of time both the conditions under which the justices worked and their relationships with the professional judiciary and the staff were greatly improved, but in the new climate it was not possible to re-establish the congenial atmosphere which had appealed to the justices attending Quarter Sessions.

There was a considerable difference between the effectiveness of the new system in the rural counties and in the large cities. In the former the scheme worked reasonably well, though numbers of justices were obliged to travel greter distances than before to reach the Crown Court which sat in fewer centres than Quarter Sessions. It was a different matter in the main urban areas where the work was heavier and where the magisterial element was composed entirely of justices who had had no previous experience whatever of sitting in a higher tribunal than Petty Sessions. Apart from feeling somewhat daunted by their new surroundings these justices, who numbered about 12,000 throughout the country as a whole, were not inspired by the same dedication to the higher courts as their county colleagues who had always regarded sitting at Quarter Sessions as an essential part of their office.

The various difficulties which beset the new system were never completely overcome. Pressure began to mount for the elimination of all justices from the Crown Court, particularly for the hearing of cases at first instance. This could be effected, as mentioned above, by amending the directions of the Lord Chief Justice under s. 5(4) of the Act. Those who argued for the removal of the justices sought to support their case by pointing to the additional cost[19] involved in their sitting in the Crown Court and to the fact that the court could dispose of its work slightly more rapidly when a judge sat alone than when he had justices sitting with him. Both the Lord Chancellor and the Lord

---

19.   In 1976, £92,635 was paid to magistrates for travel, subsistence and loss of earnings when sitting in the Crown Court. Administrative costs brought this total to approximately £110,000. If justices had sat only for appeals and committals for sentence the amount saved would have been between £50,000 and £65,000.

Chief Justice were reluctant to curtail the justices' role in the Crown Court and for some time no action was taken, although in 1976 the Lord Chancellor asked the Magistrates' Association to identify the dificulties which caused concern to their members and to consider whether the existing Directions might be amended so that justices should no longer be called upon to sit for trials. The outcome of the Association's inquiry which followed was confused, and the only information which emerged clearly was that about one justice in four was dissatisfied with some aspect of the Crown Court system but that the great majority wished to continue to sit in trials as well as appeals.[20]

This was one of the occasions in their history when the justices made little effort to meet the challenge of a new environment. It was not altogether surprising, for the justices' work was more onerous, even at Petty Sessions, than it had ever been and most of them experienced difficulty in finding sufficient time to discharge their magisterial duties. Very few had the periods of leisure which had been enjoyed by their predecessors. They were reluctant to lose the eminent position they had reached in the judicial structure but were equally reluctant to shoulder the additional burden which would be involved in maintaining an effective presence at Crown Court trials. Inevitably, the time came when Lord Lane, LCJ, concluded that the involvement of Justices of the Peace in Crown Court trials could not be justified in the face of the greatly increased pressure of work and, in 1988, with the agreement of the Lord Chancellor, he amended the directions so as to exclude justices entirely from trials and they were therefore limited to the hearing of appeals and committals for sentence.

It seemed to many that the Justices of the Peace had at last reached the limits of their capability, at least in so far as the extra dimension of the higher courts was concerned. It was certainly obvious by the beginning of 1990 that the part they would play in the Crown Court would remain restricted for the foreseeable future, but the Lord Chief Justice's directions were not final. It still remains possible that one day the justices' functions may become even more extensive than they have ever been, but such a situation must lie a long way ahead. The justices' prospects in the summary courts will be discussed later.

The Clerk of the Peace: The Courts Act also brought about the demise of the ancient office of Clerk of the Peace which, as we have seen, dated from the fourteenth century and had been the cornerstone of Quarter Sessions. The Clerk of the Peace was the principal officer of the sessions in both counties and boroughs, but in the counties he was far more. In 1971 he was also clerk of the county council in all but

---

20.   Although appeals and committals for sentence represented around 40 per cent of the numerical case load they accounted for only some 10 per cent of the court's time, 90 per cent of which was occupied in trials.

five counties outside Greater London. He was usually secretary of the advisory committee on Justices of the Peace and Clerk to the Standing Joint Committee, the magistrates' courts committee, the confirming and licensing authority and to the Lieutenancy, as well as holding virtually every other county office which was worth having. As already mentioned, he performed many of his duties through deputies, but most clerks were personally involved in the matters which concerned the magistrates. They were present at the justices' meetings and were well known personally to them all. The justices knew that their clerk had their interests at heart and they looked upon him as a friend and trusted him as an adviser. The plurality of the clerk's appointments and the great authority which he wielded may have been wrong in principle but it had its advantages. As we have seen it meant that responsibility for all aspects of the county magistracy and for the administration and work of both Quarter Sessions and Petty Sessions was in the hands of the same individual who had a profound knowledge of all aspects of the judicial system in the county and, being also the principal administrative officer of the local authority, could act as an effective link between the two bodies. Potential sources of friction were avoided or defused by the action of the Clerk of the Peace. In particular he could do much to bridge the financial gap between the magistrates and the county council and could ensure that the magistrates received the funds that they needed. The departure of the Clerks of the Peace like that of the chairmen of Quarter Sessions created a vacuum which was never entirely filled.

Petty Sessions [21]

In 1945 there were 997 petty sessional divisions in England and Wales, including Lancashire, of which 746 were in counties and 251 in boroughs. In some divisions the court sat in more than one place. The magistrates' courts committees, which were established under the Justices of the Peace Act 1949, were empowered to submit proposals to the Home Secretary for the amalgamation of petty sessional divisions or the alteration of their boundaries, and during the first 20 years after the passing of the Act the number was reduced to 842 in spite of stiff resistance from the benches which were threatened with the loss of their separate status. During the following 20 years they were further reduced to 625.

Virtually all criminal prosecutions continued as before to be brought

---

21. Although the term "Petty Sessions" continued to be used to indicate the normal sittings of justices in their local courts "magistrates' courts" was generally applied to all the courts in which they sat other than Quarter Sessions, and later the Crown Court. The Justices of the Peace Act 1949 defined "magistrates' court" as "a court of summary jurisdiction or examining justices, and includes a single examining justice."

before the magistrates' courts and in some years 98 per cent of these were disposed of entirely there.[22] In 1945 the summary courts dealt with about 400,000 criminal charges while Assizes and Quarter Sessions dealt with less than 16,000 between them. There was a rapid increase in the number of cases tried at Petty Sessions throughout the following decades, and this was augmented by an expansion of the justices' civil and administrative work. A noticeable effect which this had on the courts was in the hours for which they were obliged to sit. In 1945 the great majority of petty sessional courts were still held only in the mornings, whereas 40 years later courts were held also in the afternoons as a matter of routine. The Royal Commission of 1946 considered the question of courts sitting in the evenings as well as during the day. It had been suggested to them that this would have two advantages: that parties and witnesses would be able to attend without interruption of their daily work, and that the field from which justices could be drawn would be enlarged. While not prepared to say that evening courts should never be held, the Commission did not recommend their introduction, and no action was taken in this direction until the 1960s when several experiments in the holding of courts in the evenings and at night were made. The object of this was to make the maximum use of limited court accommodation, but the projects were soon abandoned for a number of reasons. These were: the reluctance of court staff to work a shift system, opposition from the legal profession who required time after normal court hours to attend conferences and to deal with paper work, transport difficulties and the fact that after a long day's work elsewhere the magistrates were not in the best state to administer justice. In view of the suggestion made to the Royal Commission that the public would prefer evening courts so that they could avoid interferring with their daily work, a sample inquiry was carried out. Contrary to expectation, this revealed that most members of the public preferred to take time off from work to attend court rather than encroach upon their leisure hours.

Until 1949 there was no limit on the number of justices who might sit in one court, except in juvenile and domestic proceedings, and sometimes 15 or more were present. In 1937 the Departmental Committee on Courts of Summary Jurisdiction in the Metropolitan Area thought that there should never be more than three justices on each bench, but the Roche Committee in 1944, while expressing the view that three or five was the best number, recommended that the maximum should be seven. As mentioned earlier, the Justices of the Peace Act 1949, s. 13, gave the Lord Chancellor power to fix by rules the maximum numbers for both Quarter Sessions and Petty Sessions,

22.   This varied from year to year but was never less than 95 per cent during this period. The figures are based on those given in the annual Criminal Statistics.

and in respect of the latter he limited the number to seven,[23] but in a direction he stated that only in exceptional circumstances should more than five be present. The minimum number of justices required to form a court remained at two,[24] but a single justice could try an offence for which the maximum penalty did not exceed 20 shillings or imprisonment not exceeding 14 days.

The magistrates' petty sessional courts were not within the terms of reference of the Beeching Royal Commission because they did not suffer from delays to the same extent as the higher courts, and to include them would have delayed the Commission in making its recommendations. It was also thought that as reforms in the administration of the magistrates' courts had been introduced by the Act of 1949 it would be premature to review them 20 years later. The consequence was that there were no fundamental changes in the structure of the summary courts as there were in the higher courts. On the other hand, the jurisdiction of the magistrates' courts continued to be extended. The process which began in the nineteenth century of relegating offences to summary trial was accelerated in the 1960s and 1970s.

The chairman: From the middle of the century the significance of the chairmen of Petty Sessions was recognized more fully than it had ever been before. The Roche Committee commented upon the importance of the chairmanship in their Report of 1944[25] and they recommended that the chairmen in both counties and boroughs should be elected and that the procedure should be governed by rules. The Royal Commission of 1949 pointed out that the efficiency of a court and the reputation in which it is held depends more upon the personal qualities of the chairman than upon any other factor, and they observed (para. 177) that "good chairmanship of a court is essential to the proper conduct of its business." The commisson devoted a whole chapter to this subject and referred to the defects in the existing system. At that time there were many divisions where there was virtually no permanent chairman, it being the practice for justices to take the chair in rotation, which meant that there was no one with overall responsibility for the bench as a whole. In some divisions the senior justice always presided notwithstanding the fact, as the Roche Committee commented, that in some instances this resulted in the chair being occupied by someone "whose physical and other faculties have begun to be impaired by age."

Most chairmen were of an advanced age. The Royal Commission

---

23. Justices of the Peace (Size and Chairmanship of Bench Rules) 1950. (SI 1950 No. 1908) and Amendment Rules 1951 (SI 1951 No. 1982).
24. Magistrates' Courts Act 1952, s. 98.
25. Cmd 6507, paras 212-217.

found that 21.7 per cent of county petty sessional chairmen were over the age of 75 and 1.4 per cent were over 85. Only 1.5 per cent were under 50. In the boroughs the problem was aggravated by the provision in s. 18 of the Local Government Act 1933 (re-enacting earlier legislation) that "the mayor if present shall be entitled to preside at all meetings of the Justices of the Peace held in the borough."[26] The Royal Commission agreed with the Roche Committee that borough justices should elect their own chairman. A suggestion to this effect had been included in a Home Office circular sent to all mayors in October 1944, but although this had the effect of persuading some mayors to refrain voluntarily from presiding, there were others who disregarded the advice. The Royal Commission therefore recommended that the mayor's right to preside at meetings of magistrates should be restricted by statute to formal and ceremonial occasions. The Justices of the Peace Act implemented the Royal Commission's recommendations by removing the mayor's right to preside and by requiring the Lord Chancellor to make rules governing the election of a chairman and also of one or more deputy chairmen in every petty sessional division who would preside when present (s.13(3)). The election was to be by secret ballot. In making these rules the Lord Chancellor's principal concern was to ensure that the justice best qualified for the post was elected, irrespective of seniority or of his political or social background. It was for this reason that the rules prohibited nominations in advance.

In spite of these regulations there continued to be instances of the most senior justice being elected solely because his colleagues did not wish to hurt his feelings, and there were other occasions when justices from one political party agreed in advance among themselves that they would all vote for a justice designated from among their own number. In addition to these defects in the system there were two others which soon became apparent. The first was the influence which the justices *ex officio* were able to exercise over the elections in some areas. Many of these justices showed no interest in the magistracy except once a year when they appeared to vote at the election of the chairman. They were not in a position to compare the merits of the candidates and their sole intention was to vote for a member of their own political party. In some places there were several justices *ex officio* in the same division and their votes could be decisive. This was remedied by the Administration of Justice Act 1964 which disqualified *ex officios* from voting for the chairman or deputy chairmen of their benches and from being elected to these offices themselves. The other deficiency

---

26.   Local Government Act 1933, s. 18(9). There was a proviso that the mayor should not be entitled to preside except when the justices were acting in relation to the business of the borough. The position is explained in greater detail in vol. I, ch. X.

emerged in those divisions which were so large that it was a long time before a justice could get to know all his colleagues, and he was not therefore in a position to appreciate who was most suitable for the chairmanship. Although it was not possible to eliminate this defect entirely an attempt towards that end was made in the Justices of the Peace Act 1968, and the rules made thereunder, whereby a justice might not vote at an election of officers within 12 months of appointment to the bench.

The 1948 Royal Commission took the view that a chairman should remain in office for as long as possible provided that his faculties remained unimpaired. The rules therefore placed no limit on the length of service but merely provided a check requiring the chairman to stand for re-election each year. As time passed there was a growing feeling that a limit should be imposed, the general opinion being that a chairman should not serve for more than three years. In 1969 the Lord Chancellor sought the views of his advisory committees and of magistrates' courts committees but found that only one in four favoured a limit. The rules were therefore left unaltered for the time being, but an increasing number of benches introduced limits of their own from then onwards and finally, after prolonged discussions between the Lord Chancellor's Department and the Magistrates' Association, a limit on the length of service of bench chairmen (but not of deputy chairmen) was introduced in 1986. Rules were then made under which a chairman could serve for five years only and could not then be re-elected until three further years had elapsed. It was still possible, however, for a chairman to hold office for more than five years if his bench was anxious to retain him. The regulations contained a proviso whereby a chairman might be re-elected again after completing five years service if at least 75 per cent of all those justices in the division who were entitled to do so voted for his re-election by secret, postal ballot.

Some benches also continued to press the Lord Chancellor to amend the rules so as to allow at least sufficient advance nomination to enable justices to consider carefully the merits of those who had a reasonable chance of being elected. It was pointed out that, unless this were done, many justices in the larger divisions would waste their votes on candidates who had no chance of success and would have insufficient information about other candidates to enable them to judge their quality. Lord Hailsham remained firmly opposed to the nomination of candidates prior to an election, but he agreed to consider the recommendation of a joint working party of the Magistrates' Association and the Justices' Clerks' Society which considered the question at the end of his term of office as Lord Chancellor. Soon after Lord Hailsham was succeeded by Lord Mackay a new provisional scheme was agreed which benches were given the option of adopting. Two months prior to the annual election of the chairman there was to be a postal ballot for a short list of four candidates. The names of these four would then be circulated to all the justices in the division in advance of the election meeting so that they would have time to consider their qualificaitons before voting at the meeting itself. This arrangement was introduced on a provisional basis from the annual meetings in October 1990. Benches were then given the opportunity to adopt the short-list ballot for a period of three years, but at the end of 1990 a number of questions of detail needed to be resolved and obviously it would be some time before the success or failure of the new scheme was known.27

The rule that the chairman or a deputy chairman must invariably preside when present made it impossible for a future chairman to gain experience of presiding under the supervision of an existing chairman or deputy. The rule was therefore modified in 1977 by the Administration of Justice Act which provided that another justice might take the chair if invited to do so by the chairman or deputy who was present.

The importance which came to be attached to the chairmanship of benches was reflected in the special training arrangements for potential chairmen which have been mentioned above.

Special provisions applied to the chairmen of juvenile and domestic courts which will be described below.

The justices' clerk: Earlier chapters have shown how the office of justices' clerk developed piecemeal over the centuries and how it became the linchpin of the lay justice system. Were it not for the justices' clerks there would be good reason for the disbelief often expressed by foreigners when told that most criminal cases in the country are disposed of satisfactorily by courts composed of men and women drawn from different walks of life who are not lawyers and who serve on a part-time, unpaid basis. The work of the Justice of the Peace in the twentieth century would have been impossible were they not able to look for advice and guidance from their clerk, particularly on points of law. Unfortunately, the increase in the volume of work in the courts in the later part of the century resulted in such advice becoming unavailable in many instances; a point to which we shall return later.

As explained earlier, during the first part of the twentieth century each petty sessional division of a county and each borough with a separate commission had a clerk who was usually a local solicitor serving on a part-time basis. Where, outside London, there was a

27. Regulations governing the procedure were consolidated in the Justices of the Peace (Size and Chairmanship of Bench) Rules, 1990, S.I. 1990, 1554.

stipendiary magistrate, the same clerk served him and the justices, but until 1974 there were certain areas where separate clerks to the stipendiaries were appointed under local Acts.[28] In London the metropolitan stipendiary magistrates had their own court service with clerks who were not concerned with the JP's courts. In 1945 the basis of the justices' clerks system was still the Act of 1877 which required that clerks should be either lawyers or men who had worked as assistants to a justices' clerk[29] and that they should be salaried. The clerk had to engage his own staff and to pay them, as well as all his other expenses, out of his inclusive salary. We have also seen that the Roche Committee made a number of far-reaching proposals for the improvement of the justices' clerks' system in their Report published in 1944. These were implemented in the Justices of the Peace Act 1949. Under s. 19 of the Act clerks were appointed by the newly established magistrates' courts committees and they held office during the committees' pleasure. The committee had to consult the magistrates for the petty sessional division before appointing or removing a clerk and they also had to obtain the approval of the Home Secretary.[30] The clerk was to receive a salary plus expenses and be provided with staff, accommodation and equipment. In order to qualify after 1949 the clerk had to be a barrister or solicitor of not less than five years' standing and be within prescribed age limits. Special provisions were contained in the Act (s. 20) which, for a limited period, enabled a person who had served for a specified time in certain capacities in a clerk's office to become a justices' clerk even if he did not have these qualifications.

When the 1949 Act was passed the quality of many clerks left much to be desired, and as noted in the last chapter some were not averse to breaking the law. A great many dominated their benches, though this often arose from the inability of the ageing chairmen to conduct proceedings without relying wholly upon their clerks. The clerks still served mostly in a part-time capacity and many were important figures in their locality. They were underpaid but, as the Roche Committee commented: "The position of clerk is one of dignity and the holding of that position may itself be regarded as part of the reward."

During the 30 years which followed the 1949 Act substantial changes

---

28. Staffordshire Potteries Stipendiary Justice Acts 1839 to 1895; South Staffordshire Stipendiary Justice Act 1899; Manchester and Borough of Salford (Stipendiary Justices) Act 1878; Merthyr Tydfil Stipendiary Justice Act 1843 to 1907; Pontypridd Stipendiary Magistrate Act 1920.
29. Justices' Clerks Act 1877, s. 7.
30. Previously appointments in counties were made by the justices in special sessions (Justices' Clerks Act 1877, s. 5; Local Government Act 1888, s. 84) and in a borough by all the borough justices (Municipal Corporations Act 1882, s. 159). Under the Criminal Justice Administration Act 1914, s. 34 the appointment required the confirmation of the Secretary of State who had to take into consideration any representations made to him by the Standing Joint Committee or the borough council.

took place in the office of justices' clerk which were partly due to the even more profound changes which occurred in the office of Justice of the Peace. The greater proficiency which the justices acquired induced them to be less ready to accept without question pronouncements by their clerk, and to this extent the influence of the clerk declined, but in other respects the importance of his office and of the functions he performed increased substantially. The emphasis was on professionalism. The magistrates' courts committees, under pressure from the Home Secretary, eliminated the part-time clerks as far as this was reasonably possible, and the majority of appointments were full-time, some clerks serving several petty sessional divisions. Whereas in 1944 there were 732 part-time and only 90 whole-time clerks (excluding clerks to the metropolitan magistrates' courts) by 1977 there were 62 part-time and 312 whole-time appointments.[31] These figures also show the reduction in the number of clerkships which was consequential to the conversion of part-time into full-time posts.

The clerk's duties expanded together with those of the justices and this, as well as the larger areas for which individual clerks were responsible, had the unfortunate effect of obliging the clerks to devote more time to administration and less to sitting in court. We return to this problem later.

The new body of full-time clerks, operating through the Justices' Clerks' Society, acquired considerable influence in a wide field beyond the confines of their courts. They were consulted regularly by Government departments and other bodies on new measures which were under consideration, and if they were not consulted they soon made their views known in an authoritative manner which received due attention. The evidence which the Society submitted to the various commissions and committees of inquiry into matters relating to magistrates' courts was usually among the most cogent received from any quarter, and at least one of their members served on the body itself, including the Royal Commission of 1948.

As individuals, some clerks attained an eminence which had not been enjoyed by their predecessors.[32] Their success induced them to look for further advancement beyond the office which they then held, and in 1950 a number aspired to the post of stipendiary magistrate. This prospect would not have been conceivable before 1949 because all of those who were then serving as clerks were solicitors and only

31.   The process continued though more slowly. Figures in the 1980s were:

	1984	1986	1987	1988	1989
Whole-time	309	301	293	277	275
Part-time	27	14	12	8	7

32.   An outstanding example was Sir Sydney Littlewood who, having been Clerk to the Justices in Kingston-upon-Thames, was knighted for his work in establishing the legal aid system and later became President of the Law Society from 1959 to 1960.

barristers were qualified for appointment. The 1949 Act, however, extended the field to solicitors. The first applications by clerks for stipendiary appointments were made in the early 1950s but Lord Simmonds, who was then Lord Chancellor, would not accept any candidate who was not in active practice. His successor, Lord Kilmuir, was prepared to reconsider the matter in the light of a considerable drop in the number of applications from practising members of the profession which began from 1953 and which was accompanied by a need for additional appointments. Lord Kilmuir decided that if a clerk were to serve temporarily in a judicial capacity and proved himself to be satisfactory, he would be considered for a permanent appointment as a stipendiary magistrate. Accordingly, arrangements were made for clerks to sit as deputy stipendiary magistrates during the unavoidable absence of a permanent stipendiary. The first justices' clerk to become a stipendiary was appointed in 1956[33] and by the end of 1983 12 such appointments had been made.

This was not the end of the clerks' aspirations, and when the Crown Court was established in 1972 some looked to it as an avenue for further advancement. This again meant, however, that before qualifying for appointment, a clerk would be required to serve for a trial period as a part-time Judge in the court, and the Lord Chancellor was not willing to allow a serving clerk to adjudicate in the Crown Court as a Deputy Circuit Judge or a recorder. He felt that, even if the clerk sat only in places outside his own commission area, the fact that he presided in a higher court which heard appeals from magistrates' courts could disturb his relationship with his own justices. It was a different matter if a clerk had been appointed a stipendiary magistrate, for he could then sit as a Deputy Judge or recorder and some of them began to do so regularly. In 1980 one of them was appointed a Circuit Judge and was soon followed by others.[34]

Suggestions were made from time to time that the clerks should be given judicial duties of their own while still remaining clerks. Lord Parker, LCJ, in an address to the Justices' Clerks' Society in 1966, suggested that the clerks should be placed on the Commission of the Peace so that they might exercise minor judicial functions. Ten years later the Society of Conservative Lawyers recommended that clerks

---

33. He was L.M. Pugh, clerk to the Sheffield justices, who became stipendiary for Huddersfield, having just completed his year as President of the Justices' Clerks Society. He was also the first solicitor to become a stipendiary. Eleven years later E.L. Bradley, a barrister, was the first justices' clerk to be appointed to the metropolitan bench. He was clerk to the Poole justices and was formerly on the staff of the Home Office. After appointment to the bench Bradley became a keen member of the Magistrates' Association and served as chairman of its legal committee, later becoming a Vice President of the Association.

34. The first was Kenneth Cooke. He was clerk to the Bradford city justices when he was appointed a metropolitan stipendiary magistrate in 1970. He was a recorder from 1972 to 1980 when he became a Circuit Judge. He was also chairman of the legal committee of the Magistrates' Association and honorary secretary of the Association's London branch.

should sit as deputy magistrates and that their clerical and administrative duties should be transferred to other officials. Although these proposals were popular with many of the clerks they were not accepted by the Government. It was seen that to place the clerk on the bench would sow the seed of the destruction of the lay magistracy, and with it the office of justices' clerk itself.

Those clerks who did not join the professional judiciary found that the scope of their work was constantly expanding. We have seen that they had an important part to play in the training of justices which increased steadily from 1949, particularly after the introduction of compulsory training in 1966. They also had charge of the training of their own staff. Again, they became deeply involved in the administration of the magistrates' courts through the magistrates' courts committee, but here the progress was slower. This was because, although Clerks to Justices became clerks to most of the committees in boroughs from the beginning, in counties it was usually the Clerks of the Peace who served in this capacity until they were abolished in 1971. Immediately afterwards, the Local Government Act 1972 altered the areas of all magistrates' courts committees and combined the borough commission with those of the new counties or metropolitan districts. This was followed by the appointment of clerks to the new committees, and in every one of the 36 metropolitan districts and in 27 of the 47 non-metropolitan counties a justices' clerk was appointed clerk to the committee. For this work the clerk received an additional salary. Yet another addition to the clerk's responsibilities was the power to grant legal aid (though not to refuse it[35]) which he was given in 1968, thus relieving the justices of some of this task.

In addition to these new functions the clerk, or his office, had many administrative duties to perform. These included the collection of fines, licensing fees, legal aid contributions, and maintenance and compensation payments. Registers had to be kept and summonses and warrants issued. A number of extra duties arose in connexion with both liquor and betting and gaming licences, and the clerk arranged the special sessions, processed the applications and issued the licences. The clerk had to maintain contact with the prosecution, probation and social services and with the legal profession and the police. He was the taxing master in indictable cases. Many clerks were secretaries of their local advisory committees on the appointment of justices.[36] This list is not exhaustive and proposals were constantly being made, sometimes by the clerks themselves, for further extensions of their duties.

All this was in addition to the clerk's primary function of advising

35. If they did not grant legal aid they were obliged to refer the application to the justices.
36. In 1989 justices clerks were secretaries of 41 advisory committees and 97 sub-committees.

his justices on points of law and procedure, which became of still greater importance as the law which the courts had to administer became more complex. In spite of this there was no retreat from the principle that the justices' decisions on points of law were theirs and theirs alone, and that they and not the clerk were responsible. It was therefore a common phenomenon for advocates to address their legal arguments to the justices even though the justices probably did not understand them, while the Court of Appeal referred to justices "misdirecting themselves" when, in fact, they had probably been misdirected by the clerk. In view of this, both justices and clerks attached the greatest importance to the clerk retiring with his justices when they had a question of law to consider. They were dismayed therefore when in 1952 Lord Goddard, LCJ, in the Court of Appeal in *R. v. East Kerrier JJ., ex parte Mundy,*[37] ventured to observe, *obiter dicta,* that a clerk ought not to accompany his justices as a matter of course when they retired to consider a case. Until then it was the practice in many courts for the clerks to retire with their justices whenever they thought their advice might be required. Lord Goddard was somewhat surprised by the furore that his remarks caused, and he endeavoured in several subsequent cases to water down to some extent what he had said.[38] He also issued a Practice Direction[39] in which he stated that justices must consult their clerk in four sets of circumstances: (1) on questions of law or of mixed law and fact; (2) on questions regarding the practice and procedure of the court; (3) for information as to sentences imposed by their bench or by neighbouring benches; and (4) so as to refresh their memory as to any matter of evidence which had been given. Regrettably, Lord Goddard also stated on another occasion that disregard of his instructions by the justices would be ground for complaint against them to the Lord Chancellor. The consequence was that justices were inhibited by this threat from asking their clerk to retire with them in all but the most clear-cut cases. Lord Goddard's two immediate successors, Lord Parker and Lord Widgery, both had reservations about the doctrine propounded by their predecessor and, in 1973, Lord Widgery stated that

"It must be stressed that in these days, when legislation becomes more and more complicated, and when problems of law and practice become more and more oppressive, that justices should not be

37. [1952] QB 719.
38. In *R. v. Welshpool JJ, ex parte Holley* [1953] 2 All ER 807, Lord Goddard explained that in the *East Kerrier* case he had not meant that "if a point of law had been raised during the hearing the justices should not ask their clerk to come into the room with them so that they could at once consult him. In *R. v. Barry (Glamorhgan) JJ, ex parte Kashim* [1953] 2 All ER 1005) h;e said "We did not mean, of course, in the *East Kerrier* case, that if a question of law were raised the clerk ought to stay in court until the justices said: 'Come out with us'."
39. [1953] 2 All ER 1306.

discouraged from seeking the assistance of their clerk within the legitimate field in which he can advise them."[40]

The principle behind the doctrine was based on the famous dictum of Lord Hewart, LCJ, in *R. v. East Sussex JJ* in 1935 that "justice should not only be done but should manifestly and undoubtedly be seen to be done," but as Lord Parker observed when LCJ, the continued citation of the principle "may lead to the erroneous impression that it is more important that justice should appear to be done than that it should in fact be done." At the instigation of the Justices' Clerks' Society, the Justices of the Peace Act 1968 (s. 5(3)) contained a declaration that the clerk's function included: (1) giving advice on law, practice and procedure, at the request of the justices, on questions arising in connexion with the discharge of their duties; (2) giving such advice on request when not personally attending on the justices; and (3) bringing to the attention of the justices any point of law, practice or procedure that is or may be involved in any question arising in connexion with the discharge of their function.

The Act therefore confirmed the clerk's right to draw his justices' attention to the fact that a point of law might arise, but it was not always possible to foresee that such a point was going to arise in the retiring room, and the position remained unclear.

The great expansion of the clerk's administrative duties, in addition to the increasing volume of court work which required more courts to be held at the same time, made it impossible for the clerk to maintain the close relationship with his justices which he had done in the past. At best he could attend only one court at a time, leaving it to his assistants to staff the others, but occasions when the clerk himself did not have time to appear at all in any of the courts became ever more frequent, especially in the larger court complexes. The extent to which this occurred, however, depended to a considerable degree upon the views of the individual clerk as to where his principal duty lay. In 1946 the clerk himself was present in about nine courts in 10. Thirty years later the average was not more than one in 10. In the absence of the Clerk to the Justices his duties were performed by deputies and court clerks. An undesirable aspect of this situation was that some courts had to be staffed by court clerks who had little experience and were not qualified for the job. Moreover, these clerks often sat with the least experienced justices, an arrangement that was far from conducive to the efficient administration of justice.

Another undesirable aspect of the new situation was that many clerks became managers of large and complex offices and that, whereas they were well qualified as lawyers to advise their justices and

40.   *R. v. Southampton JJ, ex parte Atherton,* 137. JP 571.

to manage their courts, they had comparatively little training in administration.

As the shortcomings of the system became more apparent remedial proposals were put forward. Prominent among these was the suggestion that there should be a division of duties between two separate clerks, one responsible for administration and the other for the traditional court work. More will be said on this subject in the following chapter.

The appointment of clerks to judicial posts skimmed off much of the cream and many of those who filled their places were not of the same standard as their predecessors. This was largely because the level of pay dropped behind that of other posts which rose rapidly in the employment market. Those who might otherwise have joined the magistrates' courts' service were attracted to careers elsewhere. As already mentioned, clerks had been entitled to receive salaries from 1851, but at the time of the Roche Committee in 1944 the level of their pay was low. There was little improvement following the new system introduced by the Justices of the Peace Act 1949, whereby salaries were paid through the magistrates' courts committees from local authority funds. After a drive by the Justices' Clerks' Society during the years following 1949 a national scale was introduced in 1953 under an agreement reached by a joint negotiating committee which had been appointed for the purpose. From then onwards, however, the remuneration of those in the public servcie generally fell behind that of the private sector, and this was accelerated in the 1970s and 1980s. The clerks' salaries barely kept up with inflation and were far from reflecting the increasing scope of their duties, with the result that recruitment was adversely affected. The same applied to the clerk's staff, and the magistrates' courts, both lay and stipendiary, suffered appreciably from lower standards of efficiency at a time when much greater demands were being placed upon them. Reference is made later to the continued importance attached to the localization of magistrates' courts whereby their organization and funding was retained on a local basis. A consequence of this was that justices' clerks had no national career structure. Once they had reached the principal post in their own division the only means of gaining further promotion or advancement to another post which drew a higher salary was to apply for appointment in another area. There was no effective means of interchange of professional staff between courts, and a magistrates' court could not even borrow staff from a neighbour on a temporary basis if its own were away ill. A solution might have been found in centralizing the administration of magistrates' courts under the Lord Chancellor's Department as was done in 1972 in respect of all the other courts. In 1966 the Justices' Clerks' Society had urged the Government to adopt such a course but without success, and the antiquated principles upon which the system was based were retained even after a national court service had been established in 1972 with wide career opportunities. The administrative functions of the clerks, especially in the management of their courts, would be altered fundamentally if the proposals made in 1989 by a Scrutiny team appointed by the Home Secretary were to be implemented. These proposals will be described in more detail in ch. IX when considering the administration of the magistrates' courts in general.

Practice and procedure

Criminal trials

The trend which had begun in the previous century of relieving pressure on the higher courts by bringing more business to the magistrates, continued after 1945 when it was accelerated by the spectre of increasing delays in the trial of the more serious offences.

We have seen the steps that were taken to transfer work from Assizes to Quarter Sessions. Moves were also made to extend the magistrates' summary jurisdiction, but these always met with strong opposition from those who claimed that it curtailed the citizen's right to trial by jury and was even an abrogation of Magna Carta. In 1933 the Administration of Justice Act had removed the right of a jury in civil cases except in a limited class, and there were many who advocated similar action in respect of criminal trials. They pointed to Continental systems which appeared to work satisfactorily without juries. Holland, in particular, had developed a criminal justice system which had been applauded by penologists. Some changes were indeed made in this direction, notably by the Criminal Justice Act 1961 which extended the list of indictable offences triable summarily, and the Theft Act 1968 brought the stealing of horses, cattle and sheep into this category. Political opposition, however, prevented any appreciable advance being made. In 1975 a Committee on the Distribution of Criminal Business between the Crown Court and the Magistrates' Courts was set up under the chairmanship of Mr Justice James for the express purpose of finding ways to relieve pressure on the Crown Court by extending the jurisdiction of the magistrates. The committee made a number of recommendations,[41] but only the least important were implemented. The Criminal Law Bill, when introduced in 1977, sought to implement the James committee's proposal that minor theft should be triable only summarily. This aroused heated argument where it was claimed erroneously that all citizens in the country had an ancient and inalienable right to trial by jury. In fact there was no

41.   Cmnd 6323 (1975).

constitutional right to be tried by jury and it was largely fortuitous whether some of the offences created by statutes during the previous hundred years had or had not been made triable on indictment. This argument also implied that a jury was more likely to give a fair verdict than a court composed of lay justices, an assumption which was highly questionable, and it ignored the care which was then being taken in the selection of candidates for the bench and in the extensive training they received after appointment, and it also ignored the extent to which they studied the social and economic problems which affected the cases coming before them. It was also generally assumed that lay Justices of the Peace were more prone to convict than juries, but as the Home Secretary pointed out in the House of Commons on January 27, 1977, the acquittal rate for a number of offences was greater in the justices' courts than in the Crown Court.[42] The civil rights lobby, however, triumphed and the Government were obliged to drop much of what they wished to introduce, and which they abandoned with reluctance as trial in the magistrates' courts would have brought a substantial reduction in cost.[43] Successive Governments lacked the courage to pursue the matter to any appreciable extent.

A major piece of legislation which was to govern for a long time the procedure of magistrates' courts in civil as well as criminal matters was passed in 1952. The Magistrates' Courts Act of that year consolidated certain earlier enactments and made a number of improvements. The Act prescribed the pre-trial procedure and confirmed that, whereas the most serious offences, such as homicide, arson, rape and burglary, could be tried only by the higher courts, there were four categories of offences which might in appropriate circumstances be disposed of summarily. These were:

(1) Less serious indictable offences, such as stealing and various forms of fraud, might be tried summarily subject to the consent of the accused who must be informed of his right of choice. The court had to be satisfied that the case was suitable for summary trial, taking into consideration the nature of the case, the appropriateness of the punishment they could inflict and any representation made by

42. For thefts the rate varied according to the type, but in those of items valued at less than £5 the justices acquitted in 64 per cent of contested cases while juries acquitted in 61 per cent. For offences in the public order group, justices acquitted 57 per cent as against 28 per cent acquitted by juries. In assaults on the police, justices, in spite of an inclination to believe police witnesses in preference to others, acquitted 27 per cent of cases while juries acquitted only 20 per cent.

43. The James Committee found that the average cost of a number of selected cases was £431.39 when tried on indictment while the estimated cost of trying them summarily would have been £136.44. In the case of *R. v. Lawrence* [1981] All ER 983, which had taken four days to try in the Crown Court, Lord Roskill said when it came on appeal to the House of Lords, "It is difficult to believe that any magistrates' court would not have dealt with this case, if not in a morning, at least within one full day and reached the correct answer."

the prosecutor or the accused.[44] It was also provided that the justices, after a finding of guilt, might commit the accused to Quarter Sessions for punishment if his character and record were such that they felt that their own powers of punishment were inadequate.[45] Justices often availed themselves of this option, though it was not uncommon to hear them complain that Quarter Sessions, and later the Crown Court, failed to impose a higher sentence than they could have done themselves. In 1962 the Criminal Justice Administration Act (s. 13) enabled justices who had begun a summary trial and then found that the case was more serious than they had thought, to discontinue the summary proceedings and begin a preliminary examination with a view to committal for trial.

(2) Some offences were stated in the statute under which they were created to be triable summarily and on indictment.[46] These offences were tried on indictment unless, on an application by the prosecution, the court decided to try them summarily.[47]

(3) Whenever a summary offence carried a maximum punishment greater than three months' imprisonment the accused had a right to be tried by jury on indictment, and he had to be informed of this right.[48]

(4) Other offences were triable summarily only.

As already mentioned, a person convicted by a summary court had a right of appeal against conviction or sentence to Quarter Sessions, and since 1971 to the Crown Court. In each case the appeal was heard without a jury. Appeals to county Quarter Sessions were taken by a specially constituted committee, while in boroughs the recorder heard appeals alone. The Crown Court had to be composed of a Judge or recorder sitting with not less than two nor more than four justices. At both Quarter Sessions and the Crown Court appeals involved a complete rehearing of the case. An appeal, by either the prosecution or the defence, also continued to lie direct to a Divisional Court of the High Court by way of "case stated." Appeals from Quarter Sessions and the Crown Court lay to the Court of Criminal Appeal.

---

44. Magistrates' Courts Act 1952, s. 19.
45. *Ibid.,* s. 29. After the passing of the Courts Act 1971 committals for sentence were made to the Crown Court.
46. For instance, under the Road Traffic Act 1960, a person who drives a motor vehicle on a road recklessly, or at a speed or in a manner dangerous to the public is liable (a) on conviction on indictment to a fine or to imprisonment for not more than two years or both; (b) on summary conviction to a fine not exceeding £100 or imprisonment not exceeding four months or both.
47. If, however, the justices decided to try the case summarily, or if they decided to inquire into it as examining justices with a view to subsequent trial on indictment, they might change their decision if the nature of the case showed that the alternative procedure would be more appropriate. Magistrates' Courts Act 1952, s. 18.
48. *Ibid.,* s. 25. Cases of assault and under the Vagrancy Act 1898, s. 1, were excepted.

Rules governing the procedure of magistrates in both criminal and civil courts are described in ch. IX.

Committal for trial

The justices continued to exercise the power which they had always possessed of issuing warrants to bring before the courts persons charged with crime, but after the establishment of regular police forces in the mid-nineteenth century they had lost their responsibility for arresting criminals and bringing them to trial. On the other hand, it remained their function to decide judicially whether the prosecution had produced sufficient evidence to justify sending the accused for trial on indictment; and this could be done by a single justice sitting alone. Depending upon the justices' conclusions the accused would be either discharged or committed for trial. For this purpose the justices took and recorded oral evidence, and when doing so they were not required to sit in open court, but usually these proceedings took place in the ordinary magistrates' court. The justices' powers and the procedure they were to follow on such occasions were set out in the Magistrates Courts Act 1952 (ss. 4-12). They were extremely time-consuming and tedious and, as the justices' overall workload increased, suggestions were made for relieving them of this unpopular work.[49] It was feared, however, that any diminution of the justices' role would jeopardize the accused, and it was some time before any reform was introduced. It came to be realized in the course of time that preliminary inquiries might themselves be detrimental to an accused person by revealing to the trial jury in advance much of the evidence for the prosecution and little if any for the defence who usually did not wish to disclose its case until the trial itself had opened. In 1967 therefore, the Criminal Justice Act provided for a person to be committed for trial on written statements, with no oral evidence being adduced, but there were safeguards in favour of the accused who could demand old-style committal proceedings if he wished. This new method certainly had the effect of reducing considerably the amount of time spent by justices on this wearisome work because it enabled them to commit without considering the evidence, but it soon led to claims that the higher courts were being overburdened with cases which ought never to have reached them and which would not have done so had the justices been able to dismiss them under the old procedure.

Apart from cases which could only be tried by Assizes and Quarter

49. Such a suggestion was made by Lord Goddard LCJ in an address to justices on November 5, 1959. A step was taken in this direction in the Children and Young Persons Act 1963 which provided (s. 27) that in preliminary hearings of charges of sexual offences against children, written statements of the child's evidence should be admissible and the child should not give oral evidence unless the defence objected or the child's attendance was required to establish identity.

Sessions there were also those indictable offences which could be tried by the justices at their discretion, and here too an increasing number of offenders were committed to the higher courts. The criminal statistics for 1987 show that the number of adult defendants in "either-way" proceedings had increased by 16 per cent in the previous 10 years, but during the same period the number of such defendants committed to the Crown Court increased by 69 per cent. In 1988 a Home Office Research Study, *Triable either-way cases; Magistrates' Court or Crown Court*, found that 40 per cent of defendants sent to the Crown Court were committed by the decision of the magistrates. Understandably, the Home Office was alarmed by this trend and, in 1989, they pointed out to the Magistrates' Association that every increase of one per cent in the number of cases sent up for trial meant an increase in the workload of the Crown Court of about 1,000 cases a year and an extra expenditure of £6-8 million in addition to the appointment of three additional full-time Judges. The Home Office also pointed out that, as more defendants were committed for trial in custody, pressure built up on remand accommodation with serious consequences to the prison system. The Home Office urged that magistrates should give the matter immediate attention and should consider the reasons behind their practice, especially having regard to the fact that in over half the cases committed to the Crown Court by the magistrates' decision the defendant eventually received a sentence within the sentencing powers of the magistrates' court.

Sentencing and the treatment of offenders
Penal policy underwent conspicuous changes after World War II. From the outset it was dominated by public reaction to the upsurge in crime which struck the country within a few years after the end of the war and which continued unabated throughout the following four decades. In 1947 indictable crimes known to the police numbered 498,576. They dropped by some 40,000 in the next two years but more than doubled to 1.2 million between then and 1967. Thereafter the rate of increase was even greater and, in 1981, the total reached three million and 3.7 million in 1988. Society was puzzled not only by the size of the threat but by the nature of the criminals, who were usually young and often came from well-to-do families, thus disproving the established theory that crime was only a product of poverty.

In 1949 the only sentencing options open to magistrates were imprisonment, corporal punishment and fines. Corporal punishment was abolished by the Criminal Justice Act 1948[50] but an era soon began in which the courts were presented with an extensive list of alternative options.

50.   Except in prisons where it survivied until the Criminal Justice Act 1967.

Imprisonment: Penology had been influenced by a reformative philosophy since the Gladstone Committee at the end of the previous century had proposed that imprisonment should be used to reform and rehabilitate criminals. This trend accelerated after the end of the Second World War and the sentencing policy of both Labour and Conservative Governments became engrossed in reform and rehabilitation to the exclusion of other previously accepted objectives, such as deterrence and retribution. Punishment became a pejorative word. At first therefore the Government and other authorities, instead of reacting in the traditional manner of imposing harsh punishments, adopted a paternalistic approach based on the reform and rehabilitation of the criminal. Under this policy custodial sentences could be justified only in so far as they offered the prison authorities an opportunity to reclaim and re-educate the offender. The courts were therefore urged when imposing prison sentences to make them of sufficient length to give the prison and probation officers, social workers and others concerned with the treatment of offenders ample time to turn criminals into new, reformed beings. This meant that a prison sentence should be of sufficient length to allow the prison authorities plenty of time to complete the conversion.[51] Magistrates were discouraged by the Lord Chancellor and the Home Secretary from imposing short custodial sentences, and the Lord Chief Justice gave similar advice to the High Court Judges.

This policy, which was implemented without sufficient preparation and research, was orientated entirely towards the offender and ignored the primary object of criminal law which is the protection of society. In any event, the new system proved to be totally ineffective in achieving its objective. Both hardened criminals and new offenders staunchly refused to be converted, and the latter, after lengthy terms in prison, became as hardened as the old-stagers. In spite of statutory restrictions on the sentencing powers of the courts and the genuine efforts of most Judges and magistrates to avoid custodial sentences, the prison population increased so dramatically[52] that the Government was led to a complete reversal of its previous policy. Prison sentences, if imposed at all, should be short, and alternative forms of treatment should be chosen wherever possible. Even this did not curb the growth of the prison population which reached 45,500 in 1981[53] and which was

51. In 1913 over 80,000 prison sentences were for two weeks or less and in 1945 such sentences were still common, but by 1960 they had dropped to about 3,000 in spite of a huge increase in the number of prison sentences.

52. Having numbered 18,600 in 1947 it rose to 42,000 in 1977. In 1957 the Home Secretary's Council on the Treatment of Offenders produced a report entitled *Alternatives to Short Terms of Imprisonment,* which resulted in (1) increase in the maximum time spent at attendance centres (described below) by those aged 17 to 21 (Criminal Justice Act 1961); (2) Attachment of wages for maintenance orders (Maintenance Orders Act 1958); (3) Restrictions on imprisonment for first offenders (First Offenders Act 1958).

53. By 1989 it had increased further to 49,500, the highest figure during that year being 49,562 on February 28.

relatively higher than almost any other country in western Europe.

The size of the prison population was also increased by those who were remanded in custody pending trial and by those sentenced to imprisonment in enforcement of certain orders in civil matters. Those remanded will be referred to later when discussing bail. Civil debts incurred in a County Court were enforceable by imprisonment until. this procedure was abolished by the Administration of Justice Act 1970, but it remained open to magistrates to imprison in default of payment of maintenance orders and of rates and taxes.[54] A year later the Attachment of Earnings Act 1971 empowered the courts to ensure the payment of debts by attaching earnings in the hope that this would reduce the number of committals to prison for non-criminal matters, but the effect was marginal, and from 1974 receptions of non-criminal prisoners began to rise.

Magistrates' powers to impose prison sentences were being curtailed as early as 1948 when the Criminal Justice Act prevented them from sending anyone under the age of 17 to prison; nor could they impose a prison sentence on a person aged 17 to 21 unless no other method was appropriate and they recorded their reasons.[55] Ten years later the First Offenders Act 1958 placed similar restrictions on magistrates' powers to imprison a first offender over the age of 21. Thereafter magistrates' courts could not pass a sentence of imprisonment on any first offender unless they were of the opinion that no other method of dealing with him was appropriate, and they were required to state their reasons and enter them in the court register and on the committal warrant. Further restrictions were added by the Criminal Justice Act 1961[56] and the Criminal Law Act 1977. In 1967 the Criminal Justice Act provided (s. 60) for prisoners to be released on licence (ie, on "parole") after serving one-third of their sentence (or 12 months, whichever was the longer) subject to recommendations by local review committees in each prison and by a national Parole Board. This came into operation in April 1968.[57] The older concept of remission as something earned by positive good conduct and industry was replaced by a system which credited a

---

54.   The Committee on the Enforcement of Judgment Debts (1969 Cmnd 3909) recommended that enforcement offices should be established to deal with the enforcement of civil debts and fines, but this was not implemented.
55.   The number of persons under 21 sentenced to prison had risen sharply during the previous 10 years. It dropped immediately after the 1948 Act, but then increased again as many youths were sentenced by the higher courts for indictable offences. The 1948 Act abolished the distinction between imprisonment and penal servitude, although for many years there had been no difference in the treatment of persons serving the two kinds of sentence.
56.   This Act authorized the transfer to the Home Secretary of the functions of the Prison Commissioners, which was carried out in 1963.
57.   In considering whether a prisoner should be granted parole account was taken of his previous record - occupational, social, domestic and criminal - his response to prison treatment and training, the nature and circumstances of his offence and his circumstances on release.

prisoner with remission at the beginning of his sentence, and this could be forfeited only as a punishment for a specific offence against prison discipline. Where, however, a licensee while on licence committed a further offence punishable on indictment with imprisonment and was convicted by a court of Assize or Quarter Sessions, the court might, under s. 62 of the 1967 Act, revoke the licence whether or not it passed any other sentence on him. Where he was convicted of such an offence by a magistrates' court the court might commit him to Quarter Sessions for sentence and Quarter Sessions then had power to revoke the licence. Automatic remission of detention centre sentences (described later) was raised in 1968 from one-sixth to one-third of the term, and in 1975 the Home Secretary enraged magistrates by raising it for junior centres to a half. Not for centuries had there been so much involvement by the executive in the sentencing process. The authority of the courts to decide upon the appropriate length of sentence in each case was undermined both by the limitations placed on periods spent in custody and by virtually eliminating all the differences between medium length custodial sentences.

An exceptional situation arose in 1980 when industrial action by prison officers made it virtually impossible for further prisoners to be accepted by the institutions, and as a temporary measure the Government usurped the authority of the courts by empowering the Home Secretary, in the Imprisonment (Temporary Powers) Act, to suspend prison sentence for a limited period.

In spite of all these measures the prison population rose steeply and the Government sought desperately to find other means of reducing the numbers. It became preoccupied with the need to reduce the number of prisoners partly because of the rising cost of keeping them in custody and partly because the prisons were becoming so overcrowded that there was virtually no room left to receive further inmates. The courts, and especially those of the magistrates, were blamed unjustifiably for this situation which was in fact due to the increase in serious crime coupled with the failure of successive Governments to increase prison accommodation. Between 1918 and 1959 not a single purpose-built prison was constructed in England and Wales. The conditions in the prisons was appalling, but the magistrates, although involved as prison visitors as well as sentencers, were less to blame than almost anyone. Published statistics, including those for the Crown Court after 1971, showed that the higher courts were far more likely to imprison for serious offences than the magistrates' courts. From 1950 onwards it was rare for magistrates to impose custodial sentences save in a very limited number of serious offences which were of a kind that the Court of Appeal had stated to be normally appropriate for imprisonment. The Justices of the Peace were also alert to the problems facing the criminal justice system. The Magistrates' Association was among the first to draw attention to the deteriorating situation and to propose ways of dealing with it, and they were quick to respond to any guidance given by the higher judiciary.[58]

Suspended sentence: A means of reducing the prison population which had been proposed for some years before it was adopted in 1967 was the suspended sentence. The Criminal Justice Act 1967 provided that where a court passed a sentence of not more than two years it might order the sentence to be suspended for a period of from one to three years. If, during this period, the offender committed another offence he became liable to serve that sentence in addition to any other he might receive, but the court also had a discretion at that point to reduce the suspended sentence or not to let it operate. The introduction of the suspended sentence had the immediate effect of reducing the number of persons serving prison sentences after conviction by magistrates' courts.[59] The number of those fined also diminished at the same time, but this was due partly to the courts applying suspended sentences contrary to the meaning of the Act by imposing them in cases where, before 1968, they would have imposed a fine or conditional discharge. It had been Parliament's intention that suspended sentences should be used only in cases where the court would otherwise have ordered immediate imprisonment. The result was that a number of suspended sentences which ought never to have been imposed had to be activated when the offender committed another offence, and ultimately more rather than fewer offenders

58.   In 1980 Lord Lane LCJ in *R. v. Bibi* laid down that imprisonment should be avoided if possible, but if it was unavoidable it should be for as short a period as possible. There was an immediate and striking reduction in the average length of sentence imposed in magistrates' courts.

59.   The use of suspended sentences after they became available on January 1, 1968 is shown in the following tables:

I Persons proceeded against at magistrates' courts

Year	Total proceeded	Found guilty	Imprisonment	Suspended sentence
1967	1,663,877	1,554,068	25,529	-
1977	2,161,947	1,944,857	18,466	22,975

II Persons tried at the higher courts

Year	Total tried	Found guilty	Imprisonment	Suspended sentence
1967	30,265	25,585	10,450	-
1977	68,721	57,225	19,505	10,864

III Persons sentenced at higher courts after conviction
at magistrates' courts

Year	Total sentenced	Imprisonment	Suspended sentence
1967	10,640	3,893	-
1977	15,727	4,121	1,230

ended up in jail. The Government, however, in its desperate efforts to clear the prisons, carried the process a stage further by partly suspended sentences which were introduced under the Criminal Law Act 1977. This again did not result in the desired reduction in the prison population, and some disenchantment in the concept of suspended sentences became apparent with the Government although the option remained popular with the magistrates. In a further attempt to reduce the time spent in prison, the Criminal Justice Act 1982 reduced from six to three months the minimum sentence to which a partial suspended sentence might apply, and it also reduced to 28 days from one-quarter of the total sentence the minimum period that had to be spent in custody.

There were other results of the post-war enlightened approach to sentencing which were more gratifying. The 40 years which began in 1950 witnessed some of the greatest changes in penal policy in the history of the courts. Although there were increasing limitations on the magistrates' powers to impose custodial sentences, the period was marked by an unprecedented expansion of alternative methods of disposal. The new era began with the Criminal Justice Act 1948 which replaced the Probation of Offenders Act 1907 and provided new methods of disposal in lieu of imprisonment, of which the most important were *attendance centres* and *detention centres* for young offenders.

Attendance centres: Offenders who were aged 12 (reduced to 10 in 1961) and were under 21 could be obliged to attend an attendance centrea for certain number of hours which did not interfere with school or work. The regime provided "physical exercise and useful occupation." The centres were open on Saturday afternoons and were recognized as particularly useful for dealing with young hooligans at football matches. The centres were an immediate success in so far as boys were concerned,[60] and by 1969 there were 61 centres for boys under 17 and two centres for youths over 17 and under 21. The total number of attendance orders made by the courts in that year was 7,438. In 1984 it was 15,300.

Detention centres were for offenders aged over 14 and under 21. They provided residential training for periods of three months for

---

60.   At first no attendance centre was provided for girls because there was an insufficient number of girl offenders to make it worth while, but from the late 1960s there was an alarming upsurge in delinquency, including criminal violence, among girls which presented a new challenge that oculd not be met effectively by the courts owing to lack of suitable facilities. By 1984 there were 127 centres in England and Wales, of which 89 catered for boys aged 10-16; seven for girls aged 10-16; 13 for boys and girls aged 10-16 and 19 for young men aged 17-20.

younger offenders and six months for older ones. They were intended to give a short, sharp shock with hard work and strict discipline. The courts regarded detention centres as a valuable form of disposal and would have liked to have had a larger number of such centres available. By 1969, however, there were only 14 senior detention centres and five junior centres. Magistrates would also have liked to see detention centres extended to adult offenders, but this was never done. In 1967 the Advisory Council on the Penal System reviewed the operation of the detention centre principle and redefined its aim and philosophy. The Council's recommendations, which were accepted by the Home Secretary, resulted in the "short, sharp shock" principle (which had been based on the Army "glasshouse" principle of punishment during the war) being abandoned and replaced by emphasis on rehabilitation. Ten years later the pendulum seemed to be swinging again towards a more harsh régime.

Conditional discharge: The Criminal Justice Act 1948 also enabled a court to discharge an offender without punishment on condition that he committed no further offence within a specified period. Conditional discharge was a useful option which became widely used by magistrates.

Confiscation and criminal bankruptcy: In 1972 the Criminal Justice Act introduced a number of further options. First, it empowered magistrates' courts to confiscate property, including vehicles, used in the course of committing a crime. Second, it introduced criminal bankruptcy whereby convicted criminals could be prevented from profiting from their crimes, but this was available only to the Crown Court and not to Petty Sessions. In addition to these innovations the Act introduced two new non-custodial methods of treatment: *community service* and *day training centres.*

Community service orders were inspired by a report in 1970 by the Advisory Council on the Penal System under the chairmanship of Baroness Wootton. This was one of the most promising developments in the social history of the era. The primary purpose of community service was to provide a constructive alternative for those offenders who would otherwise have received a short custodial sentence. Those aged 17 and over who had been convicted of an offence punishable with imprisonment could be ordered to carry out unpaid work of service to the community during their spare time, up to a maximum of 240 hours. The offender was therefore deprived of his leisure time but was obliged to work for a constructive and outward-looking purpose which gave him an opportunity to make reparation to the community against which he had offended. The new system began modestly in six experimental areas, but it soon gained the confidence of both magistrates and the probation service, with the result that the number of referrals increased rapidly, rising from about 5,000 in the first year after the scheme began in 1973 to 12,133 in 1977.[61] One of the aspects of the scheme which appealed to magistrates was that, under the 1972 Act, the court itself could lay down the régime which the youngster was to follow. Previously this rested largely with the social workers or probation officers, and the courts, through lack of confidence, often imposed a custodial sentence where it was not really necessary. An important feature of a community service order was that it gave an offender a sense of responsibility, which was generally recognized as one of the most important elements in the war against crime.

Community service was the success story of this period and it was extended to offenders aged 16 by the Criminal Justice Act 1982. Six years later an extensive review was carried out into the operation of the system with a view to identifying ways in which it could be further improved. This led to the introduction of new standards from April 1, 1989 which, among other objectives, were aimed at insuring that work carried out was tough and demanding. The standards required closer supervision of offenders through weekly reports and they introduced a stricter policy and more consistent approach towards offenders who failed to satisfy the conditions of their orders. This reflected the Government's strategy at the time which, on the one hand, favoured longer prison sentences for serious and violent offenders, but on the other promoted the use of non-custodial penalties for less serious offenders who did not present a danger to the public. The Government hoped that the new standards would induce magistrates to make still greater use of community service orders and would apply them in the right circumstances. It was felt at that time that the orders were used too often as substitutes for a fine, yet their object was to provide for more serious offenders who would not usually be fined.

The Govenrment view was summed up by a Home Office Minister in the words, "They are too often regarded as 'the last rung on the ladder to custody', yet they should be used for more serious offenders, not those usually fined. They should be used again and again for some offenders who commit less serious non-violent offences." The magistrates, while welcoming the new approach, expressed caution lest the toughening process which was introduced by the national standard should lead to an increase in the number of cases of breach proceedings.

Day training centres were also introduced by the 1972 Act. Section 20

---

61.   During the six years from the inception of the scheme in 1973 the number of persons giving community service orders was 105,000. The failure rate was between 15 per cent and 20 per cent. Over half the referals were in respect of persons under 21.

provided that where a court made a probation order it might include a requirement that the offender should attend a specified day training centre. The centres were to be provided and administered by the probation and after-care committees. They were intended as an alternative to imprisonment for the socially inadequate recidivist for whom other methods of disposal seemed to have failed. Men and women between the ages of 21 and 45 could be required to attend the centres for five days a week, to a maximum of 60 days. The length of attendance on each day was regulated by the Home Secretary and amounted to about eight hours. Experimental centres were established in four places which were centrally funded by the Home Office. Those involved in the centres thought them beneficial, but annual reconviction rates varied from 40 to 60 per cent and the centres suffered from a general disenchantment with the concept of "therapeutic" sentencing. The new Criminal Justice Act of 1982 replaced them with locally funded *day centres* and courts were allowed to make probation orders requiring attendance at such centres for not more than 60 days. In practice the number of hours which offenders spent at the centres during the course of the day varied from 2½ to 6, and the Magistrates' Association suggested that attendance should be measured by the hour rather than by the day. *Day centres* proved to be more acceptable to the courts than their predecessors, and in March 1989 the Magistrates' Association suggested that they should be open during evenings and weekends as well as during the day. The Association also proposed that the term "day centre" was changed to "probation centre."

Other new options which were introduced during this period but which applied only to the juvenile courts are referred to later, but schemes designed to reduce the number of persons in custody continued apace. In 1989 they included a number of new experiments in placing restrictions on offenders' liberty without the involvement of imprisonment. Some of these had been rehearsed in a Government Green Paper, *Punishment, Custody and the Community* published in July 1988. These included intermittent imprisonment as an alternative to full-time custody and electronic monitoring whereby a device was attached to an offender left at liberty which indicated his whereabouts. There were also proposals for judicial supervision which could be exercised by a single magistrate. The approach adopted by the Government in the 1988 Green Paper aimed at changing the whole basis of sentencing which would involve the courts in considering a wide package of options. The magistrates, while welcoming the objective of reducing the use of custody, were inclined to think that this could be achieved more effectively by improving and combining the existing facilities rather than introducing yet more innovations. A major problem which faced all courts was to understand fully everything that was involved in each of the new options at every stage of their application. This was particularly acute in the case of the lay justices who, before they could operate the new schemes, would have to devote still more of their time to additional, reorientated training.

Fixed penalties and disqualification. As we have seen, the largest volume of business coming before magistrates' courts at the middle of the century was related to traffic offences. Attention was soon directed towards reducing the amount of time which had to be devoted to this boring work which was disproportionately time-consuming because defendants ignored summonses more often than in any other type of case. The establishment of special traffic courts was considered on several occasions, but the idea was abandoned for practical reasons.[62] In 1957 the situation was greatly improved by the Magistrates' Courts Act which enabled the accused to plead guilty by post and to be dealt with in his absence. In 1960 the Road Traffic and Road Improvements Act introduced a system of "ticket fines" for the least serious motoring offences.[63] A constable, or in later years a traffic warden, might place a notice on a car setting out the fixed penalty, which would be less than the statutory maximum to which a first offender would otherwise be liable, and which could be paid to the justices' clerk for the district within 21 days. If the motorist did not pay within this time he might be prosecuted in the normal way.[64] The Transport Act 1982 extended fixed penalties to some of the less serious moving traffic offences such as speeding. Although proposals were put forward to relieve the courts by enabling police to levy fines on the spot for certain motoring offences these were never implemented because it was thought that it would be wrong in principle to place these powers in the hands of the police alone.

An extra dimension in the sentencing of road traffic offenders was the power to endorse the driving licence of an offender or to disqualify him from driving for a specified period. These powers were exerciseable by magistrates in the first half of the century and were extended later. Wherever a court had a duty to endorse a driving licence it also had a discretionary power to disqualify, but in respect of certain offences the disqualification was obligatory. There was reason to think that the fear of disqualification was often a greater deterrant than a fine. It was an option much favoured by the Government, and for this reason the magistrates were obliged to disqualify in certain cases by statute and were not allowed complete discretion. The Road Traffic Act 1962 set out (sch. 1, Part 1) a list of offences for which the

62. See *The Changing Image of the Magistracy*, 2nd ed., p. 86.
63. Illegal parking, obstruction, leaving vehicles without displaying lights as required by law and non-payment of charges due at parking meters.
64. The procedure was prescribed by the Fixed Penalty (Procedure) Regulations, 1950.

court was obliged to disqualify a convicted offender and to endorse his licence unless it found special reasons for not doing so. The special reasons had to relate to the offence and not to the offender. The court had a discretionary power to order disqualification if it thought fit in respect of a further group of offences set out in Part 2 of sch. 1 to the Act, though in these cases it was obliged to order the endorsement of the offender's licence unless it found special reasons for not doing so. The group included such offences as exceeding the speed limit and careless driving. The court was also required by the 1962 Act to take into account previous convictions for motoring offences and to order disqualification unless they thought that there were mitigating circumstances.65 This was called the "totting-up" system which was extended by the Road Traffic Act 1972, whereby magistrates were required to disqualify an offender for at least six months when he was convicted of a third endorseable offence within three years unless there were mitigating circumstances.

"Totting-up" was replaced by a "penalty points" system introduced by the Transport Act 1981. An offender incurred a number of penalty points for each offence he committed, and these were fixed by statute, though in certain cases such as careless driving the number of points could be varied according to the gravity of the offence which was actually committed. If an offender incurred 12 points or more within three years the court was obliged to disqualify unless it was satisfied that there were sufficient mitigating circumstances.

Probation: As mentioned earlier the Criminal Justice Act 1948 replaced the Probation of Offenders Act 1907. The new Act ended the old method of probation whereby conditions were inserted in a recognizance and instead an order was made by the court requiring a person to be under the supervision of a probation officer for a period of not less than one year nor more than three.66 The order might also contain such other conditions as might be appropriate. The offender had to express his willingness to comply with the requirements. He would then be brought before the court again if he failed to comply or if he committed a further offence. Where there was a breach of a requirement the offender might be fined, ordered to attend an attendance centre or dealt with for the original offence. If he committed a further offence he might, in addition to being sentenced for the new offence, be sentenced also for the one for which he was put

---

65.   When an offender was convicted of any offence in schl. 1 to the Act as amended and at the time of the commission of the offence his licence had been endorsed on two separate occasions within the preceeding three years for any offences in the schedule, the court was obliged to order his disqualification for not less than six months unless it considered that mitigating circumstances existed which justified a shorter period of disqualification or none.

66.   The Children and Young Persons Act 1969 replaced probation orders with supervision orders for anyone under the age of 17.

on probation or discharged conditionally.

For the next 20 years the courts continued to place a sizeable proportion of convicted persons on probation, but by the end of the 1960s the numbers of probation orders, which had been growing since 1967, began to drop, partly because of the larger number of sentencing options which were open to the couts, especially following the Criminal Justice Act 1967, and partly to the diminished confidence felt by some magistrates in the probation service which was passing through a critical stage. The future of the probation service was discussed at the time of the Seebohm Committee on Local Authority and Allied Personal Social Services in 1968,[67] and it was suggested that it should be combined with local authority staff, but this was not thought to be practicable. The Probation and After-care Service was expanded (from 3,400 to 4,400 between 1970 and 1975) and continued to be increased in order to deal with some of the non-custodial sentences which were introduced subsequently. The Government expected the probation service to play a key role in reducing the prison population. Unfortunately, the high reputation which the service gained in its earlier years was not maintained and by 1967 both magistrates and Judges showed a lack of confidence which was one of the causes of diminished use of probation. After 1972 some courts were deterred from resorting to the alternative options provided by the Criminal Justice Act, notably community service orders, and although the proportion of sentences in which probation officers were involved rose from 9 per cent to 16 per cent between 1977 and 1987, this was not accompanied by a reduction in the proportion of offenders being sent to prison.[68]

Bail: Reference has been made to the number of persons remanded in custody while awaiting trial. During the nine years 1966 to 1975 the number of such persons rose by 50 per cent, whereas there was an increase of only 20 per cent in the total daily population of all prisons. Large number of the remand prisoners did not subsequently receive custodial sentences. This naturally attracted the attention of those concerned both with the overcrowding of the prisons and with the liberty of the subject.

Until 1967 bail had to be applied for and magistrates had an almost unfettered discretion, but most courts granted bail except in the case of grave offences or where there was a positive reason why it should be refused. The Criminal Justice Act 1967 provided expressly that bail

---

67. Cmnd 3708 (1968) Previously the Departmental Committee on the Probation Service, under the chairmanship of Sir Ronald Morison QC, had conducted a comprehensive survey of probation and reported in 1962.
68. In 1989 the deficiencies of the probation service were discussed in an article in the *Law Society's Gazette* of April 12; "Doubts about the effectiveness of the probation service."

should not be refused except on one or more of a number of specified grounds, and that the reason for refusal should be given if the accused was not legally represented or if his representative required it. After the passing of the Act the number of remands in custody declined appreciably.

In 1976 the Act was replaced by the Bail Act which advanced the rights of the accused still further by providing that a defendant awaiting trial or remanded for inquiries pending sentence should be granted bail unless he fell within one of the exceptions listed in the schedule. The magistrates were therefore faced with the statutory presumption in favour of the grant of bail which they were obliged to consider whether or not an application had been made.

Deliberations on the grant or refusal of bail occupied more of the magistrates' time than might be supposed. They found this to be one of their most difficult tasks, as they had to weigh public interest against the rights of the accused who must be presumed innocent until found guilty. At that stage there was often little information on which to base a conclusion. Unlike a decision on guilt or innocence their function here was to forecast the future and not to make an assessment of past conduct. They were also under considerable pressure from several quarters. The Government, through the Home Office, urged magistrates to grant bail almost as a matter of course, yet if they did so and the defendant absconded, or committed another offence while on bail, they were reprimanded by the higher courts and accused by the police of making their task impossible.[69]

Binding over: The justices in the twentieth century still possessed their ancient power to bind over to keep the peace. This function, which they had exercised from the fourteenth century and from which the probation system was developed, was one of the curiosities of legal history, its object being not to punish for past misconduct but to discourage future breaches of the law. Coke and Blackstone refer to it as "preventive justice." It could be used after a conviction either in addition to or in place of a penalty, and it was often employed in civil as well as criminal proceedings, especially in domestic cases and disputes between neighbours.[70] There were many occasions when the device was used in attempts to prevent breaches of the peace which it was feared would result from public demonstrations. The application of the law in such instances had been reviewed by a Divisional Court of

69.   A study by the Metropolitan Police in 1977 showed that, excluding juveniles, about 4,000 persons absconded from bail in the London area in a year and 3,000 indictable offences were committed while on bail.

70.   As previously, the procedure was for the person who was to be bound over to give a written recognizance whereby he promised to pay a specified sum of money to the Crown, but with a clause that if a certain condition were complied with the bond would be void. The court might require a defendant to produce sureties who would be bound over in the same way.

the High Court in 1913 in the case of *Lansbury v. Riley* of which an account was given in ch. VI (p. 240). This confirmed that where a magistrates' court was satisfied that a person had incited others to commit breaches of the peace and that he intended to continue to do so, they might bind him over in recognizances to keep the peace and could order him to find sureties. In default they might commit him to prison. The magistrates might exercise this power even though the person concerned had not caused anyone to go in fear.

Soon after World War II, the device was employed on a number of occasions against the supporters of the Campaign for Nuclear Disarmament, but the leaders of the movement, including Bertram Russell, refused to be bound over and were sentenced to short terms of imprisonment. Sometimes, however, magistrates used the power in a manner which clearly did not come within the terms of the statute and applied it in cases where a speaker himself was not likely to cause a breach of the peace. In these circumstances they were induced by the police to bind over a speaker solely on the ground that other persons who might be present at the meeting were likely to cause a disturbance entirely at their own volition. As an order binding a person over to keep the peace was not a conviction there was no right of appeal to Quarter Sessions, and the only means of challenging the magistrates' order was by case stated to the High Court as was done by George Lansbury. In 1956, however, a Private Member's Bill which became the Magistrates' Courts (Appeal from Binding Over Orders) Act provided for an appeal to Quarter Sessions - later to the Crown Court.

All members of the judiciary attached considerable importance to this original power, and its use was not confined to the magistrates' courts. It was generally assumed, no doubt rightly, that when a Judge bound a person over he was exercising the power conferred on all Justices of the Peace by the 1361 Act because he was a Justice of the Peace *ex officio*. When therefore, as we saw in the last chapter, under the Justices of the Peace Act 1968 all Judges ceased to be justices by virtue of their office, steps were taken in the Act to preserve their power to bind over to keep the peace.

Fines: Whereas fines were not imposed by the justices in earlier times, by the late twentieth century they were by far the commonest form of sentence in the magistrates' courts, amounting in some years to 90 per cent of the sentences passed. In contrast, fines imposed by Assizes and Quarter Sessions were comparatively few, especially before the passing of the Criminal Justice Act 1948, for until then these courts had no power to order fines for felonies, although they could do so for misdemeanours. Magistrates' courts, when imposing fines, were required by the Magistrates' Courts Act 1952 and subsequent legislation to take the offender's means into account.

A current phenomenon from the 1960s onwards was a fall in the value of money, but for a time both the Government and the magistrates failed to take account of it, and consequently the level of fines became unduly low. At last, legislation was passed to increase the maximum financial penalties which the summary courts could impose, and periodical guidance from the Lord Chancellor made justices more inflation-conscious. The Criminal Law Act 1977 enabled the Home Secretary to vary fines by order to take account of inflation.[71] The maximum fines that magistrates could impose for indictable offences triable summarily with consent was fixed in 1925 at £100 (and/or six months imprisonment). This was not changed until 1967 when the figure was raised to £400, and in 1977 to £1,000. There were a few exceptions to these limits, the most notable being offences against foreign currency and fishing regulations. Under the Fishery Limits Act 1976 penalties of up to £50,000 could be imposed on summary conviction for breaches of fishery regulations. In cases involving foreign currency frauds the financial penalty was limited only by the size of the sum involved in the illegal transaction as we have seen in ch. VI.[72] From 1982 most fines were placed on a five point scale set out in the Criminal Justice Act of that year.[73]

In default of payment of a fine magistrates had power to order imprisonment, but whereas during the five years following 1945 the average number of committals for non-payment were under 5,000 annually, it had reached more than 13,000 by 1967. This induced Parliament to take action in the Criminal Justice Act 1967 which, in addition to increasing the maximum penalties which might be imposed,

71. The most common cases in which fines were imposed were those of motoring offences. The average fine for speeding rose from £6.8 in 1967 to £9.6 in 1972, £17.7 in 1975, £20.04 in 1977 and £29 in 1981. The increase between 1967 and 1972 was in line with changes in the Retail Price Index. The average fine exceeded the Index in 1975, but this was mainly the result of large increases in maximum fines under the Road Traffic Act 1974, and after 1976 the increase of fines dropped behind the rate of inflation. Between 1977 and 1981 the average annual rate of increase in fines for motoring offences was 10 per cent compared with 13 per cent inflation.

72. In 1973 the City of London justices, in *DPP v. Stanley and Others* which took four weeks to try, imposed fines of £300,000 (£200,000 on one charge and £100,000 on a second) on two companies for offences under the Exchange Control Regulations, the financial penalty in such cases being limited only by the sums involved in the illegal transaction. These proceedings could have been brought before the Crown Court but the City magistrates, who were able to field a full team of financial experts, were thought to be the better tribunal.

73. In 1989 the standard scale under the Criminal Justice Act 1982 (s. 37(2)), of maximum fines on an adult on conviction for a summary offence was:

Level 1	£50
Level 2	£100
Level 3	£400
Level 4	£1,000
Level 5	£2,000

restricted further the magistrates' powers to commit to prison by requiring them to find that all other methods of enforcement had been inappropriate or unsuccessful. This Act also gave magistrates the power to remit fines and to enforce them by attachment of earnings, but the latter device proved to be less efficacious than had been expected mainly because of the speed with which employees were able to change their employment. The 1967 Act also made magistrates responsible for enforcing fines imposed at trials on indictment by the higher courts. The Act did have an immediate effect in reducing the number of committals to prison which fell in the following year to 8,720, but this was due to a large extent to the reluctance of magistrates to apply immediate enforcement and instead they allowed longer time for repayment with the result that the total amount of outstanding fines mounted considerably. The number of committals for non-payment also increased in the following years and by the early 1980s about 20,000 defaulters were jailed each year. The courts therefore came under increasing pressure not to impose this sanction but it proved impossible to find an effective alternative if the fine was to be a valid penalty. The subject was examined in 1981 by a NACRO group headed by Lady Howe (a London justice who was married to Sir Geoffrey Howe the then Chancellor of the Exchequer). They came firmly to the conclusion that prison should be retained as a final sanction for those who wilfully refuse to pay fines.[74]

At the end of 1976 unpaid fines amounted to about £15 million, but six years later it was nearly £40 million.[75] A fine was potentially the most promising alternative to a custodial sentence, but its value depended upon prompt and effective enforcement measures, and many courts gave it low priority. Inquiries revealed that the rate varied considerably from court to court. A Home Office study in 1982 showed that performance was closely related to efficient organization and to the quality of the staff engaged in collection, and also to the speed with which action was taken after default.

A new method of assessing the rate of fines was introduced towards the end of the 1980s. *Unit fines* as they were called, were the subject of a pilot scheme conducted by the Basingstoke justices and those in three other divisions. The fines were based on the seriousness of the offence combined with the defendant's ability to pay. The amount was measured by assessing the number of weeks which represented the

---

74. In 1965 the Lord Chancellor had appointed a committee under the chairmanship of Mr Justice Payne to consider the enforcement of judgment debts. It recommended (Cmnd 3909 (1969)) that there should be Enforcement Offices which would deal with enforcing both civil debts and also the payment of fines. This recommendation was later endorsed by the *Report on Non-Custodial and Semi-Custodial Penalties* (HMSO. (1970), ch. 2).

75. This sum included fines imposed by the higher courts as well as by magistrates and it also included fines which were not yet due because the court had allowed payment by instalments.

gravity of the offence and a unit per week which represented the person's spare weekly income, the precise formula being left to the discretion of the magistrates in the division. For example, careless driving was rated by one bench at five weeks; driving with excess alcohol in the blood, 10 weeks; theft, five to 10 weeks; assault, 10 to 30 weeks. This was multiplied by the weekly rate of the spare income of the individual defendant which was calculated in accordance with a means form which he had to complete. Unit fines were a success from the start, and in 1990 they were included in a Government White Paper and later in the Criminal Justice Bill. They seemed destined to become a standard approach in the magistrates' courts.

Disparity in sentences: Almost 90 per cent of the complaints about the conduct of magistrates which were received by the Lord Chancellor from the middle of the century onwards related to the sentences which were imposed, and most of these alleged undue leniency or disparity. Many were unjustified because they were based on the limited reports of cases which were published by the media, but there were many others for which there was ample foundation, though it is also true to say that divergence of views on sentencing was not markedly greater among the lay justices than it was among of the professional judiciary at all levels. One of the objects of the sentencing conferences and exercises for justices which were organized on an increasing scale from the mid-1950s was to minimize disparity in the level of sentences imposed by different justices and different benches, while recognizing that there might be good reasons for variations in sentencing policy in different areas.

It was in the sentencing of motoring offenders that divergent views among the sentencers became more apparent than in any other types of case.[76] The Magistrates' Association had recognized the importance of the problem by 1960, and in 1965 they prepared a list of what they termed "basic penalties" for the principal motoring offences. This was intended to give an indication of what would be appropriate where there were neither aggravating nor mitigating circumstances. It was emphasized that the suggestions were subject to variation according to the circumstances of each case and the previous record of the offender. The list was approved by the Lord Chancellor and the Lord Chief Justice in 1965 and was then circulated to members of the Association throughout the country. This was attacked from various quarters on the ground that it attempted to fetter the court's

76.   Disparity in the sentencing of motoring offenders was the subjects of detailed study by Dr Roger Hood of Cambridge University in 1972. At the beginning of cha. I of his book *Sentencing the Motoring Offender* he comments that many of those convicted of motoring offences felt a grievance, but although they blamed the police for prosecuting their main complaint was against the magistrates because they believed that there were gross disparities in the sentences imposed.

discretion, but it was defended by the Lord Chancellor, Lord Gardiner, and the Association issued further lists at intervals from then onwards. The suggested penalties were later termed "starting points" to emphasize that no attempt was being made to lay down standard tariffs, and later still similar guidance was given for some of the other common types of offence in addition to those relating to traffic. Many benches drew up their own lists of "norms" based on the Association's guidelines. There was good reason to believe that sentencing exercises and the issue of lists of "starting points" had an appreciable effect on reducing unreasonable disparity in sentences for motoring offences.

There remained marked differences between benches in different parts of the country but these could often be justified by differing local conditions and the prevalence or otherwise of certain types of crime in the area, and also by the extent to which the police cautioned the least serious offenders instead of bringing them to court. In vol. III, ch. I attention is drawn to differences in sentencing between the English and Welsh justices.

The juvenile courts

The seperate courts which were first established by the Children and Young Persons Act 1908 to deal with juveniles continued to operate in the second half of the century in much the same way as they had done before. The justices' jurisdiction when sitting in these courts was hybrid, and included both criminal and civil business. About four-fifths was criminal and the procedure in these cases was the same as that in the adult courts. The remaining one-fifth was unique and consisted of care proceedings.

The composition of the juvenile courts continued to be governed by the Children and Young Persons Act 1933, as amended by subsequent legislation, in particular the Children and Young Persons Act 1969, and rules made thereunder by the Lord Chancellor. As before, the courts were drawn from a juvenile panel elected every three years by the justices in each division, except in the county of London (later Inner London) where they were appointed by the Home Secretary until 1964 and thereafter by the Lord Chancellor[77] on the recommendation of a specially constituted advisory committee. Those elected to the panels were supposed to be the most suitable of the local

---

77. The transfer of responsibility was effected by s. 12 of the Administration of Justice Act 1964 after a clash between the Lord Chancellor, Lord Dilhorne, and the Home Secretary, Mr Henry Brooke. Lord Dilhorne took the view that as the Lord Chancellor was then responsible for virtually all judicial appointments those of the London juvenile court justices should also be in his hands. Mr Brooke and the Home Office on the other hand were reluctant to lose this function and claimed that the existing system worked effectively. Lord Dilhorne was able to gain the support of most of his Cabinet colleagues and the transfer was made.

justices for this specialized work, but until the mid-1960s this was often not the case, and in many instances the panels were composed mostly of those justices who could afford to give the extra time that was required.

Until 1949 there was no statutory age limit for justices serving on juvenile panels, though in London it was the normal practice of the Home Secretary not to appoint anyone to the panel who was over 70 or who would attain that age during the life of the panel. Justices were also encouraged to resign from the panels when they reached 75 and in a few places the justices themselves fixed an age limit, sometimes below 70. We have seen in the last chapter that the Royal Commission of 1948 regarded the ages of justices sitting in juvenile courts as being of the utmost importance, and they considered that the most suitable age for appointment was between 30 and 40. They also recommended that every justice should be required to retire from the panel on attaining the age of 65. The Lord Chancellor, in exercise of powers confined upon him by the Justices of the Peace Act 1949, made rules which disqualified lay justices (but not stipendiaries) from serving on a panel after reaching 65 unless specially exempted by him.

As mentioned earlier, from 1933 each court had to consist of three justices who were to include at least one man and, so far as practicable, one woman. The reason for this sex discrimination was that until the 1950s there were not sufficient numbers of women on the commissions to staff all juvenile courts. Shortly after the war, however, there was considerable agitation by women's organizations aimed at correcting this discrepancy, and the Lord Chancellor instructed his advisory committees to take positive steps to increase the proportion of women justices. By 1954 it was decided that the rules could safely be amended. Accordingly, a new set of rules[78] provided that a juvenile court should comprise both a man and a women, but in case of emergency it was also provided that if at any time no man or no woman was available the court might proceed with only men or only women present.

The chairman of a juvenile court played a particularly important part. His role required considerable skill and experience in handling children, and it might be more demanding than that of the chairman of an adult court. Throughout England and Wales, except London, the chairman of a juvenile court was elected by the members of his panel to preside during the three year period for which the panel was constituted. In London the chairman was either a metropolitan stipendiary magistrate or a lay justice appointed by the Home Secretary or later by the Lord Chancellor.[79]

78. Juvenile Courts (Constitution) Rules 1954.
79. AS explained in ch. IV, stipendiary magistrates sat alone in the London juvenile courts from their inception in 1908 until 1933 when, if they sat at all, they were required to do so with lay justices. In 1945 none of the stipendiaries were doing this work, but from then onwards some began to do so again, and in the 1980s six or seven were usually on the panel.

The most extensive piece of legislation relating to this branch of the justices' work was the Children Act 1989 which made a fundamental change in the juvenile court itself. This Act, in spite of a strong movement aimed at abolishing the magistrates' jurisdiction in juvenile matters, preserved their prominent position but in a reformed structure. The previous juvenile courts were retained but only for criminal proceedings, and the Act transferred care, custody and adoption, together with the justices' previous domestic jurisdiction, to a new Family Proceedings Court composed of magistrates drawn from family panels which replaced the existing domestic panels. This will be described more fully when dealing with the justices' civil work in the next chapter.

Treatment of young offenders

Throughout the period there were more significant changes in the treatment of young offenders than in any other area of the criminal justice system. No other issue aroused greater feeling among magistrates and their clerks as well as the public. There was also a great advance in the social services, and whereas in the early years of the juvenile courts such services as existed had been totally inadequate, from the end of the war they were vastly strengthened and expanded. Previously the juvenile courts themselves had tended to act as a kind of welfare agency, but now work was assumed by officers of the local authorities.

In 1945 the procedure of the juvenile court when dealing with young offenders was essentially the same as that in the adult courts, and was adversarial, but far less formal. The young who appeared before the juvenile courts were either children, who were under the age of 14, or young persons aged between 14 and 17. They were tried summarily in the juvenile courts for all offences except those involving homicide, unless they were charged jointly with an adult. The minimum age at which a child could be prosecuted under the 1933 Act was eight. Before then it was seven where, as mentioned earlier, it had remained since the Normans reduced the age of criminality from 12 where it had been under the Saxons. In 1960 the Ingleby Committee (mentioned below) recommended that the limit be increased to 12. This was never implemented, but the Children and Young Persons Act 1963 raised it to 10, where it remains, though provision was made in the Children and Young Persons Act 1969 to raise it further, first to 12 and then to 14. There was therefore the curious phenomenon that, as the seriousness of offences committed by children increased, the age of criminality was also raised. After 1969, however, opinion hardened against raising the prosecutable age, and it was allowed to remain at 10.[80]

Some of the sentences which might be imposed on juveniles have been described earlier in this chapter in the context of sentencing in general. They included attendance centres and detention centres which were introduced by the Criminal Justice Act 1948. The Children and Young Persons Act 1969, which had been passed by the Labour Government, provided for the abolition of attendance centres and detention centres and also of Borstals, but this part of the Act was not brought into force immediately, as the Conservative Government which came into office in 1970 had different views on the value of these disposals. By the time a Labour Government was returned in 1974 opinion generally was more favourable to their retention. However, in 1982 the Criminal Justice Act finally abolished Borstal training and also imprisonment for offenders under 21. The 1982 Act also introduced new determinate sentences including a revised system of detention centre orders. In broad terms the courts were able to impose these orders from three to four months in length. When longer sentences were necessary the court could impose *youth custody*. A youth custody sentence was usually served in the same institution which was previously used for Borstal training. An important innovation was that magistrates could thereafter send an offender direct to youth custody whereas previously they had been obliged to commit to the Crown Court for a Borstal sentence.

From 1945 onwards the previously accepted theories on the treatment of young offenders underwent extensive reappraisal. Attention was focused to an increasing extent upon the care aspects of the proceedings in the juvenile courts and upon the need to remove the young as far as possible from the atmosphere of the criminal courts. This coincided with the expansion of the social services mentioned above and with a movement to transfer welfare work to officers of the local authorities, who were given new powers in both welfare and education by the Children Act 1948. One of the most important provisions of this Act from the point of view of the magistrates was s. 5, which placed an obligation on local authorities to accept any child who was placed in their care by a court under what was called a "fit person order." Previously an authority could refuse. Where a child was placed in the care of an authority the latter was responsible for his welfare and education while the order remained in force.

80.   Between 1969 and 1973 the number of children under the age of 17 dealt with (either by the courts or by police caution) for indictable offences rose from 165,000 to 205,000. At the same time, the degree of seriousness of the offences increased and by 1975 boys and girls aged 10-16 were responsible for nearly one-sixth of all offences of personal violence, one-fifth of all theft and handling, a quarter of criminal damage, 30 per cent of robberies and 45 per cent of burglaries.

The Children and Young Persons Act 1933 made certain provisions for the care and protection of children, as already described. The definition of being in need of care and protection was widened further by the Acts of 1952 and 1956. The powers of local authorities to deal with such children were also enlarged by the Family Allowances and National Insurance Act 1956. This movement towards increasing the local authorities' involvement culminated in the Children and Young Persons Act 1969 whereby much of the responsibility for young offenders was moved from the courts to the social services administered by the local authorities.

Efforts were already being made in the early 1950s to keep the young out of the courts entirely. One of the earliest moves in this direction was a Police Juvenile Liaison Scheme which was adopted in 1951 by the Liverpool police authority and which was based on cautioning instead of prosecuting the juvenile first offenders. So impressive were the results that they were soon followed by authorities in other areas.

The pace increased during the 1960s. In the autumn of 1960 the Children and Young Persons Committee, under the chairmanship of Viscount Ingleby, issued its report[81] which supported the retention of the magistrates' juvenile courts but recommended a further move away from the concept of criminal jurisdiction. The recommendations were partly implemented in the Criminal Justice Act 1961 and in the Children and Young Persons Act 1963.[82] The latter extended the welfare powers of local authorities and required them to do preventive work on behalf of children. At the same time the causes of crime, especially among juveniles, and the welfare of deprived children began to form part of the Labour party's political platform, and in 1964 the party produced a paper *Crime - a Challenge to Us All,* which contained recommendations by a group headed by Lord Longford and including Lord Gardiner, the future Lord Chancellor. The paper had a considerable influence on the Labour Government which came into office in October 1964, and in 1965 they published a White Paper, *The Child, the Family and the Young Offender.* This went so far as to propose that juvenile courts should be abolished and that offenders under 16 should be dealt with by "family councils" and those aged 16 to 21 by "young offenders courts." A family council was to consist of two social workers from the local authority's children's department and other suitable persons. These proposals ran into heavy opposition and were dropped, but a further White Paper, *Children in Trouble,*

81. Cmnd 1191 (1960).
82. These Acts applied to England and Wales, but developments were also taking place in Scotland. In 1964 the Committee on Children and Young Persons; Scotland, under the chairmanship of Lord Kilbrandon, reported (Cmnd 2306) and its recommendations were implemented by the Social Work (Scotland) Act 1968.

published in 1968, was better received and formed the basis for the Children and Young Persons Act 1969, which can be seen as part of the continuing process that begin in 1847 and was a logical extension of the underlying philosophy of the Children Act 1908. The aim was to spare young offenders the stigma of criminality by dealing with them as far as possible outside the criminal law, and to support and treat them in their families and in the community. The Act provided for "intermediate treatment" which would allow a child to remain in his home but would also bring him into contact with a different environment. It retained the juvenile courts but removed their power to send a child to an approved school or to make a fit person order. It also abolished the sanctions which might be imposed in default of payment of fines and it substituted *supervision orders,* which carried no penal sanctions, in place of probation orders.

In some respects the 1969 Act proved to be an example of idealism out-running resources. Its provisions were brought into operation before there had been adequate groundwork, and they were therefore not given a fair chance to prove themselves effective. Experienced probation officers were replaced by local authority social workers who were not specifically trained in this type of duty, and in most cases they had no secure accommodation at their disposal. Local authorities failed in many cases to keep pace with the extra demands made on them in terms of both staff and facilities.

Although the 1969 Act was well designed to deal with the majority of young offenders it made no provision for the minority who persisted in the commission of crimes. The latter carried out their disruptive activities with impunity and with increasing contempt of authority, which led to public accusations that the courts were failing in their duty to administer the law. This caused deep resentment among the magistrates who were placed in a virtually impossible position. When dealing with a child under the age of 14 there was nothing they could do beyond making a care order placing it in the care of the local authority. What happened thereafter depended entirely upon the authority, and frequently the child was returned to his home and immediately proceeded to commit another offence. It became quite normal for a child who appeared before a court to have been found guilty of three or four similar offences within the previous few weeks and for the magistrates to find themselves obliged to make the same order at each hearing.[83] The police often took the view that it was a waste of time to bring a child before the court.

It is not surprising that this state of affairs caused disillusionment among many of the magistrates, especially as they were accused of exaggerating the juvenile problem and of being motivated purely by resentment at losing their former powers. This was a gross distortion of the truth. Since well before the 1948 Act, a number of juvenile court chairmen, of whom the most outstanding were Basil Henriques and John Watson, had been among the leaders of the movement towards greater understanding of the problems of young people, and there can be little doubt that the great majority of the justices who served in the juvenile courts were dedicated to their work and were genuinely concerned with the problems and welfare of the children who appeared before them. They were wholly in sympathy with the philosophy underlying the 1969 Act and were at the opposite end of the spectrum from the callous sadists which some of their detractors tried to make them appear. Many were involved in social work and a significant proportion were in the teaching profession and had had long experience of young people. They readily acknowledged that the new Act provided a sound framework for dealing with children in trouble, but they were critical of the method of implementing, or failing to implement, the new policy.

In 1972 several juvenile court justices resigned in desperation at not being able to discharge what they saw as their public duty, but the great majority continued to serve. While agreeing whole-heartedly that the care of juvenile offenders was of the utmost importance, they pointed out that this could never be the sole consideration. They were particularly concerned that the interest of the victims and of the public in general should be protected. In 1976 the House of Commons Expenditure Committee suggested that courts should be enabled to make a "secure care" order which would oblige a local authority to keep a child in secure accommodation, and the Magistrates' Association urged that this recommendation should be implemented. They pointed out that the inability of magistrates to make orders for the custody of juveniles on remand when bail was inappropriate

83. In 1976 the Lord Chancellor's attention was drawn to a boy of 13 who had committed 81 burglaries and was brought before the court, who placed him in interim care pending full consideration of his case. In the space of 10 days he escaped six times and committed nine further burglaries. His parents asked that he should be sent to secure accommodation but the local authority had nowhere secure and were not prepared to turn a key in a lock. They tried keeping the boy in his pyjamas but he again escaped. This was repeated a further three times, with the boy absconding on each occasion, and at last the local authority agreed to put him in a locked room. There was, however, no secure accommodation which could contain him so that remedial and educative work could begin. This kind of situation was repeated throughout the country and it became quite normal for a child appearing before a court to have been found guilty of three or four similar offences within the previous few weeks and for the magistrates to find themselves obliged to make the same order at each hearing. *The Changing Image of the Magistracy,* 2nd ed., p. 108.

frequently resulted in the court being obliged to resort to the wholly unsatisfactory expedient of remanding the juvenile in prison while inquiries were made pending trial. This was because the local authority had no accommodation in which they could hold him. The Government, however, would not accept the Expenditure Committee's recommendation on the ground that it limited the local authorities' discretion.

Magistrates were not alone in criticizing the operation of the 1969 Act. In *R. v. D.*[84] the Court of Appeal reviewed the case of a boy of 15 who had a long criminal record. They took the view that the proper course was to send him to a community home, but they noted what frequently had been the experience of magistrates' courts in that if a care order were made the offender was often returned to his home within a short time. Lawton, LJ, observed that the decision whether the boy would go to a community home did not rest with the court but with "unknown social workers and psychiatrists," and he added that "the bureaucratic machinery is such nowadays that the courts have no control whatsoever over where the boy should go." The Court of Appeal was concerned with the safety of the public as well as with the welfare of the boy and they decided that it was not in the public interest that he should roam the streets as he pleased. They therefore confirmed an order for Borstal training as the only means of keeping him in secure accommodation, though in other respects they considered this to be the wrong treatment.

This continued to be the position until the Criminal Justice Act 1982 introduced *residential care orders.* It provided that where a juvenile who was already the subject of a care order was found guilty of an offence punishable with imprisonment in the case of a person over 21, the court might add a condition to the order that, for a period not exceeding six months, the local authority might not place the juvenile in the care of a parent or guardian or other person.

The Children and Young Persons Act 1969, though imbued with sound principles, was not well implemented, and lack of facilities denied it a fair trial. Its implementation was also made more difficult because it coincided with the amalgamation of the children's departments and the transfer of responsibility from the Home Office to the Department of Health and Social Security. This was followed in 1974 by the reorganization of local authorities upon whom responsibility was largely to rest.

Steps were taken to strengthen the 1969 Act in the Children Act 1975 and the Criminal Law Act 1977. Under the latter the *supervision order*, which had lost much of its credibility, could contain conditions

---

84.   *The Times,* October 21, 1976.

such as "regular attendance at school." The 1975 Act aimed to improve the provisions of the 1969 statute which enabled local authorities to restrict the liberty of a child "to such extent as the authority thinks appropriate." The 1975 Act also authorized the making of regulations for an annual judicial review of care orders, a course which had been urged by magistrates for some time. In 1980 the Child Care Act empowered local authorities to assume parental rights and duties in respect of a child in care. In 1982 the Criminal Justice Act introduced further substantial changes in the sentencing and treatment of young as well as adult offenders.[85]

These steps were not sufficient to satisfy public opinion, and at the end of the 1980s the Government embarked upon the most extensive reform of the law relating to juveniles since 1908, which was imbodied in the Children Act 1989. This was indeed an important milestone both for the children and for the magistrates. Some regarded it as the greatest piece of legislation concerning the young. A Government paper issued to coincide with the passing of the Act began with the words:

"The Children Act which received Royal Assent on November 16, 1989 is the most comprehensive piece of legislation which Parliament has ever enacted about children. It draws together and simplifies existing legislation to produce a more practical and consistent code. It integrates the law relating to private individuals with the responsibilities of public authorities, in particular local authority social services departments, towards children. In so doing the Act strikes a new balance between family autonomy and the protection of children."[86]

From the magistrates' point of view one of the most important of the Act's many provisions was that it retained the juvenile courts, but only for criminal proceedings, and it transfered care, custody and adoption, together with the previous domestic proceedings, to the new Family Proceedings Court composed of justices drawn from family panels which replaced the existing domestic panels. The juvenile courts retained the power, however, to make supervision orders in criminal proceedings. Details of the new care system are given in the next chapter.

---

85. As already mentioned, these included the replacement of Borstal training by a new sentence of youth custody and it also made changes in detention centres and in the law relating to compensation. Day training centres were replaced by locally financed day centres, and the Act gave new powers to impose "curfew" and residential care orders and to make financial orders on parents.

86. *An Introduction to the Children Act 1989.* HMSO, November 1989.

Borstal: Borstal training for young offenders over the age of 17 which, as we have seen, was introduced in 1908, continued to be a sentencing option until 1982. Magistrates' courts could not sentence offenders direct to a Borstal institution except in Northern Ireland. If they considered Borstal training to be appropriate treatment they could commit the offender to a higher court for the order to be made. The Criminal Justice Act 1948 encouraged magistrates to make such committals instead of imprisonment by clarifying the circumstances in which an order might be made. It provided, however, that the higher courts must be "satisfied having regard to his character and previous conduct, and to the circumstances of the offence, that it is expedient for his reformation and the prevention of crime" that the offender should undergo Borstal training.

Borstals were designed, however, for the more simple way of life of the pre-war years when, to judge from the low reconviction rate, they were reasonably successful. After the war many young adult offenders who should have been sentenced to prison arrived in the Borstals which became over populated and contained a considerable number of difficult characters for whom the institutions were not designed. Moreover, overcrowding meant that time spent in Borstal had to be reduced, and many were discharged before their training was completed. In 1974 the Advisory Council on the Penal System[87] presented a report on an inquiry it had carried out on young adult offenders. The report, which contained a very full account of the Borstal system, put forward proposals for a shift from custody to treatment in the community and recommended that imprisonment, Borstal and detention centres for young adult offenders should be discontinued and replaced by two new forms of sentence, one custodial in a prison department establishment designated by the Home Secretary, the other non-custodial which would allow release under supervision in the community. These recommendations were not accepted, but in 1982 the Criminal Justice Act abolished Borstal training and imprisonment for offenders aged under 21. These options were replaced by the two new determinate sentences of detention centre and youth custody orders mentioned above.

---

87.   An Advisory Council on the Treatment of Offenders was set up by the Home Secretary in 1944 as a standing body to consider matters he referred to it. The council was dissolved when a Royal Commission on Crime and Punishment was appointed in 1964, but the commission was disbanded in 1966 without having completed its task and the Home Secretary then appointed the Advisory Council on the Penal System.

CHAPTER IX

1945-1989 A NEW CHALLENGE
PART III - CIVIL COURTS AND ADMINISTRATIVE DUTIES

Civil jurisdiction: Husband and Wife; Children; Civil Debts - Rules of
Procedure - Legal Aid - Administrative duties - The Justices of the
Peace in a new environment

THE LAST TWO CHAPTERS HAVE DESCRIBED the Justices of
the Peace and their criminal jurisdiction in the last half of the
twentieth century. This chapter will conclude the account of the
justices during this period by describing their civil jurisdiction and
administrative functions. It will also include two subjects which were
relevant to both criminal and civil proceedings - legal aid and rules of
procedure.

Civil jurisdiction

One of the anomalies of the magistrates' courts was that, although they
were primarily concerned with the administration of criminal law, they
were also required to handle an appreciable amount of civil business,
quite apart from that which came before the juvenile courts as just
described. It would have been more logical if this civil work had been
placed within the exclusive jurisdiction of the County Courts,[1] but in
the past, Parliament had seen fit to relegate a variety of odd duties to
the Justices of the Peace as a cheap and easy method of dealing with
what were thought to be fairly simple problems. In most cases this has
remained the position to the present day, when magistrates are still
entrusted with family matters and with the enforcement of certain
debts to special creditors, notably rates and income tax. A few further
additions were made to the list after the war when the right of appeal
to magistrates from determinations by a local authority was extended.

Domestic proceedings

The bulk of the civil work in magistrates' adult courts relates to
domestic matters and is among the most important of their functions.
It is also the most confused as there has long been much overlapping
with the High Court and the County Court for which no coherent
principle is apparent. The justices' domestic proceedings include

---

1. The establishment of the County Courts in 1846 has been described in ch. V. For the first
    20 years after World War II the maximum claim that could be brought before that court
    remained at £500 but, in the face of inflation, it had risen to £5,000 by October 1981. From
    1972 County Court Judges ceased to be appointed as such and they were converted into
    Circuit Judges with both civil and criminal jurisdiction under the Courts Act 1971, s. 20.

matrimonial, affiliation and guradianship cases, applications for consent to marry, adoptions and some rare proceedings under various statutes.

Until the creation of the new Family Proceedings Courts in 1989 the magistrates' family jurisdiction continued to be exercised as before by their domestic courts, which had to consist of not less than two nor more than three justices and were required to include so far as practicable at least one man and one woman.

From time to time proposals were made to trasnfer the magistrates' family jurisdiction elsewhere. In 1974 the Finer Committee on One Parent Families recommended the establishment of a new system of specialist family courts in which all family jurisdiction should be concentrated. The lowest level of the proposed structure would be composed of justices sitting in the County Court under the chairmanship of a Circuit Judge. This proposal was not accepted because it was decided that Circuit Judges were already fully committed and could not undertake any further duties. In 1975 the James Committee[2] recommended that magistrates' civil jurisdiction and administrative duties should be removed in order to allow them to develop to the full the skills required in their primary role of administering the criminal law. This recommendation was not accepted, and in so far as civil procedings were concerned the principal reason was inability to find an alternative tribunal. The Government also recognized that in certain respects justices had advantages over County Courts in that they could normally act more swiftly, the procedure was less expensive and they usually had a higher degree of local knowledge.

In 1977 a Law Commission Working Party[3] put forward alternative proposals which were implemented in the Domestic Proceedings and Magistrates Courts Act 1978. This provided for the establishment of courts composed of justices drawn from a panel specially appointed to deal with domestic proceedings. The Act also empowered the Lord Chancellor to make rules governing the size, chairmanship and composition of the domestic courts and the manner in which panel members should be elected. It extended the jurisdiction which the magistrates were to exercise in the new courts and assimilated the law to that administered in the High Court.

Matrimonial

We have seen that the origins of the justices' concern with family matters lay in the Elizabethan Poor Law which required a man to

2.   Cmnd. 5629 (1974).
3.   Committee on the Districution of Criminal Business between the Crown Court and Magistrates' Courts, Cmnd. 6323 (1975).

maintain his family so that they did not become a burden on the parish. As the Poor Law was administered by the justices, subsequent responsibility for enforcing similar duties also devolved on them. Their matrimonial jurisdiction, however, began with the Matrimonial Causes Act 1878 which, as we have seen, empowered them to make orders of non-cohabitation and maintenance and custody of children where a husband had been convicted of aggravated assault on his wife. Their work was very similar to that of the Divorce Division of the High Court and the problems facing both courts were often the same, but whereas the High Court could grant a divorce the magistrates could only make an order of separation. The magistrates' matrimonial jurisdiction was extended by subsequent statutes[4] and was consolidated by the Matrimonial Proceedings (Magistrates' Courts) Act 1960, which was based on the report of the Committee on Matrimonial Proceedings in Magistrates' Courts.[5] Among other things the Act removed the maximum limit on the weekly amount of £7.10 shillings which could be awarded as maintenance to a wife. The occasions on which husbands assaulted their wives became less frequent than before and the wife's reason for coming to court was more often to obtain maintenance and other relief. After the 1960 Act a husband could also obtain relief against his wife. The grounds on which either a husband or a wife could obtain an order were desertion, cruelty, adultery, habitual drunkenness, wilful neglect to maintain and certain others.

The public were excluded from matrimonial proceedings and there was a severe restriction on what might be published by the press. The proceedings themselves were informal. An appeal against a magistrates' order lay to the Divisional Court of the Probate, Divorce and Admiralty Division - later the Family Division - of the High Court.

Matrimonial cases were more likely than any others coming before magistrates to involve difficult questions of law, yet whereas similar cases coming before the High Court had been carefully prepared in advance by solicitors and were presented by counsel, the magistrates were usually obliged to look after the interests of both parties and to rely for guidance solely upon their clerk. Consequently, the advice of the clerk was sought more frequently than in other proceedings. A matrimonial case could also occupy more time than any other, because it was not uncommon for an order to have to be reconsidered by the court from time to time, and this might continue for a number of years. A husband or a wife might apply for the order to be amended or discharged, or one party might fail to keep up payments and would then be brought before the court for inquiry as to his or her means.

4.   Licensing Act 1902; Maintenance Orders (Facilities for Enforcement) Act 1920; Summary Jurisdiction (Separation and Maintenance) Act 1925; Matrimonial Causes Act 1937; Magistrates' Courts Act 1952, ss. 56-62; Maintenance Agreements Act 1957.
5.   Cmnd. 638 (1959).

Failure to comply with an order could ultimately lead to committal to prison. An attempt to strengthen the magistrates' powers to enforce payment of maintenance was made by the Matrimonial Orders Act 1968 which enabled them to make an order for the attachment of earnings. This proved to be less effective than had been hoped because, as mentioned earlier, a husband could often change jobs without being traced.

The Domestic Proceedings and Magistrates Court Act 1978 extended the jurisdiction which magistrates were to exercise in the new specialist courts set up under the Act (described above) and assimilated the law to that administered in the High Court. A guiding principle which was set out in s. 26 of the Act was that, before hearing an application, a court must consider whether there was any chance of reconciliation between the parties.

For a number of years prior to 1978 the matrimonial jurisdiction of magistrates had been in decline and it was thought that the new Act would lead to a revival in this branch of their work. In fact, although the situation varied widely from area to area, there continued to be a general drift of business from the magistrates' courts to the County Court. Most solicitors favoured the County Court, but the main reason for this drift was the lack of initiative on the part of many magistrates to provide an effective service. The Magistrates' Association and the Justices' Clerks' Society, however, recognized the Act as a challenge, and in 1981 they issued a joint paper to domestic court panels making a number of suggestions on how to operate the courts effectively. They pointed out that a court composed of three people, selected and trained for the work and drawn from a range of social backgrounds, including both sexes and with the possibility of a spread of ages, all with wide experience of the local community, should be an ideal tribunal to handle domestic problems, especially in the role of conciliator. After 1981 the magistrates' matrimonial work showed signs of increasing, but the family court concept was never far from the minds of the reformers and legislators.

Juvenile
The juvenile courts and their hybrid jurisdiction was described in the last chapter. They were responsible for the trial of young offenders and also for the welfare of those in need of care and protection. The latter was part of the magistrates' civil jurisdiction and was generally regarded as one of their most important functions. It was also thought to be one that should be entrusted to a new type of family court, and this was the underlying principle applied to the novel system introduced in 1989 though, as we have seen, the justices retained responsibility through the new Family Proceedings Court.

Under the Children Act 1989 all applications for care orders, access and related matters were to start in the new court, but the Lord Chancellor was to define criteria which would decide which cases were to be transferred. A forensically difficult case would obviously be referred to a professional Judge, but the Lord Chancellor recognized that Justices of the Peace had a very important input to make into this branch of the law. The Lord Chancellor was also to make rules allocating some types of cases between courts. In particular, local authority proceedings involving the protection of children were to start in a magistrates' court but were then to be transferable to a County Court or the High Court, if their weight or complexity justified it. This would have important results for the magistrates becaues it meant that there would be far more disclosure of evidence by the parties ahead of the hearing with greater reliance on written material which would involve the magistrates in reading papers before the hearing. It would also require the magistrates to give reasons for their decision at the conclusion, in marked contrast to most proceedings in magistrates' courts where no reasons were given.

Section 17 of the 1989 Act set out three principles which were to guide a court when administering the Act. (1) The child's welfare was to be the paramount consideration when determining any question regarding his upbringing. (2) A court might not make an order under the Act unless it considered that to do so would be better for the child than making no order at all. (3) The court should have regard to the general principle that delay in deciding questions as to a child's upbringing was likely to prejudice his welfare. The Act was also based on the belief that children were best cared for within the family with both parents playing a full part and without resort to legal proceedings.

The administrative arrangements for the new system were to be supervised by a committee appointed by the President of the Family Division of the High Court which was to include magistrates. The campaign for a family court had been waged for 20 years and had got nowhere, but although the 1989 Act did not impose the comprehensive type of court for which campaigners had pressed, it did produce the embryo of such a tribunal. The new system of courts also differed from what had ben urged by some of the family court advocates in that it retained the lay justices as an essential element in the framework. In doing so it presented them with yet another challenge. The Lord Chancellor announced that he was to maintain a rolling programme of review of family law, procedure, jurisdiction and related machinery and that he had an open mind as to what further part the magistrates could play in the family law system. The magistrates therefore had a real chance to prove themselves. Yet they were also faced with a new burden involving both an exacting workload in the courts and still more intensive training. A new philosophy had to be developed, and expertise gained in the juvenile courts would not be sufficient. There was clearly a question mark as to whether sufficient numbers of justices could, or would be willing to accept the additional pressure on top of their existing duties. The most likely prospect seemed to be the establishment of a specialist body of justices, highly trained in the disciplines of family jurisdiction and engaged exclusively in this work, leaving the rest of the magisterial duties to others. In the past the Lord Chancellor had been prepared to accept such a system in the case of London juvenile courts, but elsewhere he adhered strictly to the rule that all JPs should sit regularly in the ordinary courts even if they were also members of specialist courts. When the 1989 Act was passed there was reason to believe that the Lord Chancellor was prepared to consider an extension of the London system to other parts of the country. A specialist system would probably have the advantage of attracting a number of suitable candidates who were already experienced in the welfare of children and were dedicated to work of this kind but who were not interested in the wider experience of magistrates' courts. The fact remained that at the beginning of 1990 the Justices of the Peace had a real chance to prove themselves in a new environment. Their family jurisdiction might well be extended still further if they were able and willing to seize the opportunity presented to them. On the other hand, they might fail to meet the challenge as they had done in the Crown Court, in which case they would eventually lose their family jurisdiction entirely.

Custody
In addition to an order for the payment of maintenance and directing that the spouses were no longer bound to cohabit, the magistrates could award custody to one of the parents of any children under the age of 16. After the Matrimonial Causes Act 1878 custody was always given to the wife, but following the Matrimonial Proceedings (Magistrates' Courts) Act 1960 and for some time thereafter it was normally awarded to the successful party. By the end of the 1960s, however, the primary concern of all courts was the welfare of the child, and it was not uncommon for magistrates, having considered all the circumstances, to place a child in the care of the children's department of a local authority or under supervision.

These cases occupied a considerable amount of the justices' time, but the decisions they reached often attracted adverse public comment. An instance of this was the case of *Deramault* v. *Deramault* which was heard by two justices in Gosforth in 1970. They awarded custody of a child to the father who was French and who immediately returned with it to France. The mother appealed successfully to the High Court which reversed the magistrates' decision, but by then the child was outside the jurisdiction and it was three years before it could be restored to the mother. The public obloquy which descended upon the justices exceeded any other criticism of magistrates during the period, but it was largely undeserved as the justices, both of whom were experienced and dedicated members of the juvenile panel, had spent a great deal of time on the case and had reasonable grounds for reaching their decision.[6] This was one of the many instances where public feeling was roused by ill-informed comment in some sections of the press.

Adoption

Justices of the Peace had heard applications for the adoption of children since 1926 when the first Adoption Act was passed. Until then adoption, which had figured prominently in Roman law, was unknown to English law under which one person could not adopt another. The 1926 Act enabled parents to surrender their rights and obligations over their children to other persons who were allowed to adopt them. There was considerable overlapping of jurisdiction because applications could be made either to the High Court, the County Court or the magistrates, but most came before the summary courts because they were considerably cheaper and more convenient. Although the press had the right to attend sittings of the juvenile courts this did not extend to adoption proceedings.

Changes in the law of adoption were made in several Acts during this period and local authorities were empowered to take part in arrangements for the adoption of a child whether or not it was in their care. The Children Act 1975 contained provisions which encouraged the making of custody rather than adoption orders, but this was overtaken the following year by the Adoption Act 1976 which was the last statute relating to adoption before 1989. The 1976 Act was amended and clarified by the Children Act 1989 which transferred adoption proceedings to the new Family Proceedings Courts, described earlier, which were composed of justices drawn from the new family panels which replaced the former domestic panels. The jurisdiction of these courts, however, was concurrent with that of the High Court and the County Courts.

Bastardy

As the century progressed the concept of illegitimacy and its debasement of the social and financial position of those who were not born in wedlock became unacceptable. Recognition of the new ethos was contained in the Family Law Reform Act 1987. From then onwards references to relationships were to be construed without regard to whether or not the father and mother of a person were or

---

6. A fuller account of this case is given in *The Changing Image of the Magistracy*, 2nd ed., pp. 169-170.

had been married to each other. The notion of bastardy was eliminated and thereafter affiliation proceedings were conducted without reference to the marital relationship of the parents of the child.

Affiliation

The origin of affiliation and bastardy proceedings is also to be found in the Elizabethan Poor Law under which a man was under an obligation to maintain his children as well as his wife. One of the objects of affiliation proceedings continued to be to keep the cost of maintaining children off the rates, and therefore an application could be made not only by the mother but by the local authority if the child became chargeable, but by the twentieth century the principal object was to enable a woman to maintain her child. The court was required to determine the paternity of the child and to provide for maintenance payments by the father. In the first half of the century the law was governed by the Bastardy Laws Amendment Act 1872, but thereafter the first statute affecting these proceedings was the Affiliation Proceedings Act 1957 which was a consolidating measure. Under s. 1 of this Act a woman who was single at the time of the birth of her child, or was living away from her husband, could apply to a magistrate of the area in which she resided for a summons against a man whom she alleged to be the father of her illegitimate child. The court might adjudge the defendant to be the father and, at its discretion, require him to pay a weekly sum not exceeding 50 shillings per week, and also expenses incidental to the birth of the child (or if it had died, the funeral expenses). An order could be made for the payment of periodical expenses until the child reached the age of 16 (or 21 to cover education and training). The maximum limit on the amount payable was removed by the Maintenance Orders Act 1968. Blood tests could be ordered in certain circumstances, but the legal position was confused until the matter was regulated by the Family Law Reform Act 1969.

In affiliation cases an appeal lay to the Crown Court by way of a rehearing.

Consent to marriage

Magistrates retained their power to consent to the marriage of young people between the ages of 16 and 18 where the parent whose consent was required was incapable of giving it or refused to do so. The proceedings might be heard in camera and there was no appeal from the magistrates' decision.

For 40 years the matter was governed by the Marriage Act 1949, but this was amended by the Children Act 1989 (s. 12, para. 5) which substituted a simpler and more coherent set of rules on the consent required to the marriage of a young person between 16 and 17, but the power of magistrates to permit marriage in the face of parental opposition, which was conferred by s. 3 of the 1949 Act, remained. It seemed unlikely, however, that magistrates would often have occasion to exercise this authority. A notable phenomenon was the steep reduction in the number of applications, especially in the 1980s, leading to an almost complete absence of applications to magistrates by 1989. This again was a reflection of the spirit of the age. Young people were less inclined than their parents to enter into matrimony and it became a general practice for them to live together without any legal bonds. Those who did contemplate marriage, but were unable to obtain their parents' agreement, had no hesitation in following the general trend and they saw no reason to go to the trouble of applying to the courts.

Civil debts

The jurisdiction in family matters described above has long accounted for the bulk of the magistrates' civil work. The little that remained was concerned with the payment of rates and of other debts to a restricted number of public authorities. Private individuals could not pursue their civil debts in the magistrates' courts and were obliged to take proceedings in the County Court or High Court. Under the Distress for Rates Act 1849 a local authority could obtain an order from the magistrates that the ratepayer pay, or in default that distress be levied on his goods. Similar provisions applied to gas, electricity and water undertakings. Income tax could be recovered to a maximum of £50 (or £100 for Pay As You Earn). The creditor first obtained judgment that the debtor owed a stated sum and the magistrates then ordered the amount to be paid within a specified time or by instalments. The order might be enforced by their issuing a distress warrant. In certain cases they might commit the debtor to prison in default.

Civil debts incurred in a County Court could be enforced in a magistrates' court until 1970 when this procedure was abolished by the Administration of Justice Act.

A number of statutes also gave a right of appeal to a magistrates' court from a determination by a local authority. The leading examples of such Acts passed after 1945 were the Housing Act 1961, the Public Health Act 1961 and the Town and Country Planning Act 1971.

There are two other subjects which relate to the judicial work of the justices; rules of procedure and legal aid. These apply to the criminal as well as to the civil courts and they therefore relate also to the last chapter, but it seems appropriate to combine the descriptions in the following paragraphs.

Rules of procedure

Before 1949 the procedure in magistrates' courts was governed by various statutes which had to be amended before any change could be achieved. The magistrates' courts were therefore well behind the County Courts and higher courts which had had rule committees from the nineteenth century.[7] Some procedural provisions for magistrates' courts were contained in the Summary Jurisdiction Acts of 1848 and 1879 but they were far from comprehensive, and other statutes governed the magistrates' procedure when exercising various parts of their jurisdiction.

The Roche Committee on Justices' Clerks of 1944 examined this question in some detail (paras. 220-229) and concluded that the procedure prescribed for courts of summary jurisdiction appeared to work reasonably well in practice, but they concluded that as it was "contained in various statutes and sets of rules it is needlessly complicated and is not without contradictions and obscurities. There is an urgent need for consolidation and simplification." They therefore recommended that the principles which already applied to rule-making in the Supreme Court and County Courts should be extended to courts of summary jurisdiction. In particular, detailed rules of procedure should no longer be embodied in statutes but should be made on the advice of rule committees.

The Royal Commission on Justices of the Peace of 1949 endorsed the recommendations of the Roche Committee, but this was ignored when the Justices of the Peace Bill was first introduced in 1949. The then Home Secretary, Mr Chuter Ede, within whose province the adjectival criminal law was assumed to lie, preferred to retain the old system whereby all procedure was set out in a statute. Most magistrates were convinced that this was a mistake and took steps to have the Bill amended. The Chairman of the Council of the Magistrates' Association, Lord Templewood, successfully moved an amendment in the House of Lords which largely implemented the Roche Committee's recommendations. These amendments were incorporated in s. 15 of the Act as passed,[8] which empowered the Lord

---

7. For a few years after County Courts were created in 1846 their rules of procedure were drafted by Judges of the common law courts. In 1849 this duty was given to five County Courts Judges appointed by the Lord Chancellor, and the rules became effective after being approved by the Lord Chancellor and certain other Judges and by Parliament. For the higher courts, a Rule Committee was set up under the Judicature Act 1873 and the Appellate Jurisdiction Act 1876. Under the Supreme Court of Judicature (Consolidation) Act 1925, rules were made by the Lord Chancellor together with four or more other persons described in s. 99 of the Act. Nine years later County Courts rules were placed on a similar footing by the County Courts Act 1934 under which County Court rules were made by a committee of five County Court Judges and three other persons appointed by the Lord Chancellor. The rules so made had to be approved by the Lord Chancellor and subsequently by the Supreme Court Rule Committee.
8. Re-enacted in s. 144 of the Magistrates' Courts Act 1980.

Chancellor to appoint a rule committee for magistrates' courts and to make rules of procedure and practice for those courts and for justices' clerks on the advice of or after consultation with the committee. The committee was to consist of the Lord Chief Justice, the President of the Probate, Divorce and Admiralty Division and the Chief Metropolitan Magistrate together with a number of other persons appointed by the Lord Chancellor at his discretion, but including at least one justices' clerk, one practising barrister and one practising solicitor. The committee usually included a representative of the Lord Chancellor's Department and of the Home Office, and its secretary was always a Home Office official. (The author was one of the first members and served on the Committee for 10 years). The committee suffered from the defect of being somewhat sluggish in its operation. Some of its members, like the Lord Chief Justice who was supposed to be chairman, were too busy to attend meetings and all business was therefore conducted by post and tended to fall behind changes in court machinery and in the substantive law. There was an obvious need for a more continuous and positive approach, and this could have been provided by the appointment of a small, active working group, as suggested by the Justices' Clerks' Society, to review the rules in detail at regular intervals and to report to the main statutory committee.

In spite of this, the rules of procedure in magistrates' courts were kept reasonably up to date. They could be amended at any time without new legislation, though they had to be laid before Parliament subject to negative resolution procedure. The committee's approval was also required for any rules made by the Lord Chancellor under s. 13 of the 1949 Act regarding the size and chairmanship of benches.

The existance of the rule committee did not wholly preclude the inclusion of procedural law in Acts of Parliament. The Magistrates' Courts Act 1952 consolidated all enactments relating to the jurisdiction, practice and procedure of magistrates' courts, and this was re-enacted with amendments by the Justices' of the Peace Act 1979 and the Magistrates' Courts Act 1980. Wholly new innovations were introduced by the Criminal Jusice Act 1967, which simplified committal proceedings using written statements in place of oral evidence, and the Criminal Law Act 1977 which reclassified all offences into three categories.

Legal aid

As mentioned in ch. VI, the first statutory provisions for free legal aid in defending criminal cases had been contained in the Poor Prisoners Defence Act 1903, but this was limited to trials on indictment. In 1930 another Poor Prisoners Defence Act, based on the recommendations of a committee which reported in 1926[9] extended legal aid to cases heard in magistrates' courts and provided a system whereby it was available in summary proceedings and preliminary inquiries. This scheme did not work satisfactorily, but a good deal of the failure was due to the reluctance of magistrates to grant legal aid certificates. Another committee was therefore appointed in 1944 with wide terms of references and it produced a comprehensive report in 1945.[10] Their recommendations were implemented by the Legal Aid and Advice Act 1949 which established a new system in civil cases, administered by the Law Society with the approval of the Lord Chancellor. This provided legal aid in court proceedings and also legal advice, but the introduction of the latter was postponed by the Government until 1959 for reasons of economy. At first the scheme applied only to the High Court and it was not extended to matrimonial and other civil proceedings in magistrates' courts and Quarter Sessions until 1961. Other parts of the Act affected the criminal courts and provided for legal aid to be granted by the courts themselves, but these did not come into operation until the 1960s, and in the meantime the Poor Prisoners Defence Act 1930 remained in force, though amended. It was not until 1968 that legal aid became fully available in magistrates' courts.[11] Magistrates' courts gave legal aid for summary trial and for committal proceedings, while for trial on indictment it could be given either by the committing magistrates or by the Assize court or Quarter Sessions. It was already clear, however, before the 1949 Act was extended to magistrates' courts that further changes were necessary. A committee was appointed in 1964 to review the system and it reported in 1966.[12] Its principal recommendations were embodied in the Criminal Justice Administration Act 1967 which provided a complete code for legal aid in criminal proceedings. The grant of legal aid continued to rest with the courts notwithstanding recommendations made to the committee that this duty should be transferred to an independent body on the lines of civil legal aid. The committee did not

---

9.   Cmd. 2638 (1926).
10. Deaprtmental Committee on Legal Aid and Legal Advice, under the chairmanship of Lord Rushcliffe, Cmd. 6641 (1945).
11. Increase in legal aid in magistrates' courts after it became available in October 1968 is shown by the number of applications and grants:

	Applications	Grants
1st October - 31st December 1968	20,706	17,812
1969	102,684	88,193
1972	164,553	147,181
1975	257,691	234,744
1977	333,756	296,615

From 1981 the numbers dropped following a circular from the Lord Chancellor to justices' clerks urging them to save as much as they could on legal aid.

12. *Departmental Committee on Legal Aid in Criminal Proceedings,* under the chairmanship of Widgery J (later Lord Widgery LCJ) Cmnd. 2934 (1966).

accept this proposal mainly because they thought that it would result in delay. The Act simplified the procedure and replaced the previous variety of certificates by an order which merely directed that the accused should be given legal aid. It had also been suggested to the committee that an accused person should be examined as to his means and should be required to make a contribution. This again would have been similar to the existent civil legal aid scheme, but it was partially rejected by the committee because of the probable cost of administration and of the additional delay that would be involved. Instead, the committee recommended that an applicant should be required to complete a form about his means and should suffer a penalty for false statements, and that in appropriate cases he should be required to make a down payment as a condition of receiving legal aid. They also recommended that he might be required to contribute towards the cost of the legal aid he received. These recommendations were implemented by the 1967 Act.

In spite of these improvements the task of the magistrates was not an easy one, largely because of the difficulty in reaching a satisfactory decision at such an early stage in the proceedings, especially as the accused's means could depend to a large extent on the outcome of the trial. As we have seen, however, justices' clerks were also empowered to grant legal aid, and in the larger courts the function was often delegated to deputies.

Reference has already been made to the legal aid available in magistrates' courts for civil proceedings. These included matrimonial, affiliation, guardianship and recovery of small tenements. The Children Act 1989 extended it to the new family proceedings court.

Legal aid continued to be granted on an ever larger scale in the 1980s, with an enormous increase in the cost (£68 million in 1984-5 to £152 million in 1989-90). In view of this the Government began to encourage the courts to be more frugal in their grants. Lord Chancellor Mackay told magistrates in a speech in 1990 that "no matter how precious and important justice is, as with any other service the resources available to fund it are not infinite."

Administrative functions

We have already seen that there were few administrative duties remaining to the magistrates at the beginning of the twentieth century. The position changed little during the latter part of the century, although various proposals were put forward for extending the magistrates' responsibility for granting licences of various kinds. Apart from the few duties carried out by single justices which are mentioned below, those performed at formal meetings of magistrates related to liquor and betting licences, police and the administration of the courts. They will be described under separate headings.

Licensing
The Royal Commission of 1948 were concerned only with the desirability or otherwise of having persons on the bench who were connected with the liquor trade, and they made no proposals for changes in administration or procedure. In the years that followed the magistrates retained their old liquor licensing duties which they had exercised for 400 years. An important administrative change, however, was made by the Licensing Act 1953, later amended by the Licensing Act 1961, which required each bench to appoint a licensing committee of not less than five nor more than 15 magistrates[13] to replace the throngs of justices who used to attend the annual Brewster Sessions, many of them heavily biased for or against the consumption of alcohol.

The idea had been gaining ground, however, that the justices' responsibility for liquor licensing could usefully be extended into other fields. The Government were persuaded to go a short distance along this path, and in 1960 the Betting and Gaming Act (which was based on recommendations of the Royal Commission on Betting, Gaming and Lotteries of 1949-51) gave magistrates the duty of granting licences to bookmakers, betting officers and betting agents. This replaced the Street Betting Act 1906 which had sought to suppress betting in streets and other public places, but had had very little effect. The object of the new statute was to interfere as little as possible with individual liberty to take part in gambling but to impose such restrictions as were desirable and practicable to discourage or prevent excess. The Home Secretary, Mr R.A. Butler, when introducing the Bill said that the Government's aim was to "liberalize a branch of the law which, over the years, has become outmoded and ineffective and therefore treated by many people with ridicule and contempt." The Bill therefore endeavoured to provide reasonable freedom for people who wish to bet or play games for money, while "retaining sufficient safeguards to act as deterrents against their being led into excess." Applications for betting and gaming licences were heard by the licensing committee, and the magistrates' application of the Act met with general approval.

The Betting, Gaming and Lotteries Act 1963 contained further restrictions on betting premises and empowered the magistrates to license premises for gaming and bingo. This was followed by a number of proposals for extending the justices' licensing powers beyond gaming and liquor, so as to include football grounds, transport and

---

13.   Where the number of justices in a division was less than 10 the whole body might be appointed.

almost anything else that the Government sought to regulate. The Lord Chancellor resisted these moves on the ground that magistrates were appointed for the purpose of discharging judicial and not administrative functions and that in any event they already had more than enough to do. It was not easy to convince his colleagues in the Government. Some Ministers argued that the justices constituted a unique group of citizens in that they were an uncommitted section of the community with knowledge of local affairs and reflecting diverse views who, if the the system worked as it should, maintained a reputation for impartiality. No other body of persons satisfied these criteria and therefore there was great advantage in placing upon this respected body of laymen responsibility for taking administrative decisions, especially if the decisions might be unpopular. On the whole the Lord Chancellor was successful in protecting justices from further increases in their licensing commitments, and at the beginning of the 1980s responsibility for granting licences for music, singing and dancing were diverted to the local authorities, though the justices were required to register private clubs.

There is one interesting survival from the distant past which deserves special mention, though its legal right to remain in being might be questioned. This is the *Board of Green Cloth* whose origins lie in a committee of the Royal Household. Its primary purpose was to keep the peace in the immediate vicinity of the person of the sovereign, but by the twentieth century its functions consisted only of granting licences over a small area in the neighbourhood of Buckingham and Whitehall Palaces, and in the decades following World War II the number of premises concerned numbered only four. The Board, which meets in Buckingham Palace, has long consisted of a small number of justices on the London commission, including the Chief Metropolitan Magistrate, and its chairman is normally the Master of the Household.

Police
The police system which had been introduced in the nineteenth century survived, in so far as the magistrates' involvement was concerned, until 1964. Each county had its own force controlled by a Standing Joint Committee composed of persons appointed by the County Council and by the justices in Quarter Sessions. The borough forces were under a Watch Committee appointed by the borough council and it contained no magistrates. The Metropolitan police in the London area were unique in that they were under the direct control of the Home Secretary. From the 1950s it was recognized that small police forces could not perform effectively under modern conditions and consequently some forces were amalgamated. In 1962 a Royal Commission was appointed to review the whole policing system.

In their report[14] they supported the retention of local forces but recommended that they should cover larger areas and that Standing Joint and Watch Committees should be abolished. In their place they proposed the appointment of new committees composed as to two-thirds of members of the local authority and one-third of magistrates. There were some who thought that it was wrong in principle for magistrates, who were part of the judiciary, to play any part in police administration, but the Royal Commission were of the opinion that there was a vital need for police authorities to include an element of independent and non-elected members and that this could best be provided by Justices of the Peace. They, like the government Ministers mentioned earlier, attached special importance to the unique position of the JPs. They expressed the view that the police authorities would be greatly assisted in their tasks of "enhancing the standing of the police force and appointing its senior officers if they were to include a proportion of justices," and they added that justices "constitute a body of public-spirited citizens whose services cannot be enlisted through the normal machinery of local government."

These sentiments naturally found favour with those members of the Government who wished to see the administrative duties of the magistrates expanded and the Royal Commission's recommendations were implemented in the Police Act 1964. There was therefore a reduction in the proportion of justices serving on county police authorities but they were included for the first time in those for boroughs.

There was some difference in practice between police forces in the way in which they handled prosecutions in magistrates' courts. In some areas the prosecution was conducted by a solicitor, but it was more usual for the police themselves to take their own cases except where the importance or difficulty was thought to require legal representation. This changed, however, from 1987 with the establishment of the Crown Prosecution Service composed of qualified lawyers who became generally responsible for conducting all prosecutions.

Increasing demands on the police resulted in fewer officers being present in the courts and by the end of the 1980s there were many sittings of magistrates where no member of the police was present. This presented new problems of security and the maintenance of order which were far from being solved by the beginning of 1990.

Administration of the courts
We have already seen that the Roche Committee recommended in 1944 that committees to be called magistrates' courts committees

14.   Cmnd. 1278 (1962).

should be established, principally to deal with the appointment of clerks and also to fix the boundaries of petty sessional divisions.[15] After a delay of five years these committees were set up under the Justices of the Peace Act 1949[16] on the scale of one for each county, for each county borough and for each non-county borough with a separate Commission of the Peace and a population of 65,000 or more.[17] In a county, the justices in each petty sessional division elected one member of their bench to the committee. Under the Act the duties of these magistrates' courts committees included the appointment and removal of justices' clerks and their staff (who were to hold office at the committee's pleasure), the division of counties into petty sessional divisions, the provision of courses of instruction for justices and the general supervision of court administration. In the latter context, the courthouses and other accommodation, furniture, books and other items required by the justices were determined by the committee in consultation with the council of the local authority. The latter was responsible for the payment of all expenses including the salaries of the clerks and their staff. Any council which was aggrieved by a determination of a magistrates' courts committee might appeal to the Home Secretary whose decision was binding.[18]

Before the 1949 Act, the whole of the cost of magistrates' courts was met entirely by the local authorities, except in the London Metropolitan area. Fines and fees collected by the courts were paid to the authority unless a statute directed otherwise,[19] but whereas previously these had been more than sufficient to cover the costs, from 1944 there was a deficit which had to be borne by the rates. This situation whereby local authorities were no longer beneficiaries of the magistrates' courts was to be found in some areas even before the war. To assist the local authorities, s. 27 of the 1949 Act provided that all fines and fees should be paid to the Home Secretary. Thereafter the Home Office returned to the authority an amount representing the proceeds of certain fines, plus two-thirds of the difference between these and the actual expenditure. In practice the amount of the grant usually represented about 80 per cent of the total cost. The Criminal

---

15. Although the committee did not say so, the idea was taken from the old General Purposes Committees in some boroughs.
16. Sections 16-24.
17. After the Local Government Act 1972, which altered the local government structure, there was a separate committee for each non-metropolitan county, for each district in a metropolitan county, for each of the four outer London areas and for the City of London. Inner London, with its separate system had a Committee of Magistrates. The Local Government Act 1985 abolished metropolitan counties, and thereafter the number of committees increased, with a separate committee for each metropolitan district and London borough. In 1989 there were 105 Magistrates' Courts Committees in England and Wales.
18. Justices of the Peace Act 1949, ss. 25, 26(3).
19. Fees were abolished in 1967. By that time they were small and were merely an inconvenience.

Justice Act 1972 formalized the ratio of funding between local authorities and the central government at 20:80.[20]

In performing their function of submitting proposals to the Home Secretary for the amalgamation of petty sessionsl divisions or for the alteration of their boundaries, magistrates' courts committees often met stiff opposition from the local magistrates in divisions which would lose their separate status. The Home Office urged committees to exercise this power as far as possible with a view to reducing the number and size of divisions, and considerable progress was made in this direction during the first 20 years after the Act was passed, when the number of divisions was reduced from 938 to 842. This trend continued and was accompanied by a reduction in the number of places in which magistrates' courts sat. By 1978 there were only 640 magistrates' courts centres in England and Wales.

An underlying principle of the 1949 Act was that magistrates' courts, to be effective, must operate on a local basis. There was justification for the claim that courts staffed by lay magistrates could operate to the best advantage if they were organized as local entities, but it was fallacious to asume that this necessarioy involved funding by local authorities, and from 1949 onwards the influence of local authorities on magistrates' courts was restrictive. As might have been expected, many authorities were not interested in the administration of justice, over which they had no control and which seemed to have little prospect of affecting the authority's public image, and they preferred to spend their funds in other directions. Although the initiative rested with the magistrates' courts committees whose decision to spend money could only be challenged by appeal to the Home Secretary, many committees proved to be reluctant to indulge in expenditure to which their local authority was opposed, even if it seemed to be in the interest of the courts to do so. This was particularly the case where, as frequently happened, justices serving on the magistrates' courts committee were also members of the council. In some cases the magistrates' courts committee was conducted as if it was one of the committees of the council. Consequently there was no assurance that sufficient staff would be engaged or that courts would be built when and where they were needed or that they would be properly maintained. Some court buildings were totally inadequate[21] while others were of a much higher standard than was necessary, depending upon the policy of the local authority. Reference has already been made to the effect that poor staffing arrangements had on the quality of the justices' clerks, especially the absence of a satisfactory career

20.   In 1976 expenditure on magistrates' courts, including loan charges, amounted to £43 million. By 1989 the cost was about £200 million.
21.   A depressing account of court accommodation in the London metropolitan area was given in a Law Society report in 1970. See *Law Societies Gazette,* February 1970.

structure. In a number of areas there was a general staff shortage which, among other disadvantages, resulted in ineffective fine enforcement and an absence of accurate statistics of all branches of the magistrates' work.

These shortcomings were not immediately apparent, but by the 1960s suggestions for greater centralization were being heard from a number of quarters. It was pointed out that this would lead to greater efficiency among the staff by providing a national career structure, effective training, common standards and the replacement of large numbers of part-time staff with fewer and more efficient whole-time officers. Centralized control and the elimination of restrictions imposed by local government boundaries would also result in magistrates' courts sitting in suitable accommodation where, but only where,they were required. All this would lead to more rapid disposal of work and the elimination of arrears. Although there would be substantial setting-up costs, considerable long-term saving would be gained by the greater efficiency of the staff, the more economic use of accommodation and the use of joint services.[22]

In 1966 the Justices' Clerks' Society urged the Government to centralize the administration of magistrates' courts under the Lord Chancellor. The proposal was not viewed with great enthusiasm either by the Lord Chancellor, Lord Gardiner, or by the Home Secretary, Mr Roy Jenkins. At that time the Lord Chancellor's Office was still very small and, although it had more than doubled since 1945, there were only 13 senior officers, all of them lawyers. To assume responsibility for the administration of all magistrates' courts would have involved a vast expansion, and indeed a complete transmogrification of the Lord Chancellor's Office. This was precisely what was to happen only a few years later when the Lord Chancellor became responsible for the administration of all the higher courts, but at the time Lord Gardiner did not wish to see a further widening of what he regarded as his already over-extended field of responsibility. The Home Secretary, for his part, was concerned at the repercussions which the change was likely to have on some of the institutions for which he was responsible, especially on the probation and aftercare service. There were also some among his advisers in the Home Office who resented the proposed transfer to the Lord Chancellor's Department of some of the Home Secretary's long-standing responsibilities. The subject was therefore shelved for a few years, but it was naturally revived in 1970 when it became clear that the Lord Chancellor would have to assume responsibility for administering all other courts according to the recommendations of the Royal Commission on Assizes and Quarter

---

22. An example of this was in the printing of the many forms and other documents required by the courts. This was provided by some 200 different local printers whose work varied greatly in quality and cost.

Sessions. Lord Gardiner, and his successor, Lord Hailsham, who succeeded him in June 1970, would have been willing to accept the proposal, albeit reluctantly, but in spite of its obvious advantages there were some who opposed it. It was therefore decided to test opinion by issuing a consultative document to those principally concerned. It was found that the great majority of those consulted were in favour of centralization under the Lord Chancellor. These included the Bar Council, the Law Society, the Magistrates' Association, the Stipendiary Magistrates' Society, the Justices' Clerks Society and the Greater London Council, all of whom supported centralization on the grounds of efficiency and economy. The only serious opposition to this imposing array of authorities came from the County Councils and their clerks who were motivated largely by self-interest. The councils were reluctant to lose something they had possessed for centuries, even though what they stood to lose was a financial obligation over which they had no control, but they were also influenced by their clerks who feared that the change would affect their own authority within their counties and might deprive many of them of their appointments as clerks to the magistrates' courts committees. The principal reasons, however, that were given by the county lobby for their opposition was that the transfer to central government of responsibility for magistrates' courts, which had their roots deep in local history, would be a move against the general trend for greater devolution. They emphasized the need to preserve the involvement of the local community in the administration of justice, but ignored the fact, mentioned earlier, that local involvement of the magistracy does not require local authority involvement. At this point the Justices' Clerks' Society modified its views on the desirability of change, largely because they were disillusioned by the terms of service offered to previous county officers who wished to join the staff of the new Crown Courts.[23]

Within the Government, opposition to the proposed reforms still came from the Home Secretary.[24] His department continued to be preoccupied with the future of the probation and aftercare service. Any change in the magisterial system would have made it difficult to leave the organization of the probation service, which was on similar lines to that of the magistrates' courts, as it was. It would have meant choosing between the incorporation of the service in the new local authority social work departments set up in accordance with the recommendations of the Seebohm Committee, to which the service itself would have been strongly opposed, or converting it into a national courts and prison service provided by the Home Office. Apart

23. One of the main causes of their dissatisfaction with the existing system was removed when local government reorganization resulted in the majority of the new magistrates' courts committees having a justices' clerk as their clerk instead of a Clerk of the Peace.
24. Mr Reginald Maudling had succeeded Mr James Callaghan on the change of Government in June 1970.

from these considerations, it was difficult to contemplate a fundamental structural reorganization of the probation service at a time when what was needed was a rapid expansion of the service to enable it to cope with the widening range of tasks mentioned earlier. The Home Secretary therefore felt obliged to oppose the proposed reforms, at least for the time being, and although most of his Cabinet colleagues were basically in favour of centralization under the Lord Chancellor they were deterred from taking a positive decision by extraneous circumstances which coincidentally faced the Government at that time. It was the period in which the major local government reforms that were embodied in the Local Government Act 1972 were being debated. These had not met with universal approval and it was obviously not a propitious moment to embark upon further measures affecting the local authorities. There was also another disincentive. It was assumed that centralization of the magistrates' courts would involve transforming the justices' clerks and their staff, numbering some 3,500, into state civil servants (if the probation and aftercare service had also been included the number would have been increased by 5,000), and it was a phenomenon of the time that successive Governments recoiled from anything that appeared to swell the ranks of the Civil Service. The decision was therefore taken to retain the essentials of the existing system and to try to regularize and improve it. No marked progress was made in this direction though there was some advance in staff training. Petty sessional divisions continued to be amalgamated, sometimes involving the closure of courthouses. The reduction in the number of courthouses was designed to reduce costs, but it often gave rise to strong local criticism as the public were caused greater inconvenience when they were obliged to attend court.

The basic defects of the sytem remained, and many well-informed people were convinced that it was only a matter of time before mounting arrears, unnecessary costs, shortage of experienced staff and the need to improve general efficiency would force the Government into assuming over-all control through an integrated system for all the courts. It was obvious that the most urgent reform was the transfer of financial responsibility for magistrates' courts from the local authorities to the central government, and this was precisely the proposal put forward in a report of the Layfield Committee in 1974,[25] but no steps were taken to implement it. The position remained virtually unaltered, although the Home Office tried to encourage magistrates' courts committees to adopt more economical methods, and the committees themselves and the justices' clerks in many areas attempted to improve their local machinery. Little real progress could be made within the parameters of the existing system.

25. Committee on Local Government Finance, paras. 38-9. Cmnd. 6453 (1974).

By the end of the 1980s the annual cost of administering the magistrates' courts amounted to about £200 million, a large part of which was defrayed by the Government, yet its powers of supervision were limited. It could only be a matter of time therefore before the question of central control was raised again. In March 1989 the Home Secretary set up an Efficiency Scrutiny on the management and organizational structure of magistrates' courts under the chairmanship of Mr Julian Le Vay of the Home Office. The report was publisehd in July. It stressed that the Scrutiny was focused on the management and resourcing systems for magistrates' courts and was not concerned with the judicial function of magistrates, but it made no reference to the difficulty in separating the one completely from the other. The report commented:

"The arrangements for managing magistrates' courts and their resources date from 1949 but retain the local, part-time, almost amateur flavour of an earlier age. The arrangements have never been systematically appraised, and have not adapted to take account of the enormous increase since 1949 in the volume of business and the number of permanent staff, or the fact that central Government now foots most of the bill."

The team found that there was no coherent management structure for the service, and that although the sevice itself had attempted to develop more integrated local structure, and the Home Office had tried to play a more active role in promoting value for money, little more could be achieved within the existing framework which was "narrowly limited by the ambigious role and inadequate powers of all the participants." They went on to say that:

"It would be difficult to think of any arrangements less likely to deliver value for money than the present ones. The Home Office provides most of the funds but has no say in how resources are allocated or used, or even the total level of spending, other than by operating detailed approvals which are themselves an obstacle to optimum value for money. The immediate funding body, the local authority, has too little stake in the service to provide an effective budgeting discipline, while magistrates' courts' committees are too dependent on local authorities, and their management capacity is too underdeveloped, to plan or manage resources effectively. There is little evidence of a planned relationship between work and resources, or review of performance or scrutiny of efficiency. Most justices' clerks have little control over resources and little information about costs. Spending is not properly controlled and the audit arrangements, despite improvements, are still deficient."

The Scrutiny team shared the conclusion reached by the Royal Commission on Assizes and Quarter Sessions that the administration of justice must be recognized as a central government responsibility. They therefore recommend that magistrates' courts should also "be run as a national service, funded entirely by the Government - but with maximum delegation of managerial responsibility and control of resources to the local level." To achieve this they proposed that there should not be direct management by a government department on the traditional Whitheall model, nor on the other hand should the magistrates' courts be run by a non-departmental public body. Instead, they concluded that the right solution was to introduce an Executive Agency. Such bodies, which had become popular with the Government, were responsible to a Minister but were operationally independent. The Magistrates' Courts Agency would be managed by a Director-General and would be appointed by and accountable directly to the Home Secretary in whom ultimate control would be vested.

The majority of the Justices of the Peace were prepared to accept a system of this kind so long as it came under the supervision of the Lord Chancellor. The Le Vay team were obviously right in their conclusion that the financing of the courts should be removed from the local authorities and that management should be centralized, but it did not necessarily follow that the responsible Minister should be the Home Secretary. It was not difficult to argue that to place the structure under the ultimate control of the Home Office was wrong in principle and constitutionally indefensible. The Scrutiny recognized the need to protect the magistracy from undue influence by the Government, but the Home Secretary was the Minister responsible for the police, for apprehending offenders and for bringing them to trial, and for dealing with those who had been convicted and sentenced by the courts to custodial treatment - the prisons and probation etc. The same Minster ought not therefore to be concerned in arrangements for the trial itself. The Royal Commission on Assizes and Quarter Sessions had concluded that the administration of all the other courts should fall within the jurisdiction of the Lord Chancellor, as had been done a century earlier with County Courts. As head of the judiciary and Minister responsible for judicial appointments, the Lord Chancellor was in a unique position and, being further removed from the political arena than any of his colleagues, he seemed to be the obvious authority to be entrusted with all aspects of the judicial process and correlative matters. Moreover, to have the same Minister responsible for the administration of all the courts would avoid the conflict of interests which had caused unnecessary complications in the past, especially regarding court accommodation.

The Le Vay team acknowledged the special role of the justices' clerk as adviser to the justices on points of law and procedure in and out of court, but they recommended the appointment of *court managers* to conduct the day to day management of the courts. Although the *court managers* would be required to liaise closely with the justices, they would be part of the Agency personnel, serving under chief executives and responsible to the Director-General. Many feared that this could jeopardize the delicate relationship existing between the justices and their clerks which was the pivot on which the whole of the unique lay justice system turned. At least, there could be little doubt that it would be more conducive to the preservation of this relationship if the management service were ultimately responsible to the same authority which was charged with the appointment and conditions of service of the magistrates themselves. The right solution would seem to be to bring the organization of the magistrates' courts into the system established by the Courts Act 1971 for all the other courts, but with special provisions to retain the local basis of the magistrates' jurisdiction and the peculiar position of the clerk as legal adviser. This would mean bringing the administration of the magistrates' courts directly under the Lord Chancellor's Department, but the Lord Chancellor himself, Lord Mackay, was reluctant to assume responsibility because he considered that the Department was already fully stretched. Consultations between the justices, the Government and all others concerned in the future of the magistrates' courts were continuing in 1990. There was no doubt that a new system was about to be introduced but what form it would take was still uncertain.

The future of the courts' administration was undoubtedly one of the most momentous problems facing the magistracy as they approach the end of the century. The continued survival of the lay justice system as a major factor in the judicial process might well depend upon the extent to which the magistrates' courts could operate speedily and economically.

Miscellaneous administrative matters

Magistrates might still find themselves engaged in a variety of matters of an administrative nature. There were many committees on which they might serve apart from the magistrates' courts committees such as the probation and aftercare committees, training committees, the Lord Chancellor's advisory committees or committees of the Magistrates' Association at both national and local level. They might also find themselves acting *ex officio* in some capacity not directly concerned with the courts. For instance, at the beginning of 1990 all the Caernarfon justices were still trustees of Caernarfon harbour by virtue of an Act of 1793,[26] which not only added to their work but could have led to a conflict of interest if an action was brought by the Harbour Board.

26.   33 Geo. III, C. 123, confirmed in 49 Geo. III, C. 24 and later Acts.

The single justice

Certain functions continued to be performed by single justices, sometimes in the justice's home. He might try an offence for which the maximum penalty was 20 shillings or 14 days' imprisonment but this became rare. Otherwise his principal activities consisted of the granting of summonses, warrants for arrest and search, the taking of declarations, adjourning cases without consent, acting as an examining justice in committal proceedings, witnessing documents and giving advice to the public. Fortunately for the justices the last two of these diminished sharply from 1945. Before then most documents requiring attestation were taken to justices because, it seems, there was thought to be a greater aura of respectability and confidentialtiy surrounding a matter if it were referred to a justice rather than to anyone else. It may also have been thought that justices were the only ones who would not charge a fee. For the same reasons justices were consulted on a wide variety of subjects. There was a marked decline in this sphere of the justice's work from the 1950s onwards for a number of reasons. With the object of minimizing the calls on justices to witness documents the Lord Chancellor embarked upon a successful campaign to increase the number of persons qualified to attest such papers. At the same time, the custom of turning to a justice for advice, which had been at its height in the previous two centuries, lapsed with the establishment of Citizens' Advice Bureaux and other advice centres and government information offices.

Executive functions

It remains to observe that by 1989 the justices no longer retained any executive functions. We have seen that during the nineteenth century their policing duties were assumed by the regular police forces and that the only executive power which remained to them was under the Riot Act 1715. By the twentieth century this had fallen into disuse and the 1715 Act was repealed in 1967.

Summary of the post war era

The pages in this and the previous chapter have disclosed the very substantial increase which occurred in the work of the Justices of the Peace from 1949 onwards. This was due to a number of causes of which the principal were extensions of the magistrates' jurisdiction, a massive increase in the number of cases coming before the courts with the growth in the level of crime,[27] the introduction of more complex procedures and the advent of legal aid which was also partly responsible for the larger number of pleas of not guilty. At times there were temporary spates of activity to deal with unexpected problems, and the 1990s began with a surge of extra sittings to deal with cases of unpaid poll tax.[28]

The number of persons dealt with in the summary courts more than doubled in the 20 years between 1947 and 1967 from 589,534 to 1,368,048 and it nearly doubled again in the following 10 years, reaching 2,438,212 in 1977.[29] These figures, however, do not give an accurate impression of the actual increase in the burden because by the 1980s cases tended to take much longer to try than they did in the 1940s. A better indication of the increase in the volume of work may be obtained from the time spent in court. In 1947 the average number of days on which magistrates' courts were held in England and Wales, including London, was about 870 per week. The figure reached 9,000 in 1982. Furthermore, in 1947 nearly 70 per cent of the courts sat only in the mornings, whereas by 1977 some 65 per cent continued sitting in the afternoon, sometimes until after 5 o'clock. Moreover, these figures do not include the amount of time spent by justices in the Crown Court or in attending committees or partaking in other work, which increased even more steeply than court sittings.

The rapid increase in the workload continued throughout the whole period. The 1980s saw the passing of several Acts which added appreciably to the justices' burden, notably the Police and Criminal Evidence Act 1984, the Public Order Act 1986 and the Criminal Justice Act 1988 which transferred a considerable bulk of cases from the Crown Court to the magistrates.

A vastly increased workload was only part of the scene. Those who served on the Commissions of the Peace after 1945 were obliged to meet the challenge of a wholly new environment. They had to operate

---

27.   There were considerable fluctuations. For instance, there was a rise of seven per cent in indictable offences in England and Wales between 1974 and 1975, but of only one per cent between 1975 and 1976. This led to the conclusion that the rise in crime had reached a plateau, but in the following year indictable crimes rose by 12 per cent. The most notable sectors in which this occurred were burglary, which dropped by one per cent in the year to April 1975 but rose by 15 per cent in 1977, and robbery which moved from a six per cent drop in 1976 to an 11 per cent rise in 1977. Criminal damage on the other hand mounted steadily; those cases known to the police rising by more than 10,000 a year between 1974 and 1977, and so too did violence against the person but a lowr rate.

28.   This was an illustration of history repeating itself, at least to some extent. Wat Tyler's rebellion in 1381 (described in vol. I, ch. III), which had a considerable effect on the justices, was sparked by the attempted introduction of a poll tax.

29.   During the 20 years between 1957 and 1977 the number of persons found guilty of indictable offences per 100,00 of the population aged 10 and over rose by just under 400 to about 950, but the proportion of persons cautioned by the police during this period rose by approximately 50 to nearly 250.

in a political and economic climate for which, at least in theory, they seemed unfitted. They were part of an institution which had been cosseted in previous generations when the word of the law and of the judiciary was sacrosanct and when judicial decisions were generally accepted without question. From the 1950s there was diminishing respect for the law and the courts, and magistrates and Judges had to work in an increasingly critical climate. Lord Atkin observed that: "Justice is not a cloistered virtue; she must be allowed to suffer the scrutiny and respectful, even though outspoken, comments of ordinary men," but soon many comments were no longer respectful. Yet it was also a time when greater demands than ever before were made upon the judiciary at all levels. As we have seen, the work of the courts became more intensive and its volume increased enormously, and continued to do so into the 1980s which were particularly notable for a rapid rise in drug-related crime and for violence in the inner cities.

It will have been seen that a revolutionary change occurred in the lay justice system during the 40 years following the Justices of the Peace Act 1949. This was manifest in the personnel of the magistrates themselves and in the weight and nature of the functions they had to perform. As individuals the justices underwent a transformation from amateurs to a status verging on professionalism. Had they not done so they could not have satisfied the demands of the new era. From the 1950s they were chosen exclusively, after careful scrutiny, from among those members of the local community who appeared to be best qualified to discharge their important duties. They were given a growing amount of instruction in their work, until by the 1980s they were subjected, from the moment of their appointment until their retirement from the bench, to the most intensive scheme of training that was compatible with essential demands on their time. They also came to be a more representative cross-section of the population with a wider political, social and ethnic background, though by 1989 they were still far from being a true microcosm of the local community. The upper levels of society continued to predominate, and the air of arrogance and personal prejudice, which had characterized the benches in earlier times tended to persist, though to a lesser degree.

The transformation in the quality of the justices led to an improvement in their public image, but not to the extent that might have been expected. Often they were still seen by the public in the light of what they had been 50 or even a 100 years earlier, and the majority of those coming before the courts preferred to be tried by members of the professional judiciary. This was due partly to the press which attempted to gratify its readers by reporting the magistrates' shortcomings and ignoring their achievements. Good news is no news; on the other hand a story can usually be found among the thousands of cases coming before magistrates in the course of a week which depicts them in a disparaging light and makes good reading. The Government and Parliament, however, were more aware than the public of the improved quality and efficiency of the JPs, and increasing confidence was shown in the number of enactments which extended their powers. An example of this was the radical change which occurred in the metropolitan area in the 1960s when the lay JPs, having been virtually excluded for a century-and-a-half from almost every part of the administration of the criminal law, were reinstated and placed on the same level as the professional metropolitan magistrates. The enhanced reputation of the JPs was also reflected in the Contempt of Court Act, 1981 which, for the first time, enabled magistrates to commit for contempt of their courts. Previously it was only the higher courts which were thought fit to exercise this authority. Another illustration of the improved reputation enjoyed by the justices was their confirmation as Judges of the Crown Court by the Courts Act, 1971, but this proved to be one of the few instances where they were unable to meet the challenge. The failure arose from a fundamental defect in the part-time system. Although the justices did their best to devote all the time that was required to their work and were able to attend their courts on single days, it was virtually impossible for busy men and women, heavily engaged in other activities, to give serveral consecutive days to the court sittings which became a normal requirement for jury trials.

A result of the greater confidence on the part of the authorities was a long series of statutes adding to the extent and complexity of the justices' duties, and in addition to the changes in the personnel of the magistrates there were radical reforms in the law they administered, in the procedure they followed and in the running of their courts. All this was intended to meet the demands of the changing environment in which the magistrates had to work, but many of the new schemes fell short of what was required. The enthusiastic spirit of reform and modernization failed to achieve the success at which it aimed because those responsible for the over-all operation of the system and for introducing the essential innovations were constantly looking for ways and means of retrenchment instead of expansion. It was this that resulted in failure to exploit to the full promising new developments such as attendance centres and detention centres and some of the provisions of the Children and Young Persons Act, 1969. Many potentially fruitful schemes also foundered through lack of sufficient financial backing, while some urgent reforms were delayed indefinitely by extraneous political influences, as occurred in regard to the administration of the courts.

Progress was also hampered by lack of adequate research. Although there was a considerable expansion of research activity from 1950 onwards and particularly after 1970, it still fell short of what was required. Even the findings of some of the major inquiries were based on limited information which could have been extended if more time and resources had been available. More thorough, evaluative research was needed into the operation of the courts and into specific subjects such as sentencing and the effectiveness of the jury system. It was also necessary to adopt a new approach and to give more consideration to the "consumer" - the person in the dock, the victim of the crime and the general public. Similar problems had faced earlier ages but they became more acute as the rate and magnitude of change accelerated in the twentieth century.

From 1949 all justices began to bear a far heavier burden than their predecessors in the first half of the century. Already in the 1950s the office of Justice of the Peace could no longer be regarded as a sinecure, and by the 1980s it amounted in many instances to a distinctly onerous task. Those who did not perform what the Lord Chancellor regarded as a fair share of the duties were removed from the commission, and those who remained were faced with an increasing workload. It was no longer possible for busy people to serve as justices without some detriment to their personal affairs, and as the majority were fully occupied in earning their living or attending to their families there were few who did not have to make some sacrifice. At the same time there were no material rewards for service on the Commissions of the Peace as there had been in earlier days. There were some who were gratified by the honour and reputation which attached to the office, but there was little evidence to suggest that the majority were so motivated. It followed that they undertook the onerous and sometimes boring duties because they were genuinely interested in the work and were imbued with a desire to fulfil an important public task in the best interests of the community. There were many people who questioned whether public spirited fervour on this scale could continue indefinitely. Some relief of pressure seemed essential.

By 1990 the lay justice system had succeeded once again in coming to terms with an entirely new climate, but the justices' own qualities and the various procedural and administrative innovations which had appeared with growing frequency throughout the twentieth century were not alone sufficient to ensure the system's continued survival. As the justices approached the end of the century they found themselves in yet another crucial period. If they were to survive on the same scale they and the system under which they operated would have to continue to adjust to the demands of an unpredictable world.

EPILOGUE

DURING A PERIOD of nearly five centuries from 1361 the Justices of the Peace came to be regarded as an inevitable feature of the English scene. Those, such as Charles I, Cromwell and James II, who tried to dispense with the justices in their traditional role, met with failure. Yet the JP is the kind of historical legacy that one would have expected to flounder in the reforming flood of the post World War II period. It is surprising that the system still survives in an age when established institutions, especially those identified with the "establishment" like the JPs, have been subject to constant denigration, when the amateur has been replaced by the professional and when voluntary service has become anachronistic in the prevailing climate of totalitarianism. Moreover, it is difficult to see how such a system, which seems wholly anomalous when compared with those operating in other countries, could work effectively in the modern age.

Nevertheless, in the latter part of the twentieth century, a large part of the criminal jurisdiction of the courts in England and Wales remains almost wholly in the hands of part-time, unpaid magistrates who, without any legal training, are required to decide questions of law (albeit infrequently and with the advice of their clerks) as well as of fact and who combine the roles of Judge and jury by deciding both guilt and sentence. These same individuals also deal with a not unimportant number of civil matters and licensing. At the beginning of this period C.K. Allen wrote:

"To cold, detached calculation to a mind, let us say, like that of Jeremy Bentham, our system of lay justice is among those British legacies of history, including the British constitution itself, which obviously cannot work, or at all events cannot do so except in defiance of all reason and probability."[1]

Will this unique and incongruous system survive for much longer? At each crucial point in the past history of the Justices of the Peace their system has been assumed to possess certain inherent qualities which warranted its retention. On many occasions the justices reached a point where they might well have been annihilated, yet each time they survived by adjusting to the changed climate; though their survival was usually due more to outside influences rather than to their own volition, and not until the twentieth century did the magistrates as a body make a concerted effort to improve the service they gave and to meet the needs of a new era. Fortune has undoubtedly smiled on the lay justices of England, but the question often asked is "how long will

1.   *The Queen's Peace* (1953), p. 179.

this continue?" As the twentieth century ends, the air is again filled with a spirit of reform, stimulated by the unimagineable constitutional changes that are sweeping the countries of the world. Institutions that are perceived to be illogical or incapable of fulfilling the demands of the age will be especially vulnerable.

The JP system in the modern era is not without obvious defects, even after the reforms and reorientation of the post World War II period and, as might be expected, it is the subject of critical and often disparaging scrutiny in the current censorious climate. Some of this is unfair, as when the justices are castigated by the media and the public who are unaware of the real facts or considerations that applied to a reported case; but there are other occasions when criticism is justified. The JPs can be compared unfavourably with professional magistrates in that they are too much inclined to decide cases upon a general impression and too little upon precise evidence. They are also thought to be too ready to accept police evidence and to rely too heavily upon the advice of their clerks; both of which criticisms are still valid to a degree, though far less so than they were 30 years and more ago. Again, the justices' sentencing policy is often deprecated on the ground of inconsistency, or because it is too lenient or too harsh but, as we have seen, although such disapprobation may have been fully merited in the past, the justices themselves have gone to great lengths to cure the faults and have achieved some degree of success. Moreover, they do not differ greatly in this respect from the professional judiciary who exhibit wide differences in sentencing practice.

The lay justice system is also attacked because of the secrecy that is alleged to surround the choice and appointment of those who serve on the bench. It is claimed that public confidence is undermined by the mystery that envelops the process; though inquiry among the public suggests that their concern about this issue is much less than it is generally made out to be. In this context the critics have emphasized the fact that few magistrates know for certain how they came to be nominated; but it has been pointed out that this presupposes that the office of JP is a coveted honour and that those who attain it should know to whom they are indebted. In fact, the post of magistrate amounts to an important job of work on behalf of the public. It should not be conferred as an honour or reward but should be undertaken only by those best qualified to perform the duties effectively, and it matters not whether those who serve know who was instrumental in putting their names forward. It would seem too, that those who still maintain that there is unwarranted secrecy in the appointment system are unaware of the steps taken by the Lord Chancellor and his staff to dispel the air of mystery.

Those who complain of secrecy are mainly concerned with what they term the "democratization" of the magisterial system. They judge the validity of the appointment process according to the degree to which it produces benches that are fully representative of the population, and they assume that this objective can not be achieved unless every citizen is able to play a part in the process if he or she wishes. They therefore want to see the introduction of an electorial system based on the Parliamentary or local government franchise.[2] Any institution is suspect if it does not owe its existence to the will of the people as revealed at regular intervals through an election. It is argued that if, as is generally accepted, the effectiveness of the law rests in the last resort upon acceptance by the people to which it applies, it must be assumed that the law will not be observed unless it is not only made by the peoples' representatives in Parliament but is also enforced by courts composed of magistrates elected by the people.

The aetiological conclusion that the effective enforcement of law is linked to respect for the courts does not nesssarily entail the further conclusion that those who form the courts must be chosen and appointed by the people. Many have taken precisely the opposite view and regarded the professional judiciary with greater respect than the lay justices because they have assumed that the professionals are more competent at performing the job. Most people seem to agree with the Royal Commission of 1946 which, as mentioned earlier, expressed the opinion that the qualities required of those elected to local authorities were not necessarily those requisite for the office of Justice of the Peace. It has also been pointed out that an elected body, such as a local authority, often fails to gain the respect of the electorate. It is unquestionably of the utmost importance that those who serve on the bench should reflect the opinions of the local population, but if lay justices are to hold the confidence of the people they must show that they are well fitted in ability, understanding and impartiality to perform the duties entrusted to them. In any event, there are obviously limits to the extent to which the principle of trial by one's peers can apply. If carried to its logical conclusion it would require benches to be composed largely of those who appear most frequently before the courts, from which it would follow that many magistrates would have criminal records[3] and more than three-quarters would have to be under the age of 25. If, on the other hand, the courts are to perform their prime function of administering the law in defence of the community, it may be argued with equal force that the courts should be

2.   It was on this premise that Mr Bruce Grocott based the Bill which he introduced in the House of Commons in June 1977, as mentionedin ch. VII, p. 295.

3.   Large numbers of upper class citizens of all ages are charged with motoring offences, but the great majority of these take advantage of the fixed penalty system or plead by post and do not appear in court.

staffed exclusively of the most law-abiding citizens, who may not be chosen in a popular election.

What is essential is that no group of persons should be, or appear to be, in a position to dominate a bench and, above all, that no one appearing before a court should feel that the bench is biased against him. It is generally accepted that today, with few exceptions, manifest impartiality is a salient feature of every bench. Certainly the gross injustices that were often committed by prejudiced magistrates in the past have long disappeared. On the other hand, benches are far from being precisely representative of all sections of the population, in spite of the efforts of the Lord Chancellor's advisory committees to extend the catchment area. The reasons for this were explained in ch. VII, and it seems unlikely that the scene will change much in the foreseeable future. In the meantime the Commissions of the Peace will remain predominantly middle class, male and politically Conservative.

Yet another criticism of the justices' courts has been that the cost of administration is unnecessarily high. This claim is fully justified but, as shown earlier, it is a matter that requires managerial reform and it would not be solved merely by replacing the JP by another form of judicial officer, including the stipendiary magistrate. It is true that a stipendiary system would save administrative costs by reducing the number of courts and staff, but on the other hand, as the JPs are unpaid, they are to a certain extent more cost-effective than salaried judges, as explained below.

The comparatively low cost of maintaining the JPs is one of the factors that has made the system acceptable and even attractive to successive Governments, though the saving when compared with a stipendiary system is not as great as is sometimes supposed. JPs work more slowly than stipendiaries and take longer to reach a decision, especially if they have to consult their clerk and adjourn to their retireing room. Consequently they dispose of less business than a stipenidary at each sitting and therefore need more courtrooms and staff.[4] In addition, although justices are unremunerated, the allowances to which they are now entitled can amount to a significant sum, especially when several sit together. In spite of this, however, Justices of the Peace are on the whole cheaper than any other effective method of administering justice that has so far been devised. This seemed to be confirmed by an inquiry carried out in 1965 on the instructions of Lord Chancellor Gardiner. Twenty countries were asked to provide information on the number of their whole-time judges and on the annual cost of their judicial administration. The total expenditure

4.   Research carried out by the Lord Chancellor's Departament in 1972 showed that, on average, a stipendiary disposed of about 60 per cent more work in a two hour session than a bench of three justices. Skyrme, T., *The Changing Image of the Magistracy*, 2nd. ed., p. 194.

(excluding that on police and prisons) expressed as a percentage of the annual national budget, ranged from 1.46 at the top of the scale to 0.16 in the case of England, Scotland and Wales at the bottom. As regards the number of judges, several countries had more than 200 per million of population, while Scotland with 15 and England and Wales with eight were again at the bottom.[5] The fact that England and Wales had the smallest proportion of judges was attributed to the much larger amount of court work disposed of by their unpaid, part-time lay magistrates compared with other countries.

Apart from the lower cost, the JP system also appealed to the Government because it was more flexible. Sudden fluctuations in the volume of work could be handled by calling upon justices to sit more or less often in more or fewer courts as the need arose, whereas a whole-time judge or magistrate had little scope to expand his output if the work increased, while if it diminished he might be left partially unemployed at public expense.

Other positive qualities attributed to the lay justices are their sensitivity to local problems, an ability to counterbalance the professionalism of the courts and, when comparing them with a single stipendiary, the fact that two or three heads are better than one. They are better still if they have an intimate knowledge and understanding of the problems facing different sections of their local community. Further advantages that benches of lay justices are said to hold over stipendiaries are that:

"The collective views of a cross-section of the population, representing different shades of opinion, can be more effective in dispensing justice acceptable to the public than the decision of a single individual necessarily drawn from a fairly narrow social class and whose experience of local problems may be limited. Justices also act as a check on one another and provide a balanced conclusion, whereas there is nothing to curb a general idiosyncrasy or the spasmodic whim or irritability of a single magistrate. Furthermore, as justices attend court at intervals they approach their task with a freshness and objectivity that is lacking in a professional judge who is wholly engaged in adjudicating day after day."[6]

Above all, the Justices of the Peace, like the jury, reflect the traditional involvement of the layman in the administration of justice, as they have done throughout the centuries since they were first

5.   *Ibid.*, p. 7. These figures should be treated with caution as some were based on estimates. As was expected, most common-law countries were in the lowest bracket because of their single-judge systems. Thus the United States had 34 judges per million population, Australia 29 and New Zealand 24.
6.   *Ibid.*, p. 8.

established. The system, if properly operated, provides the potential for the ordinary citizen to see that the law is his law, administered by men and women like himself, and that it is not the esoteric preserve of lawyers. Unfortunately, it seems doubtful whether the majority of the population regard it in this light.

A further asset of the lay justices, which has not often been recognized, is that they have the ability to act as a unifying factor in society as a whole. This was emphasized by Lord Chancellor Hailsham in a speech to magistrates in 1981 when he referred to their potential influence, out of court as well as on the bench, and described JPs as "one of the characteristic institutions holding our society together."

The debate for and against a lay justices system is perennial, but the arguments which have just been rehearsed are of only abstract interest if the operation of the system falls short of the criterion that is demanded. In the long term the survival of the system will depend upon the extent to which it can be made to satisfy public demand; but in the short term the surrender and replacement of the present arrangements is out of the question, if only because there is no viable successor.

At the beginning of 1990 the comment is heard among JPs that their days are numbered and that soon they will be replaced, probably by full-time stipendiaries. These defeatist prognostications, which bear some resemblance to views expressed by justices in the 1890s though for different reasons, are inspired by the conviction that part-time "amateurs" will no longer be able to absorb the increasing volume and complexity of the work that falls upon them, and partly by the erroneous belief that it is Government policy to establish a professional judiciary for all courts. In fact the Government seems far from being set on any such course, and there are some authorities, even among the professional judiciary, who foresee a promising future for the justices. For instance, Lord Donaldson, the Master of the Rolls, when addressing the Bar Conference in London, proposed that a body of civil justices, appointed in the same way as JPs, should be created to arbitrate on small civil claims. He pointed out that there was little scope for expanding the professional judiciary, and he argued that the public's demand for a quick and cheap method of resolving disputes could best be met by applying the "very old British tradition" of involving ordinary citizens in the administration of the law. Lord Donaldson's proposals would, of course, add still further to the burden that is being placed on those members of the community from whom most of the JPs are drawn, whereas the most urgent need is to relieve them of some of the tasks they are already performing. This is especially necessary in view of the current trend to relieve pressure on the higher criminal courts by making more cases triable summarily.

Moreover the justices are not inundated with a far greater volume of work than they were in the middle of the century, but it is becoming so complex and wide-ranging that it perplexes even the lawyer magistrates. Some reduction in the scope of the justices' duties is therefore essential in the interests of efficiency. An indication of the effect of this pressure has been seen in the rising rate of premature retirements from the commissions. Although the Lord Chancellor still experiences little difficulty in recruitment to the benches, there is a growing problem of retention.[7]

The necessity for the justices' load to be lightened has been recognized for some time, and certain steps have been taken in this direction. An obvious choice is to remove their licensing duties, and so end their administrative commitments. We have seen that the Lord Chancellor resisted attempts to add further to this branch of their work, but by 1990 no alternative body had been found to take over liquor, betting and gaming licensing. We have also seen that some progress has been made in relieving the pressure of criminal business, especially by expanding the fixed penalty scheme. There is an obvious

---

7.   During the 10 years between 1979 and 1989 there was a steady increase in the number of appointments from 1,500 to 1,963 annually, and the Lord Chancellor had no difficulty in finding persons of the required standard to fill all the posts; but during the same period there was a serious rise in the number of early retirements. In 1979 only about 500 justices retired before reaching superannuation, and most of these did so on moving from one area to another and not because of the weight of work. In 1989, however, retirements were 1,278, many of them because the burden of their duties were felt to be too great. The numbers of resignations, removals and retirements between January 2, 1989 and January 1, 1990 inclusive were:

	Men	Women	Total
Resignations and Removals	458	341	799
Compulsory Retirements at age 70	248	136	384
Deaths (of justices on the active list)	70	25	95
	----	----	----
	776	502	1278

Reasons for resignation or removal:

Pressure of work	125
Ill health	98
Residentially disqualified	164
Disqualified for other reasons	3
At own request	271
Financial loss	1
Employment difficulties	12
Personal reasons	89
Other reasons	29
Removal on initiation of Lord Chancellor	7

	799

need for a further extention of fixed penalties, though the number of criminal cases coming before the magistrates has also been reduced substantially by police cautioning which began on a large scale in the 1980s. Yet another proposal for reducing pressure on all the courts is decriminalization. In 1971 a working party suggested that the habitual drunkard (who is still a frequent visitor to some magistrates' courts, though to a far smaller extent than in the past) should no longer be brought before the courts but should be taken to a detoxification centre. Although two of these centres were opened little progress was made in this direction because of the alleged cost although, as the Magistrates' Association who strongly supported the proposal pointed out, it would have been money well spent. Extensive proposals for reducing the number of offences triable in the courts were contained in a report, entitles *Breaking the Rules,* which was issued in 1980 by *Justice,* the all-party group of lawyers. This suggested that there should be two classes of wrongful conduct; one called "crimes" would be triable by the ordinary criminal courts, and the other, called "contraventions," would not come before the courts but would be subject to penalties in some other way.[8] The case for at least some degree of decriminalization is a strong one and has the support of most magistrates and their clerks. Apart from delivering the courts from work which is ineffective and a waste of time it would help to reverse the current trend towards disrespect for the law; but so far little progress has been made. [9]

Further alleviation of the pressure on the justices is undoubtedly necessary if they are to retain their creditability, but whether or not this takes place there can be little doubt that the JP system will remain in existence for the foreseeable future, if only because for the present there is no feasible alternative. It is generally agreed that the only practicable substitute for the JPs are legally qualified stipenidary magistrates but, whatever advantages these may have, the supply of suitable recruits would be totally inadequate to meet the requirements of a lower judiciary composed entirely of professionals. We have seen

---

8.   For example, the Post Office would be able to impound an unlicensed television or radio set, which would probably be a greater incentive to buying a licence than the prospect of a fine, and would be more expeditious than procedure through the courts. This would not be dissimilar to the power which the police already have to tow away a wrongfully parked vehicle without resort to the courts and is known to be a greater deterrent than the risk of a fine. The *Justice* report pointed out that Parliament had found it necessary to regulate so many everyday activities that it had become well-nigh impossible for even the honest and law-abiding citizen to get through the year without infringing some regulation, and that he then found himself prosecuted in the same court as robbers and rapists and finished with a criminal record. The report also recorded that of the 21 member countries of the Council of Europe, only three (Eire, Malta and the UK) treated every breach of every regulation as a criminal offence.

9.   The Justices' Clerks' Society issued an important paper on the subject in 1982.

that as far back as 1946 Lord Chancellor Jowitt, when giving evidence to the Royal Commission on Justices of the Peace, said that it would be "absolutely impossible" to find enough barristers to do the job.[10] At the time when Lord Jowitt spoke, the pool of candidates was limited to practising members of the Bar, but during the following 40 years, although solicitors became eligible for appointment in 1949, the position became worse rather than better because of the drain on the pool of candidates caused by the vast increase in the number of full-time appointments made to all the courts, from the House of Lords to those of the stipendiary magistrates. The problem did not become acute until the 1980s, but by about 1985 the growth in the number of Circuit Judges was beginning to create serious recruitment difficulties, and potential candidates for stipendiary magistartes' posts were being taken for the Circuit bench. In 1988 and 1989 the Top Salaries Review Body,[11] which is responsible *inter alia* for advising the Government on all judicial salaries, was given a disturbing account of the situation by the Lord Chancellor, who urged them to recommend substantial increases in the remuneration of the Circuit Judges in order to encourage larger numbers of suitable lawyers to accept appointment. There were other recruitment deterrents in addition to the salary level (in particular there was a perceived lack of status associated with judicial appointments below High Court level) all of which applied even more forcefully to stipendiary magistrate appointments which were lower in the hierarchy.

There is good reason to suppose therefore that the lay justice system will remain in being for some time to come, even if it continues to be placed under such pressure that its capability deteriorates. Even at present, however, there is scope for the creation of a few additional stipendiary posts, and what seems to be the most likely way forward is through an extension of the stipendiary magistracy in an ancilliary role to that of the JPs, so that they augment rather than replace them. Both lay and stipendiary magistrates have a proper contribution to make to the judicial system. Already additional stipendiary appointments are being made in places where the courts are subject to the greatest pressure and arrears are most serious. Also, part-time deputy stipendiaries are used to handle long and complicated cases. It is in this direction that the immediate future lies.

As to the long term, there is no reason to assume that the present circumstances will persist indefinitely and that the substitution of professional magistrates for the lay justices will remain a virtually impossible contingency. If the history of the Justices of the Peace is to

---

10.   *Ante,* p. 159. Cmd. 7463, Minutes of Evidence, October 30, 1946, p. 12, Question 223.
11.   Review Body on Top Salaries, Report No. 29, Cm. 938, paras. 59-76.

extend well into the second millenium, the system must give satisfaction to future Governments and to the public. All legal institutions, like the law itself, cannot remain static, but if they are to survive they must adapt to the changing conditions in which they operate. We have seen that the system of Justices of the Peace has many distinctive assets. It could be argued that its basic characteristic of justice administered by the people should make it particularly attractive in the ethos of future generations. Moreover, the British love of tradition and continuity favours the preservation of a system which has long been established as part of the English and Welsh heritage, and it is now too deeply ingrained in the way of life of the people to be easily uprooted; but uprooted it may be one day if, like other institutions that have perished, it is unable to continue to move with the times, to adapt to evolutionary change and to satisfy the diverse demands of a progressive, democratic society.

Volume II
INDEX